Married to Laughter

♥

A Love Story Featuring Anne Meara

JERRY STILLER

A Touchstone Book
Published by Simon & Schuster
NEW YORK   LONDON   TORONTO   SYDNEY   SINGAPORE

TOUCHSTONE
Rockefeller Center
1230 Avenue of the Americas
New York, NY 10020

First Touchstone Edition 2001

TOUCHSTONE and colophon are registered trademarks
of Simon & Schuster, Inc.

Designed by Kyoko Watanabe

Manufactured in the United States of America

1   3   5   7   9   10   8   6   4   2

The Library of Congress has cataloged the Simon & Schuster edition as follows:

Stiller, Jerry.
Married to laughter : a love story featuring Anne Meara / Jerry Stiller.
p.   cm.
1. Stiller, Jerry.   2. Meara, Anne.   3. Actors—United States—Biography.
4. Comedians—United States—Biography.   I. Title.
PN2287.S697 A3 2000
792'.028'092273—dc21
[B]   00-041324

ISBN 0-684-86903-9
0-684-86904-7 (Pbk)

For information regarding special discounts for bulk purchases, please contact
Simon & Schuster Special Sales at 1-800-456-6798 or
business@simonandschuster.com

special thanks to

Peter Matson, my literary agent, whose belief in my stories gave a first-time writer the courage to go forward.

Bob Bender, whose invaluable editorial insights turned my life into a book.

Dawn Eaton, whose dedication, support, and watchful eye helped make this book a reality.

Evangeline Morphos, who took the time to read my stories, then unlocked the door to the literary world.

Barbara Buloff, who explored my soul as if it were her own and gave me the insight to reinvent my life.

Jerry Tallmer, for his valiant work on the book.

Francy Falk Phelps, for permitting me to use Professor Sawyer Falk's letters.

Esther Porter Lane and Henry Street Playhouse, and the Boys and Girls Brotherhood Republic . . . thanks for showing me the light. Ed Sullivan, who took a chance on us—thirty-six times. Erin Nemy, a journalist and friend. Rodney Dangerfield, our Mr. Chips of comedy.

Greg Fletcher, Johanna Li, and Jim Rutman, for their tireless work on the book.

acknowledgments

To Hazel and Edwin Hugh, for their loyalty and love of over thirty-five years.

To Judy, Gene, and the Collatz and Lendway families, for a seamless friendship.

To Christine Taylor, my daughter-in-law, and all the Taylor family.

To my family—the Stillers, the O'Neills, the Citrons, the Liebermans, the Sussmans, the Gartners, Aunt Nettie and the Carusos, the Raffes, the Escobars, the Abraskins, the Stollers, the Laskys, the Fidlers, the Mosses, Eleanor Dempsey Nadolski, the Greenbergs, the Kachkovskys, the Hollys, the Jungkvists, the Schwartzes, the Posners, the Zemels, the Rimers, Joanie and Charlie Robinson, Ursula and Pat Campbell, Bobbie and Mark Gordon, Mary Ellyn Devery.

To Pearl Wexler, Michael Hartig, Paul Hilepo, Norman Reich, Lee and Alan Salomon, Steve Kessler, Mike Wilkins.

To Carroll and Nancy O'Connor, Jason Alexander, F. Murray Abraham, Danny Aiello, David Amram, Jed Bernstein, Paul Crabtree, Madeline and Jack Gilford, Tom Fontana, Ken Greengrass, John Guare, Lila Garrett, Alan King, Jack Klugman, Tony Randall, Joan Micklin and Ray Silver, Rita Moreno, Dick Moore and Jane Powell, Jules Munshin, Mark Murphy, John Mahoney, Charles Nelson Reilly, George Schlatter, Gerald Schoenfeld, Larry and Norma Storch, Richard Sandomir and Griffin Miller, George Shapiro, Howard West, Jerry Seinfeld, Michael Richards, David Stone, Mort and Natalie Lachman, Chris and Georgianne Walken, Julia Louis-Dreyfus, Estelle Harris, Kevin James, Michael Weithorn, David Litt, Rob Schiller, Sheldon Silver, the Tarrants, and the Forsythes. John Randolph, Nancy Ponder Zucker, Rabbi Cutler, Byrne Piven, Marty Litke, Charlotte Rae, Kaye Ballard, David Shepherd, David Gordon, Louis Milgrom, Alyse Myers, the Gelbs, Walt Witcover, Art D'Lugoff, Donald Margulies, Isaiah Sheffer, Portia Nelson, Bea Arthur, The Berghofs, Peter Swet, Jim McKenzie, Al Hirschfeld, Bill Hurt, Frederick Schweppe, Larry King, Regis, Booby DiVito, and Richard and Zora Borwn.

To George Lichter, Steve Burn, Ron Carey, Olympia Lee Falk Yamayoshi, Pat and Jack Morris, Nat Adler, the Hittmans, Sylvia and Milton Yarensky, Bob and Marion Geller, Fielder Cook, the Paltrows, Faith Stewart Gordon, Sam Greenberger, Marvin and Sukie Gutin, Enid and Bill Hairston, Maggie and Bill Dwyer, Dione and Will Holt, Larry Holofcener, Ed Katz, Jan Morgan, Amram Nowak, John and Geraldine O'Connor, Mary Anne Page, Richard and Francy Phelps, Harold Schoenberg, Rabbi Saul Wohlberg, Morty West, Barry Zevan, Rabbi Ed and Ruth Klein, Henry Ziegler, Lewis James Rose, Norman Wallace, Ginger Andrews, and the Burns family.

To Marvin and Paul Belsky, Larry Chinitz, Billy Bob Bernstein, Frank Weiser, Michael Uris, Morton Brenner, Lester and Andrew Lutzker, Louis Angioletti, Lou Lapid.

To my Syracuse classmates who never stopped being my friends— Earl Simmons, Allan Shalleck, the Reidenbaughs, Peggy Menefee, Helen Buchta Gustafson, Rex Partington, Leo Mitchell Bloom. Richard Harris, Lee Davis, Howie Saks, Ruth Winokoor, Sally Orloff Berger, Helen Slayton, Roy Jensen, Jerry Gershman, and Jerry Adler.

*To Anne Meara, my wife, comedy partner and mother of Amy
and Ben, who loves me still, for reasons known only to her.*

*To Amy and Ben, who with Anne are the most important
people in my life.*

*To my mother, who taught me the lessons of life,
but never made opening night.*

To my father, never a faker.

*To Arnie and Lynda, Doreen and Maxine, who enrich
my life and make me proud to be their brother.*

*To Jack, Mickey, and all the Gartners, who made Anne, myself,
Amy, and Ben a part of their family.*

*I was blessed by God with uncles, aunts, and cousins who opened
their hearts to my dreams. Their loving feelings gave me
strength when I needed it. Without that love, I could
never have turned my dreams into reality.*

I love you all.

contents

No Hands

It was my fifty-seventh birthday, June 8, 1984. I was on Nantucket's Polpis Road. It was a hot and sunny day. I'd passed the lifesaving station on my left; to the right were the moors. Endless reaches of briar in budding earth colors disappeared into nothingness, creating an island eeriness that often seemed breathtaking.

My blue Motobecane bicycle was performing smoothly on this oddly windless afternoon. Did I dare let the bike do the work? I could see the heat rippling off the newly paved asphalt. Not a car in sight. Dare I let go? Allow myself to ride no hands? I had seen this deed performed hundreds of times by others but never had had the guts to do it myself.

I felt I had never earned the rite of passage into manhood by riding no hands. I equated this failure with cowardice. The need to ride no hands had been festering in me since childhood.

Pedaling on toward Siasconset, I saw nothing coming toward me, no cars, no bikers, just a few gulls soaring lazily in the sky above. I challenged myself to lift both hands off the handlebars. Immediately I imagined the bike veering out of control and myself hurled face-forward onto the pavement.

I assured myself that this could not happen on my fifty-seventh birthday, so I timidly lifted my right hand a few inches into space. My legs pumped a little harder. So did my heart. I tried to maintain a constant speed while building up my nerve. The more I pumped, the braver I tried to feel. I raised my right hand a little higher. I was riding one hand. Big deal. Now could I lift the other hand? Would a bump or a pebble do me in? What about a sudden gust of wind?

I stared at the handlebars. Were they trustworthy? Was the world trustworthy? Suddenly it hit me: They're a rudder. The handlebars are a rudder. As long as I stay centered and keep pumping, nothing can go wrong. You don't have to be Einstein. Kids in Minneapolis and Denver and Brooklyn are doing this right now.

Do it before fear overcomes logic. Before a tortoise crossing the road makes me a coward.

I did a quick *sh'ma,* the Hebrew prayer said at times of peril, lifted both hands, sat back, and let the bike do the rest. I could feel my entire being released. It was like a weight I was no longer carrying. I was feeling nothing. I'd never before experienced feeling nothing. I felt free of the need to judge myself.

The bike now had a life of its own. It didn't need me. I was a mere passenger. Everything around me was now in Technicolor. I could see flowers blooming everywhere. Judy Garland was alive.

A car was approaching. Would I panic? Would *he* panic? I waved my arms high above my head, like a cyclist I'd seen on *The Ed Sullivan Show.* "Look, Ma, no hands!" I shouted. The car passed. I was no longer afraid of being afraid.

I didn't want this to end. More cars passed, some coming from behind me. I was past Quidnet. I'd cycled more than a mile. Then it hit me. Balance. It was balance, not courage.

What next? Could I do no hands with my eyes closed? As I breezed past the lighthouse, I looked at my watch. Eight minutes. No hands. I'd done it. Leo would have been proud of me.

It was my cousin Leo who had given me my first ride down Snake Hill in East New York on his handlebars. He arrived on his two-wheeler like a shining knight out of Canarsie. He lived on Farragut Road, four stops by subway from Livonia Avenue and Hinsdale. To me, it seemed as if he'd navigated oceans to come that distance. He was fourteen and I was nine.

Leo was tall for his age. He had that smile that guys in the movies flashed to show courage when they faced danger. I loved it that someone in our family could laugh at danger.

Riding on the handlebars was a very unnatural act, I thought. How does anyone sit on a pipe while another person keeps balance? What if I shift my weight? Won't the whole thing fall over and land us on the street?

"Climb on," Leo said, with no hint of any concern that we might spill over and break our necks.

"Okay," I said like some puppy dog, acting on faith.

In seconds, we were moving. Leo's body was off the seat, his head jutting over mine like a sprinter. He was pumping steadily up toward Dumont, past Blake, past Belmont, almost to Pitkin, the wind hitting us square on. Leo was alive, seemingly out of body. I wanted to be him, but I was only a passenger and he the pilot. We spun past pushcarts, sideswiped automobiles, wove our way through kids playing ring-a-levio and kick-the-can. We had wheels and were moving, while everyone else was standing still. I had no control over what was happening. It was Leo's trip, and his spidery arms held me prisoner. It felt great.

Minutes later we were back in front of the house on Livonia Avenue at Hinsdale.

"Do you want to try it?" he said.

Before I could say "I'm scared," he took out a wrench, lowered the seat, and I was on the bike.

"Now just pedal. I'll be behind you, holding the seat."

I obeyed. I could feel Leo's hands on the seat, keeping me balanced. I felt safe.

"Go," he said.

Suddenly I realized I was on my own. Free. Moving without anyone's help. And at that moment I felt brave and powerful.

1

Anne

In 1953, I was in New York City looking for work. I was making rounds with Bea Mortensen, a tall, lovely, redheaded actress. I thought we'd be terrific doing an act together. That wasn't all I wanted to do with Bea. She sensed that my hanging out with her was not solely in hope of theatrical employment, but I never made an overt pass and did everything to disguise my biological feelings.

We'd walk down Broadway holding hands, she in two-inch heels and me in my Keds, sending out a message: "See, we're just two crazy show-business people." Bea's making rounds with me must have hinged on some bizarre expectation of hers that we'd actually strike it rich one day.

On this spring afternoon we arrived at a casting cattle call in an agent's office. The place was full of chattering hopefuls seeking employment in a summer-stock company. As we waited our turn, Bea recognized a friend of hers, a tall girl, though not quite Bea's height, with auburn hair and an angelic face. They got talking just as the receptionist announced that the agent would start seeing people. I was sandwiched between them. The conversation proceeded as if I weren't there.

"By the way, this is Jerry," Bea said.

"Hi," I said, extending my hand in a kind of manly way. The angel-faced girl shook it. She looked sort of puritanical and smelled nice. She was wearing Mary Chess perfume, I later learned.

"Anne Meara," the secretary called.

"That's me," the girl said. "I already know I'm too tall to play the in-genue and too young to be a character woman."

She's very self-demeaning, I thought.

"Okay, wish me luck," she said, disappearing into the inner office.

Bea looked at me soulfully and said, "That's a nice girl." I knew instantly that this was the kiss-off. "You'll like her," Bea said. "She's a very sweet girl." I felt like a baseball card being traded.

Before I could fully comprehend that Bea's and my relationship had ended, the agent's door flew open and Anne Meara, in tears, burst back into the room.

"What happened?" everyone asked.

"He chased me. He chased me all around the desk," she said. Her face was flushed. "I think I'm going back to Rockville Centre. My father told me New York was a tough place."

"Who's next?" the secretary said. "Who's Jerry Stiller?"

"I'm next," I said.

I'd seen this agent on many occasions, and he'd always paid me the courtesy of saying hello. His walls were full of pictures of stars he claimed he handled. He wore a houndstooth sports jacket and always seemed to be on vacation.

He was basically harmless, but he also loved to play practical jokes on me. Once he asked me to light his cigar. I hesitated. "Light it," he snapped. When I struck the match, it flared brightly. He went into hysterical laughter.

Today he asked, "What have you been up to these days?"

Suddenly, acting heroic, I asked, "Why did you chase that girl around the desk?"

"Because I liked her," he replied with great aplomb. "And I like you too. Now it's your turn." He started chasing me around the room, laughing uproariously as I ran for the door. "Nothing for you this time," he said, as I exited into the waiting room, where Anne was still recovering.

Bea indicated none too subtly that she herself had an appointment and suggested that perhaps I'd like to take Anne for a cup of coffee to help her recover her faculties. I looked at Bea sheepishly, still trying to fathom why I was being ditched.

"See you again sometime," Bea said.

I asked Anne if she would like a cup of coffee, and she said yes.

We walked to Longley's Cafeteria. I had barely enough money on me to pay for anything more than coffee and cake.

"I could bring him up on charges," Anne said as I maneuvered her past the hot-food counter and toward the coffee machine.

"Are you going to have coffee?" I asked.

"Yes."

"Nothing else?" I said prayerfully.

"Nothing else."

We sat down. I really didn't know why I was with her, except that it was the way the afternoon was unfolding.

"Have you ever been bothered like that before?" I asked.

"Once," she said. "A guy started following me down Broadway. He must've known I was an actress. I had a portfolio and was wearing makeup. When he got real close, he started saying dirty words. I started to limp, hoping it would turn him off. 'Keep it up, sweetheart,' he said. 'I love women with afflictions.'"

I laughed. She seemed so unshowbusinessy. *She's probably untalented,* I thought. *She isn't trying to prove anything because there's nothing to prove.*

"How long have you known Bea?" I asked.

"She was in love with an actor I worked with at Smithtown. How do *you* know her?" Anne asked.

"Oh, I was thinking of doing a comedy act, and she was very tall and I thought it would be kind of funny, the two of us."

"Are you a comedian?" she asked, as if she were talking about plumbing.

"Yes," I said, "I guess you can call it that."

"I hate comedians," she said. "They do such awful things."

"Like what?"

"Oh, I went out with one once. He played the Copa. He took me home and tried to attack me when I wouldn't kiss him good-night. He had terrible teeth. Then he started to cry. I felt sorry for him. He was a grown man."

"Well, I'm working on an act," I said. "I did it in college, up at Syracuse."

I felt like an athlete flexing his muscles. "Maybe you can come and see me sometime."

"Where?" she asked.

I admitted I wasn't performing anyplace just then.

"Well, I've got to go," she said.

"Let me take your check," I said like John D. Rockefeller.

"No," she said. "I only had coffee. I'll take care of it, but I could use some silverware."

"What?" I asked.

"Just grab a knife and a fork. I'll take some spoons. I live down in the Village with two roommates, and they lose silverware."

I quickly slipped a fork into my jacket pocket. I've just become her accomplice in crime, I told myself. What am I getting myself into, hanging out with New York actresses? They're all crazy. I'm a normal guy. Is this what I have to do to go to bed with someone? She's committing a crime. I wanted to escape, and yet I wanted to prove I wasn't afraid.

"Well, listen," I told her as we hit the street. "I hope we meet again sometime. Here's your fork."

"Thanks," she said, and she disappeared into the Sixth Avenue subway.

2

Growing Up Poor

The town of Frampol, Poland, existed for me long before Isaac Bashevis Singer immortalized it in his stories. The Citrons—my uncles and aunts and my mother—arrived in America in waves, each child in care of the one before. My Tanta Faiga arrived first and my mother, Faiga's kid sister, Bella, last. The entire Citron family (some of them spell it Citrin) lived in one building, a tenement at 61 Columbia Street on the Lower East Side.

Yussef and Devorah Citron, my maternal grandparents, never reached America. Having gotten their children to the land where the streets were said to be paved with gold, they were content to remain in Poland. My mother told me it was because her parents looked down on things modern; for their children, though, they knew America was the future.

My mother had been born in Poland around 1900. My father, William Stiller (called Willie), had been born in America maybe four years before that. His parents had arrived from Chijika in Galicia. When Bella Citron was in her twenties, her sisters and brothers, anxious to find a husband for the youngest sister, matched her with this young boy from Stanton Street. They were married soon after.

I was born June 8, 1927, in Unity Hospital, Brooklyn, two years ahead of my brother Arnold, three years ahead of my sister Doreen, eighteen years ahead of my sister Maxine.

We moved a lot when I was a kid: ten different places in twelve years. Then in 1939 we made the big jump to Manhattan's Lower East Side, first to a fifth-floor walkup on Goerck Street, and a year later, to the projects, the Vladeck Houses on Jackson Street, from where my father could walk to Houston Street to start his new job driving a bus to South Ferry.

My father, the oldest of ten children, never finished public school. He became a taxi driver, then an unemployed taxi driver, and later a driver for the Triangle Bus Company.

My mother's wish was to become Americanized. She taught herself to read, write, and speak English. Her optimism was undiminished by the poverty that surrounded her.

On the morning my mother was to go down to take the test to become an American citizen, I sat with her at the kitchen table, going over questions like "Who was the father of our country" and "What are the forty-eight states?" Together we drilled until she could recite them by heart.

"Who wrote the Declaration of Independence?"

"Thomas Jefferson," she said, puffing on a Chesterfield.

"How many presidents have we had?"

"Thirty-two, including President Roosevelt. I'll have to write," she fretted. "My handwriting is terrible."

"It's fine. Don't be nervous, you'll pass," I told her.

I knew she would. She spoke English without any accent.

"What do you call the first ten amendments?"

"The Bill of Rights."

"Right. What was the Eighteenth Amendment?"

"Prohibition. The Volstead Act."

"And the twenty-first?"

"Repeal, thanks to President Roosevelt."

There seemed to be something unfair about a country that allowed me to be a citizen automatically because I was born here, but not my mother. "America-*gonif*"—I was getting away easy.

"You know, my friends think you were born here," I told her. "You speak perfectly." It seemed to be just what she wanted to hear.

"It comes natural. I feel like a citizen," she said, taking another puff.

I loved it when she smoked. It made her look so modern, the way American women were supposed to look. They all smoked in the movies—Joan Crawford, Jean Harlow, Bette Davis—a certain sophistication.

"Why don't you go downstairs and play. But watch out for cars," she said. "When I come back I'll be an American citizen. Wish me luck."

I kissed her, and she headed for City Hall.

A week later she was notified: Bella Citron Stiller was an American citizen.

My mother was no longer a greenhorn.

A couple of years ago I came across a photostat of her citizenship papers. They were dated June 8, 1937—my tenth birthday. But my memories go back a lot farther than that.

Mothers in Brooklyn were always telling their kids to watch out for cars because kids were always being run over. In fact, there were so many kids being hit by cars that my public school invited Irving Caesar, who wrote the lyrics of "Tea for Two," to come and teach us at assembly to sing "Cross at the green, not in between." He'd bring a pianist, Gerald Marks, with him.

The truth was that getting run over got you lots of attention, as long as you weren't killed. To a child, it was a sort of rite of passage into manhood.

When my brother Arnie was three he was almost run over on Roebling Street. Almost. He ran out of my mother's grasp when she was pushing my sister, Doreen, in the carriage. The wheel of a car screeched to a halt just short of Arnie's head. The next day the kids came up to me and said with admiration and envy, "Your brother was almost run over."

"Yeah, almost," I boasted.

Two years earlier, when *I* was three, I really had been run over but no one but me believed it had actually happened. My mother and cousins refused to believe a laundry truck had backed up over my leg. All they saw was me sitting on the curb. But my leg was broken. What really hurt was that I was robbed of the attention that was my due.

It was a hot summer day. My cousins Dottie, Jeanette, and Bluma were walking with my mother and me up Blake Avenue toward my Uncle Charlie's house. My mother, who always had a loving ear for my cousins' stories, was totally caught up in their lives as we approached Wyona Street. I saw a laundry truck parked close to the curb. The chrome rear fender seemed wide enough for me to sit on. What if I hitched a ride? I thought. They'd all see me riding away on a truck. I'd love to see the look on their faces. I'd be laughing at them.

I timed my move. As my mother and the girls kept walking, I boosted myself onto that rear fender. Just then, the truck backed up and I fell off.

The next thing I remember, I was sitting on the curb with my mother and cousins surrounding me, asking what had happened.

"I was run over," I said.

"Run over? How?" my mother asked with disbelief.

The truck was gone.

"I was run over," I insisted, but nobody believed me.

My leg, it turned out, was broken. It was put in a cast. Days later, my Uncle Jake came to visit. He and I sat outside on a bench, with a bag full of peanuts, feeding the pigeons. The hungry creatures flocked around my uncle, fighting among themselves to reach his palm. My uncle spoke calmly to them and told me not to be afraid.

Uncle Jake, Tanta Faiga's husband, was a small and gentle man. He had no hair, no teeth, and didn't work. He and my Tanta Faiga were childless. She sold towels door to door. One day, when my father was out of a job, she came to see my mother. I could hear her begging my mother to take fifty cents for food. My mother refused it, and Faiga got upset. But in terms of her own marriage it was perfectly appropriate for Faiga to work, going door to door to sell towels, and for Jake to feed the pigeons. My aunt asked for a glass of water, then kissed my mother and me good-bye.

I once asked my cousin Sandra how my mother had got to America from Europe. "Faiga brought your mother over," Sandra said. Faiga had brought them all over, five of her brothers and sisters, and also Jake. She did it by selling towels door to door. Tanta Faiga lived to be ninety-three and never stopped selling towels.

Our family hardly went anywhere together, and never to the movies— mostly because my mother enjoyed love stories and my father couldn't stand them. He'd fall asleep. Anything with Marion Davies, Mary Astor, or Bette Davis would put him away.

But he loved vaudeville, especially the comedians. Sitting through the feature movie was murder for him, but when the coming attractions appeared just before the vaudeville acts, it was like the arrival of spring after a long Russian winter.

I was no more than five when my father, who was unemployed, took me to my first vaudeville show. We were then living in Williamsburg, a depressed part of Brooklyn, and my father, a frustrated performer, would sometimes play the saxophone, usually in the toilet to avoid the glare of my mother, who thought the time could be better spent looking for work. Unemployment being the main occupation of the entire country in the 1930s, Willie Stiller was no exception in indulging in reveries and illusion rather than facing the pain of joblessness.

One afternoon, he schlepped me with him to his favorite escape, the Follies Theater on Flushing Avenue. The two youngest members of the family, my brother Arnie and sister Doreen, were left behind.

The show consisted, as ever, of vaudeville plus news plus a movie. My five-year-old impression was that all films were fake. I, like my father, couldn't wait for them to end.

During the coming attractions my father snapped to his feet, grabbed my hand, and said, "Let's move down."

Like two jackrabbits, we leapfrogged over rows to seats closer to the stage. Others had the same idea, but my father got us there first. From my new vantage point I could see the musicians filing in, and as the lights on the music stands in the orchestra pit flicked on and the musicians began tuning their instruments, I saw my father's excitement grow. In the dark pit a party was about to begin: The boisterous trumpets, sexy saxophones, innocent violins, vulgar trombones, and raucous drums were conversing with one another, tuning up, paying no attention to what was on the screen. I became a part of it. I couldn't wait for the final "cock-a-doodle-doo" of the Pathé News rooster.

Suddenly the movie screen soared skyward and the crimson traveler curtain swept across a stage blanketed by the glare of white lights. I could see just enough of the back of the conductor's head as he raised his baton and exclaimed, "Hit it!" I could hear the electrical clicking of the golden baroque standards on either side of the stage as the cards moved up bearing the name of the orchestra. The band's vibrant energy filled the theater with excitement. When the introduction ended, the cards dropped, revealing the name of a dancer and the subtitle TOPS IN TAPS. Then came an Apache team: Three minutes of mayhem in which a man and two women in gypsy attire commit violence upon one another without getting hurt. This was followed by a monologist—a low-keyed performer who professed to be one of the best and cheapest in his line of work. I knew the last act would be someone funny.

They were a team. He came out first and told suggestive jokes, then he introduced his beautiful foil. Her blue-and-silver sequined costume shimmered under the lights. A single-strapped bra precariously contained her

flouncing bosom. Her costume disappeared at her thighs, replaced by silver tassels that sparkled as they danced at her slightest movement. Her
naive persona gave no indication that she was a steaming temptress en-
ticing everyone, including myself. Standing there wearing not much more
than a smile, she was emblazoned indelibly on my five-year-old brain.

I felt a peculiar sensation in my pants as I watched this delicious lady
succumb to the comedian's advances. What I saw made me want to climb
up onto the young woman's lap and take her away from this weird, leer-
ing beast who wanted to harm her. I could feel myself wanting to kiss and
hug her. I wanted to show her how much I could care for her. I could
smell the powder on her face, I could feel those tassels in my fingers as
she threw herself at me, telling me she was a nice lady and not anything
like the way this man acted toward her. I desperately wanted to protect
her from him. If only I could get up there and tell that guy where to go. It
really annoyed me.

It was at this point in the act that the comedian reached behind the
curtain for a large wooden plank. With it, he whacked the gorgeous lady
on the behind, causing a loud explosion and lots of smoke. She screamed
with shock and grabbed her backside and ran off. The audience roared
with laughter. The smoke clouded the first several rows of the orchestra.
The whole bizarre business and loud explosion frightened me.

To this day, I have never forgotten the board hitting the beautiful lady.
As we left the theater I told my father I never again wanted to see vaudeville when they had loud noises.

At that moment, though, I loved my father for taking me with him to
the show, loud noise or not. On the way home I asked him, "Do all the
acts go home together, Deddy?"—that was what I called my father—
"Do they sleep in one bed? Do they live in one house like a family? Do
they eat together?" My father didn't reply.

When we returned to the three-room flat on South Fifth Street, my
mother demanded to know where we had spent the afternoon.

"I took him to vaudeville," my father replied.

I was his alibi. It was my father's way to legitimatize his unwillingness
to go out to look for work. My father was a cab driver. He had at one time
been partners with a pal and they owned a Lincoln. When the Depression
hit, they lost the cab. People couldn't afford to ride in a cab.

"Why the hell don't you get a real job," my mother snapped.

"I tried yesterday. There's nothing around."

"Keep looking, I got three kids to feed."

"What do you want me to do, sell apples?" he asked. That was the ultimate bottom and he refused to see himself that low.

"I should've married a real man," she cried. "Where are you going?"

"To lie down."

"I need money," she screamed. "Go out and hack a couple of hours, you could make a few cents."

"I'm going to sleep," he said.

"Sleep? Look at this!" My mother turned her pocketbook inside-out. "Nothing, not a penny. We're broke. I don't even have money for milk. First you go to vaudeville and now you want to *sleep?*"

The day my mother said there wasn't enough money for milk was the day I really knew the meaning of poor. It must've hit my father too as he slowly put on a sweater and headed for the door.

"You hate vaudeville," he said to her.

"Maybe if I wasn't with you I'd like it."

It was dialogue I remembered all my life and that I would someday use on stage with Anne. The difference was that our audience would laugh at it.

My father, defeated, left the house to hack. When he returned a few hours later he threw a quarter on the table.

"Here," he said, "buy some milk." And then he started to cry.

Within the space of one year in the Depression—1933 to 1934—we moved from South Fifth Street to 131 Meserole then to Siegel Street, then to the end of Siegel Street. I never was told what caused these departures.

At our last Siegel Street apartment, the rickety wooden staircase to our five-room, cold-water flat turned slightly before reaching the second floor. The five of us stood on a landing that faced two apartments. The one on the right belonged to us. My mother turned the key and we were looking into a kitchen that had a gas range, a bathtub with a porcelain cover, a coal stove, and a door leading to the bathroom we would now share with strangers. A room to the front overlooked the street, while the other four led to the backyard.

Suddenly I realized we had dropped to life's lower scale. We could no longer afford the luxury of steam heat. At that moment I knew we were no longer the chosen people. It was as if God had decided to put us out of His kingdom. Jews had always had steam heat.

After my mother fully took in the bleak surroundings and digested the indignity of having to share a toilet with people of unknown origin, she said: "We're only going to be here a couple of months."

Her eyes avoided my father, who stood by catatonically, unable to control the events that had brought us to this horrible place.

We had traveled the grand distance of five blocks, transporting our personal belongings in shopping bags, the furniture by pushcart.

"Let's get unpacked," my mother said.

My father moved quickly, simulating an army going into battle, grabbing cartons of dishes, pots, whatever came into his hands. He was trying to maintain his manhood. At that moment—six years old, going on seven—I wanted to take over. I was sure I could do better than he.

"It's cold in here," my mother said. "We need some heat. Make a fire."

My father hurried into the next room and returned with some scraps of wood.

"We need coal," my mother said.

"I've found some!" my father shouted triumphantly, dropping the wood and coming back with a bucketful of coal.

The huge black stove stared at us like some monster at feeding time. We had never had to face one of these before. My father stuffed newspapers into the bell of the stove, then wood, then shiny black chunks of coal. He tossed in a lit match, and in a few seconds smoke filled the apartment, choking us.

"Can't you put it out?" my mother shouted.

"There's a thing here someplace," my father said, looking for the damper. Smoke was everywhere.

"You picked this place!" my mother screamed. "Don't you know how to work the stove?"

"I'm a nothing," he yelled back. "You made me a nothing."

My brother and sister were crying. I could hear them even though I couldn't see them. I wished I were an orphan. *I don't belong to these people,* I told myself. I placed an invisible shield between my ears and the words they said to hurt one another.

"Stop crying," I said to Doreen through the smoke. "Everything will be all right." I had to become a father to Arnie and Doreen.

Suddenly the bathroom door opened. A short middle-aged woman in a dark dress stood in the doorway. "What's wrong?" she said in a thick

Italian accent. "I'm your next-door neighbor." She headed straight for the stove.

"You no open the damper," she explained, grabbing a handle on the stove and shoving it forward. "You gotta smoke in the whole house. The fire engines is gonna come."

The smoke stopped pouring out of the stove.

"We just moved in and it was cold," my mother said. "We never did this before."

The woman looked at us as if we were immigrants who had just landed.

"You gotta start slow," she said. "Gotta have patience. Use a little bit of wood, then put the coal on one at a time. Then you got a good fire. It can go all night."

"Thank you," my mother said. "I'm Bella. This is Willie and our kids."

"I'm Mrs. Palazzo. My daughter and I live next door. We and you share the same bathroom. There's a lock, see? You want privacy, you just turn it." She pointed to the little screw latches on both doors to the bathroom, hers and ours.

"You no sleep in the back room," Mrs. Palazzo said, pointing. "The heat don't go back too far. Better you sleep together in one room, near the stove. It's nice and warm."

"Thank you," my mother said.

"Anytime you want something, you call."

From that moment the Palazzos and the Stillers were neighbors.

When she left we dropped everything and went to sleep. All five of us in one bed.

Tessie was Mrs. Palazzo's only daughter. She was a Roman beauty in her twenties. Her olive skin and classic features made her seem like a goddess. She loved kids. She'd come in and play with us. She knew what we were thinking. She could wrap us around her little finger.

My mother and Tessie got to be friends. They'd smoke cigarettes, drink coffee, and talk about things. We never knew what they were talking about, but it fascinated us. We'd watch them for hours.

It was sometime in December just before Christmas that we first noticed the lights on a tree blinking on and off in the Palazzo apartment. We could see the lights through the frosted glass of the Palazzos' bathroom door. And, as it turned out, Tessie could see the silhouettes of our faces against her frosted glass. One night she pulled open the door.

"What are you looking at?" she said, as if catching us in some forbidden act.

"Your tree," we whispered.

"Don't you have one?" she said, peering into our apartment. She saw we didn't. A revelation.

A couple of nights later she knocked on our door and very apologetically, seemingly on tiptoe, asked my mother if it would be all right to invite the children in to sit under the tree.

"They don't have to do nothin'," Tessie said. "They can just come in and sit there under the tree."

My mother's face turned white. Arnie, Doreen, and I sat waiting for her answer. The doors between both apartments were now open. We could see the lights on the tree twinkling on and off, the peppermint candy canes, the colored balls, the icicles, the little Santa Clauses, the stockings filled with gifts. My mother looked at the three of us and very quietly said, "I'm sorry, I don't want to offend you, Tessie, but in this house we don't celebrate Christmas. That's why we don't have a tree. I hope you understand."

Tessie stood for a moment, then silently walked back through the bathroom into her apartment.

"I hope you kids will understand someday," my mother said to us. "We don't celebrate Christmas."

We watched the lights on Tessie's Christmas tree blink on and off, and then we went to bed.

A few nights later, while listening to Eddie Cantor on the radio, we heard what had to be loud arguing in Tessie's apartment; lots of crying and cursing. There was a man in the apartment.

"Marry you? I wouldn't marry you," we heard Tessie say. "Besides, you're already married, you bum. You're nothing to me."

"I love you, Tessie. I'll get a divorce," the man's voice pleaded.

"You lied to me, you SOB."

"But I love you."

"I don't love you," Tessie said. "Even if I'm carrying your child, I don't love you. Understand?"

"*Make* her understand," the man begged Tessie's mother. "I'm good. I make a good dollar. Tell her not to treat me this way."

As the argument grew more intense, we turned up the radio to blot it out, so as not to be eavesdropping. We couldn't help but notice through the frosted glass the shadows of Tessie, Mrs. Palazzo, and a small man moving frantically back and forth in front of the Christmas tree.

"Don't you understand?" Tessie screamed again. "I'll have the baby but not you."

The man said, "I won the race today. I rode a winner at the track. I'm giving you everything."

"I don't want your fucking money!" Tessie screamed.

All of us in our own apartment forgot Eddie Cantor. We were now glued to the drama going on next door.

"Okay," the man said. "If you don't take the money I'm flushing it down the toilet."

There was a silence, and then Tessie's bathroom door swung open. We could make out the figure of the little man through the frosted glass of our own bathroom door as he reached into his pocket and pulled out a wad of bills. I could see him waving them over his head, as if it were some bomb he was about to throw. There was another silence, then the sound of the toilet chain. I could visualize the bills falling into the toilet. Without saying a word I yanked open our bathroom door and screamed, "Take the money, Tessie, take the money!" as the bills went swirling to a watery grave.

During those early days in Brooklyn the fights between my mother and father were almost always about money. When the battles became physical, I assumed the role of protector over Arnie and Doreen.

I remember pushing both of them under the kitchen table when fists started flying. I hoped that the sight of Doreen's blonde ringlets and blue eyes streaming oceans of tears would cause my parents magically to kiss, make up, and live happily ever after, as in a fairy tale. Instead, it only seemed to intensify their combat.

My biggest dread was that the neighbors would hear. Jewish people don't fight, I thought. I would tiptoe between my mother and father, acting as a buffer, hoping that would make them stop. They almost hit me as they flailed clumsily at each other.

It was usually my mother who would initiate the battle, daring my father to strike her. His response was to turn his back, in protection against the fingernails that tore at him. He was usually in some sort of undershirt, so a considerable amount of skin was exposed. He would duck his head as her hands lunged for his face. "Why don't you move?" my mother would scream at my father.

"And go where?"

"To the baths."

"I'm going."

"When?"

"Tomorrow."

During the Depression, many husbands left their homes and moved into the bathhouses, establishments normally occupied by alcoholics and womanizers drying out after a night in the bars. The spaces were just large enough for a cot covered with a sheet. It was just a place to dump your clothes while you took a steambath. For a dime, a Polish attendant would pour buckets of water on you and beat you with twigs and leaves, both cleansing you and punishing you. It was a sort of self-inflicted punishment for boozing and/or adultery, acts my father could never have committed.

"I don't drink and I don't fool around with other women," he'd declare as Bella chased him around the kitchen.

"Why don't you?" she'd yell. "Then I wouldn't have to see your face." She'd land a fist on his shoulder. He'd curse and start to strike back, with a cry that seemed to rise from deep within him. He'd hit her with the backs of fists curved inward.

"*Ktsop!*" he'd scream. It was an expression used in the old country to describe Cossacks during a pogrom.

Arnie and Doreen huddled under the table, bawling.

"*Greener Zoodic!*" My father, born in America, was falling back on Yiddish.

"Call the police!" my mother shouted at me.

"No," I pleaded. The shame. Jews did not call the police—Jews fighting among themselves. The police would only watch and laugh. Encourage us to kill ourselves. How could my parents be so stupid? They've lost their souls.

"Not the cops," I begged.

"Then make him get out."

"Why don't you leave," I begged my father.

"Where can I go?" he asked me.

"Go to the baths!" my mother yelled.

"Okay."

"When?"

"Tomorrow."

"Always tomorrow. And I want you to send money. Seven dollars a week for us to live on."

"What am *I* going to live on?" my father would ask. "I can't live on two dollars a week. I need at least seven dollars myself."

"Stop smoking cigars!" my mother yelled.

"A nickel a day," my father said. "I smoke two cigars for a nickel, and you want to take away my pleasure."

It was the cigars that made her furious. Smoking cigars and listening to the radio as if there were no Depression, no troubles.

I loved the smell of my father's two-for-a-nickel cigars. I remember the look on his face as he sat listening to Eddie Cantor on the radio while my mother snapped his cigars in two. My father switched to a pipe and Union Leader tobacco, a nickel a pouch.

My father, like many, wanted to work. When we moved from Williamsburg to East New York, he became part of the WPA, the Works Progress Administration. He helped build the Palisades Parkway. At 5 A.M. I'd watch him get dressed. He'd put on huge leather lace-up boots that extended almost to the knee. I asked why he wore boots. "Copperheads," he said. New Jersey had copperheads. A dangerous job, I thought. Deddy then waited for the truck that would pick him up and take him along with other men to New Jersey. My father had never held a shovel in his hands until then. When he got home from the Palisades he'd plop himself into a chair, light up his pipe, and turn on the Atwater Kent radio, a large metallic black box with a lid and a horn. Comedians were my father's favorites. On different nights there were Eddie Cantor, Jack Benny, Fred Allen, and Edgar Bergen and Charlie McCarthy. He didn't understand Fibber McGee and Molly.

Laughter seemed to dissipate the pain of being unemployed. Even my mother's anguish subsided when Eddie Cantor sang, "Potatoes are cheaper, tomatoes are cheaper, now's the time to fal-l-l-l in love." More than anyone else, Eddie Cantor made us aware that the entire country was in a Depression and we weren't alone.

My mind danced when Eddie was on. I wanted to be Eddie Cantor. I thought he could change the whole world. I too could change the world if I were a comedian. Eddie said, "When I'm the president, when I'm the president." I thought, *Wow, what if we had a Jewish president?* We could go down to Washington, D.C. We'd live with him in the White House. He'd take care of us like cousins.

My dreams were real to me. I wrote a letter to radio station WEAF, requesting tickets to see *The Eddie Cantor Show* live. Six weeks later five tickets arrived in the mail at our new apartment on Alabama Avenue, Brooklyn. Had Eddie Cantor read my letter? I felt like I had reached someone for the first time in my life. I was about nine years old.

The day we were to see the show I became the head of the family. We left from East New York, taking the subway at Livonia Avenue, then changed at Broadway Junction for the Broadway local, and went over the bridge into Manhattan. Life changed once I was over that bridge. It was a new world.

We arrived at Rockefeller Center and waited in the lobby with hundreds of other free-ticket holders. An usher, looking very formal, motioned to all of us and removed the felt-covered chain. Like a hungry army, we crowded into the elevators that took us to the eighth floor. There, in the studio where the Conan O'Brien TV show is broadcast today, was where we'd see and hear Eddie Cantor. We quickly moved into our seats, hungry for the excitement to start.

The clock on the wall said 7:00 P.M., an hour before the show was to go on. The musicians strolled onstage and took their places. Jimmy Wallington, the announcer, appeared before us. "Before Eddie comes out," he said, "we want you to know this show is going out all over the country. So what we need is lots of applause, and we want you to laugh *loud* at the jokes. Let's see you applaud." Everybody applauded enthusiastically.

Suddenly, Eddie Cantor bounded onto the stage. Everyone clapped. His energy, his bulging eyes, his jet-black hair seemed to burst out of his body. Eddie talked directly to the audience.

"Would you like to hear a song?" he said.

"Yes!" the audience answered.

"How about 'Makin' Whoopie'?" he said. Big applause. "This is Bobby Sherwood, our orchestra leader. Bobby, take a bow. Bobby's from the South. A lot of you are probably from the South. South Brooklyn." He continued speaking to the audience. "How did you get here tonight?"

"Subway!" somebody yelled out.

"Was it crowded?"

"No."

"Did you pay?" Laughter.

"Come on, who went under the turnstile? You, what's your name?" Eddie Cantor was talking to my brother Arnie! "How old are you?"

"Seven," Arnie replied.

"Are you married?"

"No," Arnie said shyly.

"I've got five daughters," Eddie Cantor said.

The audience laughed.

"I'm just looking for a *shiddach*"—the Yiddish word for a marital match. "How much time do we have, Jimmy?"

"Half an hour."

"Let's do 'Susie.'"

More applause. Cantor started to sing. His body seemed to surge as if it had been hit by electric current. His feet and hands were moving vertically and horizontally like piston rods. He looked like a puppet that had been given life and wanted us all to wonder at it.

I saw my mother and father turn to each other. They smiled. I had brought them together. I had done something that seemed impossible. Eddie Cantor could bring peace to my family.

From that moment I really wanted to become a comedian.

At three minutes to 8 o'clock, just before the show went on the air, Jimmy Wallington said to all of us out in front, "Remember, you're supposed to laugh."

Eddie ran across the stage, took a flying leap into Jimmy Wallington's waiting arms, and kissed him on the cheek just as the program went on, live.

To call it a radio show was a misnomer. When Eddie came to a joke he'd roll his eyes, which meant for us to laugh. He nodded his head when a joke didn't go over, which meant laugh anyway. When the show ended, Eddie seemed exhausted, but he performed a few encores. He gave us a great show, a great evening.

It was late when the Stiller family arrived home. I had gotten my family out of Brooklyn to see the world's greatest comedian. My mother and father had an unwritten truce; there were no fights for three whole days. I felt I had accomplished something wonderful.

Years later, when Eddie Cantor died, I wondered why there wasn't a national day of mourning. He died as if he had never been around. What he did for my family that night was never expressed in the obituaries, but my memories of Eddie Cantor—and my debt to him—never died.

I still remember the clang of the wheels of what we referred to as the Tanta Annie train, which ran along Pitkin Avenue, taking us to the home of the Citrons. The wheels clanging on the track sounded like the beat of a snare drum, din-da-din-da-din-da-din.

"We'll be going on the din-da-din train," I'd told Arnie and Doreen, excitement in my voice. "Let's be in the first car."

My father and mother sat with my little sister Doreen on the seats made of woven, wicker straw while Arnie and I became explorers discovering America through the front window. The thrill of being in the first car was heightened when we emerged from the tunnel. As the sunlight hit us, we marveled at how we could go from darkness to the fullness of light.

We were heading to the Citrons for Passover. Since my father never conducted a Seder, each year the five of us would take the subway to the home of someone in our family. This was done without an invitation. This particular year we arrived unannounced at my Uncle Charlie and Tanta Annie's house, 965 Sutter Avenue, Brooklyn. The Seder dinner was already on the table. The sight of five hungry faces standing at the door triggered a burst of laughter. Their smiles removed any embarrassment we might've had. The warm and effusive welcome, this year as all other years, filled us kids with the belief that our not being there would cause disappointment, heartbreak, grief. To this day, I wonder what really went through the minds of my various uncles and aunts.

Uncle Charlie and Tanta Annie's children were our cousins Joe, Dottie, and Jeanette Citron. They were older than us, and when we were at their house they became our loving caretakers. They seemed to enjoy taking us by the hands, buying things for us as if they were our mothers and father.

My Uncle Charlie had a seltzer route. He supplied families in East New York with the elixir of the poor: carbonated water in a bottle. He owned his own truck. Boxes of seltzer sprouted on two sides at 45-degree angles, making the truck look like a portable pagoda. The truck had non-inflatable hard-rubber tires. The cab stood above an engine that gasped when it turned over, then sputtered without letup, once started. I always recognized the sound when the truck was near our house, and I'd run into the street to greet it.

When I spotted my uncle he was usually on the way up to an apartment with a seltzer box on his shoulder. On his return he'd ask me how everyone was, and reach deep into his pockets and pull out a fistful of coins. He'd invariably hand me half a dollar.

"Here, buy something," he'd say. "For everybody."

The amount was unbelievable: a half dollar. On one occasion I immediately ran to the candy store and bought twenty-five pieces of penny gum that came with Indian picture cards. I knew my mother would kill me if I told her in advance, so I didn't. When I arrived at our apartment with twenty-five pieces of gum and pictures of Indian chiefs, my mother was furious.

"Where did you get the money?"

"Uncle Charlie gave it to me."

"What? Come with me," she said. "Take the gum and the cards." We went back to the candy store.

She confronted the owner. "How could you sell a kid twenty-five pieces of gum?" She turned to me. "Give him the cards."

I quietly took out the cards and handed them back to the store owner.

"What do you want from me?" the man asked.

"I want the quarter back."

The man looked at my mother, her eyes afire. He sheepishly gave back the quarter.

"Don't ever do it again," she said to him.

Uncle Charlie continued to slip me money from time to time, and I would buy what I wanted. And hide it.

Although the country was in the depths of the Depression my aunts, uncles, and older cousins still managed to have family meetings once a month. Each month the gatherings of the Devorah Faiga Jake Club—named for those aunts and uncles—were held in a different Citron household.

There was food, card playing, and discussion. In the middle of an evening of schmoozing and camaraderie, the bedroom door opened and a man dressed in a woman's fur coat, a lady's hat on his head and a rose in his mouth, burst into the living room singing the flower song from Bizet's *Carmen*.

He started to dance the flamenco, whirling around the room, grabbing my cousin Beady, who seemed to be a willing partner. Of course the shock of seeing my father in drag brought on a state of hilarity. No one could stop laughing. *Where did this come from?* I wondered.

Everyone laughed but my mother. This was a side of him we had never seen. He loved to dress up and shock the hell out of everybody, and he did.

I didn't know what to think. I didn't realize that my father's dancing was his way of denying there was a Depression. He wasn't going to let being jobless stop him from enjoying life. My mother could not understand this, and neither could I. I was ashamed at watching him make a fool of himself.

My father died at 102. Whenever I would ask what kept him going, he'd answer, "I never worry."

The get-togethers of the Devorah Faiga Jake Club never grew tiresome. They were full of warmth, good food, spontaneous singing, card-playing, and coffee and cake prepared by the many cooks and bakers who swarmed all over the kitchen. In the basement of my Uncle Max's house on Farragut Road in Canarsie, children would play games. My mother and my older cousins would always go off in some corner. Their conversations became intimate little gatherings that, as with Tessie and my mother, kids were not meant to overhear.

When the entertainment part of the evening began, there was an air of anticipation. My cousin Joe Lieberman, looking like an elegant compere, would introduce the show. His introductions were serious, as if he were presenting the greatest talents in the world. Chairs would quickly align themselves on either side of the room, creating an informal nightclub.

"Tonight we're going to hear from some members of the family," Joe said one night, as if at heart we were all artists whose talents had been hiding underground till this moment. "Who's going to be first?" he asked.

Doreen, who was five years old, blonde, blue-eyed, and terrified, suddenly bolted out of a corner into center stage, singing fervently, "Ay, ay, ay, they call her Minnie from Trinidad." Her rhythm was twice as fast as the written score. Her body was shaking and gyrating like a wound-up Judy Garland. "Ay, ay, ay, she wasn't good but she wasn't bad." After sailing through the chorus in record time, Doreen immediately sat down on a chair and joined the audience. She had broken the ice.

Uncle Abe had promised he would do a number, Joe announced as he scanned the room. An operatic piece, no doubt. Uncle Abe, however, was nowhere in sight.

"Where's Uncle Abe?" someone asked.

"He's in the bathroom warming up," somebody else said.

"Well," Joe said. "We heard from one member of the Stiller family. Now let's hear from Jerry."

Less shy than Doreen, three years older, and full of poise, I moved to the center of the room.

"What are you going to sing?" Joe asked.

"'Wagon Wheels,'" I said proudly. I began singing: "Wagon wheels, wagon wheels, keep on rollin' along. Wagon wheels, roll along, sing your song, carry me over the hill. Go long, mule, the steamer's at the landing, waitin' for to carry me home. Go long, mule, the bosses is a-waitin', waitin' for to carry me home."

The fact that I was singing a Negro spiritual to my family never fazed me or them. It was the only song I knew, and I sang it with feeling. When it was over and the cheering subsided, my cousin Leo—the one who had taken me on his bike—sang "Once I Built a Railroad." Joe himself followed by singing in Yiddish "Beltz, Mein Shteitle Beltz," Beltz being a small town in Poland.

A quiet settled over the room. "Where's Uncle Abe?" someone asked again.

"He has a cold," someone said.

"Well, he'll sing next time," Joe said. "Let's all eat."

We feasted on platters of salmon salad, tuna fish, egg salad, seeded rye bread, fresh-whipped butter, tomatoes, lettuce, and onion, all prepared by Abe, Hymie, and Max, restaurateurs who loved food and what it could do for the soul.

Abe owned the Madison, the biggest and classiest delicatessen on the Upper East Side. He and my Aunt Anne were the family aristocrats and lived on Park Avenue, but they were as generous as they were well off. Being good to the family seemed as important to them as being good in business. You always knew you could drop in at the restaurant without an invite.

Uncle Abe was small and feisty, quick to smile, and could speak positively on any subject. Even when the country was in the throes of the Depression, there was never a hint of negativity in his thinking. Though he was successful in business, the story in the family was that his true ambition was to be an opera star.

When I first told Uncle Abe that I wanted to be an actor, he never blinked. He looked at me with the unshakable belief that I would someday make it. "At least you'll never starve," he said. "If you're hungry, you can always come into the restaurant." It was a vote of confidence.

Some years later, during World War Two, Senator Harry Byrd of Virginia visited Uncle Abe's restaurant. It was during the days of rationing and the Office of Price Administration. The senator ordered a turkey sandwich. The check came to a dollar. The senator, feeling he'd been taken, reported it to the OPA. The story made page 3 of the *Daily News,* under the headline "Senator Byrd Gets the Bird." The flap devastated my uncle. He was characterized by some customers as a war profiteer, and was bombarded by hate mail. The barrage never ended. He finally sold the restaurant.

We were now living in East New York, Brooklyn, a neighborhood that was like a Jewish Brigadoon. It was warm and *gemütlich*. I was nine years old. What sticks in my memory was that our apartment doors were always open. Kids in the building were always running in and out of each other's apartments.

On Blake Avenue you could find appetizing stores, fish and poultry markets. On Sutter and Pitkin Avenues were movie palaces like Loew's Premier and Loew's Pitkin. On Hopkinson Avenue across the subway tracks in Brownsville were the Stone and the Stadium, where on weekdays anyone could get into a double feature two for a nickel.

The pushcarts on Blake Avenue were not unlike shtetl scenes Isaac Singer described in Frampol. They were a reminder that I was Jewish. Peddlers were up each morning screaming their wares half in Yiddish, half in English. They'd argue over a customer.

"I had her first," one would say.

"Gey in Dreyet." ("Go to hell.")

They'd shout, and grab people by their sleeves as they went by.

"Hey lady, I got something for you." A peddler was pulling my mother by the arm. It made me very uncomfortable.

"Leave me alone," she said, removing his hand. It was usually the beginning of bargaining.

"You're a nice-looking w[...]
mantic. My mother knew it [...]
loved it. "What are you so mad [...]
mediate attraction. Being poor [...]
very attractive. She turned men [...]

"*A sheine veible.* You're a goo[...]
the peddlers enjoyed the banter. [...]

We loved East New York. But i[...]
Leo's mom, won $2,500 in the Iris[...]
and my father used our half of the [...]
to move again.

So in 1939, the year Hitler inva[...]ved to Goerck
Street on the Lower East Side. As a fiv[...]old, I had not been very nice
to my younger brother, Arnie—in fact, I had once pushed him down a
flight of stairs and on another occasion had done nothing while he almost
drowned in Prospect Park lake. But now, I felt I was my brother's keeper.
So at age twelve I became Arnie's protector from kids who might take advantage of him.

Ralphie Stolzman was a tall, angular boy about a year older than me,
and was a terrific stickball hitter. He was quiet and wore glasses. He
looked like a misplaced Eton student. His grace reminded me of Joe
DiMaggio as he stepped up to the plate to take his incredible whacks.

The first fistfight of my life was with Ralphie in the schoolyard next to
the Rubel Ice plant on Mangin Street. I was a full six inches shorter than
Ralphie, and full of conviction that I could kill the guy. This was to be my
baptism into manhood on the Lower East Side.

The argument that started the fight had to do with a ring belonging to
my brother that Ralphie had absconded with. Ralphie denied stealing the
ring. I called him a liar. In front of friends I goaded Ralphie into the fight
by calling him "four eyes," then accusing him of being yellow. He seemed
to take the provocations calmly, as if giving me a chance to take them
back even while saying them.

"You're yellow, Ralph, you know that, don't ya?"

Ralphie kept listening with a sense of disbelief.

"You took my brother's ring," I said.

"No, I didn't," he finally replied.

"Yes, you did. You stole it."

"So where do you want to fight?" he asked. "In the schoolyard?"

...eel fear creep up my shoulders into my neck
...w he hated me.
...ed.
...Friday, after school."
...ere," Ralphie said.
...as about five days before showdown, and the news really got
...und. Excitement rippled through the whole neighborhood. I heard rumors that Ralphie had obtained a second, an older fat boy I knew from
school, a loudmouth know-it-all.

The fat boy was spreading it around that Ralphie was out to kill me.
Fat boy confronted me two days before the fight to alert me that I was in
a lot of trouble. I asked him what he meant.

"Ralphie's in training."

"What does that mean?" I said.

"He's doing roadwork."

"Yeah?"

"Yeah. He wants to teach you a lesson. How did you get into this,
Jerry?"

"He stole my brother's ring."

"Your brother gave it to him. Do you really want this?"

Ralphie's trying to get out of it, I thought to myself. *He's trying to back
out; he really* is *yellow.*

"Tell him I'm waiting for him," I said.

My words seemed to fill me with courage and anticipation of what was
to be the great triumph of my twelve and a half years on the planet. I was
going to make it on the Lower East Side.

The next day I got a report that Ralphie was dipping his hands in cement to toughen them, and that the fat boy had gone to Stillman's Gym
to bone up on some tricks of the trade.

Friday arrived at the schoolyard, and so did I. A thin spray of water
was spritzing from the ice-making machinery atop the Rubel plant, and
the last rays of the sun through the mist gave everything an eerie reddish
tint. The concrete ground was the color of rust.

I could see a few curious faces hovering around. There were a couple
of others peering from behind a wire fence. They seemed skeptical that
anything violent was going to take place. Ralphie was nowhere in sight.
My dream of this being another Dempsey-Willard fight went up in smoke.

Suddenly Ralphie arrived with the fat boy. Ralphie seemed very con-

centrated. He hardly noticed me. Methodically he removed his glasses
and handed them to the fat boy. He looked kind of innocent without
them, and also a little blind. Fat boy whispered something into Ralphie's
ear. Ralphie nodded. I suddenly felt all alone. Now people started coming
in from behind the fence. Someone in the yard shouted, "You need a referee."

Fat boy said, "I'll be the referee."

I said okay.

"Shall we have rounds?" someone asked.

"Sure," I said.

No mention was made of how many rounds, and how long. I stared
up at Ralphie, who now seemed even taller than the six inches he already
had on me. I figured if I crouched he'd never lay a hand on me. I tried
looking at him. He showed no emotion. He seemed a little hurt. Maybe
he was right, I thought; maybe my brother did give him the ring. It didn't
matter. I wanted this fight. I had provoked it because I wanted somebody
to beat up, someone I thought I could lick and prove myself a man on the
tough Lower East Side. Ralphie looked so easy. At that moment I knew
that fear had made me act like a bully so I would not appear a coward.

Somebody said, "Bong." The fight started.

Ralphie just stood there. He looked strong, tough, unafraid. I was
scared. I charged into him, trying to convince myself I could fight. Ralphie stood his ground. I tried to get under his long arms and land a blow
to his head, which I thought would make him quit. I missed.

He stood and measured me as I prepared for another onslaught. His
right hand hit me in the face, and I could feel his knuckles against my
skin. It hurt. I looked at his hands. They were chalk white. They *had* been
dipped in cement. He hit me a shot above the left eye. I was bleeding. I
tried hitting him in the stomach. I couldn't touch him. He was moving
around me. I lunged again. Now he was hitting me at will, like an *angry*
Joe DiMaggio. The only thing he didn't have was a bat.

As I ducked a left and fell into a clinch, his fist came around with a
roundhouse right that caught me in the spine. It was like an electric
shock, like voltage going through my entire body. It straightened me up
to my full height. Tears stuck in my throat. I could feel pain and humiliation. He hit me again. I refused to give up. I moved forward. I remember
hanging onto his two fists as supports. Fat boy tried to separate us to keep
the fight going.

I don't remember much more except that the beating didn't stop, and the cement on Ralphie's fists had done its damage. At one point he must have had some mercy, or maybe someone off the street stepped in and stopped the massacre. I was bleeding, and could feel my upper body hanging from my waist.

The crowd started to break up. My shirt was ripped and bloody, and I tucked it into my pants as I made my way down Stanton Street, walking as fast as my body would carry me, trying not to look in the faces of the people staring at me.

I reached Goerck Street and climbed the flights to our apartment. The door was open and I walked straight to my room, fell across the bed face-down, and started to cry. My mother appeared in the doorway.

"What happened?" she asked.

"I was in a fight."

I lay there, waiting for her to say something.

"I heard about it," she said. "It was with Ralphie. Why?"

"He stole Arnie's ring," I said, as if I had saved the family jewels.

She went into the kitchen and returned with some ice wrapped in a dish towel. She lifted my shirt carefully so as to not tear the skin. I felt her fingers touch my back. She applied the ice to the welts. I waited for her to say something, but she didn't say a word. I wanted her to hug me, tell me I was brave, make me feel less ashamed of having taken a beating.

She put her face next to my ear and whispered, "Next time you'll know better."

She went to get some more ice. I started to cry, then stopped myself. I knew she was right, and I fell into a deep sleep.

Some five years later, I was in basic training at Fort Knox. There was a sergeant in charge of us—Sgt. Ralphie Stolzman, one and the same. He was the most docile guy in the world, so sweet. He got me off KP. After his discharge I think he became a schoolteacher.

Just before my thirteenth birthday, my mother said, "We're going to get you a nice Bar Mitzvah suit."

She took me down to Orchard Street. Orchard Street made Baghdad seem like kindergarten when it came to bargains, but my mother's bargaining skills were honed to razor sharpness.

We passed a few stores. "Let's try this one," she said, and led me inside.

"He wants a suit," she said to the owner, as if this were not her idea. "Have you got a suit for him?"

The store was loaded with suits. There were racks on top of racks. The quiet-spoken man with a European-educated voice asked, "What kind of suit?"

"A wool suit," my mother said, wool being top-of-the-line material, not to be confused with rayon or some synthetic.

"I've got a beautiful suit for him here."

He reached up with a stick with a handle that worked movable claws, and he took down a brown wool suit from the rack. He showed it to us.

"It's got knickers, one pair of pants, and a vest. Do you want to try it on?"

"Yes, I'd like that," I said, unable to control my feelings.

"Then try it on. There's a fitting room over there."

My mother took me into the fitting room.

"Don't say you like it," she told me.

"Why not?"

"Because he's going to want more money if he knows you like it."

"How much will it cost?" I asked.

"Just keep your mouth shut and let me handle this. Try the suit on."

When I came out of the dressing room, she asked, "Do you like it?"

"Yes, I love it."

"Don't tell him that," she mumbled, giving me a look.

The owner said, "How do you like it?" a smile lighting up his face.

"He says it's okay," my mother said in a sullen voice.

"That's 100 percent pure virgin wool, you know."

"Yeah," she said cutting him short. "How much?"

"Thirteen dollars."

"What? Thirteen dollars!" my mother screamed. "Take off the suit."

"What?" I said.

She looked at me with that look. "Take it off."

I went back into the dressing room.

"Wait a minute," the man said. "That suit costs me thirteen dollars, lady. I'm giving it to you for thirteen dollars."

"Thirteen dollars? Who's got thirteen dollars?"

"Okay, how much do you want to give me for the suit?"

"You're going to have to do better."

As I changed back into my own clothes, I was listening.

"All right, take it for twelve dollars."

"Twelve dollars!" Her voice sounded as if she were being strangled. "Come on, let's go." She yanked me out of the booth by the hand.

"Where are you going?" the man said.

"Out of here." She was pulling me. As we hit the street I heard, "Ten dollars." He had come down three dollars. My mother said: "Keep moving." I turned to look at the man following us. "Come on," she said. "Keep walking."

"What are you doing, lady?" the man cried. "Do you want to kill me?"

He was chasing her.

"I gotta make a living too. All right, nine dollars. Take it for nine dollars."

"Take it, Ma," I said.

She hit my shoulder with her hand. "Shut up."

"Look, how much do you want to give me?"

"I'll give you five dollars," she said.

On the street for everyone to hear, he yelled, "Five dollars! Go, get out of my sight." He was no longer the quiet-spoken man. "Walk. I don't want to see you again!" he was shouting.

"Come on." She pulled on my sweater and started to run.

"Ma, why don't you take it?"

"Shut up," she said. "And run."

We were at the end of the block. We'd passed three other clothing stores. Breathless, he caught us. Tears in his eyes.

"Okay, you can have it for seven dollars."

"Six," my mother said.

"Six-fifty."

"It's a deal," my mother said.

We walked back to the store. They talked. Suddenly, there was friendship, warmth.

"I would never do this for anyone else. I want you to know I'm losing money on this," the man said. "You'll tell your friends?"

"Yes," my mother said. "I'll tell the world."

I could sense she still felt she'd gotten the bad end of the deal. He folded the beautiful suit in a box. Six-fifty, I said to myself. How did she do it? I felt sorry for the man. He got some twine and tied the box.

"What is the suit for?" he asked me.

"My Bar Mitzvah."

"Wear it in good health. Is this your first suit?" He was searching for some reason for giving the suit away for so low a price. "I want you to know you got a real bargain. I wouldn't do this for just anybody."

"You're a wonderful man," my mother said. "A sweetheart."

What she had done was extraordinary, but I could not help feeling she had taken advantage of this poor man. Later I learned that the money for my suit had been borrowed from my Tanta Faiga.

As we walked home, my mother said, "You should've listened to me when I told you to be quiet. Do you know how long your father has to work for thirteen dollars? Did you know that fellow was overcharging us to begin with? Look around," she said pointing to other store windows.

Sure enough, there were suits going for nine and ten dollars, before the bargaining.

"It's all an act. One day when you have to go to work you'll know."

Work? I thought. *Who wants to work? Someday I'm going to be an actor.*

We moved from Goerck Street to the Vladecks about the same time as the New York World's Fair arrived in Flushing Meadows in 1939. The projects were a dream come true for many families. We had courtyards, elevators, washing machines in the basement, and no more bathrooms in the hall.

By the time I was thirteen, Arnie and I had spent two summers outside New York at summer camps. One was the Boys Club camp, Camp Carey, at the tip of Long Island. The other was the Educational Alliance Camp, also called the Eddie Cantor Camp, at Surprise Lake, on the New York/New Jersey border.

I hated both places. The Boys Club camp seemed totally devoid of Jewish faces, while Surprise Lake had nothing but. Boys Club seemed structured and cold, while Surprise Lake was warm and supervised and full of wonderful food. Much too nice for me. I couldn't handle it.

At Boys Club, Arnie and I bunked together with ten other kids. When lights-out occurred at 9 P.M., the entire camp was expected to obey the rule of silence. The sound of crickets quickly replaced the sound of the human voice. The edict was strictly adhered to by everyone. "Lights-out, no noise." The order, shouted in the dark by a counselor, put a damper on everything, and was also a little scary.

One night, as the counselor's voice bellowed, "No noise," I could hear Arnie's chatter at the far end of the bunk area.

"Quiet, and I mean it," the counselor yelled.

Whereupon my brother shouted, "Give me liberty or give me death!"

"Who said that?" the counselor demanded.

"Patrick Henry," my brother answered.

The bunk exploded with laughter. The counselor was not amused. He ordered Arnie to stand outside. Arnie threw a blanket across his shoulders and obediently walked outside to face the night's formations of mosquitoes. I asked the counselor if I could join him. I was given permission, and together we stood outside for twenty minutes. After that, I knew I would never return to that camp, and I didn't.

My father was a part-time driver for the Triangle Bus Company. This was the job he had bought a few years earlier, when my mother and her sister Chaila (Leo's mother) won the Irish Sweepstakes. My father was able to get off the WPA and through an uncle "buy" a job with the bus company. He stayed with them for twenty years.

The owner of Triangle was a Democratic Party captain in our district. My mother thought political influence would help get me into another summer camp. The Eddie Ahearn Club, a Tammany Hall branch on East Broadway, was accessible to any of the party faithful who might need a favor, and my mother felt my father was owed one of those favors. During the summer months he was asked to "volunteer"—without pay—to drive busloads of loyal Democrats on excursions to Coney Island. In return, the club owed my father a favor, namely to get me into camp. But when it became clear that no help was forthcoming, my mother was livid.

This inspired me to investigate a settlement house on East Third Street known as the Boys Brotherhood Republic. The BBR was at the bottom rung of the settlement-house ladder. It was a renovated six-story tenement run by the boys themselves, a kind of mini-democracy. George Ogourlian, the adult supervisor, was ensconced in a small office. The young members were called "citizens," and they elected a mayor, a district attorney, a police commissioner, a judge, and ten councilmen. Council meetings were held once a week. Taxes were collected, fines levied in cases of criminal conduct, and court trials of the accused were held every Friday night. "Where Boys Rule" was the motto.

This self-administration created responsibility for boys from seven to eighteen. The BBR, though a good half-mile from Jackson Street in the projects, excited me enough to walk or skate to East Third Street every afternoon to take part in the activities. I was very comfortable there.

The BBR allowed me to take responsibility for my own life. I ran for city councilman and won. I was elected number-one councilman by a record number of votes. The BBR took me off the streets. I was paid twenty-five dollars to write a story that would be published in Denmark that spoke of my BBR experience. What a thrill. At fourteen I was paid to write. It was a leg up into life. It gave me a sense of self.

Eddie Egan, a former amateur boxing champion, was married to a member of the Colgate toothpaste family. He had visited the BBR and was impressed enough to convince his in-laws to donate land for a summer camp. Camp Colgate was several acres of land near Pompton Lakes, New Jersey. There was no electricity and no counselors, just older BBR boys who took care of us younger ones. Food was prepared by a guy who claimed he could cook. We were like pioneers awakened by a bugle sounding reveille. We had breakfast cooked on a huge coal stove. We all had jobs clearing the land, building the camp. We also had a baseball team that played other camps in the area, treasure hunts that I had a knack of winning, and campfire shows that I started putting on, satires of camp life.

When the two weeks were up, I hated having to go home. When World War Two broke out, two of the older boys, Moishe Bader and Mac Mandel, became flyers. Both were killed over Germany. Ralph Hittman joined the marines and later married Moishe's sister, Rose. Ralph took over for George Ogourlian as supervisor and remained in charge for forty-three years. We have stayed close to this day.

I had learned pride. The BBR opened me up and made me aware of life's possibilities.

When I was in high school, I started attending performances of Yiddish theater, which at that time was vying for an already dwindling audience as Yiddish became less frequently spoken. Necessity dictated that I catch a breath of it before it expired. Maurice Schwartz was considered one of the greatest stars of the Yiddish theater, and one Saturday afternoon I headed to Second Avenue, the Great White Way of Jewish theater, to see one of his shows.

The lobby was alive with people looking for one another, husbands looking for wives, wives for husbands. Everyone seemed related—was it possible they were all one family? I felt like an orphan. For one thing, I did not speak Yiddish, although I could understand it.

A man in a dark suit and a felt hat suddenly appeared next to me and asked if I had a seat.

"Dir hust a seat?"

"Nicht," I said, trying to affect the Yiddish equivalent of the word "no." He then told me that some members of his burial society did not show up and I could have a $2.40 orchestra seat next to him. I handed him fifty-five cents and he handed me a ticket. At once, much of the magic of theater disappeared. The theater was supposed to be artistic, above the level of *hondling*. I had often bought a balcony seat and then snuck down to the orchestra, but this was different. I felt Yiddish theater was sacred. Nevertheless, I went into the theater and seated myself next to my benefactor.

The curtain rose on a painted backdrop depicting a home in a Polish shtetl. The first act centered around the impending arrival of a Hasidic rabbi who was bringing the forlorn people news that would change their lives. The stage suddenly became alive with actors and actresses in colorful costumes. I could see beards that had been hurriedly glued on—the actors were obviously doubling in parts. They delivered most of their lines out front, setting up the plot. I cringed and wanted to leave. The man who sold me the ticket grabbed my arm. He must have guessed what I was thinking and shook his head as if to say, "stick around." I now sat straight up in my seat and pretended to be intensely interested.

The play progressed, and every few minutes there would come a knock at a door onstage, heralding another character's entrance. The audience was waiting for Schwartz to appear and so, at every knock, would begin to applaud wildly—but it would only be another bit player announcing that Mr. Schwartz was on his way. This happened again and again. I too fell into the trap, clapping for the wrong actor each time, and each time my benefactor looked at me soulfully, his eyes telling me it was not Schwartz. His look seemed to imply that I might as well be a Gentile.

At one point he turned to me and whispered: *"Fer shtaite Yiddish?"* (Do you understand Yiddish?) I replied meekly, *"A bisselle,"*—a little.

I knew I had just signed on as his pupil. He started filling me in so I could understand the plot.

"Soon," he said, "you'll see Schwartz."

At the next knock a huge man with great presence and a dark beard strode on stage. Just as my hands came together the man stopped me.

"Schwartz?" I muttered.

"No, no mein kint." He referred to me as his child and he grabbed my arms.

Suddenly the lights dimmed. A knock. All eyes turned upstage. We heard wind, thunder, lightning. The door flew open, but mysteriously, there was no one there. Where was Schwartz? As the moment was about to pass, the door slammed shut and a small mole-like figure scurried from the wings across the stage unobtrusively. *"Ich hat bikimin"* (I have come), the man whispers. The curtain falls. The old man turns to me and says with a smile, "That's Schwartz."

Years later I was asked to read for Maurice Schwartz, who was about to do an English-language version of Molière's *The Miser*. I was up for a small role. The audition began and I read with the stage manager. In the middle of the reading the phone rang. Schwartz asked the stage manager, Terry Becker, to answer the phone.

"But I'm reading with an actor," Terry said.

"He can read both parts himself," Schwartz said, as I stood in quiet amazement.

"I can't read a scene between two people by myself, Mr. Schwartz," I said.

"Yes, you can. I can tell," he said. I read both parts and didn't get either one but I did meet the great Maurice Schwartz.

But theater was less important to me than girls. Adolescence was starting to kick in.

In the Cellar Club on Pitt Street the smell of Pall Malls made us feel like big guys. This was the place where a girl's lipstick on a cigarette butt meant make-out. Fifteen was an age where you tried to go all the way. Pall Malls—the longer, taller cigarette—were a weapon of seduction. When she saw you light up, she'd know this was no foolin' around. Man, who knew *what* she might do once you got her to puff one of those bombolinos. If she wasn't supposed to be smoking in the first place, then what else might she be willing to do?

The scene would always play out something like this: A guy and a girl are sitting on the couch. He reaches for a butt in his shirt pocket. With one hand he lights up, closing the matchbook with his thumb and fore-finger. (How many times has he rehearsed that one?) He takes a drag and inhales. The smoke's coming out of his nose now, like some kind of dragon. She takes a puff as he casually ambles over to the hi-fi and drops a 45 of Glenn Miller onto the turntable. "Wanna dance?" It's "Moonlight Serenade," a slow Lindy.

She can kind of go with this. He's not comin' on too fast. She likes this. Just enough to get her in the right frame of everything. She can't come off as being easy. He's a good dancer, nothing too fancy, just do-ing steps. Now he spins her into a twirl. She's a little shy, but goes with it. He's playing it cool. Now she's smiling. When the record ends, she's in his arms. He goes into a dip. Nobody dips when you Lindy.

Suddenly the Cellar Club empties. I take the hint, because I know they're gonna be doing it soon on a damp couch.

At sixteen I had a high-school sweetheart, the first girl I was serious about. She was definitely not one of the girls from the Cellar Club. I re-member saying good-night on the stoop of her house. I kissed her softly on the lips, as if contact with them would betray the passion she had ex-cited in me. I felt this restraint would win her love. Her body would arch against the door, awaiting a move on my part. I'd purse my lips and swear to myself that if she never put out, I could love her anyway. The good-nights left me satisfied that I had not violated her purity and that one day she would marry me.

My interest in theater was growing, and I decided that I would be an actor. I was proud of the fact that, unlike most kids my age who had not yet made a life choice, I had.

I broke the news of my secret ambition to my sweetheart during a per-formance of the Ice Capades at the Center Theater in Rockefeller Center. We were high up in the balcony. I felt the glamour of show business would somehow rub off. The ice skaters were marvelous athletes who thrilled the audience.

At intermission I made the momentous announcement. I'd deliber-ately led my sweetheart to the candy concession and bought some Goobers. And, like a munificent millionaire, I had put some of them in her hand.

"I'm going to do that someday," I said.

"Do what? Skate?"

Suddenly I realized I had picked the wrong setting. This was an ice show, not a stage play. Making this announcement at a Broadway show would have been more appropriate, but I couldn't afford the ticket.

"I've decided . . . I'm going to be . . . an actor," I said a bit hesitantly.

She gave a disbelieving laugh, then fell silent. I was desperate. I wasn't kidding.

"I do these impressions," I said in a low voice as people moved about us, talking away. "I have the information," I said, doing Peter Lorre.

She stared at me, puzzled.

"I also do Jimmy Durante," I said. "'Ya gotta start off each day with a song, inka dinka doo,' I got a million of them," I said, waiting for her to respond.

A bell sounded the end of intermission. I wanted her to say something like, "That was wonderful. I think you're great." I would then have said, "With you behind me, I can go to the top." But this wasn't turning out like an MGM movie.

"The second act is about to begin," an usher said. We headed back to our seats, which now seemed even farther from the ice than before. We watched the second act of the ice show in complete silence. I had proposed marriage and she didn't know it. I still pursued her.

Two years later, while I was stationed in Italy, I received a letter from her saying she could no longer write as she was seeing another boy. He worked in the post office, and they planned to get married. I guess being an actor could not compete with delivering the mail. But could he do Peter Lorre?

While still in high school I signed up to participate in amateur night at the Educational Alliance. I wanted to show my mother I had talent.

The auditorium had folding chairs placed in rows and a microphone on a stand. The emcee was the Alliance social director. "Who knows, we may find a future star here tonight," he announced.

I asked my mother to sit up front and I went backstage, awaiting my turn. I vaguely thought of what I would do. A surge of confidence filled me as I waited, fearless, for my name to be called. I had no script, no plans, no music. I would just get up and take the microphone and entertain. Dreams of Eddie Cantor making people laugh floated through my head. Just talking to the audience would make them love me. Maybe, I thought, I'll do my Jimmy Durante and Peter Lorre impersonations.

I heard my name, ran out on the stage, grabbed the mike, and started talking. I don't remember a word I said except that I paced in front of everybody saying, "Good evening, ladies and gentlemen" and whatever else came into my mind. I expected laughter to burst upon me, crushing me with its deafening roar.

Nothing.

Then the people out in front started talking to one another, ignoring me.

I started to do my imitation of Jimmy Durante singing "Inka-dinka-doo." No one cared. I looked out into the audience for my mother. She seemed mystified, bewildered. I turned away. The emcee came out and asked me if I was finished.

"Yes," I said.

My mother was walking toward the staircase. Very fast. I chased after her.

When I caught up, I said, "How was I?"

"You stunk," she said, continuing down the stairs.

I couldn't believe she would say something like that. I was her kid. How could she say that to me? I wanted to be great for her, but I had only disappointed and shamed her.

What had gone wrong?

Despite my disastrous amateur night appearance, my interest in show business didn't flag. I was on my way home from Seward Park High School when I passed the Henry Street Playhouse on Grand Street. A friend, Nat Adler, had told me he was acting there. On this warm spring day I decided to walk in. I entered the lobby carrying my books and could hear a piano playing inside the theater. Nobody stopped me so I opened the door and ambled in. The theater was empty. The stage was bathed in a blue light and someone was playing "Night and Day."

I stood for a moment. Suddenly the music and the blue lights enveloped my senses. I felt a sereneness I had never experienced before. It was like I had been transported into a land that was trouble-free. I sat down and listened. When the man stopped playing I quietly walked up the steps of the stage and said to another man with a paintbrush and overalls, "How do I get a chance to act?" I was speaking to Richard Brown, the scenic designer and technical director of the theater. He looked at me very sympathetically.

"Why don't you see Mrs. Lane," he said "She's upstairs."

And that's how, at age fifteen, I met Esther Porter Lane, a beautiful woman who made me aware for the first time how beautiful theater was. This was to be the most fateful moment of my life.

"Come back next week. We're doing *Many Moons* by James Thurber. You can play the king."

"My friend Nathan Adler told me about this place," I said.

"Nat is playing the wizard," she said.

Esther Lane was an assistant to Hallie Flanagan Davis, one of the founders of the Federal Theater. Mrs. Lane was from Maine. What possessed her to come to Manhattan's Lower East Side and work with disadvantaged people I'll never know. It must have been that brand of social consciousness that was aflame in those days. It was the Eleanor Roosevelt thing, helping the people who needed it most. I always thought of Esther Lane as a Protestant woman who loved the poor of all faiths.

My first laugh as an actor came when as the King in *Many Moons*: I pulled the bell cord and it accidentally fell to the floor. A big laugh. I liked that. I did nothing and people laughed. It took away the hurt of the amateur night. Next I played Hsei Ping Kwei in *Lady Precious Stream*.

Esther directed a show that included music by Earl Robinson, who later wrote "The House I Live In." The show was a living newspaper called *It's Up to You* that was about winning World War Two. I sang and acted. Joan Woodruff did the choreography.

One day Esther got us free tickets to see Uta Hagen, José Ferrer, and Paul Robeson in *Othello*. I'll never forget sitting in the fifth row. How wonderful. Now I really wanted to act. She introduced me to her husband, David, an Army Air Force officer who came in on furlough. Both of them got me started in theater.

3

GI Jerry

By the spring of 1944, the United States had landed troops in Africa and Sicily. D-Day was still two months away, but it was clear that we were going to invade Europe somewhere across the English Channel. We kept hearing Gabriel Heatter declare on the radio, "There's good news tonight." The Russians were holding on, though their casualties were enormous. Rommel was on the run in Africa, and the Fifth Army was winning in Italy. But in the Pacific there were Guadalcanal, Kwajalein, Guam. If it were to happen, we assumed, we would have to lose at least 100,000 men in the invasion of Japan.

Four of my older cousins were now in the service. Leo, the biker, enlisted the day after Pearl Harbor, at age seventeen. He rose to the rank of staff sergeant and landed in the second wave at Omaha Beach on D-Day. He would later be awarded the Bronze Star, the Combat Infantryman's Badge, and the Presidential Citation. He was wounded twice, the second time in the Battle of the Bulge.

One afternoon I came home from Seward Park High with a form from the U.S. Army Specialized Training Reserve program. I needed my parents' signatures to join. I had already passed the special high school armed services test. I would be seventeen on June 8, 1944. I could join the Army Reserves, and the government would send me to an Ivy League college. I'd learn Japanese, become an officer, perhaps an interpreter, ready for when we invaded Japan. Landing in Japan seemed a very remote possibility to me, but my mother and father were appalled.

"We're not signing." It was the first time I'd ever seen them in agreement about anything. They looked at me in disbelief as I held the paper in my hand. "Sign it," I said.

My father sat at the edge of the bed. He had just come home from work.

"Talk to him," my mother said, tears in her eyes. "You can't join the army," she said. "You're sixteen years old. The war is on. Do you know what that means? They want you to join up and they'll send you over-seas."

"They can't. I'm seventeen years old."

"You're sixteen."

"It's a trick," my father told me. "Once they get you in, they can do what they want with you."

I had never seen him so upset. "I'm seventeen," I said again. "They can't send me over." I could not comprehend the possibility that I'd ever get killed. I could only think of the free education I would receive at Harvard or Yale. I could see ivy-covered walls. I really wanted to get out of the Lower East Side, away from the fights between the two of them—yet here they were, fighting over me, begging me to stay out of the army.

"Tell him," my mother pleaded. "Tell him not to join."

"I could get a college education," I said, "and you won't have to pay."

"They could call you up and ship you out tomorrow," my father re-peated. "They just cut basic training from twenty-six weeks to thirteen weeks. It can go down further." He was right. "And they can change the law to take you in the regular army. Don't join," he said.

"I need your signature," I said. I loved this moment. It made me feel brave. "I can go to Yale, Cornell, Harvard, all the places that have Army Specialized Training Reserve Program (ASTRP) programs. Clemson. Georgia Tech." Just hearing the names of these schools was a dream come true.

"*I'll* send you to college," my father said. I had never heard him say that before.

"How can you? It costs money."

"I work, I'll pay for it," he said. It was like a cannon exploding in my heart. I knew my mother and father really loved me.

"You can't, it's too much money," I said. The thought of going to a college in New York City, which was free, was out of the question. I really wanted to run as far away from them as possible. We argued the entire night. By morning I finally got them to sign.

I received my orders to report to City College of New York (CCNY), 137th Street and Amsterdam Avenue. I was less than an hour from home on the IRT subway. The army lied. My dream of going to Yale had not materialized. However, CCNY was at the top of the country scholastically.

On June 6,1944, two days short of my seventeenth birthday, I was readying myself for battle with integral and differential calculus, chemistry, and a course in Japanese for an inevitable landing at Tokyo Bay.

Then on August 6, 1945, we dropped the bomb—the landing in Tokyo Bay was not to be. I was ordered to report to basic training at Fort Knox, and was looking forward to a chance at qualifying for Officers' Candidate School. Everything was going well until an episode during the third week of training. I had just been chosen the best soldier in my company. I performed the manual of arms and recited the articles of war, which I had memorized. My reward for being chosen best soldier was to be a three-day pass.

But first I was made an honor guard and given an MP armband and a .45 automatic, which I had not yet learned how to fire. I was then introduced to a sergeant wearing lots of ribbons who was to be discharged the following day. Together we were to circle Fort Knox in a jeep, for twenty-four hours, in four-hour shifts.

We started our tour. The sergeant asked me if I would mind driving; he'd take over later. I agreed, and we circled the perimeter of Fort Knox. Our MP presence was a deterrent to GI speeders.

As I drove, we chatted. The sergeant related how he'd been wounded in North Africa. Upon leaving the hospital he was sent back into action in Sicily, and was again hit. He was getting a medical discharge the next day, and was aching to get out. I told him my story.

The sergeant said he was twenty-seven, an infantry rifleman promoted to sergeant on the battlefield. "They wanted to make me an officer, but I didn't want it."

"Why not?" I asked.

"It would've been a battlefield promotion. You know what that is, don't you? They give you the bar. Right on the spot you're a second lieutenant. Two minutes later you're out in front, and you're dead."

"By the way," he added, "would you mind if we dropped over to the package store in Elizabethtown? I want to pick up something. My company's throwing me a farewell party tomorrow night."

I knew this excursion was off limits, but sitting next to a battlefield veteran with a slew of medals, including a Purple Heart, a Bronze Star, and more, led me to believe nothing would happen to us.

"Just sit here," the sergeant said as he pulled up at the package store. "You'd better take off the MP band and get rid of the .45."

I obeyed, stowing everything in the rear compartment of the jeep. I got back in the jeep. It was one of those blistering hot days when the rising dust particles reflect and the sun creates a Hollywood sunset.

I waited in the jeep just as a civilian car drove up and an elderly major got out and also entered the store. He gave me an odd kind of glance. A woman, no doubt the major's wife, remained in the car. The sergeant emerged carrying a brown paper bag. He handed it to me and asked me to stick it in the back compartment as he jumped behind the wheel. The major, carrying a purchase himself, bounced out the door of the package store.

"Let's go," the sergeant said, the wheels screeching as he put the pedal to the metal.

"Do you think he'll follow us?" I asked.

It was now dusk, and through the dust I could see headlights. The vehicle behind us speeded up. It was the major's car. The sergeant slowed down. "We'll see what he wants." He seemed unperturbed.

The car pulled alongside, forcing us off the road. The major got out and advanced toward the jeep.

"Dismount," he ordered. The sergeant and I obeyed, then saluted. We were silhouetted against a moon that was just beginning to rise on one horizon as the sun was disappearing on the other. The major looked directly at me and said, "What were you doing in that liquor store, soldier?"

I didn't answer.

He repeated, "What were you doing in that liquor store, soldier?"

"I was not in that store, sir," I answered.

"Are you calling me a liar?"

"No, sir."

"Is there any liquor in that vehicle?" he asked.

"I don't know, sir."

"Why don't you open the hatch."

I walked hesitantly to the back of the jeep.

"Open it," he ordered. I did.

"Take out what's in there."

I reached in and pulled out the MP band.

"Why aren't you wearing it?"

"I thought I'd take it off," I said.

"What else is back there?"

Once again I reached in and lifted out the .45 automatic.

"What's it doing back there?"

"I don't know, sir."

"Is there any liquor in this jeep?"

"I don't know, sir."

"Why don't you look."

I removed the brown paper bag.

"What's in the bag?"

"I don't know."

I stopped calling him sir. Was he trying to get me to pin it on the sergeant? Why wasn't he questioning him? Why didn't the sergeant own up? Nevertheless, Lower East Side ethics were in force: Never squeal.

"Take it out of the bag," the major said.

I removed a bottle of bourbon from the bag.

"What are you holding in your hand?"

"I don't know, sir." I was calling him sir again, hoping he'd let up.

"Hold it up," he ordered.

I lifted the bottle above my head.

"What's in that bottle?"

"I don't know, sir."

His wife had got out of the car. I was on trial on a dirt road in Kentucky. Do I tell the truth? Blame the sergeant? This major can't be serious.

Grabbing the bottle from my hand, he waved it above his head, and using the rising full moon to illuminate the evidence, he shouted, "What do I have in my hand?"

"I don't know, sir," I said quietly.

"You're under arrest. Mount." The sergeant and I got back in the jeep.

"Take me to your company commander."

We drove back. I drove, the sergeant sitting next to me, tight-lipped. When we arrived at company headquarters, the major told me to remain in the jeep while he and the sergeant entered the office. I could overhear him telling the lieutenant that I'd been purchasing liquor. The three of them emerged from the office. The major again asked me if I'd bought the liquor.

I said again, "I was not in that store, sir."

He said, "Are you calling me a liar?"

The sergeant, standing right next to me, never said a word.

The lieutenant said, "You're under arrest. Don't leave the barracks."

I was relieved of all duties and left wondering what would come next. Two days later I was called in by the lieutenant, who informed me that the sergeant had admitted his guilt. He'd been afraid of losing his honorable discharge if he admitted anything. He could have been court-martialed and might have lost his GI benefits.

"What made him tell you the truth?" I asked.

"He just felt sorry for you when you wouldn't turn on him. We're going to drop the whole thing and make out it never happened."

"What about Officers' Candidate School?" I asked. "Do I have a shot?"

He looked at me and said, "This incident is not going to go on your record, but OCS is not going to happen. By the way, I'm still giving you a three-day pass."

Was somebody trying to make up for something? I wondered whether he was trying to compensate for having arrested me. I hitched a ride on a C-47 army transport plane at Godman Field, Kentucky. I wanted to get back to New York and away from Fort Knox. I was starting to feel lonesome for my father and mother.

When I arrived home I wanted my parents to see me in my army uniform. I was eighteen years old, serving my country. That night we were invited to the house of my grandparents, Bobbi and Zeidi, for the Passover Seder. Both of them were bigger than life. When I was around five or six years old they would arrive on Sunday afternoons at our house on South Fifth Street in Brooklyn and advance into the kitchen with large brown bags, like the National Recovery Act, dispensing food to the starving poor. They'd speak a truncated Yiddish, a shorthand that only they seemed to understand.

There was always a smile on my grandmother's face as she eyed me with a special glint meant only for her favorite, as it appears I was. Grandmother looked like a queen out of Genesis. Her shiny black hair was pulled back in a bun and her eyes burned like coals when she looked straight at you.

My grandfather, a tall, smiling, bashful man, would remove reddish frankfurters from the bag. They were strung together and wrapped in heavy waxed paper. The franks were thrown into a kettle of boiling water. Twice the size of ordinary frankfurters, they were called "specials." Minutes later they burst. Our mouths watered. The seeded mustard, wrapped in cylindrical brown waxed paper, oozed out onto the rye bread in swirls, like toothpaste. We hungrily devoured all the franks.

My grandparents' impromptu visits would elevate our lives on a Sunday afternoon. But they depressed my mother, who watched silently as our daily meals were eclipsed by my grandparents' grandstand play for affection.

On Friday nights my father would take me for dinner at my grandparents' house. The family sat at a long table with a white tablecloth.

The Friday night candles were always in the center of the table. My grandmother would put a handkerchief over her head, *"Tsindt lecht,"* light the candles. My grandfather struck the match and lit them, and my grandmother would wave her arms over the brass candle holder and say a prayer, more of an incantation. My grandfather would make a funny aside to take the seriousness out of everything, and all ten of their children would laugh.

First we'd sip the soup. This was chicken soup like none I'd never tasted. My grandmother cooked all day Friday in preparation. She made the noodles herself. If I arrived early I'd see her flattening the dough with a rolling pin. She would slice the dough into strips with a Lukshen knife and then drop the strips into boiling water.

At the table, she sat me closest to her. My father, the eldest, came next, then the rest of the family.

"Ehr iz zoi veir Villie," she told everyone in Yiddish.

"He looks like his father," my aunts would repeat in English.

I took this to mean that because I resembled my father I was special, unlike my brother, who looked like my mother.

When the meal was finished and the evening ended, everyone took home cake. This was for the in-laws. My grandmother's dinners went on for years.

When I was fifteen my grandmother took ill. She needed a transfusion. I arrived at Memorial Hospital, where the doctors checked my blood and found that I was O-negative, the same type as my grandmother. I was scared but as I watched my blood filling the jar, the fear disappeared. When the family heard that I'd donated blood, cries of joy went up. "Jerry gave blood," they said. This made me special. My grandparents had instilled a fear of doctors in my father's family, and it had paralyzed them. Ironically, most of them lived into their late eighties and rarely went to a doctor.

Three years later, I arrived at my grandparents' apartment in my uniform and sat at the same table with my aunts and uncles. My grandfather sat alone at the head of the table. I waited for my grandmother to appear and light the Sabbath candles. When she didn't, I asked where Bobbi was. There was silence, and I knew.

"Why didn't anyone tell me?" I asked. I could have seen her before she died.

At the time it upset me. Today I think of it as my grandparents' way of protecting their grandchildren from pain.

When I returned to Fort Knox, I was assigned to an eight-week course in radio at the Armored School. That's where I met Joe DiSpigno.

Joe and I were the only New Yorkers in our company at the school. We were both 5-foot-6, weighed about 150 pounds, and when standing next to each other looked like twin fire hydrants.

On the first day of class the T/4 instructor explained the international Morse code: "Dit-da is A, da-dit-dit is B, da-da-dit is C . . ."

Joe was in the row in front of me and turned around, rolling his eyes back in his head as if seeking help. His eyes met mine. I seemed to be the only one who could read his thoughts. "Can we take eight weeks of this?" I knew he was thinking.

When the class was over, he said, "I'm Joe DiSpigno. I'm from Astoria. You're from New York too?"

I told him I was.

"Thank God. We're the only ones. How'd you get here?" he asked.

"It's a long story," I said.

"Let's get together tonight at the Post Library," he said. "It's nice and quiet. We can look around. You know, pick up a few books."

That night, for want of anything else to do, I met Joe in the library. As we browsed we told each other about our eighteen and a half years on the planet.

"I lived on the Upper West Side when I was a kid," he said. "West Sixty-seventh Street, near Ederle's Pork Store. His daughter Gertrude swam the English Channel."

"I'm not into pork," I said.

"Neither am I," Joe said. "Jews are right about that. You can get trichinosis. Why'd you join the army?" he asked.

"To get away from home. My parents were always fighting. It made it hard," I said.

"I thought Jewish families didn't fight," Joe DiSpigno said. "Didn't they love you?"

"Sure. They just fought with each other. They never laid a hand on us kids."

"You're lucky," Joe said. "When Italian families fight, kids better go hide someplace."

There was a pause.

"You're Jewish and I'm Italian. Being from New York makes us exactly alike. Different from the other guys here."

That was the truth.

"So. What are you going to do when you get out?" Joe asked as we were leaving the library.

"I want to be an actor."

It didn't shock or surprise him. It seemed to interest him.

"You really want to be an actor?"

I don't know why I'd told him. It's not something you tell everybody. It's more of a secret wish that you harbor inside yourself. People usually would laugh when I mentioned it.

"What kind of actor?" Joe said.

"A comedian." There was another pause.

"Why a comedian?"

"I like to make people laugh."

We reached the barracks.

"I'll see you in the morning," he said.

From that moment on, he was my friend. A real friend. I didn't know what he'd thought when I told him my secret ambition, but he never blinked.

We seemed to know instinctively that we were different from everyone else there. We felt smarter than everybody in the company. But we knew we couldn't act like we were smart. In the next few weeks we were both taking international code at the highest speeds, and enjoyed being the best at it in the company. We'd go out in army half-tracks, which were like tanks, and practice sending messages, Joe in one half-track and I in another.

It was strictly forbidden to send anything out into the air other than official material. During a battle exercise, Joe sent a message telling me he'd met a WAC at the PX, and she had a friend for me that night. Everybody in the unit heard the message. The CO sent a message back, warning us that the next man who did that would be court-martialed. Joe's next message was something to the effect of "Go fuck yourself." Sending a message like that over the air, in code, and knowing everyone was taking it down, was like bringing the army to its knees. No one except me could believe that Joe had the nerve to pull it off. Fortunately for Joe, there was no way to figure which vehicle the message was coming from.

That night I said, "Why did you do it, Joe?"

"I hate officers," he said. "Don't you?"

"I wanna be one," I said.

He looked at me. "Yeah, well, if you become one, it would be the end of a friendship. I hate them. I hate having to salute them. Look at this— what do you think of this salute."

He raised his right arm then bent it slowly until his hand, palm out, came to rest, over his right eye, covering it as if he were taking an eye test.

"Isn't this ridiculous," he said. "I'm saluting another human being like he's better than me. Fuck him. He's no better than me."

At the end of Armored School training we were both shipped to Italy on the *General Howze,* a troopship. We left Staten Island at night with upwards of a thousand men. The war had ended and we were replacements for guys who had won battles, eighteen-year-olds sprinkled in with regular army guys who had reenlisted after being through battles in Africa, Sicily, and mainland Italy.

As the ship pulled away from land, one of the enlisted men put on a life preserver and, with Bible in hand, proclaimed we were going to sink. We were to be lost at sea. Joe said the guy was bucking for a discharge.

The ship sailed and details were organized. Men were assigned to stuff like KP and guard duty. Rules were announced over the PA system as to expected behavior. Officers were to be saluted as they would be on land. The enlisted men were to eat in shifts, at counters, while standing. The officers would eat seated in a shipboard mess hall.

We slept in the hold of the ship on canvas hammocks, triple decked. The smell of the sleeping quarters was close to unbearable. To escape this, I would sleep on deck.

The GI with the life preserver walked the decks, Bible still in hand, proclaiming to everyone in a prophetic voice that the ship would sink before we reached Livorno, Italy. We paid him little attention as he made his rounds.

Music was played over the loudspeaker system, interspersed with warnings against gambling which, though they were repeated and repeated, were never enforced. Gambling was actually encouraged—it was a distraction that kept us from going bananas and committing whatever mischief men create on a ship that has no women on board. Soldiers would play crap games on deck. It was impossible to walk on deck without stepping on a blanket that was someone's card game or crap game.

The ship's library had books that could be borrowed. The most popular was a single copy of Erskine Caldwell's *God's Little Acre,* which kept making the rounds. It was the closest to pornography that any of the books came. I eventually got to read it.

As the *General Howze* slowly moved across the Atlantic, life on board took on a day-to-day monotony. We'd get up in the mornings, go to breakfast, and kill time until lunch.

During the trip, Joe and I befriended a tech sergeant who was a veteran of North Africa and Anzio. He was a rifleman, and his decorations included a Purple Heart. He buddied up to Joe and me, assigning us duties that were less demeaning than cleaning latrines. We were made MPs and assigned by him to guard duty. Our job was to patrol the decks. It felt good to be walking around in charge.

We'd finish a tour and take naps, four hours on, four off. At midnight we arose from our nap, put on our MP armbands, and walked the decks.

One night Joe said to me, "Come on, let's go to the back of the ship. I want to show you something."

At the stern of the ship we looked down at the huge wake churned up by the ship's propeller. The moon lit up the sea around us. Joe looked out. "Beautiful, isn't it."

There were four steel chairs with leather upholstery. Across the backs of these chairs were the words: "For Officers Only."

"Come on," Joe said, "let's throw them overboard."

"What?!"

"We'll throw them overboard."

"Why?" I asked.

"Because those bastards are no better than us, and they've got chairs that say 'For Officers Only' on them."

After checking that no one was in sight, Joe lifted one of the heavy steel chairs and threw it over the stern into the ocean. I could see the moon reflecting on the white backwash of the sea churned into foam by the ship's propellers.

We took turns hurling the chairs into the ocean. As each chair hit the water I imagined the bottom of the Atlantic infested with chairs that one day would be found saying "For Officers Only."

The next morning the voice on the loudspeaker asked, "What happened to the officers' chairs?"

Of course they never found out.

A few days into the trip the *General Howze* slowed to a crawl and began listing heavily. No one informed the troops what was going on, and in the ensuing days the ship almost ground to a halt—because of engine trouble, as it turned out. The rumors now had us going to Bermuda, but in the meantime we just struggled along, feeling like we were getting nowhere.

I was now assigned KP—kitchen duty. I decided to steal some of the food from the officers' mess—huge unlabeled cans of sliced turkey. I stashed a couple. When my dishwashing tour was over, I snuck the cans to the hold of the ship and told Joe to get the guys together for a feast. Eight guys surrounded me as I opened the first can. It was . . . ketchup. What the hell? I tried the next one. It was green . . . relish.

"You got ketchup and you got fucking relish," Joe said. "That's worth a court martial?"

"Well, I tried."

"We'll have to throw it overboard," Joe said. "Feed it to the sharks."

Everyone was on edge, and even our beneficent tech sergeant started baiting me, saying "Jews are cowards" in earshot of the other men.

At first I ignored him, but the invectives continued. His battle decorations seemed to give him privilege. I tried to think of Jewish war heroes. My mind focused on my cousin Leo, who'd been awarded the Purple Heart twice and later a Bronze Star. I needed to prove Jews were heroes.

One of the activities on board was boxing matches. I found myself going down to the ship's gym, putting on gloves, and trying to learn the manly art of fisticuffs. I was quietly punching the bag, shadow boxing, and sparring with guys who looked very much like they'd done this before. I was trying hard to learn courage. Joe became aware of my workouts, and watched as I sweated for the next few days.

"What are you going to do?" he asked.

"I think I'm gonna box."

"Because of him?"

I kept silent.

"You're crazy, Stiller," Joe said. "Some of these guys are good."

"Hey, I'm just fooling around."

"Well, he heard about it," Joe said. "He's telling everyone on the boat that you and him are gonna fight."

"Really?" I said.

"Yeah."

"Well, I haven't made up my mind," I said. "There are some bouts coming up tomorrow night. I want to see what they're like. See if I can deal with it."

The following night Joe and I watched the bouts. Hundreds of GIs jammed tight around a makeshift ring in the ship's belly, smoking cigars and betting. The first bout seemed tame, two guys just managing to touch one another, to the derision of everyone. The evening turned ugly, though, when a kid from Ohio, fat but brawny, left his corner at the bell and pulverized his opponent for two minutes, nonstop. The bout was not halted until the bloody loser crawled to his corner on his knees.

The kid's fury scared me. I knew at once I could not enter the ring. The sergeant who baited me sensed this, and the next day, as I was standing on the fantail, he approached me in front of the others and asked whether I was going to fight. I didn't say anything.

"What can you expect from a Jew," the sergeant said.

I don't know what possessed me, but I grabbed his hand and marched him to the fantail. Even though the ship was almost motionless, the propeller was still turning over, churning up the ocean.

"Come on," I said, "let's do it. Let's both of us jump into that propeller."

He looked at me in shock. I took off my tie and unbuttoned my shirt. His face turned red.

"Come on, let's see who's got the guts."

For the first time in my life, I knew I was bordering on committing suicide. Guys were starting to gather around. I took off my shirt.

"Okay, take off yours," I said. When he didn't move I did it for him, unbuttoning his shirt and untying his necktie. He was in even deeper shock. I started to unbutton his pants. Would he take me up on it? The entire ship seemed to be gathering around us. Would he go the whole route? Would I? Now our combat boots and pants were off, and we were standing in our underwear, the wind blowing hard. *What the fuck,* I said to myself. My life was miserable. I was thinking of my parents fighting all the time. *Look where it's taken me,* I thought.

I took his hand as I would that of a schoolchild, and walked with him to the very edge of the stern. I couldn't believe what I was doing. Nobody said anything. They just watched, mesmerized.

"Okay," I said. "You and me, we're going into the propeller together."

I tightened my grip on his hand. I was proving to myself I could do it, and praying someone would stop us.

Suddenly DiSpigno appeared behind us with the officer of the day.

"What are you guys doing?" the OD asked.

"They're going to jump overboard," Joe said.

"Okay, both of you come with me. I oughta put you both in the brig," the OD said. "It'd keep you out of trouble. Look, gamble, do something, but don't do this again."

The tech sergeant never baited me again.

The *General Howze* finally broke down completely off the Bermuda coast, and we remained stationary as repairs were made. Three days later we started back to the States, to Staten Island. There, we went down the gangplank of the *General Howze* and right up the gangplank of the *Newbern Victory.* Ten days later we arrived at Livorno, Italy, and were immediately transported to a former POW camp in the Tuscan countryside. We played softball in the warm Italian sun, surrounded by barbed wire. Outside the fence we discovered a watermelon patch. The game stopped, and we crawled under the barbed wire to pass small watermelons back into the field, fire-brigade fashion. Like teenagers on a rampage, we devoured the stolen watermelons, pits and all.

That night the entire company sneaked out of the compound, and an hour later we were in the waiting room of a whorehouse in Pisa. The matronly signorina in charge asked each of us for 20,000 lire or a carton of American cigarettes, and instructed us to sit still until called.

This was to be my rite of passage into manhood. Minutes later, a hand appeared through the beaded curtains and a woman with golden hair and dark roots stood above me. She wore just enough makeup to highlight her soft face, and a negligee that revealed she was voluptuous and slightly overweight. She beckoned me as a kindergarten teacher would beckon a child on his first day at school.

"Vieni qua"—come here—she commanded in a husky voice.

I obeyed.

"Come se gama?" What's your name?

"Joe," I lied.

"You like me, Joe?" she said, removing her negligee, exposing her breasts.

"Yes," I said. "You're nice."

"Okay," she said. "Take off your clothes."

I stood for a moment, then unbuckled my belt and struggled to remove my pants without first taking off my combat boots. The pants fell to the floor, hiding the boots. I finally untied my shoelaces and pushed off the cumbersome footwear. She watched patiently as the battle ended and I stood opposite her in my khaki shorts and stocking feet.

"Okay," she said, waiting for the dance to begin.

"Okay," I said, staring at her, knowing something was to take place, but not what. It seemed clear that nature was not taking over.

"What's the matter?" she said, clearly upset by the unexpected turn of events. "You no like?" she said, her voice heavy with hurt.

"Yes, I like," I said.

"Come on," she said urgently. "Make love."

I felt totally out of it. I tried to tell myself to do something, commanding my thing down there to do something. It seemed totally autonomous.

"Come on, Joe," she said, getting angry. It was getting personal. I was insulting her. I could feel her desperation; her womanhood had been challenged.

"Wait," she said. She called into the next room: *"Vene car."* Suddenly our room was filled with girls. She spoke to them in Italian, explaining what was (not) going on. I could feel a wave of compassion sweep through all of them. It was totally incomprehensible to them that this could happen. It would clearly give the place a bad name.

"Come on, Joe," one girl urged.

"You can do it, GI!" cried another.

After each utterance their eyes dropped to my groin, hoping some sign of life would appear. The more they urged, the more inert I felt. I could feel myself trying to make something happen.

The blonde—my blonde, with the dark roots—was now almost in tears. "What's the matter, Joe?" she asked.

"It's my mother," I said. "I look at you and I see my mother standing next to you."

"Mother," one of her friends said. *"La mama."*

"Oh . . . oh . . ." A sigh that sounded like a symphony orchestra went up as they stared at me.

They left the room, one by one, knowing their womanhood was still intact. I dressed as quickly as I could. As I slipped out the door, the signorina in charge handed me back my 20,000 lire. "No charge, Joe," she said.

I was assigned to the 977 Signal Company at Allied Force Headquarters, Caserta, and was put in charge of a film exchange whose library consisted of popular Hollywood pictures and VD films. *Eight Triple Zero,* in color, was designed to make GIs aware of the dangers of VD.

At one point I answered a call for recruits to the company football team. The ever-present hunger to be some kind of hero impelled me to put my name on a list to try out.

Football was a game I had never played before, except for the touch variety. Ignorant of any of the fine points of the sport, I lied and said I'd played guard in high school. Guard seemed to me to be a position I could learn quickly and which demanded the least amount of skill. I figured I simply had to stop an opposing player when he had the ball, or create some kind of hole for our own guys when we had the ball. I immediately made the team.

Being 5-foot-6 and weighing about 150 pounds seemed to be a great advantage. I was small enough to see through the legs of almost everyone in front of me, and my speed allowed me to be in the right spot to read the opposition's plays and shout a warning to my teammates. In practice my sharpness surprised everyone, including myself. I suddenly seemed to fit into this peculiar game. I experienced a rush of good feeling from the men around me, a feeling of warmth and respect.

We had a couple of ringers on our team. The halfback was someone who had distinguished himself in college ball. It was our job to get him the football. Our first game was played in Victor Emmanuel Stadium, Caserta, before a full house of GIs, British Tommies, Mihailovich Yugoslavs, and Italians who worked for the occupying U.S. Army. Also present were German prisoners of war who now were working in U.S. Army kitchens or PXs.

The match between the 977th and the MPs had a built-in drama, and provided great pregame excitement. The MPs, as traffic cops of the Caserta area, had tyrannized the comzone with their meticulous enforcement of army regulations regarding traffic rules and the wearing of uniforms.

The architect of these harsh policies was a Lieutenant Cranshaw, who came off as an MP bully. The sight of his yellow scarf and his motorcycle was the scourge of every GI for miles around. One day I had made an illegal left turn onto a dirt road off the main highway. Cranshaw hauled me over to the side, gave me a ticket, and, as the saying goes, chewed out my ass. His reputation as an unredemptive son of a bitch made him the center of conversation in every GI bar in the Naples area.

The name Lieutenant Cranshaw, playing fullback for the MP team, blared over the public-address system. His presence seemed to be one of the main reasons for the size of the crowd in the stadium.

We listened to "The Star Spangled Banner." Then came the referee's whistle. The MPs won the toss and elected to receive. The moment filled me with wonderment. What the hell was I doing here? I thought of football as a Neanderthal sport played by animals, and now here I was, wearing shoulder pads and a helmet, playing it myself.

I decided that I had to prove I was no longer a little Jew by playing the part of a tough guy in an all-American sport. Football was a battlefield that allowed me to hit, smash, and even maim. I could feel a real joy in all this. The chains of Talmudic teaching were no longer binding me. I was pure goy and beginning to love it. No apologies.

The whistle blew. Kickoff. On the first play from scrimmage the ball was snapped to a quarterback who handed off to fullback Cranshaw. Their guard opened a hole between me and our center. Cranshaw came charging through the line of scrimmage. I fell. He was lumbering past me and was as wild on the field as he was on his motorcycle. I was up on my feet. He was plowing through our secondary, with the open field just ahead. Being small, I circled around my teammates. I had seen this move in a Ritz Brothers movie. Suddenly there I was, the only man between Cranshaw and the goal line. His head sank into his shoulders. He was coming straight at me. He wasn't trying to avoid me. No sidestep. On the contrary, he wanted to take me with him.

In a split second I decided I could tackle him if I had the will. I also knew that if I tackled him at the ankles, he would fall like a tall oak in the forest. He kept coming. I was short enough to aim directly at those ankles. *Get him!* I screamed at myself. *Don't be afraid.*

I dove and caught one ankle. I heard a crack, and Lieutenant Cranshaw shrieked in pain. As his body hit the ground, I felt sorry for him. I heard the crowd screaming deliriously at the sight of the guy lying on the field, writhing in agony. What the hell had I done? There was another roar from the stands as a stretcher came out and Cranshaw was lifted onto it and carried off the field.

I played fifty-eight minutes that day, both offense and defense. When I left the field, two minutes before the game's end, a roar went up in the stands that to this day I can still hear. Italians who were new to American football and who didn't know my name stamped their feet and shouted my number: *Ootan doate, ootan doate*—eighty-eight, eighty-eight. I was so moved, I wanted to cry.

I played the following week, on Thanksgiving Day, when we went up against the team from the aircraft carrier *Franklin Delano Roosevelt*. My nose got broken, or at least some cartilage got misplaced, but I never knew it. I enjoyed every moment.

In the years since, theater has been the only other place where I could find the same kind of warmth and gratitude from total strangers, but I don't think anything that ever happened to me in show business could rival the moment of sheer exhilaration I experienced in Victor Emmanuel Stadium that afternoon.

4

Syracuse, Sawyer Falk, and Theater

Shortly after my army discharge, I moved back home with my parents. They were now living in another city housing project, Ravenswood, in Astoria. Deddy was still driving a bus, although he was no longer with the Triangle Bus Company, but with Fifth Avenue Coach.

One day, I went to the garage on 145th Street and Lenox Avenue and watched him check out. He seemed to be a favorite among the drivers. They'd call him Butch. They thought of him as some kind of sweet little puppy that somehow got misnamed. Since my father had been working steadily, and rent in the housing projects was determined by income, each pay increase had forced my parents to move. Living in Ravenswood was a little like being exiled. Astoria was a ghostly Siberia after the volatile Lower East Side. The apartments were essentially the same: five rooms with thin walls for a family of five. The project itself extended for blocks. The sameness of these buildings and apartments tore at your sense of individuality. My mother sensed this and hated it.

"Let's get out of these projects. Why do you have to tell them your salary? Why should anyone have to know how much you make?"

My father didn't seem to mind, but for my mother, the projects were a constant reminder that she could no longer dream.

I knew that it was time to contribute to the household. I read a want ad promising huge weekly salaries for highly motivated men who could sell. "Veterans please take notice." Since my only means of supporting myself was twenty dollars a week from veterans' entitlements, the ad intrigued me.

I arrived at an office on West 42nd Street and was met by a sales manager whose first question was whether I had ever sold door to door. I told him no, but because I was a veteran he said he was willing to train me. A few hours later I was out on the street with a young man named Tommy who would be doing the actual selling. Tommy had a great smile. I could see his teeth every time he spoke.

We drove down to a quiet neighborhood in Flatbush, Brooklyn, where we went to a restaurant and joined four or five other guys sitting at a table. One, the district manager, assigned the territories that were to be taken by each of us. Tommy got his blocks and we hit the streets.

As we were leaving Tommy told me, "Put on your ruptured duck."

The ruptured duck was the gold pin the army issued that indicated you were an honorably discharged veteran.

"Just listen when I knock on the door."

We approached a two-family house. Tommy rang the bell and a woman answered.

"Excuse me," he said smiling, his teeth flashing. "I'm taking a survey. I'm a veteran and my friend Jerry is one also. Was anyone in your family in the service?"

The war was over and anyone who had had a member of the family in the service was quick to let it be known.

"You know, veterans are having a tough time of it now," Tommy continued. "They've given a lot for their country and many are out of work. By the way, are you receiving any magazine subscriptions right now?"

The woman said no.

"Well, what my company does is offer you a two-, three-, or four-year subscription to *Life, Look, Pic,* and *Liberty* magazines. What you're doing is getting a discount on the magazine which you'd be buying anyway and giving something back to the veterans who gave so much."

"How much is it?" the woman asked, reaching into her bag.

"Why don't you take it for three years. You save a lot. You Italian?" Tommy asked.

"Yes," she said.

"Me too," Tommy replied. *"Uno mano lavo nada"*—one hand washes the other. In minutes the transaction was completed.

"Thank you," Tommy said, handing her a receipt. "You'll get your first magazine in a month." They shook hands.

We said good-bye and were knocking on the next door. It was like clockwork. The next day I was out doing it myself. I was no Tommy, but I did the spiel and it worked. Part of the magic was the neighborhoods. Two-family houses, Italians, Jews, and Irish were very receptive. For about ten weeks I was selling and making about $125 per week. I was living at home and making more than my father.

On one occasion I knocked on the door of the DeMarcos. The De-Marco sisters were a family that sang on Fred Allen's radio show. The door opened and one of the sisters invited me in. I didn't have to say two words. The checkbook was out and I had my order for four years.

One man was not so receptive. He said he had placed an order a couple of months back and not received his magazine. That disturbed me. Of course, it could've been a slipup, but it made me suspicious. I went to the sales manager's office and told him about this man who had not received his magazine. "It's in the mail. Sometimes it takes a while."

Suddenly my territory was now shifted to the Inwood section of Manhattan with mostly six-story apartment houses. The tenants were largely Jehovah's Witnesses.

I knocked on a door.

"Are there any veterans in the family?"

"Come on in," the woman said. "You a veteran?"

"Yes."

"Would you like a cup of coffee?"

"Why not," I said. This job was turning into an adventure. She introduced me to her daughter.

"Please sit down," they said very sweetly. They sat me down at a table and listened to my pitch. When I finished the mother said, "I really can't do anything until I consult my husband. He doesn't come home till 4 P.M. He's a motorman on the IRT.

"You're Jewish?" she added.

"Yes," I said.

She handed me a Bible. "You know, we have many Jewish people in the Jehovah's Witnesses. The Jewish people were the ones who gave us the Torah."

For the next two hours I listened as she tried to convert me. She brought me food, coffee.

Finally I said, "I really have to leave."

"Would you like to come to a meeting this Thursday night?"

"I don't think so," I said.

"Why don't you keep the Bible." It was very hard to say I didn't want a Bible, so I took it.

"Could you make a donation?" she asked.

"How much?"

"Twenty-five dollars."

"I can give you ten," I said.

"We'll accept that." She gave me a receipt and a notice of the next meeting. I thanked her. "You'll be getting *The Watchtower* in the mail," she said, and as I left she added, "The Jews were the chosen people."

The next day I was again assigned the Inwood section, but I didn't have the heart to knock on another door. I ended up going to a movie, *Duel in the Sun.*

The next day another person claimed they had never received their subscriptions. I called the sales manager and said, "We have to talk."

At the office I said, "I can't go on selling when people aren't getting their magazines. Are people getting their magazines?"

"The trouble with you, Jerry, is you ask too many questions."

"Well, I quit. I can't sell knowing they're not getting what they paid for."

"What are you going to do?"

"I'm gonna be an actor," I said. If I could sell magazines I could sell myself.

"You'll never have a better job," he said. "I'm sorry you're leaving."

So I took the subway down to Greenwich Village wondering what I was getting myself into.

Off-Broadway theater was a new concept in 1947. It wasn't Broadway, but it was theater. The Cherry Lane, a small, old theater on Barrow Street in the Village, seemed an easy mark. I was sure that there I could find something with no trouble at all.

There was a young fellow outside sweeping the street. He was the producer. I asked if he knew whether they needed actors. "Can you paint scenery? I can't offer you any money," he said, "but if you want to make yourself handy, you might also be able to play a couple of roles during the season. I'm the producer."

Al Hurwitz was a cherubic, sweet-faced guy fresh out of Yale. He led me into a tree-filled yard and introduced me to a barrel-chested, shirtless man in shorts with a paintbrush in his hand. "This is Rod," Al said. "This fellow's going to help you backstage, Rod." Then he left.

"What's your name?" Rod asked.

"Jerry," I told him.

"So you want to be an actor, Jerry?"

"Yes," I said.

"Have you ever worked in theater?"

"Henry Street," I said. "I played Hsei Ping Kwei in—"

"Have you ever painted a flat?"

"No."

"Up and down, up and down. You paint it sideways, it looks like scenery. Up and down, it looks like a wall. This is a dutchman," he said, running a strip of glue-soaked canvas between two flats. "You paste it over the hinges. That way, the audience doesn't notice the break in the wall."

"You're an actor?" I asked.

"Yes."

I wondered why anyone with ability would stoop to painting scenery.

"Here," he said, handing me a paintbrush.

At that point someone yelled, "Rod, telephone for you."

"Okay, I'm coming," he yelled back, handing me the brush. "Just remember, Jerry, up and down."

So Rod Steiger taught me to paint my first flat. He returned a few minutes later, shoving his shirt into his pants. "I gotta go," he said. "Nice meeting you, Jerry."

I asked him where he was going.

"I'm playing Christ at the Rooftop Theater."

The Cherry Lane is losing one hell of a set painter, I thought.

I struck up a friendship with a 6-foot-2 Texan lady while we were both painting. She was several years older and a full eight inches taller than me, but painting scenery must have made me attractive, because one night she invited me to her Greenwich Village flat. As I watched her frying chicken she looked at me with kind, motherly eyes. I was going to be fed before being led into the bedroom.

Her cooking was wonderful. The chicken was heavy with breadcrumbs, dipped in batter, then drowned in hot grease. I kept wondering what I was doing there and how I got into this. I was an aspiring actor, working on Barrow Street for no money. This was the payoff.

When we finished our chicken, she looked at me languorously. Her lids grew heavy and seemed to say, *Now.* It was my turn to do my stuff. She took me by the hand and led me into the small, darkened bedroom. A cot with a madras spread over a thin mattress loomed in front of me. Her towering body slowly sat, pulling me next to her. I sat, saying nothing, waiting for something to happen. She removed her blouse. I slowly got up and unbuckled my pants. She lay back, pulling off her blue jeans, revealing her panties. Her shoes were off. I was acting as if I knew my way. I was upon her. Her eyes looked at me with the expectancy of a woman experiencing a seasoned lover. It was over before it began. I looked at her sadly and thought, *All that wonderful chicken, and for what?*

I finally got on stage that summer in Auden and Isherwood's *The Dog Beneath the Skin.* I played a guy swinging a little girl on a swing. As I was leaving the theater that night, a man stopped me at the stage door. "I saw you up there on stage," he said.

"Did you like my performance?" I asked.

"Forget the performance, what happened to those magazine subscriptions you sold me?"

I knew by then that I had to study to learn how to become an actor, so I returned to the Henry Street Settlement Theater and asked Esther Lane for advice.

"Where do I go to become an actor? I got the GI Bill."

Mrs. Lane said, "Go to Syracuse. They've got a wonderful teacher—Sawyer Falk."

So, in the fall of 1947 I entered Syracuse University. The glut of students on the GI Bill created housing problems. For many months I lived in barracks on the state fairgrounds and had to be bused to and from the campus many miles away.

Auditions were held for a university production of *Blossom Time,* and I went up for the role of Papa Kranz. I was confident, sitting outside the rehearsal room, waiting to read, knowing I would get the part.

The audition was presided over by Professor Frederick Schweppe, a giant of a man whose manner was theatrical in every way. He had toured for the Shuberts and been a protégé of Mary Garden, the famed opera star. After I'd read a few lines, he broke into a crackling laugh and ran from the room, saying, "I found him!" to everyone on the floor. During the next several weeks, I took courses by day and rehearsed at night, commuting between the fair grounds and the campus.

"Schwep," as he was affectionately called, teamed Barry Mendelsohn (later known as Julian Barry, who wrote *Lenny*) and myself as the low comics. In rehearsals Schwep would give us stage business that he knew from his early days with the Shuberts. There was a particular shtick he said would guarantee applause if we did it right. Barry and I were to exit the scene imitating a choo-choo train. The whole thing started with my sneezing, saying, "A-Choo!" It built from there, with Barry moving behind me and putting his hands on my hips, after which the two of us, in lock-step, made like a locomotive picking up steam, going "Choo-choo-choo . . ." Just as Schwep had said, it got great applause.

It was the first time I realized that applause could be manufactured. As Papa Kranz I wore grotesque makeup that included a putty nose, a cutaway coat, and an application of zinc oxide to my hair, which gave it a silvery glow. I penciled my eyebrows to twice the normal size, and in a Viennese accent emphasized each word as if it were a punch line. I exaggerated my walk and hadn't the slightest feeling of self-consciousness about what I was doing.

We opened, and the downtown Syracuse newspapers said I had stolen the show. Professor Schweppe said I would someday be a star if I continued on the right track. Making me a star was his goal during my three years as an undergraduate at Syracuse. Being "made over" by a teacher was probably the highest form of stroking I'd ever received.

On occasion the professor would take Bernie Piven, Bette Wolf, Carmine Albino, and myself to Kiwanis luncheons, where he'd introduce us as performing students. We'd do ten-minute scenes from *Blossom Time* and then Schweppe himself would do a great rendition of "Old Man River," which put the audience away. We students each ended up with ten bucks, which made us feel like pros.

He cast me as Gieber Goldfarb, the cab driver, in *Girl Crazy,* at the Civic Theater on Salinia Street. To this day, it remains my most exciting moment on stage. My need was simply to make people laugh, to be another Eddie Cantor. Though my work was praised, I was told by one faculty member that my characterization made fun of Jews. I was hurt, and protested that Willie Howard and Fanny Brice used Yiddish accents. I just wanted the audience to love me.

In those musicals I learned firsthand what happened to my emotions when I heard an audience laugh. It was like being alive for the first time. My need to hear laughter became addictive. I wasn't holding back, and the audience loved it. I never looked at the other actors on stage. They didn't exist. I played everything straight out, and the audience ate it up. I worked with some good people: Sue Benjamin, who became Sue Bennett, the host of a TV show in Boston; Bill Clotworthy, who became the head censor at NBC and later an executive at Benton and Bowles.

Opening night, they gave me two encores for my singing of George and Ira Gershwin's "But Not for Me." In the number I did impressions of Chevalier, Peter Lorre, and Jimmy Durante. If only my mother could see me now. The impressions must have been terrible, but I did them all-out. When I went home that night, I couldn't sleep. I'd wake myself up each time I dozed off. I was reliving my performance. I entertained the thought of having my mother and father come up to Syracuse to see me. The love I was getting onstage had been mind-blowing. I couldn't wait to do it all over again the next night. The footlights were for me. I'd march out like a conquering soldier, accepting this warm glow that bathed me in love.

Larry Parish, whose father, Mitchell Parish, wrote the songs "Deep Purple" and "Stars Fell on Alabama," was one of my roommates. Larry knew show business. That night he woke me up to say, "You were great tonight, Jerry."

Syracuse, the hometown of the Shubert brothers, was reputed to be the toughest show-business town in America, but the next night I again stopped the show. I called my mother and father in New York and told them to take the train up to Syracuse. They arrived on the Empire State Express the following Saturday in time for the matinee.

So, there my parents were in the audience for the Saturday matinee, and I'll never forget this: It was the first time the audience didn't laugh. It was like playing in a vacuum. I couldn't understand what was happening. I did everything the same way, but nothing came back.

When it was over I brought my father and mother backstage and introduced them to the cast and to Professor Schweppe. A pall had fallen over the place, but everyone acted properly, as if at a funeral. The gloom was palpable. I wanted to disappear.

"Let's go eat," I said to my parents.

We found a Waldorf cafeteria and grabbed some food. Not many words were spoken. I knew they'd be leaving on the next train, but I wanted to know how they felt, seeing me up there. I didn't expect much praise, if any, but I was hoping for something.

Finally I asked, "How did you like it?"

My mother looked up and said, "We were sitting behind the Mills Brothers."

I knew the Mills Brothers were playing at Andre's, the big-time Syracuse nightclub.

"Did they like the show?" I asked.

"They were asleep," my mother said.

The Mills Brothers were asleep? They must've had a tough night, I thought.

When we finished eating I saw my parents off at the train station and went back to the theater for the evening show.

Schweppe came backstage, his face less bright but not discouraged.

"What happened, Mr. Schweppe?"

He looked at me and said, "It was a matinee. Matinees are different."

I couldn't understand why. *I* wasn't different, but now I could feel a loss of faith in myself. I couldn't control everything the way I had the night before. At the evening performance, the laughs came back, but not as strong.

My performance in *Girl Crazy* brought me to the attention of Professor Sawyer Falk. He and Professor Schweppe were dramatic opposites. Schweppe was showbiz while Falk was academia. As the first president of the National Theater Conference, Falk had been instrumental in establishing theater as a course in the Syracuse University curriculum, separate from the Speech Department. His leadership set the precedent for drama courses at Yale, Harvard, and Northwestern. The surprising thing for me was to learn that, after watching my performance in *Girl Crazy*, he thought I might one day become an actor. Obviously, he'd missed that matinee.

Falk's Syracuse class, Drama 101, dealt with the origins of theater in ancient Greece. Sawyer Falk was fluent in Greek. He could speak it, but never did so in front of his students. He kept all his notes in Greek. In class we talked about catharsis, a connection to feelings hidden deep within oneself that rise to the surface while one watches a great play or listens to a great joke. *Oedipus Rex,* Professor Falk kept saying, was a play you should read every year, because each year you will understand more about its description of the human condition.

The theater was his religion. Soon it was to become mine.

For the first time I understood theater was not just a place to entertain. I learned that theater was a battlefield to capture people's hearts and minds. I was now reading Sophocles, Euripides, Aeschylus. Professor Falk used words like *proscenium, perioktoi,* and *stykomythia.* Suddenly I realized theater was not just a place to get laughs, but could also be a way to connect to myself. Professor Falk said that through artistic integrity we'd learn personal integrity. I wondered what this had to do with learning how to act. He had us read Edith Hamilton's book on Greek mythology, then had us adapt *Hamlet* into a Greek tragedy. Wasn't this getting heavy?

Professor Falk would quote Talma, the great French writer and actor, as saying, "Middling intelligence makes for great actors, while great intelligence makes for middling actors." Was this a reference to me, I wondered? Talma was a man after my own heart. Professor Falk also said, "It takes twenty years to make an actor." Why so long? I'd ask myself. He said a true comedian was not afraid to make a fool of himself, and pointed out to the class that Jerry Stiller was an example. When I did the lead in *The Rising of the Moon,* an Irish one-act, he said I was terrible, but added that I wasn't afraid to make a fool of myself. He said I'd never be able to do Shakespeare, though I might someday become great, but only if I could develop good taste—which, he was quick to point out, can't be learned.

Each day he'd arrive on campus in a green Studebaker, his wife Kay at the wheel. I watched as he climbed the steps of the Hall of Languages. He came prepared to teach. I was always on guard when it came to teachers. Teachers could destroy my confidence. I'd put up a screen to allow some learning to find its way in and keep out what I didn't like. When Falk praised me in class, I sensed the desire to think of him as a father figure. But he did like me, and I was fast becoming the fair-haired boy of the Drama Department.

During my sophomore year I auditioned for an off-campus nightclub. I'd always loved the ghost-white spotlight, the cigarette smoke, the desire to make it with the crowd, the tough guys who accompanied saloon performing. I loved the cockfight atmosphere, the "You better be funny, kid, or we'll break your knees" thing.

Since I knew a little Italian from my army days, I worked up a five-minute routine for an Italian soap opera called *Maria Malone, Female Dottore*. It was loosely based on *Mary Malone, Woman Doctor*, a daytime soap of that era. The bit started with me as an announcer saying in pigeon-Italian, "Bona Sera, Signores, Signorinas. Questa sera I presente la day-time seriale, 'Maria Malone, Female Dottore.' I ahora al hospitale Bellevue y 'Maria Malone Female Dottore.'"

I then imitated an ambulance siren and then, in a loudspeaker voice, I said "Maria Malone, reporté a surgery." The bit went on into five minutes of two doctors killing a patient, leaving a watch in his stomach. "Una Malangara in de la Bonza."

Club Candee was on the outskirts of Syracuse, near Solvay, New York. I took a long bus ride, and in a pair of sneakers I auditioned for the owner while he sat in the back eating a bowl of spaghetti. Without ever looking up or saying hello, he informed me, "You got the job." It was for one weekend. I was to be paid $25 a night plus a percentage for every student I brought in. To make a long story short, I filled the place, and was held over the following week. I was ecstatic. I did one-liners stolen from Robert Orben's joke book. I did the impressions of Chevalier, Lorre, and Durante that I'd been doing since I was fifteen and had done in *Girl Crazy*. The audience, mostly my fellow students, loved it.

Three weeks later the owner asked if I'd perform on a Sunday night for civilians following the headliners, a team called "Jerry and Turk." I said yes. I came out, did the same act, and bombed. What had happened? My student fans were missing.

I continued my education, but I kept working on new material, waiting for another crack at the clubs. I felt that the clubs were ready for something different. *Dragnet* was a big hit on TV, and I decided to parody it. For a booking at the Casablanca, a club on Genesee Street, I wore a detective hat and found a recording of Grieg that sounded a little like the *Dragnet* theme. In full view of the audience, I put the needle on the record, which skipped, and I did my Jack Webb imitation.

To my amazement, the audience was listening to me. They weren't laughing, but listening. I considered this a triumph. I closed with my three impressions, and once more escaped with my life.

Between shows I'd retreat to the cellar, where I'd now rigged up a device to make the record skip a little more. This added a few laughs, and I was held over for a second week. I attracted many hoods and hookers, who seemed to like my originality. I'm still convinced I was the first comic ever to do a *Dragnet* takeoff.

I now felt confident enough to ask Professor Falk and his wife to come down to see me. I'd realized Falk was gradually becoming my father, and Kay, my mother. I wanted them to see me in front of people who paid. I wanted him to know I wasn't just a college actor. To my surprise, he and Kay agreed to come. There they were, sitting before me in the audience.

I did my *Dragnet*. When it was over, I took a lot of bows and knew the audience loved me. The lights went up. A three-piece band played. People danced. I went over to Professor Falk's table. I didn't say anything. He looked at me and said nothing.

"Well, what did you think?" I finally asked.

"You've got to get out of this place," Professor Falk said.

"Why? I did great," I said.

"Bad habits." It was like the voice of God. "This place will get you into bad habits. You can't play here anymore."

I wanted to laugh. I had just conquered Everest, and he wanted me to quit.

"I'll see you in class Monday," he said, as he and Kay got up and left.

God, he really cares about me, I thought.

On Monday he called me into his office and said he'd like me to produce and direct a musical revue. Revues were often discussed in class. "You could star in it," he said. "Anyway, that's your next project. I don't want you in nightclubs."

I stood wide-eyed.

"I don't want you in nightclubs," he repeated.

I didn't have time to argue. I was in charge of a university production. I was responsible for putting on a revue. *Long Live Love* was born.

The weeks that followed were consumed in writing sketches—both words and music—plus casting. I assembled the best talent at Syracuse. They included Leo Bloom, Evelyn Feldman, Vince Gerbino, Rudy Marinetti, Hal Venho, Jackie Wenz, and the very gifted Arnie Duncan, who would much later re-enter my life.

The first rumblings of discontent over my newly created position came from Professor Schweppe, who headed the Musical Comedy Department. My appointment by Professor Falk had hopscotched Professor Schweppe completely. I was now the nominal head of a musical comedy production. This created the seeds for the near demise of the *Long Live*

Love student production. Another revolution was in the offing when the students who wrote the music and lyrics disagreed with my staging of the curtain call and insisted that the cast storm up the aisles and hiss the audience. I violently disagreed, whereupon they took their music and left the show.

Professor Falk, hearing of this, was awakened from his sleep and arrived at the theater. It was past midnight. The actors, who remained loyal, gathered around awaiting his words. I expected to hear the death knell to the show. Then he quietly asked me what I wanted to do.

"We'll need music," I said, as if it were an easily replaceable part.

Suddenly the rear doors of the theater opened, and Professor Schweppe, every inch an impresario, stormed down the aisle. He, too, had heard the news and was here to put the pieces back together again. Without waiting to be asked to speak, he suggested that the dissenters be taken back. He would take over and direct the show.

Professor Falk listened, then quietly said, "I run this school and Stiller's directing the show." It was as if an ax had fallen on Professor Schweppe's head. He was in shock and so was I. I couldn't think straight or begin to examine my feelings.

Professor Schweppe, totally devastated, turned and strode out of the theater. "I'm resigning," he said. Once he was out the door, I asked myself what the hell was going on. Was this my fault? A professor leaving the university on account of me?

Falk said, "Jerry Stiller's directing the show," and he left.

At that moment my life took a new turn. It was up to me to make good on my dream of being an actor, the dream that had brought me to this place. For whatever it was worth, for the next few days I cut all my classes and searched for a student composer. I remembered that while living out at the state fairgrounds I'd met an ex-GI named Ross Miller, a fine arts music major. I called him and he played me a trunkful of beautiful ballads he had written while overseas. End of story. Three nights later, we opened to rave notices. I was recognized by everyone on the campus.

Soon after, Professor Schweppe resigned. Weeks later, he informed me he would be teaching at the University of Iowa and he would get me a scholarship there if I'd leave Syracuse. Iowa had a great reputation in drama, but I refused the professor's offer. I never mentioned this to Professor Falk or anyone. I love both my teachers to this day.

In class, Professor Falk discussed student productions he might direct. He asked me to prepare to read Tesman in *Hedda Gabler.* I said sure. Ibsen seemed so much simpler than trying to be funny. So, a couple days later, in a class where I had been lauded for my willingness to make a fool of myself, I now read a major role in Ibsen.

After ten minutes, Falk stopped the reading and proceeded to attack me. His comments were biting. I tried not to appear devastated as one barb after another pierced my sensibilities. When it stopped I couldn't believe I had once had the reputation of fair-haired boy on the Hill. It seemed like Dr. Jekyll had become Mr. Hyde.

"How long did you work on that?" Sawyer Falk finally asked.

I thought a moment. "A lot, I guess."

"How much time?" he asked.

I couldn't supply a specific answer.

"How long on that last speech?"

"Fifteen minutes," I said.

"Hours!" he exclaimed. "Actors spend hours on a single speech," he said, as if I were now the pitiful example of a hack actor.

Some weeks later, Amram Nowak, a friend and dramaturge, informed me that he'd suggested the professor allow me to read for Molière's *Le Bourgeois Gentilhomme.* I knew this would be an audition, and I spent many hours on the part. After my reading in class, Falk announced that the final university production would, in fact, be *Le Bourgeois Gentilhomme,* with myself as Monsieur Jourdain. And so I got to play one of the great classic roles in theater.

After weeks of rehearsal, we opened to much campus publicity. The hoopla, however, exceeded my performance. I was a dull Monsieur Jourdain. I had not made the transition from nightclub comedian to actor. The *Daily Orange,* one of whose staffers was an undergraduate named William Safire, ran a front-page headline: STILLER DISAPPOINTING.

I had gone from campus hero to total flop. When I signed into some new classes, "Ha-ha" was scribbled next to my name. The show drew very small audiences, and the school pressured Falk to close it. Falk insisted on keeping it open.

When I asked why, he said, "This play will someday help you become an actor. That's the reason I'm keeping it open."

As graduation day drew near, I had cut so many classes during *Long Live Love* that I failed three subjects and lacked credits to graduate. A Quaker teacher in my Comparative Religion class permitted me to take a makeup exam with an open Bible in front of me. I wrote down all the answers word for word straight out of the Old and New Testaments. I'll never forget that teacher. He was a true Christian. My ASTRP credits put me over the top, and I received my degree, Bachelor of Science in Speech and Dramatic Art.

On graduation day I overslept. I can only guess that it was because I didn't want to leave college. At any rate I ran out to the field where the ceremony was already in progress, and rather than disrupt the proceedings by running across the field to where the School of Speech and Dramatic Art students were seated, I joined the school nearest me—the School of Forestry. When my name was called I raced from among the trees, mortarboard hat flying, tripping on my black robe, then grabbed the diploma and joined my classmates in the proper school.

At the end of the ceremony I asked Professor Falk if I could walk home with him. He said yes. It seemed like something out of Mickey Rooney and Lewis Stone in the "Andy Hardy" series.

We started walking toward his house at 128 Circle Road, a good distance away. For ten minutes I said nothing. I knew I didn't want to leave the safety net of the university but also knew that telling him this would not please him. I remembered him once saying, after he and Kay and I had watched *Inside USA,* a Broadway revue, that I was funnier than one of the show's stars, Jack Haley, the great Tin Man of *The Wizard of Oz.* I was thrilled, because I knew Sawyer Falk would never lie. He believed in me, and now I had to go for it.

We reached his house, and I stuck my hand out to say good-bye. I wanted to hug him, to thank him for all he had done for me. But I didn't. He looked at me squarely. *This is all I can do,* he seemed to be saying. *The rest is up to you.*

At that moment I vowed that I'd live up to the belief he had in me. He'd be with me in the wings every time I went on.

"If I write, will you answer?" I asked.

"Yes," he said.

I turned and started back. That night I left Syracuse University.

While still at Syracuse I had written letters to professional stock companies, asking for work as an actor. I received a reply from the Shady Lane Playhouse in Marengo, Illinois, offering me $35 a week to apprentice and play small roles. My first summer out of school, and I landed a job in an equity stock company. Not bad, I thought.

Marengo was a town in the middle of some cornfields fifty miles west of Chicago. Great trees shaded the streets and the little houses. I had a room in the home of Brenda Peterson, a handsome woman who liked theater people and was glad to house some of them. My rent was $8 a week, which included a huge breakfast.

The company's director was a silver-haired gentleman named Harry Minturn. He staged a new play every week, bringing in the lead while rehearsing the resident company.

The first show of the season was Garson Kanin's *Born Yesterday*, starring Frank Stevens as Harry Brock, the bullying junk-king. My job for that week was to locate props and furniture for the show, and play the role of a barber. I had no lines. I simply had to lather Harry Brock's face and shave him while another apprentice shined his shoes. In the course of driving a pickup truck to Rockford, Illinois, to locate props and furniture, I created my character. In this small role I saw a chance to create something funny. I modeled my barber after Henry Armetta, a movie comedian. He was Italian-American, with an exaggerated accent, and had one shoulder that that always seemed to droop as he walked.

Since little or no rehearsal was set aside for apprentices, I was told on the night of the opening just to walk on with my mug and shaving cream, and get off. Mr. Stevens had done the play before and was familiar with the routine. That night I made my entrance with a pronounced limp and sporting a black mustache, my shoulder hunched like Henry Armetta.

"Gimme a shave," Stevens barked, staring at me with disbelief. I mixed the lather till it foamed, and ad-libbed, in broken Neapolitan, "Coming right uppa, Mr. Brocka."

"Make it snappy," Stevens urged.

I lathered his face with the shaving cream, and just as he started to speak his lines, the brush "accidentally" fell into his mouth. He looked at me, hate in his eyes, foam spewing from his mouth. The audience snickered. The cast was in shock. Stevens managed to wipe the foam from his mouth and said in a whisper to someone onstage, "Where did *he* come from?"

The audience seemed sympathetic to Mr. Stevens. When the act ended, no one said a word to me. The next morning the producer called me into his office and asked what I'd had in mind when I was putting shaving soap in Harry Brock's mouth. I told him that I felt the role of the barber, though small, allowed some leeway to play around. "I guess Mr. Stevens is upset," I said.

"Yes, he's upset all right. He wants me to fire you."

"Well, I'm sorry," I said, "but that's the way I see the part."

He paused, taking note of my seriousness. "Well, I'm going to have to let you go."

"Why?" I asked. "I'm an actor. The theater is a place where you can try things you wouldn't do in real life."

He looked at me for a moment, didn't say anything, and started to walk away.

"Are you going to fire me for trying to be funny?" I asked as he reached the door.

"No, Jerry, I can't fire you for that. I'm letting you go because you tore a piece of furniture when you brought it in from Rockford."

He was right. I *had* ripped a couch. I was given bus fare back to New York and $35. It just so happened that Maryanna Siskind, an actress working in the following week's show, was also fired. She was a tall, dark-haired girl whose only previous stage experience had been the role of Mary Magdalene in a tour of *The Passion Play*. She was in tears when she too was given her Shady Lane walking papers.

I asked her what she was going to do.

"I don't know," she said. "I live in Chicago, but I hate going back home a failure in the theater."

Her despair made me feel like something of a hero. "Look," I said, "there are a lot of stock companies in Wisconsin and Illinois."

"Where?"

"There's a theater in Williams Bay, Wisconsin. Let's give it a try."

Maryanna said okay.

I quickly packed and said good-bye to my Marengo landlady, Mrs. Peterson.

"What happened?" she asked.

"Oh, you'll hear about it. What do I owe you?"

"Nothing," she said. She must have guessed how hard up I was. I told her I was hitchhiking and asked her the best way to Williams Bay. She gave me the route.

A few minutes later, Maryanna and I were on the highway with our suitcases, just like Claudette Colbert and Clark Gable in *It Happened One Night,* except that Maryanna was a full eight inches taller than me. Her beautiful face got us some quick rides (just like Claudette Colbert's legs), and we arrived a few hours later at a church in Williams Bay, where a community theater was rehearsing a production of *Two Blind Mice.* We walked in. The director, a young man named Sam Johanson, was looking for someone to play the lead, the Melvyn Douglas role. When the local people finished auditioning, I approached Johanson and asked if Maryanna and I could read. To my amazement, he handed me a script. Before I finished my first speech, he shouted, "He's got it! I want him for the Melvyn Douglas part!"

At that pronouncement, the members of the resident company bolted out of their seats, and a fight erupted. They were infuriated by his having cast someone (me) who had just walked in off the street. Maryanna and I just sat there as the mood grew angrier and uglier. Finally Sam Johanson said, "I'm the director here, and I make the decisions. I think this fellow is right for the role, and if you don't go along with it, I quit."

I couldn't believe what was taking place. Here was this man I'd never before met in my life, quitting his position over me.

"Come on, let's go, we're leaving," he said. The three of us strode out of the church. As we hit the street I said, "You're not quitting on account of us? You know, we've just been fired from the Shady Lane. We're on a roll."

"No, it's more than that. I'm the director and I know I'm right. I just can't let this ride."

I said, "Well, I guess I'm hitchhiking down to Chicago now. You want to come along?"

"No thanks. But you can try the Lake Zurich Playhouse. It's on the way."

"We will," I said, thanking him. "Can I get your address?" I asked. "I'd like to send you a note."

"I have no address," Johanson said. He disappeared up the street. I never saw him again.

Maryanna and I were back on the highway.

"Wow," I said, laughing. "He really wanted me. A guy quit on account of me and he never saw me before in his life. What do you think of that?"

"I think I'm going back to Chicago," Maryanna said.

"Come on, let's try the Lake Zurich Playhouse first."

She looked at me a little uncertainly, then said yes.

That night we arrived at Lake Zurich. Although we knew no one at the Playhouse, out of the goodness of their Midwestern hearts they fed us and put us up for the night. During the night we were almost eaten by mosquitoes, and I decided that even if I were offered work, I could not survive another night of those little dive bombers. Maryanna was in agreement.

The next morning, when Maryanna and I arrived at the Loop in Chicago, we said good-bye. We had never slept together or even kissed during the brief period we knew one another. We were friends. She may have played Mary Magdalene in *The Passion Play*, but she had no passion for me.

In Chicago I found a room in a baronial brownstone on North Wellington, just off Lake Shore Drive. I had enough in my pocket for two weeks' rent. I loved the quiet, tree-lined street and living in what felt like a castle. I could easily see myself surviving indefinitely on liverwurst and Wonder bread. The craziness of the previous few days only whetted my appetite for new adventures.

Early the next day, I hustled down to the lakefront to see if they were doing any casting at *Frontiers of Freedom,* a pageant at the Chicago Railroad Fair. The pageant was an extravaganza, pure Americana with live music, choreographed and performed with great precision. It had Columbus discovering America, barges moving up and down the Erie Canal, a race between a horse and a Tom Thumb steam engine, Lincoln signing the Emancipation Proclamation, a Pony Express rider carrying the mail, and a Keystone Kops sequence.

Walking around, I learned that the director of the pageant was Joan Woodruff, who had taught dance at my youthful stomping grounds, the Henry Street Playhouse on New York's Lower East Side. I located her office and introduced myself. She remembered me and asked what I was doing in Chicago.

"Looking for a job."

"You were fifteen when I saw you last."

"Yeah. I took it up. Acting!"

"We don't pay much around here, Jerry, but where can I reach you?"

My heart jumped. Then out of the blue she asked, "Do you know any-thing about horses?"

"No. I'm from New York."

"Well, that's good, because you're not afraid of them, are you?"

"No," I said recklessly. "Of course not."

"We need somebody to stop the Pony Express horse."

"Hey, I can do that."

"Okay, you're hired. You start tomorrow. You get $55 a week. You also play William Penn, a Keystone Kop, and an Indian, and you drive Tom Thumb."

"Why are you giving me this job?"

"Because no one is willing to stop the horse. Go out and watch, and let me know how you feel about it."

I went into the grandstand, reveling in my luck. Soon I would be part of all this. *Three days ago I was out of work,* I thought, *and tomorrow I stop a horse and I'm getting fifty-five bucks a week. I'm making more than my father.*

When the Pony Express rider roared across the stage at full speed, the crowd hushed. The rider, a sack stuffed with mail on his back, barely broke stride as he gracefully switched from one horse to another. He sprinted alongside the fresh mount and with one hand reached for the saddle bow, then pulled his body upward, in fetal position. As the new horse picked up speed, the rider thrust his legs downward, just long enough to propel his body skyward. There was a discernible gasp from the spectators as the rider's legs arced high over the horse and split apart. Only his hands, locked on the pommel, kept him from leaving the planet. Like rubber bands, his arms stretched and pulled him safely back to earth—as beast and man galloped westward to grand applause.

My job was to stop the first horse and walk it into the stable. Simple enough. "Don't be afraid," the stable man told me. "Just grab the reins and lead him back. Only, when it rains he sometimes slips and falls on the train tracks. When he does that, get out of the way. Just hang onto those reins."

How do I do both? I asked myself. But I nodded yes.

At the first show I went from being an American Indian to William Penn, complete with powdered white wig and buckled shoes. The quick change came close to disaster. No one had given me a belt for my William

Penn pants. The wig did not fit. I ran onstage discovering Pennsylvania while pulling up my pants. The audience applauded as, taking wide, wide steps, I exited. It took a long time for me to get offstage.

I then changed into my cowboy outfit, ready to stop the horse. The rider, whom I'd never met or rehearsed with, came galloping down the asphalt pavement. I jogged far enough behind the animal so as not to frighten him. As the rider switched, I grabbed the horse's reins.

"Come on, horse," I said. "Come with me."

The horse stood motionless.

"Please," I said, half-begging. "Please come with me."

The horse finally obeyed. I could hear the audience cheering the Pony Express guy right on cue as he rode off on Horse No. 2.

At the next performance the horse—my horse—slipped on the pavement. It had rained between shows. He landed squarely on his side. The sound of him hitting the pavement was frightening. He got up by himself. I never let go of the reins, although I was only inches away from becoming a steak sandwich . . . rare.

The finale of the pageant depicted the glories of America at the turn of the last century. It was a colorful montage of the period. The stage was filled with automobiles, riverboats, horses, actors, singers, dancers, alive with the sounds of boat whistles, band music, fireworks, and a performance by an actor named Richard Lee in the Keystone Kops sketch that stole the show.

Physically, Richard Lee was a man of extraordinarily large proportions. He seemed like someone you'd meet in the pages of a Hemingway novel. He had gray curly hair and muttonchop whiskers that curled below his chin as if they were about to shake hands. He immediately made me feel at home, asking, "How did you get started, Jerry?" as if I were a big-time actor.

I said, "I've just graduated college, and I want to become a comedian." Richard didn't laugh at me or put me down.

"Listen," he said, "we'll rehearse together. We'll have some fun. You saw the Keystone Kops scene with me and the other guy. You just do what he did—arrest me and take me into custody."

The Keystone Kops scene in the finale of the pageant starts on a peaceful Sunday afternoon. Ladies in bustles, gentlemen wearing dusters and spats. An air of civility exists until Richard, half-potted, wearing an orange blazer, goggles, an aviator cap, and driving a backfiring Stutz

Bearcat that's billowing smoke, breaks the tranquillity. Keystone Kops fly out of the woodwork to restore order. Resisting arrest, Lee is hilarious. His comedy was the size of Greek tragedy. I wondered if I could match him.

Just before the show, Richard, as if to boost my spirits, remarked, "You know, I'm not an actor, Jerry."

"What are you?"

"I fooled around a little in the Navy," he said.

I tried to play it cool. This guy was funny and he had never taken a lesson in his life. What good was I, I asked myself, if I couldn't be funnier than him? What the hell was I doing? Stopping a horse, I told myself.

I changed from my cowboy outfit to my Kop outfit for my entrance in the Keystone scene. In this buffoonery I try to take charge and restore order. Richard, spotting me, beckons me with his finger. I'm half his height but I naively obey. He bounces me off his stomach like a Ping-Pong ball. I fly high in the air, landing on my bum. He laughs uproariously, as does the crowd. I then proceed to chase and apprehend him, escorting him by the seat of the pants to the paddy wagon. As I open its door, he grabs *me* by the bottom and tosses me into the wagon. The audience is in stitches. As a coup de grace he leaps onto the rear running board, signaling the paddy driver to drive off. As the driver hits the accelerator and the wagon bolts, Richard fakes teetering backward, then lunges at the last possible moment, miraculously grabbing at two vertical poles attached to the running board. He lifts his leg like Nijinsky doing an arabesque as the wagon pulls away. He smiles genially as the audience applauds.

The paddy wagon driver and Richard were always in synch. At the screech of the wheels when the wagon pulled away, Richard's hands would reach for the two poles. His timing was uncanny. He knew just how long to wait. He had every eye in the grandstand on him. He could practically hear the people out there holding their breaths. It was the high point of the show.

Several weeks into the summer, at one performance the paddy wagon pulled away a microsecond sooner than usual. From where I was sitting inside the wagon I could see Richard's hands grab for the poles, and the startled look on his face as his 250-pound frame lifted into the air, arching as if he were doing a backward dive. For a moment, he seemed to levitate, his hands reaching to heaven for the poles.

I saw his head hit the ground first. When I heard the sound I knew he was gone. The music and the laughter stopped. The crew, stable people, singers, dancers, actors, all converged upon him where he lay. The audience stood silently watching, then slowly started filing out. Two hours later we performed again, on schedule—minus the bit.

The following Sunday there was a memorial service for Richard Lee. The chimes of the Chicago Railroad Fair played "Somewhere a Voice Is Calling." That summer I learned, among other things, that timing is everything, the show really does go on, and funny people die.

About midsummer Paul Killiam, who produced *Billy Bryant's Showboat*, one of the other fair attractions, announced he was auditioning actors for *The Physician in Spite of Himself.* Since I had done Monsieur Jourdain in *Le Bourgeois Gentilhomme* at school, another Molière play, I felt qualified. I read for Sganarelle and got the role. We rehearsed between performances of *Frontiers.* Two weeks later we went on in the music tent between performances of *The Merry Widow.* The show was a huge hit. All the laughs I never got doing Molière in school had at last arrived. Over the following years, I kept in touch with Professor Falk. These are some of the letters we exchanged.

OIL INDUSTRY
SERVICE CENTER

CHICAGO, ILLINOIS
AT THE CHICAGO FAIR OF 1950

Dear Professor Falk:
  The Molière play is coming along fine. I could never have done it without the Bourgeois Gentleman *under my belt, however.*
  As for this pageant extravaganza, I'm beginning to be noticed. The director paid me a compliment for my work in one of the comedy scenes . . .
  Give my regards to the family, faculty, and students.

  Sincerely,
  Jerry

OIL INDUSTRY
SERVICE CENTER

CHICAGO, ILLINOIS
AT THE CHICAGO FAIR OF 1950

432 W. Wellington Ave.
Chicago, Ill
August 13, 1950

Dear Professor Falk:

Things have been happening so fast that it has been difficult for me to find time to write. In a nutshell, The Physician in Spite of Himself *was a smashing success. We played it before 1,000 people as a free attraction after our final performance. . . . I didn't think I had the strength to play that night, but I went out and absolutely killed them. As a result, I've become a sort of an overnight sensation at the fair.*

The show itself was nowhere near The Bourgeois Gentleman. *It lacked style, but as an individual I felt comfortable and funny.*

But the good news is this: The producer of Billy Bryant's Showboat, *here at the fair, a fellow named Paul Killiam, saw me and liked me. He wanted me to do the villain in* The Sin Man, *an old fashioned melodrama. I accepted. It pays ninety-five dollars a week. I go into the show Friday, replacing an old comedian in the role. Right now, I'm trying to learn the lines.*

In the meantime the demand to see the Physician *has been so great that I arranged with Killiam (who is also special-events director for the fair) to put it on again. Mr. Falk, I've invited every agent and drama critic in Chicago down to see it. The show gives me a great chance to act, and act I do. I'm beginning to get the things you were talking about and the value there is in not dawdling when doing Molière. Believe me, Mr. Falk, those rehearsals and pounding were worth it. I've put those lessons to good use.*

The melodrama plays four shows daily, seven days a week. I'll be in the American Guild of Variety Artists by the end of this week. There is a rumor the fair may be extended till September 30. Do you think this will conflict with meeting Cheryl Crawford?

*Well, this has been a chaotic summer, to say the least. I started out
as an apprentice and I end up making $95 a week. I've never had so
many ups and downs in my life, Mr. Falk.*

> *Your ever-striving student,*
> *Jerry*

My chaotic adventures at the Chicago Railroad Fair continued
throughout that summer. I was never happier. I was working all the time.
First *Frontiers of Freedom,* then *The Physician in Spite of Himself,* then I
was making $95 a week in *The Sin Man.*

The Sin Man started with a series of "olios," vaudeville bits that each
performer had in their personal repertoire—a novelty song, a poem, an
eccentric dance. It familiarized the cast to the audience, who would next
see them as characters in the melodrama. I had no olio. I was just introduced as "The Villain" by the master of ceremonies, who told the audience to hiss me, which they took a delight in doing.

My villain was hissed at throughout the entire show. In one scene I'd
chase the heroine from one side of the stage to the other, each time strip-
ping her of a piece of her clothing—first her sleeve, then her skirt. As this
happens, she'd say, "Sir, what are you doing?" and I'd turn to the audience and say, "Now isn't that a silly question."

When I'd finally have her down to her blouse and pantaloons, she'd
turn to the audience and reveal an American flag across her chest. As the
piano player plays "Hurrah for the Red, White, and Blue," she'd say, "Vi-
olate me if you will, desecrate me if you wish, but dare you desecrate our
country's flag?" and the audience would cheer madly.

I'd take one look at her, then look at the audience and say, "Just call
me Benedict Arnold." A big laugh, and I'd say, "The sun has set, Nellie;
the flag must come down."

The Sin Man had its origins at the Old Knick Music Hall in New York.
Mr. Killiam told me Ernie Saracino created my role and Jack Lemmon
played the hero.

When the Chicago Fair closed, I returned to New York from my summer
adventures, hell-bent on cracking the Broadway stage. I was living at

home with my mother and father in the Ravenswood Project in Astoria, Queens. My brother Arnie and my sister Doreen were on their own. My younger sister, Maxine, was almost five. It occurred to me that I would have to contribute something to the house, but I also needed a job that would allow me the time to make rounds. So I applied for work at Nedick's, a New York institution that sold hot dogs, orange drinks, and coffee all over the city. I worked first at Penn Station, then in Times Square. But I kept trying to find work in the theater.

25 Jackson St.
New York, New York
November 17, 1950

Professor Sawyer Falk
Director of Dramatics
Syracuse University
Syracuse, New York

Dear Mr. Falk:
Just a few lines to say things are moving along. The only thing tangible is that I managed to get a walk-on on The Colgate Comedy Hour, *which stars Jack Carson. It'll be televised coast-to-coast this Wednesday from 8 to 9. I'm in the subway scene. I don't say anything, but this morning I practiced climbing all over Jack Carson—which I later did at the rehearsal. Carson nearly threw me out of the International Theater . . .*
I'm getting lots of laughs at the Blackfriars [a theater company run by the Catholic Actors' Guild]. In addition I'm getting a reputation, the trend of which seems to be similar to the one I picked up in Syracuse. I don't know if this is good or bad, but the audience seems to like me. The other man who plays the role doesn't seem to come near to this phenomenon. The purpose of this show, Mr. Falk, is to get seen by some agents. I have no other choice.
I may be starting from the pit, Mr. Falk, but I want you to know that your standards are well preserved in this carcass. It is a great advantage to have been inculcated with those standards.

Well, suffice it to say that I'll make this league, and it won't be too long either. Thanks to you, I feel equipped.

Sincerely,
Jerry

25 Jackson St.
New York, New York
December 3, 1950

Dear Mr. Falk:

Thank you for going to bat for me with Mr. Alexander Cohen. I've already finished the letter to him that you suggested.

I'm supposed to sing for Cheryl Crawford this week. I'm going to do "The Song of the Open Road," only like it's never been done before. I will give you the results as soon as I get them.

I'm also in line for an audition with Rodgers and Hammerstein. The only trouble is they are all singing auditions. It's the only way I can get a crack at nonsinging roles. In other words, I have to do something unusual enough in the singing audition to warrant their asking me who I am and where I've been all these years. And that's exactly what I'm going to try to do. Without elaborating too much, Mr. Falk, I think it's the funniest five minutes I've ever done. And if I get the job, it will be.

Your devoted student,
Jerry

On the crucial day I arrived for the *Paint Your Wagon* audition for Cheryl Crawford at the Martin Beck Theater with a small suitcase. The doorman, eyeing the valise, ominously asked, "What's in the case?"

"My music," I said.

"What's your name?"

"Jerry Stiller."

"Sit down," he said. "They'll call you."

I sat, waiting my turn, as some of the best voices in New York filled the theater with operatic brilliance. When my name was finally called, I walked on stage with this suitcase, which had been crammed with reams of sheet music. I peered out into the darkness of the almost empty theater. From the last row, Cheryl Crawford, one of the premier Broadway producers, called out in a no-nonsense voice, "What are you going to sing?"

"What do you wanna hear?" I said.

"What have you got?" she said.

"I got them all," I said, opening the suitcase. " 'Bibbidi-bobbidi-boo,' 'Zena-Zena,' 'The Ocarina Song.' " The sheet music slalomed lazily to the floor as I read off each piece.

"Sing the next one you come to," the faceless voice, turning icy, commanded.

"Okay," I said, dropping everything ever written by Cole Porter and Irving Berlin in a heavy heap, and reaching inside my jacket for "Song of the Open Road," which I had folded neatly into eighths.

"I also do origami," I said, handing the wadded paper to the shocked piano player. "And would you mind raising this an octave?"

"I'll give it a try," he said acidly.

"This'll take a minute," I noted, as the piano player slowly unfolded the music. I could sense the shock waves as he began the arpeggio. I heard my note and burst into, "What in the world could be so sweet as the thundering clatter of horses' feet and the song of the oopen road . . ."

When I reached high C, I sneezed, pulling out a handkerchief loaded with gum drops, keys, cufflinks, and what have you. Nickels, dimes, and pennies showered the stage. I heard gasps from out front.

"Keep on playing," I begged as I went to my knees, singing away while picking up change. "I'm on the road to Mandalay . . . let me travel on with no more love and no more care, just like a vagabond . . ." I urged the piano player to keep playing away. He did. "I'll let the blue sky cover my head . . . why should I want a feather bed . . . ?"

"Thank you, thank you!" someone in the seats shouted. "That'll do. Stop. Stop." I kept going. "Please stop!" I finally stopped.

"I'm a comedian," I said, as if what they had just seen needed explanation.

"We're not seeing comedians," Cheryl Crawford said.

"It's the only way I could get in to see you for a part."

"Thank you," she said.

"It'll take a minute to get my stuff together," I said, picking up my music and carfare home as quickly as possible, and whatever coins I could. From the pit, the piano player handed me my music.

"Here," he said, "I folded it for you."

"Sorry," I said. "Just trying to be funny."

"Ha-ha," he said.

(The following Broadway season, when I was a year out of Syracuse University, Bill Liebling, the kindly agent of the Liebling/Audrey Wood agency, unwittingly sent me to read for Miss Crawford's new musical *Flahooley*. When I arrived at the Martin Beck, the doorman stared at me for a minute, then asked, "Where's your music?" When my name was called, I confronted the same group of people. There was no recognition that I'd ever been there before. Or maybe there was. They were frozen. I read well, but did not get the part. A man named Professor Irwin Corey did.)

In those days actors would make rounds together, usually in twos and threes. We were never the same type. Essentially it was to support one another and keep our egos alive. We went from office to office and did shtick for the secretaries, who might someday be promoted to casting agents. Hopefully, through these mini-auditions, they would remember us.

One day John Cassavetes, Harry Mastrogeorge, and I were making rounds. It was in the era of live television: *Studio One, Danger,* Ernie Kovacs, etc. We walked into an office on Madison Avenue. It had a marble floor, and John, who didn't look like an actor and dressed in suits that were a size too big because they belonged to his father, asked to see the producer. The receptionist took a look at the three of us and said, "He's not in."

John suddenly got very angry. "What do you mean, he's not in?" he said. "I saw him coming in on the elevator." Without warning, John fell flat-faced to the floor like a slab of stone. We were horrified.

The receptionist looked at me in shock and said, "What happened?"

I looked at John's lifeless body and said, "I think he's dead."

She ran into the producer's office and came running back with the producer.

"What happened?" he asked.

"I think he's dead," I said.

At that point Cassavetes jumped up and said, "Do you know how long I've been trying to get to see you?"

The producer, his face livid, said, "Get out of here and don't ever come back again!"

Cassavetes pulled out a flock of 8 x 10s and threw them in the air.

"Here," he said. "In case you need me."

And then we left for Chock Full o'Nuts.

I continued to make rounds constantly.

Word got around that Mike Todd was producing *Mexican Hayride* with Bobby Clark. I figured that with my musical comedy background I'd be right for Clark's understudy. Todd's office on Broadway was there for me to attack. I mustered all my swagger, walked through the room, and approached the woman at the desk.

"I'd like to see Mr. Todd, please."

"Are you an actor?" she asked.

"Yes."

"I'm afraid Mr. Todd is out of town, but can I get you a sandwich?"

A sandwich?

"No, thank you," I said. "I really would like to see Mr. Todd." I figured they were trying to buy me off when Todd was in the next room. If I took the sandwich I'd never get to see him.

"Well, he's out of town at the moment. You sure I can't get you a sandwich."

"That's very nice," I said.

I was totally confused. Rejection could buy you a sandwich?

"Does Mr. Todd always offer sandwiches to actors?" I asked.

"Yes. I'm an actress myself. My name is Belle Flowers."

"Haven't I seen you on stage?"

"Yeah," she said.

"Well, tell Mr. Todd I'll be back. And thanks." I didn't take her up on the sandwich but I walked away with a warm feeling about Mike Todd. I knew this guy understood how tough it was to make rounds, and the gesture of a sandwich made looking for a theater job less painful. Belle Flowers was terrific in her role.

On another day, I decided to visit the Shubert office. I entered the building on West 44th Street. The offices were in the same building as the Shubert Theater. I asked the elevator operator to take me up to see Mr. Shubert. We traveled several floors. The operator opened the door, and I was in the presence of an elegantly coifed woman behind a desk.

"What can I do for you?" she asked.

"I'd like to see Mr. Shubert," I said.

"Mr. Lee or Mr. Jake?"

"Mr. Lee," I said without missing a beat.

"Do you have an appointment?"

"No," I said. "I'm an actor."

"What's your name?"

"Jerry Stiller."

She flipped a switch on the intercom. "Jerry Stiller to see you."

"Send him in."

I actually was getting in to see Lee Shubert, the most powerful producer on Broadway. I opened the door. There behind a desk was Lee Shubert. His head was barely visible above the desk.

"Mr. Shubert?"

"Yes?"

"I'm Jerry Stiller."

"Yes?"

"I'm from Syracuse."

"Yes."

"*You're* from Syracuse."

"Yes."

"I'm a comedian."

"Are you working right now?"

"No."

"When you find work will you call me?"

"Yes."

"Thank you very much."

Out on the street I felt the warm glow of success. I couldn't get over my amazement that I'd actually gotten to meet Lee Shubert.

The Playhouse
Erie, Pennsylvania
March 14, 1951

Dear Mr. Falk:

I hope this letter finds you in fine fettle. . . .

William Liebling, the agent, saw me in the Blackfriars show. He shook my hand and said, "You're a comedian, all right. You're going to

*be all right." He said he would certainly keep me in mind if the right
thing comes up. . . .*

*I have been lucky. William Liebling has sent me up for three shows.
Two of them I just wasn't right for,* Billion-Dollar Baby *and* The
Gramercy Ghost; *the third show,* Flahooley, *is a new musical by Fred
Saidy and Yip Harburg.*

*I was sent to see Mr. Saidy, who looked at me and immediately said
I was too young. I whipped out some pictures from B.G. [Syracuse
production of* The Bourgeois Gentleman*], showing how old I could look
under fire. He was very impressed with the pictures, and asked about
their history. I told him. He gave me a script and locked me in a room
for ten minutes. It was the role of a comic Arab. He had me read, he
laughed, then he hollered into the other room, "Hey, Yip, come here and
look at this kid."*

*I read it over again. They said it was a good reading, but I was too
young.*

*In the meantime Newell Tarrant of the Erie Playhouse arrived in
New York. He had me read The* Gentle People. *I read Jonah and some
other characters. He seemed impressed—and here I am in Erie.*

> *Your devoted student,*
> *Jerry*

Syracuse, New York
March 20, 1951

Mr. Jerry Stiller
The Playhouse
128 West 7th St.
Erie, Pennsylvania

Dear Jerry:

*Thank you very much for your letter telling me about your doings. As
you quite rightly say, this business has its ups and downs, and the main
thing is to hang on. I feel quite sure that you will come through with
something in New York before long. I am dropping Liebling a note about*

you. Of course he knows you are ready, but an extra word won't do any
harm.

I should think you would find Erie a pleasant and profitable place
for the rest of the season. Tarrant is a wonderful person and an
especially good theater man. I am sure your stay in Erie will be mutually
beneficial. Please give him my warmest regard.

This must be short and hasty, as I am getting ready for my European
trip. I fly to Paris on Thursday.

Cordially,
Sawyer Falk

You learn to act by acting, I thought, and I did just that. I pursued employment in the theater the same way a person would look for work as a
sand hog. You apply for the job. I was never insensitive about this. I figured you just kept knocking on doors until you were hired. Then you'd
act. I had gotten my first Equity role in 1951 by virtue of a good word put
in by Professor Falk. He simply called Paul Crabtree, who was with the
Theatre Guild, also an ex-Syracusan.

"Hire him, Paul," Falk said, and Crabtree cast me for a role in *The Silver Whistle,* which starred Burgess Meredith, touring in summer stock. I
played a hobo who perched on a wall. We played Fayetteville, East
Rochester, and Watkins Glen in New York state. I got my Equity card.
My performance must have been college level, but the older members of
the cast liked me. Ruth McDevitt, Anne Ives, Fred Ardath—all wonderful
performers—treated me like a son. Working with Meredith was like being part of a fairy tale. I never knew he was acting. His language seemed
natural and poetical. As his sidekick, Emmett, I was twenty years too
young for the role. Meredith would call me "Emmett" on and off stage,
which I considered a compliment. It never occurred to me he might not
have known my name. On one occasion he called me aside after doing the
play for a week and suggested I read the lines a little faster. "Make it all
one thought," he said. "You'll get a huge laugh."

"Are you sure of that?" I asked him in a manner bordering on incred-
ulous, questioning his judgment. He looked at me for a full three seconds.

"Try it tonight," he said.

It did not occur to me that I was questioning the boss of the show.

I thought he was wrong about the reading of the lines. He didn't try to intimidate me or tell me that because he was the star. He merely said, "Try it." That night I said the lines as he suggested, making it one thought. The laugh started in the first row of the house and grew like a huge wave as it rolled to the back of the auditorium. I waited for it to subside so that I could continue. It wouldn't. It lasted for a full twenty seconds.

Finally, Meredith turned his back to the audience and looked up at me, and said in a full voice over the laugh, "I told you if you said it my way you'd get a big laugh." He then wiggled his ass, which topped the laugh I got.

My learning experience continued at the Erie Playhouse, a cultural oasis in northwestern Pennsylvania. There I first had the opportunity to work with Henderson Forsythe, and learned for the first time the meaning of trust onstage.

In Irwin Shaw's *The Gentle People,* Hank Forsythe was playing Jonah and I played Philip. We were two Sheepshead Bay residents who plot to kill a racketeer who is trying to shake us down. Opening night, as we sat in a rowboat in the opening scene, waiting for the curtain to rise, Hank leaned forward and whispered, "Tonight, Jerry, talk to me."

"What?" I said. I had no idea what he meant.

"Talk to me," he repeated.

"Haven't I?" I asked in shock.

"No, you haven't." Hank's eyes stared straight through me.

My initial reaction was anger. People don't come to see actors talking, they come to see a performance. Why is he telling me this now?

As the curtain rose I realized in that split second that Hank was right. I had never really spoken to anyone onstage; worse yet, I had never listened. I was always Acting, with a capital A. Had my success in college been a gigantic hoax?

Now, before saying my first line, I looked into Hank's eyes. I knew at that instant he was there to help me. I had never been told this before. From the opening curtain to the play's end, I had no memory of time. But I did know something wonderful had taken place. The evening sped by. The next day the Erie newspaper review said I was an actor who would someday be heard from.

Late in the 1980s, my son Ben and I were driving back to New York City from Cincinnati, where Ben had finished filming *Fresh Horses* with

Molly Ringwald. On a whim, I said, "Ben, let's go back by way of Erie, Pennsylvania." I knew we'd have to detour a couple of hundred miles, but I wanted to share with him some of my early theater experiences at the Erie Playhouse.

It was a foggy Saturday night as we cruised off the interstate into downtown Erie. I could see the town had changed. Lots of malls. I looked for the Playhouse. It was gone. The bar where Hank Forsythe had taught me how to drink boilermakers (another learning experience), the police station, the Playhouse—all missing in action. Something I loved had been stolen.

"Gone, all gone," I kept muttering. Ben just kept driving. I was talking to myself.

"Wait, there was a peninsula," I said. "They can't take away a peninsula." It was an elbow of land downtown that jutted into Lake Erie, and on that peninsula I had learned my lines. I could talk to myself there and no one would interrupt.

"There was a seafood restaurant where you could get a fish dinner for a buck," I said to Ben. "This is it—we're coming to it!"

The street narrowed. It jutted right into Lake Erie. I could smell the lake air. I could see ships all lit up.

Cars were now crawling along behind us and ahead of us. It was midnight. Teenagers in tight jeans and tank tops rode atop the roofs of their Saturday-night chariots. Some sat cross-legged on the hoods, while others lay flat on their backs as if sunning themselves on a private beach to the blare of heavy-metal music.

"Are you hungry, Ben?"

"Sure."

We pulled out of line, parked, and went in.

It was like entering a nautical museum. The walls had paintings of old sailing ships and lighthouses. The waitress seated us, then lit an imitation oil lamp. Pad and pencil in hand, she asked if we would like anything to drink.

"A Diet Coke," Ben said.

As she started to write, she looked at me and said, "Are you . . ."

"Yeah," I admitted, figuring she recognized me from television. I no longer felt like a dinosaur. If nothing else, fame saves you from extinction.

"Morey Amsterdam! What are you doing in Erie?"

"I'm Jerry Stiller," I said, correcting her. "I spent two seasons at the Playhouse in the fifties. This is my son," I said.

"He looks like you. Are you in theater too?" she asked.

"Yeah," Ben said, expressing proper humility.

"What street was the theater on? Was it Sixth Street?" I asked.

"Seventh Street," she said. "It's gone."

"Did you ever go there?"

"Lots of times. We loved it."

I never asked if she remembered seeing me in anything.

When we finished I paid the check and left a nice tip.

"Tell Mary Tyler Moore hello," the waitress said, smiling. She still hadn't got it straight that I wasn't Morey Amsterdam from *The Dick Van Dyke Show*.

"I will," I said. "I'll tell her you asked about her."

Ben and I took one last look at the cars circling in the peninsula, then left Erie for New York.

It must have been somewhere around Thanksgiving of 1951 that I heard someone at the Cromwell Drugstore, an aspiring-actors' hangout at Radio City, mention that Frank Corsaro was directing the national company of *Peter Pan* and was looking for pirates who could sing and dance. I had seen Jean Arthur and Boris Karloff do the Leonard Bernstein version on Broadway.

"They're looking for someone short," Howie Dayton, an aspiring actor who was short, said.

"Where's the audition?"

"The Majestic."

I arrived at the theater just as the casting call was over. I asked the stage manager, Morty Halpern, if the show had been completely cast. "I don't have an appointment, but I'm funny," I said.

He smiled. "Do you sing?"

"Kinda."

"Can you dance?"

"A little."

"Well, you've got to do both," he said.

"Let me audition. I won't disappoint you."

Halpern seemed sympathetic. "Okay, wait here," he said, walking out onto the stage.

"Can you see one more person?" he asked into the darkened seats.

"We're all set in the casting," a voice answered from the back of the theater.

"Please," I said, running on stage. "This will only take a minute."

"Okay, go ahead. One minute."

"This is the way I see radio in a couple of years. You know, now we have soap operas. Well, someday we'll have foreign-language soap operas." I began singing "Sorrento" and did my Italian soap opera routine. They must have thought I was crazy, but I was just showing them I could sing.

The whole audition lasted about five minutes. I could hear them laughing. They did not stop me. They let me finish. Frank Corsaro, who had acted and directed at Yale, and whom I had seen in *Mrs. McThing*, came up on stage with Ben Steinberg, the musical conductor. They were both little guys, my size. They looked me over. Ben Steinberg said, "We know you can't sing and you probably can't dance, but you're very funny and we need one more pirate."

Corsaro said, "The only problem is that the guy who did it on Broadway hasn't made up his mind if he wants to tour. If he says no to our show, you've got the job."

"When will you know?" I said.

"Well," Steinberg said with a shrug, "he's singing in the chorus at the Roxy. Why don't you go down there and ask him."

I couldn't believe what had just happened. I almost had a part in a Broadway show—or at least the national company of a Broadway show. I ran to the Roxy stage entrance and waited for the actor.

As he emerged I said, breathless and excited, "You were in *Peter Pan* on Broadway, right? I just auditioned for your part in the national company, and I get it if you keep working at the Roxy. Are you going to stay here or go out on the road?"

It seemed an eternity before he answered.

"You've got the part," he said. "I told them I wouldn't go on the road unless they hired my wife."

"Thanks!" I yelled. "And thanks to your wife. You don't know how much this means to me."

The tour starred Veronica Lake as Peter Pan and Lawrence Tibbett as both Mr. Darling and Captain Hook. I played Cecco, a pirate. I embellished the role with a pratfall. I flew in through a swinging door, bouncing on my bum, talking while moving. As I could neither sing nor dance, I felt the least I could do was fall well.

Peter Pan was the first integrated musical ever to play the South. We hit Baltimore, Louisville, Memphis, Oklahoma City, Dallas, New Orleans, and Chicago. On tour, Veronica Lake, a close friend of John Carradine—the wonderful Hollywood character actor who was Casey the preacher in *The Grapes of Wrath*—was caring for one of his sons, Keith or David, I forget which. Just before we were to open in Baltimore we rehearsed one of the scenes in Veronica Lake's suite. One of the Carradine kids was asleep in bed.

Alvin Ailey, who later founded his famous dance company, and Frank Neal, two of the black members of the cast, stayed in a separate hotel from the rest of the company and could not eat in the same restaurants with us in the southern cities. On matinee days, we'd all send out for food and eat together in the theater. In Memphis we were told we would not be allowed to open with a mixed company.

Just before curtain, the company manager came backstage, gathered us together, and said he'd just spoken to someone at City Hall, and it was okay to open.

We couldn't believe it. Everyone wanted to know how he'd made it happen.

"I told him we were going to open, and if they didn't like it, they could go fuck themselves. He didn't answer me, so we're going on."

We opened at the Memphis Auditorium to very few people. At one Saturday matinee we couldn't end the first act. The curtain line was J. M. Barrie's classic "If you believe in fairies, please clap!" The line never failed to get applause. One had to be dead not to respond. This time, nothing. Veronica Lake, a little dismayed, said again, "If you believe in fairies, clap your hands." Still nothing. Once more she said, "If you believe in fairies, clap your hands." The rest of the company was now gathering in the wings. Still no applause. Veronica Lake finally turned to Morty Halpern with a look of "What shall I do?"

"Say it again," he whispered.

"Please, please, clap your hands if you believe in fairies!" she begged.

Two men seated in the balcony got up and skipped down to the orchestra, waving handkerchiefs and saying, "We do, Miss Lake, we do." And the curtain came down.

In every city there were parties thrown by wealthy patrons who wanted to meet Lawrence Tibbett and Veronica Lake. The two stars would agree to this on the condition that the entire cast was invited. Mr. Tibbett had been with the Metropolitan Opera for years, but his voice had faded. As Captain Hook he had the opportunity to talk his musical numbers—as Rex Harrison would do in *My Fair Lady* a few years later. But Tibbett rarely did this. He attempted to sing as well as he could, to oblige his expectant audiences. Most of the listeners did not know he was struggling. At each of the post-show parties, the host or hostess would invariably tinkle a glass and ask if Mr. Tibbett would mind singing "On the Road to Mandalay." Tibbett, having been through this many times before, would magnanimously decline, saying, "Thank you, thank you, not tonight, but Jerry here will entertain you. Do the 'Italian Soap Opera,' Jerry." Then when I did my thing and Lawrence Tibbett started laughing, everyone else laughed too.

New Orleans, Louisiana
November 1951

Dear Professor Falk:
   Just a quick note. We have wended our way through Baltimore, Pittsburgh, Bloomington, Louisville, Memphis, and now New Orleans. Peter Pan has gotten excellent reviews in all the cities except Louisville, but business is below par. . . . It is rumored we have to gross $21,000 per week to stay alive. We have been averaging $18,000.
   Incidentally, my bit, which takes approximately twenty-five seconds, is the biggest laugh in the show. I've injected my own line and some business, which although not Barrie, is good enough to remain in.
   Bobby Barry, the little comic, has been showing me lots of tricks and thinks a lot of me.
   My duties in the show constitute everything from singing to dancing, and I do a pratfall. . . .
   We have been rerouted for a long stand in Chicago starting November 20th. It is believed the show would have folded long before this but for the fact the Shuberts put their dough in and we are now playing a Shubert House (New Orleans) and will be playing the Great Northern in Chicago. It is theorized the Shuberts like low-budget shows

and would rather play to a two-thirds house than to keep their houses dark.

While in Memphis I met Tom Fitzsimmons and Sam McCulloch, who you had teaching at Syracuse. They're about to venture into a commercial theater.

They saw me in the show, and Tom said of my performance, "It was a neat bit of comedy." The long hours of toil are crystallizing into clean, sharp, emphatic moves that have good effects on the audience.

At any rate they have asked me to consider becoming part of their resident company as comedian/stage manager. They hope to open the first of the year, with many stars.

As things stand right now, I think it's a good opportunity, and I will accept the offer, leaving Peter Pan if necessary. . . .

Regards to Francy, Mrs. Falk, and faculty.

> Your devoted student,
> Jerry

THE CROYDON
AT RUSH AND ONTARIO STREETS
CHICAGO, ILLINOIS
DE-LAWARE 7-6700

November 24, 1951

Dear Mr. Falk:

A lot of things have happened, the biggest being that Peter Pan folded tonight in Chicago . . . But I have a job with Tom Fitzsimmons and Sam McCulloch in Memphis starting tomorrow. . . .

I know that Memphis may never make me a star, but the value of the experience might make me more eligible for stardom when the opportunity beckons later on.

Mr. Falk, how do you feel about this reasoning?

> Your devoted student,
> Jerry

The 200-seat Memphis Arena Theater, in the shape of a half-moon, with the audience encircling the actors, had once been a swimming pool in the basement of the King Cotton Hotel.

To ensure an audience their first season, Tom Fitzsimmons and Sam McCulloch had instituted a star policy. Eva Gabor, John Carradine, James Dunn, Arthur Treacher, Vicki Cummings, Signe Hasso, and Margie Hart, a famous burlesque stripper, were among the many who signed on for one show or another.

The resident company included Rex Partington, my schoolmate, who later inherited the directorship of the Barter Theater from Robert Porterfield, its founder. Barter launched the careers of both Gregory Peck and Jeffrey Lynn. In 1949, I and hundreds of other hopefuls lined up on West 45th Street to do a one-minute audition for Shirley Booth and Robert Porterfield. Miss Booth was appearing in *Come Back, Little Sheba* at the Booth Theater. I had one minute to prove I could act. Be funny, I thought. I started by saying, "Miss Barter, I mean Miss Booth, thank you for letting me audition for you and Mr. Porterhouse, I mean Mr. Porterfield, here at the Barth Theater. I mean at the Booth for Mr. Barter." I got them laughing but didn't get the job.

At the Arena I was hired as stage manager and supporting cast member at a salary of $75 a week. My stage-managing duties were mainly being responsible for coordinating lights and sound and running the show. I soon discovered I was completely unsuited to this work. I was more interested in trying to be wonderful in my few limited minutes on stage. At 8 P.M. I'd slap on my makeup, jump into costume, and at 8:30 call "Places," then await my moment—the one that might someday make me a star. The thrill of acting with stars was enough to fill my cup.

In *The Second Man*, my inventiveness took over. I played a butler—a small role, but not small to me. In one scene I merely had to clear away some silverware. I pre-stashed knives and forks and dishes and so forth in every nook and cranny of the set. On cue, I entered carrying a tray. When I finished clearing the table, I'd head to the kitchen, only to discover a spoon I'd overlooked, and then a plate, and then a glass. The scene now turned into a little treasure hunt, with the audience, seated in the half-round, joining in and pointing to places on stage I had missed. When the tray resembled Pike's Peak and could no longer hold another saucer, I triumphantly marched out through the swinging doors to applause and laughter.

Offstage, I had pre-set a box of broken crockery. As the clapping faded, I dropped the crash box. The scene ended. More laughs. I felt being an actor was the greatest profession in the world.

Although my theatrical inventions hardly ingratiated me with the regular company, the disapproval never dampened my enthusiasm. I had indeed developed a following. Small, but a following.

Rosemary Murphy, whom I had a crush on, put it this way: "Jerry, you have so much creativity. Have you ever tried masturbating before you go onstage?"

The arrival of a new star each week aroused in all of us a sense of adoration, almost worship. I did all I could to make things smooth for them, on and off stage. They, of course, were unaware of my personal internal combustion.

When Arthur Treacher arrived to do *Clutterbuck,* the Benn Levy farce, with Vicki Cummings as his costar, he immediately announced to the resident performers, "Say your lines, buzz off, and collect your money. That's what this business is about." We all laughed. Of course, this did not apply to Mr. Treacher, who did much more than say his lines. He was a master farceur, and milked the script for every chuckle, to the delight of everyone.

That week I was assigned to the title role, i.e., Clutterbuck, who simply walks across the stage a few times to a recording of the "Third Man Theme." The budget did not allow for an assistant stage manager. Backstage, before making my entrance as Clutterbuck, I had to drop the needle on the record, then on cue amble nonchalantly across the stage. Once in the wings, I'd race behind the backdrop to stage left to lift the needle off the recording. Mr. Treacher had no idea I was also working the turntable.

On the night of the dress rehearsal, Mr. Treacher in his veddy English way said, "You'll always get a laugh on your entrance, dear boy."

Opening night, right on cue, I dropped the needle and walked on as Clutterbuck. There was a huge laugh, something I hardly expected, and then applause. Applause for my simple entrance and exit? How wonderful. I did nothing funny. I checked to see if my fly was open. I *kvelled,* which is Yiddish for being very happy inside, at this incredible reaction to my entrance.

As I continued to *kvell,* the music continued, right into Mr. Treacher's next speech.

"My God," I said, racing around behind the set. I hastily removed the needle as it scratched loudly over the amplifying system.

At the end of the act, Treacher was apoplectic. "What in God's name happened with that music?"

I told him I got caught up in my applause, and I was very sorry.

"My dear boy," Mr. Treacher said, "if you do that part right, they always applaud. But they're not applauding you. They're applauding my reaction to you. Now remember, just make your entrance, get your money, and pip off. That's what this business is all about."

My favorite star was James Dunn. He had won an Academy Award as the alcoholic father in *A Tree Grows in Brooklyn,* Elia Kazan's first movie, and with us he was playing Elwood P. Dowd in *Harvey.*

Dunn must have spent most of his Memphis Arena salary on parties for the cast. Each night he'd invite us to his suite and regale us with food, drink, and funny stories.

"I win the Academy Award and I've got no work next week," he told all of us. "It doesn't bother me. They just don't have any roles."

In *Harvey* I played Wilson, the psychiatric attendant, a role I felt eminently at home in. It was great being onstage with an Oscar winner. He was brilliant as the man who holds conversations with a large imaginary rabbit, and I never failed to tell him so. Before returning to Hollywood, Dunn said, "Kid, if I ever get back on Broadway, you're coming with me, even if you have to hold a stage brace." Again I *kvelled.* For all I knew, James Dunn was just being nice and nothing more, but it was also nice to hear it.

One of the pitfalls lying before a young actor in the theater is the love we have for stars. It borders on being dangerous to the adorer and the adoree.

Jeffrey Lynn, the Hollywood leading man who had appeared opposite Priscilla Lane, Claude Rains, and John Garfield in the much-cherished 1938 *Four Daughters* and then in a spate of 1940s films, was to come to Memphis to do S. N. Behrman's *The Second Man,* the one in which I played the overzealous butler.

Lynn's opening-night performance was wonderful, and we were shocked to read the horrible notices the following day. When he arrived that night for the second performance, we figuratively tiptoed around his dressing room. I wondered how he could possibly go on.

After putting on my costume and makeup, I gave him a quiet, "Half-hour, Mr. Lynn."

"Thank you," he said smilingly, in the best chin-up manner I thought possible under the circumstances.

"Anything I can get you, Mr. Lynn?"

"Nothing, Jerry, and please call me Jeff. You've been calling me Jeff all week, haven't you?"

"Yes, Jeff," I said.

"Then don't stop calling me Jeff now."

"Okay, Jeff, fifteen minutes," I said.

"Thank you, Jerry," he replied. I was stunned by his ability even to function.

The ability to keep going is what this business is all about. I made a mental note to remember that.

"Okay, five minutes, Jeff," I said a little later, sticking my head in. "And don't let anything get to you; you were great last night," I added.

"What are you talking about?" he asked, suddenly turning serious.

I stood silent.

"Get to me? Are you talking about reviews? What did they say about me?"

"Nothing," I said. "They said . . . nothing."

"What did they say? You've got to tell me."

"Didn't you read them?" I asked.

"No, I never read them."

"Well, I do," I said. "I've got to read them. I thought everybody reads them."

"No," he said, "I never read them. A lot of actors don't read their notices."

"Well, I can understand that," I said, and I called out, "Places!"

"Not before you tell me what they said."

"You can read them after the show."

"No, tell me. Now that you've mentioned them, I've got to know. They were bad, weren't they?"

"They weren't good. Now you've got to go on, Jeff," I said.

"What did they say?" he asked. "Don't you understand? I have to know."

"They said you were . . . I don't know. Please," I said, "I've got to get ready. I do this bit in the second act. I've got to get my props together."

"I want to talk to you later about the reviews," he said.

"Okay, okay," I said. "We'll talk."

I couldn't understand an actor not reading reviews. Today I don't read them either. I learn the bad news from "friends," the same way Jeffrey Lynn learned.

Even at this early stage of the game I was landing some odd jobs on television. Back in New York, Alixe Gordon was the casting director for *Studio One,* a live one-hour Monday-night dramatic show produced by Westinghouse. Alixe had seen me in Sidney Kingsley's *The World We Make* and *Men in White* at Equity Library Theater. She liked my work enough to cast me as a Japanese soldier guarding a rice paddy. The show was about the war between China and Japan in the 1930s.

Caucasian American actors were asked to play Asian roles. Sidney Lumet was the director, Olive Deering the star. Extra makeup artists were brought in the night of the show to make us look authentic. As show time drew near, the makeup people were busily sticking adhesive tape over our eyelids, to give us a somewhat Asian look, then covering them with Max Factor makeup. Of course, it would've been easier to cast Asian actors, but that pool went unexplored. My eyes went on without incident. I had no lines. Easy enough. I walked back and forth in a rice paddy. No close-ups. Olive, the star, had a major problem. The adhesive strips would not stick to her eyelids. As the stage manager started counting down to show time, Olive, on the set, shouted to Lumet, "Sidney, these lids are coming off, get a makeup person out here!"

Sidney shouted, "Get someone out there!"

Now we were a minute away from airtime. Olive started screaming, "They won't stick, Sidney, these fucking lids won't stay on!"

Ten-nine-eight-seven . . .

"Try!" Sidney implored.

"I can't! I'm taking them off!" She ripped off her eyelids just as the show started. The music came up, and Olive Deering was the only one on the show looking like the girl next door.

Alixe Gordon called me again some time later. "I've got a small role for you in a show with Margaret Sullavan," she said. "It's five lines."

"I'll take it," I said.

The story was written by Paul Crabtree, a Syracuse grad who'd cast me in my first Equity show opposite Burgess Meredith, at Sawyer Falk's prompting.

Margaret Sullavan played a nun who learned to fly an airplane during World War Two. During rehearsals, Miss Sullavan was having difficulty learning her lines. I, being an actor who was in love with Hollywood, if only through the silver screen, actually had a crush on her. I remembered seeing her in the MGM movies *The Mortal Storm* and *The Shop Around the Corner.* On a lunch break when everyone else had split, Miss Sullavan sat on a chair in the empty hall with a script on her lap going over her lines.

"Can I cue you?" I asked meekly.

"No thank you," she said, "I'll be all right."

"I'm here if you need me," I said. And I took off.

As the week went on, it appeared she was still having trouble with the words.

On the afternoon of the show, the cast went out for lunch. When we returned, she was nowhere in sight. After a while, it was apparent she was not going to be there for the show that night. Margaret Sullavan had disappeared. David Susskind, the producer, tried in vain to get one of the other actresses to go on in the role. So that night, a kinescope of a previous *Studio One* show went on instead.

Some time later it came out that during the lunch break on the day of the show, while Miss Sullavan was on the set, someone in the control booth remarked, "When will that bitch learn her lines!" The microphone key was open and she heard it on the floor.

Later, I learned that Margaret Sullavan was losing her hearing. The full story is better told by her daughter Brooke Hayward in her memoir, *Haywire.*

5

Anne: Act Two

*I*n the spring of 1953 life took another twist. I was walking on West 40th Street in Manhattan when I bumped into Anne Meara, whom I hadn't seen since we were in Longley's absconding with silverware.

"I want you to meet my father," she said. "He works in this building right here." I'd met a lot of girls, for better or worse, but none had asked me to meet her father.

We walked into the offices of the American Radiator Company, across from the New York Public Library. How did she get me here? You meet a girl in the theater, you don't need to meet her father.

"This is Big Ed," Anne said, introducing me. "He's the stock-transfer agent for the American Radiator and Standard Sanitary Company. They make the church seat toilet seat. My father calls it 'the best seat in the house.'"

I was with the daughter of a man whose company made toilet seats. I was getting a lot of background, considering I'd just met Anne a couple of weeks back.

"Jerry's an actor," Anne said, introducing me to Big Ed, who at that moment was talking to another big man with a handsome Irish face and the deepest of blue eyes.

"Are you in any show right now, Jerry?" Big Ed asked, breaking away momentarily. I suddenly felt he knew me.

"No, not right now."

"This is Tom Brennan," Anne's father said. "Tom, this is Jerry— what's your last name?"

"Stiller," I said.

Tom Brennan was close to Ed's age. He seemed in perfect condition, as if he skipped rope all day at the New York Athletic Club.

"Tom's with Robert Hall Clothes," Ed said.

An Irishman in the clothing business. It struck me as funny. They went back to talking. My presence seemed to animate them. They were each six inches taller than me—the kind of guys you'd one day remember seeing at the bar at Toots Shor's, the tough Irish who survived the streets of New York and made it in business or politics.

Was I just one of the many strays whom Anne, a young actress also trying to make it in New York, introduced every so often to her father to prove that she was a good girl who didn't fool around? I could feel them looking through me. In my mind I could hear, "What the hell is she doing with a guy like that? He's three inches shorter than she is. He's got to be Jewish. They're all Jewish in show business. Is she sleeping with him?"

"How about some lunch?" Ed said. "Tom's leaving."

"We've got to be going too," Anne said. "We've got some appointments."

"Keep making the rounds," Ed said to us, "and maybe we can all have lunch someday."

"Okay, Pop. So long, Uncle Tom," Anne said, as she and I headed for Broadway.

She's just legitimized our relationship with her father, I figured. I felt a little uneasy, as if I'd just become a member of her family. She never asked permission. There was nothing wrong with it, except that I felt a bit now as if I was under some kind of surveillance. God, what if I tried to sleep with her? This meeting could be a kind of warning, I thought. A deterrent.

"So Tom Brennan is your uncle?"

"No, he's my father's best friend, and he just got fired. He wanted to hit his ex-boss, and Dad talked him out of it. Tom used to box," Anne said.

Yeah, oranges, I thought. A joke I couldn't use at this moment.

"Your father's a big guy," I said.

"He's five-eleven."

"He seems much taller," I said.

"That's because he talks loud. He's got a punctured eardrum. It kept him from going overseas in the First World War."

History seemed to be pouring out as we approached Broadway.

"I hate making rounds," Anne said.

"I love making rounds," I said, suddenly feeling superior to her.

There were, I thought, two breeds of actors among the unknowns who tramped the streets looking for work: those who could knock on a door, and those who couldn't. Those who couldn't, no matter how talented, seemed destined for obscurity. I couldn't understand what it was that stopped any actor from saying, "I'm looking for work."

"What do you do all day?" I asked her.

"Sleep mostly," she said.

"How do you pay the rent?"

"I get jobs. I worked at Best & Co. for three days. I got fired for not being helpful to some woman who complained. I was an usher at the Trans-Lux newsreel theater."

"Didn't that drive you crazy?"

"It never got boring. They changed the newsreels every day. They caught me smoking a cigarette and fired me. I ushered at the Shubert, the second balcony. You know how steep that is?" she asked with a laugh. "I finally turned in my flashlight because I got so dizzy. It was so high you could get a nosebleed. I worked for an answering service, too. I took messages for Cliff Robertson," she said.

The list went on. *She's funny,* I thought. *Maybe we could do an act.*

"I ushered at the *Ballet de Paris* at the Hellinger. I'd come in early and watch Roland Petit warm up every night. The last job I had was testing detergent in a research laboratory. You had to dip each hand in a different detergent. One was harsh and made it red, the other was soft. See, this hand is still red."

"Yeah," I said, unable to see the red. "How do you pay the rent?" I asked again.

"I've got two roommates . . . I got to run," Anne said.

"So do I."

"See you again sometime."

She disappeared into the Times Square crowd. I headed uptown to my room on West 89th Street, which I had moved into. It was on the top floor of a brownstone, with just enough space for a single bed, a dresser, a table, and a floor lamp. It had a small bathroom. The skylight was the best feature. The landlord said Gershwin had lived in this room. I could see Gershwin writing *Porgy and Bess* on that very table. But I could also feel the loneliness for the first time in my life. I never thought I would experience it. I was alone in New York. Except for the army and college, I'd lived here all my life. I always thought the city was mine. It was, when I could dream. But it was different now. I was out of the army, out of school, out of work. I was shifting from dream to reality. I could no longer fantasize to Gordon Jenkins's musical tribute to New York City, *Manhattan Towers*. I was no longer living at home, telling my parents, "Someday I'm going to . . ." This was someday. It had arrived and I was empty. I had nothing except what was in my head.

Alone in the room, I thought of this girl I'd met. She liked me. I'd never met a woman who just liked me. There didn't seem to be any game-playing. What had happened that day was so spontaneous. I didn't trust it. What else would I have done today if I hadn't run into her? Does everything in life follow a plan? This girl had no plans. Nothing could really happen for her, I thought, as I dozed and finally fell asleep.

Several days later I was sitting at the Cromwell drugstore, sipping coffee.

Anne came over to sit with me. "I'm in a play!" she said. "I play a bird, an egret. We open down in the Village at the Theatre de Lys."

"What play?" I asked.

She was laughing, alive, excited. *"Which Way Is Home?* Three one-acts." She seemed to be telling everyone at the Cromwell.

"That's wonderful, great," I said, trying to match her enthusiasm. "Who's in it?"

"Nobody famous. Jerry Anspacher. An Irish actor, Milo O'Shea. It's the Touring Players. Peg Murray is the producer. It's Off-Broadway, and I play this bird. Will you come to see me?"

"Yeah, sure," I said.

"John, John," she said, hugging an actor named John Marley. "John, I'm in a show."

"Great," Marley said.

"I stayed with John and Stanya at their apartment when I first came here from Rockville Centre," Anne explained to me.

She seemed to be kissing everyone in the place. Why did she have to do that? So much affection. She seemed to love everybody equally. What did that make me? I felt a twinge of anxiety. Was it jealousy, or was I just being possessive? I had no proprietary rights to her affections. How do you tell someone whom to hug or not hug? It worried me. Was I actually beginning to like her? I didn't like the way she showered all this affection. It made me suspicious. If she liked everyone, then I was just like everyone.

One night soon afterward Anne invited me over for dinner. Her ground-floor apartment nestled in a yard between Jones and Cornelia streets in Greenwich Village. There was no sunlight. Up the street was Zampieri's Bakery, where every morning the smell of fresh bread would awaken the neighborhood.

"You cook?" I asked.

"Yeah," she said. "I make spaghetti."

For the first time I noticed the walls were frescoed, plastered and painted over in light blue, with little squiggles.

"What are those little things sticking to the plaster?"

"That's the spaghetti. I throw it against the wall. It sticks if it's al dente."

During the following weeks we spent many nights together. On some nights her roommates were present, and we just talked. On others, when we were alone, she'd often read.

"What do you read?" I asked.

"Plays," she said. "Poetry. You don't like to read?"

"It's not that," I said. "I just don't seem to have the time."

"Didn't your mother ever read to you?"

"No, but I remember her taking me to the library and having me read *Black Beauty*. It was her way to teach me—I didn't know she couldn't read. She came to America when she was sixteen and learned English by going to night school."

"My mom read to me a lot. She was a schoolteacher," Anne said.

"I feel guilty when I read. I don't ever remember ever finishing a book."

"Why do you feel guilty?"

"It's like I'm wasting my time. I should be doing something, like making money."

"Don't you enjoy reading?" she said.

"I guess so. I started reading Dostoyevsky, *The Brothers Karamazov*. I'm doing a play from it in some basement with Steve Gravers, Arthur Storch, and Stefan Gierasch. Do you know them?"

"They're good actors," Anne said.

"Yeah, I know. I play Smerdyakov, the idiot brother who's an epileptic."

"Is that why you're reading the novel?"

"Yeah, I guess so."

"What's it about?" she asked.

I started to explain, and mentioned a town in the book called Obodorsk. Anne started to laugh.

"That sounds funny," she said. "I'll be right back."

Anne disappeared into the bedroom. I picked up a copy of *The Rubáiyát of Omar Khayyám* that was lying on the table and started reading. "A loaf of bread, a jug of wine and thou . . ." When Anne reappeared she was wearing a pink flannel nightgown and holding a glass of milk. A glass of milk at a time like this.

"It's warm," she said, offering me the glass.

She was angelic. The flannel nightie suddenly seemed erotic. I looked at her face. This wasn't the way I had envisioned it. *She's an actress,* I thought. *This is supposed to be a torrid affair, and I'm getting a warm glass of milk.* I took a sip, mostly to satisfy her, and handed the glass back.

"I like milk," she said.

I stood quietly, waiting for something to happen.

"My roommates are gone," she said, taking me by the hand. Was this really happening? This was bland, milky-white sex. *I think she loves me,* I was telling myself. Is it possible any woman could love me, someone besides my mother? What could she see in me? I'm an unemployed actor. She has never seen me on stage, and yet she likes me enough to want to go to bed with me. Maybe I *am* something.

I noticed the ridges on the green chenille bedspread. An old table lamp on the night table threw off the only light in the room. The glass of milk was still in her hand. She placed it on the night table.

We looked at each other for a moment. I hesitated before daring to touch her. Her eyes told me it was all right to do something, so I took both her hands. Like two automatons, we slowly perched on the edge of the bed. I heard a squeak. It seemed like the bed would collapse if our full weight were on it. We both sensed the comedic possibilities of this moment. Our bodies slid lengthwise onto the bed, as if testing it. The bed didn't collapse. Then we pushed back with the palms of our hands till our backs touched the cold wall. I turned to kiss Anne, who was at least two inches taller than me, even in bed.

"You have soft lips," she said to me, "and I love your hands."

I had never heard anyone say anything so endearing to me in all my life. It was funny how words could turn me on. Moments later, we were making love.

The bed squeaked. Whatever guilt I may have had seemed dissipated by the funny sounds that filled the apartment as we desperately tried to create romance to the accompaniment of noisy bedsprings. Despite all this, we salvaged some joy in our first intimacy.

We looked at each other and I said, "Obodorsk." Anne laughed, we turned out the lights, and made love once again. From that night, every time I mentioned the name "Obodorsk," Anne and I made love.

We were sleeping together without being married. It was what actors and actresses did. It made you mature. In theater, anything goes, I thought. It didn't matter whether it wasn't legal. As a matter of fact, it was more fun because it was *illegal,* very Hollywood. But I was also feeling like a cad, taking advantage of a poor innocent girl. But I was so lonely, a killer loneliness that Anne's presence changed.

One late evening I was sitting on the couch while Anne was making supper. Through the bars on one window in her apartment you could see into the courtyard. The lights from the other apartments illuminated a tree that stood in the red-tiled yard. Anne noticed a shadow running behind the tree.

"There he is," she said.

"Who?" I said.

"The guy. He's been coming here for weeks every night. He looks through the bars and hides behind the tree."

"Where?" I said, pretending bravery.

"There," she said pointing.

Sure enough, I could see a white-shirted figure peeking out from behind the tree.

"He scares the hell out of me," she said.

Seeing a chance to show some manliness, I said, "I'll get him."

"Be careful," Anne said.

Before allowing my own fear to take over, I ran out into the courtyard, straight to the tree, expecting to see some huge guy with a knife or a gun.

Instead a small wretch of a man in a white shirt pleaded, "Please, don't hurt me! I'm sorry!"

His cowering was pathetic. He seemed ready to be beaten to a pulp.

"I tell you what," I said, "pretend I'm beating you. Scream loud and get the hell out of here."

"Yes, sir," he said and started to scream. "And don't ever show up here again," I shouted as he disappeared into the night.

I re-entered the apartment. Anne looked at me with admiration.

"What happened?"

"I let him go," I said, "I could've killed him. He'll never bother you again."

During those days, I'd come by often. We loved to take walks in the Village, past bookshops and the craft people selling their crazy jewelry. We were strolling down Cornelia Street just past the bakery when Anne said, "Listen, I've got to tell you something. I've got a job in summer stock out in Smithtown. I don't think I'll be able to see you too much this summer."

I felt a sudden rush of loneliness. There was a warm feeling in my throat like someone hitting me, and I had to hold back the pain. What if I lost her? I saw her with someone else. It was like a changing wind I had no control over.

"Listen, we'll write and we can phone each other," she said.

She seemed sincere.

I decided to put on a good front. "It's not as if this is over," I said. "I'm up for Sitting Bull in a tour of *Annie Get Your Gun*. If I get it I'll be out this summer too. Ten weeks altogether. I can call you."

"Okay, we'll keep in touch," Anne said. But I wondered if this was the end of it.

A week later Anne started rehearsing at Smithtown, Long Island, and I was upstate in Binghamton playing Sitting Bull. I called her seven times and she called back three. We joked about spending our salaries on Ma Bell.

Six weeks later she said, "I'm finished in Smithtown. I can visit you."

"You can?" I said, detecting a flutter in my heart. Was I actually in love? And did she still love me? It was Romeo and Juliet time. We were being kept apart by circumstances, and circumstances seemed to have intensified our feelings. I was thrilled. I was really in love.

At the Matunuck, Rhode Island's Theatre by the Sea, producers Don Wolin and Harold Schiff gave me free room and board in an old New England house facing the ocean in return for performing in their cabaret adjoining the theater. I did my Italian soap opera routine every night after the regular show.

My landlady—I'll call her Mrs. Grenfell—was close to eighty. Her beautiful gnarled face reminded me of a character out of *Great Expectations*. She informed me that I could stay in the one available room in her house.

"It's my husband's room," she said. "All his things are still in place. So please don't move anything. I hope you like to talk."

"I don't mind," I said.

"We face the sea. We can have tea in the morning."

"Do you mind if my wife comes up and spends a few days with us?" I asked.

"Are you married?" she said, with more than a hint of suspicion in her voice.

"Yes," I said.

I knew she knew I was lying. But it didn't seem to faze her.

"Come, I'll show you to the room," she said. "It was my husband's," she repeated. At the foot of the staircase was a plaster-of-paris dog. "That's Creseus," she told me with a smile. "He's named after my husband," she added, but gave no further explanation. "The room's on the third floor. I'm one floor below you. You can go up by yourself. I'm sure you'll like it."

The room contained a four-poster bed, an oak dresser, and a matching mirror. It was huge. In the bathroom a mirrored cabinet perched over the porcelain sink. Opening the cabinet door, I saw a shaving mug, shaving brush, straight razor, some combs in a glass, and a dangling razor strap. Just above one of the shelves there was a four-inch square cut out of the wall, as if by a coping saw.

I spent an uneventful night in the room. The next morning I could hear Mrs. Grenfell preparing breakfast. When I finished dressing and went downstairs, she asked how I'd slept. "Fine," I said.

"Come out on the deck," she said. "There's hot coffee, toast, and marmalade. Do you like cranberry juice? I'll get it."

"So you slept well?" she said as I sat, mesmerized at the sight of the waves crashing on the beach just a few yards away.

"I saw you in the play last night," Mrs. Grenfell said, pouring coffee out of a pewter pot. "You were very good as that Indian. You didn't overdo it. A lot of people would have overdone it."

"Thank you."

"Those Indian words that you use. Are they really Indian, or did you make them up?"

"You mean when I initiate Annie into the Sioux tribe? Those are real words," I said.

"How do you know?"

"I got on the phone to an organization called ARROW. I mentioned I was an actor playing Sitting Bull and I wanted to know the meaning of *Ne-tro-wa key*. 'Hold the phone,' the person on the other end said, and then yelled, 'Ma, what does Ne-tro-wa key mean?'"

Mrs. Grenfell laughed. "Did his mother know?"

"Yes. He explained that ARROW was an apartment in the Bronx, but they were members of the Sioux tribe and their apartment was an information bureau as well."

Mrs. Grenfell looked at me and said, "Is your wife an actress?"

"Yes, she is."

"When is she coming?"

"The day after tomorrow."

"I'm anxious to meet her," Mrs. Grenfell said, looking at my third finger, left hand, and seeing no wedding band.

I sipped some coffee and looked out at the Atlantic. "That's beautiful out there," I said after some silence. The silence seemed to be part of our conversation.

"Did you hear anything in the room last night?"

"No," I said.

"Good. Then he likes you."

What was she talking about? I didn't ask her.

"Tell me, do you like Barry Gray?"

Her question took me by surprise. It seemed almost like an exam question. Barry Gray was a very thorny New York City radio talk show host of that era.

"I had no idea you heard him in Rhode Island," I said.

"Oh, I get him all right."

I could tell she did not particularly like Barry Gray.

"His program is on all night," she said, "and I can't stand the man."

"Why not?" I asked hesitantly.

"He's so opinionated."

"Opinionated" was always a code word for being Jewish. I hoped she knew that I'm Jewish and didn't say anything terrible.

"It has nothing to do with his being Jewish," she said, as if reading my mind. "What do you like about him?" she asked, as if seeking some avenue of controversy we could explore together. "Do you really believe he's being chased by Nazis?"

"I think so."

"He sounds like he's about to be gunned down every night. He's always dodging around cars. Why does he always antagonize me?" she said.

"He's controversial," I said. "You seem to like him enough to listen."

"Maybe you're right," she said.

"Thank you for breakfast." I got up to leave.

"Be careful of Creseus," she said. "He's in touch with my late husband."

Hoolie Woolie spirit guide stuff, I thought. And on that cryptic note I left to go to the theater to pick up my messages.

That night Anne arrived, a day earlier than I'd expected. Her arrival lifted me. She looked beautiful. Her smile was beautiful.

"How are you?" she said. "I missed you. It's been six weeks."

"I missed you too," I said. I could smell that sweet fragrance of hers. Her openness suddenly overpowered me. She had come all the way from New York to be with me. Someone in the universe was giving me serious attention. I could not remember ever having been that important to anyone.

"You'll see the show tonight, then I do my act in the club. I get meals and a place to stay for doing it. You can't beat that. I feel so successful."

Her face lit up. I'd finally found someone who liked me and was chasing me. I couldn't understand it.

That night, after doing *Annie Get Your Gun,* I did my act in the club. The audience, having just seen the theater show, loved seeing the actors now do their cabaret stuff. The room was bathed in candlelight. There were white tablecloths. Sara Dillon, who played Annie Oakley, opened the cabaret show, and I closed it with my Italian soap opera and my parody of *Dragnet.* When I finished I wanted Anne to hug and kiss me for what I had just done. The audience loved me, and now I wanted her to love me because *they* loved me.

Anne said, "Where do you stay?"

I took her bags and we arrived by car at Mrs. Grenfell's house.

"Come on upstairs, I'll show you where we're living," I said.

"What's that?" she said, looking at the plaster dog.

"He's called Creseus. I'll tell you about it."

"Does the landlady know I'm coming?"

"I told her we were married," I said.

"Good. I'll wear my wedding ring. I bought it at Woolworth's for five bucks."

She took out a gold wedding band and put it on her finger.

Once up in the room I said, "How do you like this place?"

"Spooky," she said.

"Look at this." I opened the bathroom cabinet. "There's a hole here in the wall. It's been cut out, and all these shaving things are her husband's. His name was Creseus."

"Like the plaster dog?" Anne said.

I explained the whole strange business of the husband who was dead but somehow still around.

We were in bed. "Do you think Creseus can hear us through that hole?" Anne asked.

"No, but Mrs. Grenfell will if we make too much noise."

The next morning Mrs. Grenfell met Anne. I knew immediately that she was aware we weren't married. She said nothing, and permitted Anne to stay for the remainder of the week.

When I got back to New York at the end of the summer of 1953, I was in love with someone whose impulses were pure and trusting. I couldn't believe what was happening to me.

I started wondering if this was permanent. One night after Anne asked me over for dinner, I remarked casually, "Have you ever been with any-one else?"

"Yes," she said.

I paused. I hadn't really expected she would say no.

"What was he like?" I asked, almost not wanting to hear the answer.

"He was an artist. He wore glasses and his eyes ran."

Was it a joke to make me feel better? To reassure me that their rela-tionship was over?

"What happened?" I asked.

"He left." There was sadness in her voice.

I asked myself if I could be with someone who had been with another man. Was she still in love with him?

"He was the only one," she said, as if guessing my thoughts. "I must tell you something else."

"What?"

"My mother committed suicide."

We silently looked at one another. I took her hand and held it.

"Do you still want to see me?" she said, as if everything we'd had would end.

"Of course," I said. I couldn't comprehend anything that was happening. I could only sit and listen. For a moment I wanted to escape. What was I getting myself into? Until now this had been crazy fun, a crazy adventure. A girl I'd met in an agent's office liked me. Now it was becoming a little too much. She was so free and open about her feelings. I was scared. Should I stop something beautiful, or should I trust? I wanted to leave, but I knew there would be tears if I did. Did I want to see her cry? Could I say, "I never want to see you again"? But I couldn't leave. I didn't know why.

The following weeks we said little but saw each other a lot. I started thinking about my parents, and what my mother, who was ill with cancer, would do if she knew I was seeing a Christian girl. Although Anne had introduced me to her father, I couldn't bring myself to do the same with my mother. So I kept putting it off, thinking nothing was going to come of the relationship.

I tried to stop seeing Anne because of this, but she'd call or I'd call and we'd meet and walk around the Village. It felt so good being near her.

One day we were on a bus that made its last stop at Fifth Avenue and 23rd Street. We had been to a museum uptown. I had literally spent the last dime that I'd made that summer. While still on the bus I looked at the Flatiron Building and thought, *I know how to lose her. I'm busted, no job. When I tell her, she'll leave me. I'll tell her I want to break it off.*

"We're breaking up," I said.

"This you tell me on a bus?"

"Yeah."

"Why?"

I looked at her. Her face was like that of a beautiful spaniel with sad, sad eyes. "I'm broke. I can't support you. There's nothing going for us."

"Why don't you marry me?" was her answer.

"What?! That's crazy."

"Why? I love you and I want you to marry me."

"What if I said I can't?"

"Then we can't go on like this."

I felt something drop inside me. I saw myself without her, and a feeling of emptiness suddenly swept through me.

"How could we live?" I asked.

"Don't worry about it," she said. "My father will help us. We'll live in my apartment. I own the lease."

What was happening? She had just proposed to me. I was penniless, but she loved me. It was a moment I never dreamed would happen.

"We can do it right away," Anne said. "We can go to City Hall. We'll get married. I want to meet your mother."

I wasn't sure how meeting Anne and the news of our upcoming marriage would affect my mother.

"She's got cancer and she's going to die, Anne." It was the first time I had allowed myself to talk about my mother.

Then my fear of really losing Anne frightened me.

"Okay," I said, "you'll meet her."

At the apartment in the Ravenswood Project in Queens, my mother was sitting at the kitchen table by the window. She didn't look well. My father had not yet come home from work.

"Mom, I'd like you to meet Anne."

"Forgive me," my mother said in perfect English. "I can't get up."

"I understand," Anne said.

"Please, won't you sit down?" There was a formality in my mother's voice that I had never noted before. I could tell she knew why we were here.

"You love my son?" she said. The question was so immediate and direct that it pierced my sensibilities.

"I want to marry Jerry," Anne said.

There were no answering words, no cry of protest. I could see tears in my mother's brown eyes. They steadfastly refused to fall; my mother's eyes seemed magnified.

"You love each other?" she finally said.

"Yes. I'll make Jerry a good wife."

My mother looked at me. I could not tell what was going through her mind.

"Do you like matzohs?" she said after a while, breaking off a piece and handing it to Anne. "We keep them around even if it's not Passover."

Anne broke a little piece off that piece and ate it.

"Two people must really love each other," my mother said after another long interval. "That's all that counts."

"Will you come to the wedding?" Anne asked.

"We'll be there."

Anne and my mother kissed.

Three weeks later, on September 14, 1953, we were married. The wedding took place at City Hall. The judge's chambers were in an office high up in the Municipal Building. It was a space with file cabinets and wooden desks. There were civil-service employees bustling about. Why this bland setting to consummate the feelings we had for each other? As the ceremony was about to begin, the office emptied. The clerks sensed the need for privacy and disappeared into the hallways.

Willie, Bella, Ed Meara, and Ursula Campbell and her husband, Pat, arrived. Anne had known Ursula ever since arriving in Manhattan at age eighteen from Rockville Centre to study acting with Alfred Linder from the Dramatic Workshop. Willie and Bella were meeting Ed for the first time. There were smiles and polite conversation. They were standing together in a corner of the room. What could they be saying? At least they were speaking. They could have been ignoring one another, destroying us by silence. As I went over to them I overheard my mother saying, "What do you think, Mr. Meara?"

"They're just a couple of crazy kids," Ed said.

Suddenly all three were laughing out loud. I wanted to hug all of them. I could feel the leap they had made to get to this juncture.

"When this is over," Ed said, "we're going over to the Republican Club for a wedding breakfast."

My father, the lifelong Democrat, asked, "Are we going to have bacon?"

Was it a joke to break the ice another inch?

"No, Mr. Stiller," Ed said earnestly. "We don't eat bacon in our house. It can give you trichinosis."

Judge Ben Shalleck, the uncle of Alan Shalleck, a close buddy of mine from Syracuse, was a former husband of Lillian Roth, the legendary saloon singer. He arrived to perform the ceremony. It seemed to stamp the moment with some sort of showbizzy significance.

"Did you pay the clerk?" Judge Shalleck asked.

I told him I hadn't.

"That's okay, it'll be my wedding present to you. What about the blood test? You've got the results?"

"I do," I said. Ten days earlier Anne and I had gone to Bendiner & Schlesinger, the pharmacists near Cooper Square, and the results were fine.

"Good." The judge's voice now took on an official tone. He conducted a simple ceremony, and Anne and I exchanged vows. When it was over we all piled into a car and headed for the Republican Club. I looked over at Anne and knew I would never be alone again.

6

Life in the Theater

Anne and I were married three months and still living in the Village. I got a call from Ray Boyle, who, before I knew Anne, had directed Jack Klugman, Gerry Jedd, and myself in a production of *The World We Make* at Equity Library Theater. Ray was now casting for John Houseman at the Phoenix Theater. Houseman needed three Volscian servants for *Coriolanus,* which he was directing with Robert Ryan in the title role. The Phoenix producers T. Edward Hambleton and Norris Houghton were bringing classic theater with Hollywood stars to Second Avenue. Ray thought that Jack Klugman, Gene Saks, and I would be perfect as the three servants. Without auditioning, we were cast in those roles.

Addressing the cast on the first day of rehearsals, Houseman spotted the three of us sitting in the orchestra.

"I'm told you boys are the funniest guys in New York," he said. "I've never seen your work, but Mr. Boyle says you're terrific, and I trust Mr. Boyle. I'm also aware that if you leave comedians alone, they come up with the right stuff. We've got four weeks' rehearsal. Your scenes are all self-contained. Come back in three weeks and we'll see what you've got. Good-bye."

As we hit the street Jack Klugman asked, "What does he mean, our scenes are self-contained?"

"We have no director," Gene said.

We agreed to meet the next day to rehearse in a rented space. From the outset it was clear we were coming from three different directions in style and interpretation, and in short order our rehearsals ground to a halt. Three days before we were to present our results to Houseman, Gene, the elder statesman of our trio, said: "We have nothing to show. We need a director." He suggested Frank Corsaro, which suited me fine since Frank had directed me in *Peter Pan*.

As a favor, Frank came down to help us. In a few hours he put a scene together for us. When John Houseman watched it the next day, he shouted, "Marvelous! I knew when you leave comedians alone, they'll always come up with it."

My parents had just moved to another project, the University Houses in the Bronx. It was yet another mandatory move forced by the city because of my father's increased salary. My mother's condition was worsening.

One of her breasts had been removed. She was being treated with male hormones, one of the therapies being tested on cancer patients at the time. Her face, once beautiful and womanlike, was growing hairs. She was appalled at her appearance. Her womanliness was being taken from her.

"Look at me, I'm becoming a man," she would say. "They didn't tell me it would be like this."

"It's to make you better, Mom," I tried to persuade her.

She would hear none of it.

"I'm a woman," she said. "What are these hairs doing on me?"

"It stops the cancer, Mom," I said, hoping against all hope that I was right.

One day I arrived in the Bronx and discovered crowds of people in front of my mother and father's apartment building. There in front of me was my mother lying on the street in front of a truck, on her back but alive. As I rushed toward her I asked the police what had happened.

"She walked right into it."

"It looks like she tried to kill herself," some idiot shouted.

My mother, seeing my face, looked up, struggled to her feet, and said, "I'm all right, Jerry. Let's go upstairs."

The Phoenix Theater meanwhile kept me working by casting me in its Critics Circle Award winner, *The Golden Apple*. After the evening performances Anne and I would drive to the Bronx and spend the nights with my mother. My father was driving a bus at night, so we watched over my mother in shifts.

The Golden Apple was so well received that it moved from Second Avenue to the Alvin Theater on Broadway.

I like to think that my mother was proud of my being on Broadway. On the days there were no matinees, I would drive her around the city, take her to a park, or to eat in a cafeteria. I'd often pull the car onto an abandoned Hudson River pier, and together we'd watch the sun set over New Jersey before the evening show. At these moments I dreamed there'd be a miraculous cure, and that she would live, but I also knew that was unrealistic. Was I hastening her death by marrying Anne?

One day I thought I could cheer my mother up, so I drove her to the Alvin to show her my picture outside the theater with other cast members of the show, my first Broadway show. As we approached the Alvin, I glanced back at my mother, who was seated in the rear of the '47 Plymouth that had been loaned to my parents by my Uncle Oiza.

"I want you to see something," I said as I pulled up in front of the theater. Among the many pictures out front was a huge cutout of myself and Portia Nelson. We were dressed in white, and stood in front of a time machine. Portia was singing a song about the day we would visit the moon. The handle of the time machine in the background protruded at an angle which made it appear that I had a giant erection—a photographic accident, only noticeable when anyone looked two or three times. Nonetheless, this picture had found its way to the 52nd Street marquee. It was the proof that I had made it to Broadway.

It was the afternoon; that night I'd be working in the show. The electric lightbulbs spelling ALVIN extended vertically over the marquee.

"I thought you might like to see the theater I'm playing," I said.

She said nothing.

"It's the same theater I took you to to see Shirley Booth in *A Tree Grows in Brooklyn*. Remember?"

"Mom," I said. "You want to see my dressing room? That window up there. Next to the 'A' in ALVIN."

She looked. There was a long silence.

"That's my picture," I said, pointing to the huge cutout.

At that instant I thought it would comfort her to know that her son had made it to the big time, Broadway.

She looked for a moment and said, "Big deal. Take me home."

A few weeks later my mother died at Sloan-Kettering Memorial Hospital. My father was at work paying hospital bills. I had just stepped out into the hall to get some water. While I was outside, she slipped away. Anne was at her bedside when she passed.

My Uncle Abe and Uncle Charlie arranged to have my mother buried in the Frampol Society Plot in Montefiore Cemetery in Queens.

Ten days later, Jack Landau asked if I would replace someone in *The Clandestine Marriage* at the Provincetown Playhouse. I had to get back to work. I would play opposite Frederick Warriner, a brilliant character actor whom I greatly admired. Fred was especially wonderful playing fops. He must have had some emotional pipeline to the Restoration period. I was in awe of his work.

Fred, Janice Rule, Farley Granger, Blanche Yurka, Larry Gates, and I were later cast in Chinese roles in *The Carefree Tree*, a drama by Aldyth Morris at the Phoenix. I played a property man. Some makeup experts were brought in to put Oriental faces on each one of us. It normally took two hours—the most painful part of the job. I wondered if anyone in the Phoenix audience who was Chinese would take offense. Fred Warriner, being the true artist, always did his own makeup.

Just before one Saturday matinee, Fred had a grand idea. "Why don't we all go down to Chinatown and eat dinner at Wo Ping's between performances?"

Farley Granger said, "What about the makeup? We'll never get back in time to put it back on."

Fred said, "My friends at Wo Ping's would understand if we came down and had the makeup on."

We all agreed. Why not? After the matinee we all piled into a couple of cabs and traveled down to Mott Street. We gathered outside Wo Ping's in our theatrical Chinese makeup, exaggerated eyes, and high cheekbones. As is the case in New York, people took no notice. Fred led us in.

"They know me here," he said.

We entered, and the look on the maitre d's face told me immediately that this incident could affect Chinese-American relations for a long time. The restaurant's owner took us to a table way in the back, where we ordered one from group A, one from group B, etc. Eating with the makeup on almost did us in, but it had seemed like a good idea at the time.

At the close of the Phoenix season I was taken on as an actor in the first season of the American Shakespeare Festival in Stratford, Connecticut.

I had had an audition with John Burrell at the Theater Guild. The

Guild's huge baronial interior on New York's West 53rd Street was subsumed in oak. *Oak is English,* my inner voice kept whispering. *You're Jewish. You don't belong in this forest.*

Burrell, dressed in tweed, sat at a table with some other people.

I bounced in on sneakers. It was my way of telling myself not to be intimidated.

"I hear you're a very funny man," Mr. Burrell said.

I suddenly felt at ease.

"We'd like you to play Trinculo in *The Tempest,* Publius and the Second Citizen in *Julius Caesar,*" Burrell said. "We've got Raymond Massey doing Brutus, Jack Palance as Cassius, Chris Plummer as Mark Antony, Fritz Weaver as Casca, and Hurd Hatfield is Caesar. Roddy McDowall is Ariel in *The Tempest.* Are you interested?"

Interested?

"Yes," I said, practically leaping out of my Keds.

"Do you have an agent?" Burrell asked.

I didn't, but I said I could get one. They laughed. Suddenly everyone started talking in front of me as if I weren't in the room.

"He's wonderful," someone said.

"Marvelously funny," another said, giggling.

"Just what we need."

They were congratulating themselves on some marvelous find. The job was cinched.

My first day of rehearsal for *Julius Caesar* was at the ANTA Playhouse in New York City. Anne was in Norwalk, Connecticut, on tour with Uta Hagen and her husband, Herbert Berghof, in *Cyprienne.* For some time Anne and I, Steve McQueen, William Hickey, Zohra Lampert, Olga Bellin, Shelley Berman, and Jules Munshin had been taking classes with Uta, the best acting teacher in New York. The Berghofs were notorious for their unbridled loyalty to their students. They actually hired them to perform in plays they were starring in; Uta Hagen does that to this day. It is an umbilical relationship that many of us have found difficult to sever. That summer Anne and I barely saw one another, both of us working, a perfect marriage.

On the day of the first *Julius Caesar* rehearsal, Anne called from Norwalk, asking if I could pick up Letty Ferrer, Uta and José Ferrer's ten-year-old daughter, at Grand Central Terminal at 9:45 A.M. I said okay, knowing my rehearsal at the ANTA wasn't to start until 10:30 A.M. The train was delayed. I waited till Letty appeared, and put her in a cab. I arrived seven minutes late for rehearsal. The director, a pillar of the Old Vic, had already introduced himself to the company. My tardiness was greeted with a derisive, "My, my, my, what have we here?"—the English inflection cutting through the theater like a knife.

"What, no apology?" he declared.

Silence. I remembered *The Browning Version,* a Michael Redgrave movie in which schoolmaster Redgrave punishes a pupil in front of the kid's classmates for a minor infraction. This director's chastising me publicly made me hold back any apology. You apologize for doing something wrong, and I'd done nothing wrong—he was just making an example of me. This could go on all season, Jerry Stiller as his little whipping boy.

"In England, we apologize," he continued.

I wanted to say, "Guilty with an explanation, Your Honor," but I would have come across as a smart-ass.

I stood dumbfounded at his display, then said, "I had to pick up Letty Ferrer at Grand Central, and the train was late." I resorted to dropping the name Ferrer, and this seemed to satisfy him.

Sitting with the cast, I listened to his preamble about American actors being new to Shakespeare. Wally Matthews, whom I roomed with in Stratford, told me this attitude goes back to the American Revolution. They still think we're part of the Colonies.

In *Julius Caesar,* Jack Klugman and I played the First and Second Citizens. We were Brooklyn versions of Elizabethan rustics. Raymond Massey, cast as Brutus, was famous for his brilliant pre-war Broadway and Hollywood portrayals of Abraham Lincoln. Mr. Massey continuously joked about his being typecast in movies as the Great Emancipator. He said, "Of course now they'll say I'm playing Abe Lincoln in Rome."

At the first preview of the show, the temperature at Stratford rose into the high 90s. Robert Fletcher's costumes were giving us problems. I, as Publius, the oldest of the conspirators, was to enter with the other conspirators from beneath the stage. Our long velvet gowns weighed a ton and trailed far behind us. On cue, we started up a narrow spiral staircase to kill Caesar. Tripping over our gowns, I could hear my fellow actors cursing in iambic pentameter, attempting to keep in character. Directly in front of me was Raymond Massey. As Mr. Massey reached the top step he tripped and started to fall backwards. I shoved my hands against his shoulders to stop him, then pointed to a box in the theater and said, "Ray, that's where Lincoln got it." He broke up. When the scene ended, I apologized. Mr. Massey, in magnanimous fashion, said, "Jerry, it's okay. And thanks. I could've hurt myself. Besides, it wasn't like I was about to do the Gettysburg Address."

Jack Klugman, Rex Everhart, and myself were New York types, throwbacks to Will Kemp, the legendary Elizabethan clown. We spoke for the masses. Klugman, as the First Citizen in *Julius Caesar*, shpritzing all over Chris Plummer—with a lot of "whereforths" and "forsooths"—was sowing the seeds of his masterpiece Oscar Madison in TV's *The Odd Couple*. Nobody questioned our New York accents. Anyway, all eyes were on Christopher Plummer and Fritz Weaver, whose performances were establishing them as future stars.

As Publius, the oldest and most decrepit of the conspirators who assassinate Caesar and live to walk away untouched, I took two minutes to leave the scene of the dastardly crime.

That first season at Stratford was some kind of debacle. The dream of having American movie stars performing Shakespeare did not make it with the public or the critics, who had a field day swiping at John Houseman's Hollywood upstarts. No *rachmones*. No pity.

In *The Tempest*, starring Mr. Massey as Prospero, Palance as Caliban, and Roddy as Ariel, I played a jester named Trinculo. My onstage relationship with Jack Palance was rocky. He had already played the black hat in *Shane*.

As Trinculo, the fool, I discover Caliban on the beach of a mystical island called Ilyria. My monologue had me poking fun at this strange creature that was not man, beast, or fish. At one point in the scene I mimic Caliban—but I was actually doing an impression of Jack. It must have hit a nerve because he asked me to stop doing it. When I continued, he got angry. I realized that if I did it again Jack could possibly pick me up bodily and hurl me into the orchestra pit. Don't screw around with the black hat, I figured. I don't remember the English director standing up for me.

Professor and Mrs. Falk saw the show. They were following my career. Despite a nice mention of me by Brooks Atkinson in *The New York Times*, Mr. Falk was not overwhelmed by my performance. Some weeks later I received the following letter:

Syracuse, New York
October 3, 1955

Mr. Jerry Stiller
135 W. 67th St.
New York, New York

Dear Jerry:

I owe you something of an explanation and an apology for not
having come back to see you when I was at Stratford for The Tempest.
Mrs. Falk, Francy, and I went up on one of those package deals that
Alex Cohen was running: transportation by bus, "a delicious turkey
dinner," and tickets for the theater. In consequence, we had to leave
when the bus pulled out immediately after the performance. As it turned
out, the whole expedition took ten hours as it was. And for your sake, I
regret to say that I do not think the performance was worth that amount
of time nor the $30 or so that I expended on it. I was totally disinclined
to go back the next night for Julius Caesar, as we had planned.

I found The Tempest to be indescribably bad. As I told many people
beforehand, the kind of stage which was built into that elegant theater
would make any performance of Shakespeare a difficult proposition, but
the wise guys from [Lawrence] Langner on down think they know all the
answers. So as it turned out, the staging was wrong, the setting was
extremely bad in design and poorly used even for what it was. The
acting, for a company that yearns to be called the American
Shakespeare Festival, was frightful in the extreme. Massey never could
read Shakespeare and never will be able to, no matter how long he tries.
After seeing him, I retitled the play Abe Lincoln in Bermuda. All the rest,
including the "Ariel," were bad in my book. . . . Above and beyond all,
nobody concerned with the management and directing seemed to have
the faintest concept about the play, neither its style nor its theatricality.

As for you: I felt that you were the best actor on the stage. But I must
say in all candor that I felt you were terribly miscast. Your performance
was the only vital and exhilarating part of the entire proceedings, but it
couldn't possibly be Trinculo. I was proud of you for what you did, but I
felt unhappy that your abilities were not put to better purpose.

I saw Norris Houghton the night I was at Stratford, and from the
conversation that we exchanged, I would imagine he was of similar

mind about the performance. In any case I'm sure he saw the value in
your work, as is quite evident in his bringing you back into his
production [at the Phoenix]. Also I think that this [Stratford] has been a
definite step up for you: It brought you to the attention of a great many
people, and the words of praise given to you in The New York Times
will undoubtedly be of great value. . . .

> *Ever yours,*
> *Sawyer Falk*

The New York Times, **Wednesday, August 3, 1955**
Theater: "The Tempest"
by Brooks Atkinson

Let it be said that the production of "The Tempest" is an improvement
on "Julius Caesar," and has several things to recommend it. . . . Best
of all, Roddy McDowall plays the difficult part of Ariel with genuine
skill. . . . Count also on the credit side Christopher Plummer's ro-
mantic Ferdinand. Mr. Plummer is one who can speak up like a man
even when the dialogue is verse. He makes a splendid hero. There is
an amusing jester in the Shakespeare idiom by Jerry Stiller. He is
small, compact and wide-eyed—all good things in a wag. With Rex
Everhart as the drunken butler and with Jack Palance as a clumsy, sin-
ister Caliban, Mr. Stiller manages to play the low comedy scenes with
some talent.

Maurice Evans, one of America's most popular classical actors, now a
producer, came backstage after seeing *The Tempest* and offered me my
first speaking role in a Broadway show, one scene. T. Hambleton and
Norrie Houghton let me out of my obligation to the Phoenix so that I
could take part in the new play, *No Time for Sergeants*.

Long story short: I was fired from *No Time for Sergeants* on my first
day of rehearsal. The five-day tryout period, which allows a producer five
days of rehearsal to decide on a cast change, was finagled in my case. Because I was in only one scene, I was brought in on the fifth day to re-

hearse. I never met the cast or sat in on the first read-through. Script in hand, I read my scene with Myron McCormick. When I finished I was told to go home; I wouldn't be needed for the rest of the day. Upon arriving home, I got a call from my agent (whom I'd acquired in the months since my audition for John Burrell) asking what had happened.

"What do you mean?" I asked.

"They let you go."

I couldn't believe it. I explained that I never got to rehearse. "I came in on the fifth day." It seemed so unfair.

No Time for Sergeants opened on Broadway and made a star of Andy Griffith in the lead role.

The shock of being fired rocked me. Emotionally, I was in Siberia. Anne and I had moved from 11 Cornelia Street in the Village and were now living on West 67th Street in a five-room, sixth-floor walk-up, sharing a bathroom in the hall with a nice family. They had a French name and a Coca-Cola route.

"Sharing the bathroom, you can't get any closer than that," Anne said.

We'd moved from a $55 three-room Greenwich Village back apartment with a courtyard to a $65 five-room railroad flat. "Why did we move there?" I asked Anne years later.

"You wanted more space," she said.

I must have been depressed for weeks. Something happened between Anne and me. We fought over something that neither of us can now remember. The fight seemed to spring out of the realization that our lives were going nowhere.

One night things came to a boil. We couldn't stand each other, and we decided to split. The question was, who would leave whom, and what would become of our kittens, Squeaky and Sniffles? There was nothing else to be divided.

After hours of talk, Anne said, "I'll call Dolly"—the actress Dolly Jonah, who had recently split with *her* husband, Norman Fell—"and ask if I can move in with her." Dolly lived on Bank Street in the Village. Since I had no one to move in with, I agreed. I could also feed the cats.

Anne packed two suitcases with her belongings. It was now about midnight.

"How are you getting downtown?" I asked.

"I'll take the subway."

"At this hour?"

"Yeah."

The subway wasn't safe. "Let me walk you to the station," I said.

She agreed.

I carried one of Anne's suitcases to the 66th Street IRT station. It was very quiet on the street, and I started to worry.

"Let me ride downtown with you."

"You really want to?" Anne said. "I thought we were breaking up."

"We are," I said. "But I'll ride down with you."

We arrived at the Christopher Street / Sheridan Square station in the Village. "Let me walk you to Dolly's. You can't lug two bags."

"Okay," Anne said. "But we are splitting."

"Yes," I said, "we can't go on like this."

We reached Dolly's house, a walk-up on Bank Street. We schlepped the bags upstairs, knocked on the door, and Dolly answered. Dolly was a girl we'd both met in Uta Hagen's acting class, a comedienne brought up in Philadelphia. (Her father had invented the wall panel you see on every light switch.) Dolly was a shoot-from-the-lip person who could say wonderfully caustic things and still make you laugh. She didn't have a bad bone in her body.

Now Dolly's raspy voice, exacerbated by cigarette smoking, welcomed Anne, me, and the suitcases. "What, are the two of you moving in? I can only take one. Make up your mind. It's almost midnight. Why don't you come inside and have some coffee?"

We couldn't help laughing.

"Yeah, I'm breaking up with Norman. I know what it's like. But you two? What's going on? Drink some coffee," she said, pouring cups for both of us.

We talked about everything and nothing. It seemed to me that Dolly's therapy was bringing people's lives together. People like us. Her own life was another story.

During the next two hours she took no sides. "Do you want to go on together or do you wanna go your separate ways? What's better for you?" she said, puffing away.

We had been married only three years and things were falling apart. I had just been fired. I had no job. I was so sad I wanted to cry, but I couldn't. I figured the only thing that kept our lives afloat was that we were both working, and when the work was gone, so was our marriage.

Could show business be the only reason Anne and I were together? If there was something else, I couldn't figure out what it was at the time.

Looking back, it was one of the many tests that we were to meet in staying married.

At one point, maybe three in the morning, Dolly said, "I want you two to go back and work it out. I'm kicking you out of here."

Anne didn't seem to object, I wasn't too happy over the prospect of occupying five rooms with two pussycats, and so our marriage was saved, at least temporarily, by Dolly Jonah.

One day soon after, Dolly herself was wavering over whether to marry Will Holt, the wonderful actor/singer/composer with whom she was then doing an act. They played the same circuits Anne and I did, singing Brecht and Weill and Holt's own compositions. They finally got married. One day Will wrote "Lemon Tree," and they lived happily ever after until Dolly died. But Dolly was something.

Anne and I never planned a career together. We were dreamers, but there was certainly no Lunt and Fontanne in our dream factory. Certainly not a Burns and Allen comedy act. It was just nice to have a job, and jobs did come our way, but never playing opposite each other in the same show.

After the *No Time for Sergeants* debacle I replaced Eddie Lawrence, the comedian known for his character of the old philosopher, in the long-running smash-hit *The Threepenny Opera* at the Theatre de Lys (now the Lucille Lortel) on Christopher Street. I played Crook Finger Jake and read a newspaper while guarding a brothel. Lotte Lenya sang "The Black Freighter." The cast included John Astin, Ed Asner, Bea Arthur, Tige Andrews, Jo Wilder, Joe Elic, and William Duell.

I was in the show for thirteen weeks; that allowed me to compile and combine enough weeks for unemployment insurance the following year. Mr. Rector, who worked at the unemployment office in the West 90s, loved actors. He was a genius at combining the twenty weeks of eligibility necessary for collecting unemployment benefits. The laws of the states varied, but Mr. Rector would often read through manuals until he nailed down the rule that would insure us actors our thirty-five bucks a week.

I hated standing in line and waiting to sign up. I felt that everyone would know I was an out-of-work actor. I remembered my mother and father turning down Home Relief during the Depression. They'd battle each other rather than accept the shame of a handout. Mr. Rector knew that unemployment insurance money was an entitlement that came from what actors had earned, that it wasn't a dole. He removed the burden of shame.

Being in *The Threepenny Opera,* I decided to show my gratitude. While still working, I paid him a visit at the unemployment office. I said, "Mr. Rector, I'm in a show, *The Threepenny Opera,* down in the Village."

He said, "Congratulations."

"I'm inviting you down to see me in it. I'm leaving two tickets for you, all paid for, for the Saturday matinee at the Theater de Lys. Can you make it?"

He thanked me.

"Be sure to say hello after the show," I said. "I'd like to buy you dinner."

That afternoon, following the final curtain, I waited for him to come backstage. He never did. I figured he either hated the show, hated me, or both.

Some months later, once more unemployed, I was on Line C, Mr. Rector's line, to sign up once again. He took out my file and did the paperwork. Finally I said, "Mr. Rector, did you get to see me in the show?"

He said, "No, Jerry. I never see actors when they work. I just like seeing them here."

Morton DaCosta, the director of *No Time for Sergeants,* told me, "I didn't cast you, Maurice [Evans] did. I'll call T. and Norrie at the Phoenix and ask them to take you back." He was as good as his word, and they did take me back. I appeared in seven of their productions over two seasons. I will forever be grateful to those two world-class mensch-like producers.

The Phoenix Theater brought in two Shakespearean productions from the American Shakespeare Festival at Stratford. John Houseman and Norman Lloyd were directing. I got to do Barnadine in *Measure for Measure* and Biondello in *The Taming of the Shrew,* playing alongside Nina Foch, Hiram Sherman, Ellis Rabb, Morris Carnovsky, Arnold Moss, and John Colicos.

All of them could handle verse. I was never entrusted with poetic passages. But playing Shakespearean clowns was becoming my bag, and the clowns never spoke poetically.

When I was at school in Syracuse, Charles Laughton had visited the university and Sawyer Falk had invited him to conduct a class. Mr. Laughton confided to us that he was turned down by the Old Vic because the bigwigs there said he could not speak in iambic pentameter—a circumstance which had motivated his departure to Hollywood. I found myself wistfully identifying with the great Charles Laughton. Clowns and bumpkins need only speak prose.

At the Phoenix, Norman Lloyd encouraged me to be inventive. As Biondello, I did six pratfalls just walking across the stage once. At dress rehearsal I fell into the orchestra pit, an eight- or nine-foot drop, and was shaken up. Rehearsal stopped.

Norrie Houghton and T. Hambleton had me on the couch in their office.

"Are you okay?"

"I'm fine," I said.

"We can call a doctor."

"No, I'm okay."

"How did this happen?" they both asked.

"Trying to be funny," I said. "I had a good time on the way down." A few minutes later I was back onstage and grateful I hadn't broken anything.

In the summer of 1957 I received a call from Joe Papp, who asked if I'd be willing to join his fledgling New York Shakespeare Festival, touring parks in the five boroughs and ending up in Central Park. "Very little money," he said. I'd be working off a flatbed truck with a side panel that let down so the truck could open into a stage.

Where's this glamour I've been dreaming about? I asked myself.

Joe offered me Peter in *Romeo and Juliet* and the Porter in the Scottish play, known to playgoers as *Macbeth*. The salary was thirty-five bucks a week, a comedown from the $55 at the Phoenix and the $125 at Stratford, but Joe had a kind of messianic look in his eye. I felt connected to Shakespeare in the Park because of Joe Papp. He was the kind of wild-eyed young guy who had the balls to fight. He'd been a CBS-TV stage manager whose ambition to direct on network television was thwarted by his being blacklisted for his politics. He too was adrift and trying to stay afloat. Central Park to him was the battlefield of Agincourt, and he was Henry V leading his ragged little army in battle against that all-powerful enemy—who turned out to be Parks Commissioner Robert Moses.

Moses opposed performances in the park, one reason being that they would ruin the grass. Papp overcame Moses's objections by getting the public behind him.

Our first stop was an amphitheater in Corlears Hook Park, where I had once played softball. I was three minutes from where I had lived in the Vladeck Housing Project, and here I was, wearing a codpiece and leotard, suiting up to do Peter in *Romeo and Juliet*.

The mostly black and Hispanic audience sat silently in the amphitheater. As the sky darkened, actors in Elizabethan attire traipsed on stage carrying torches, recreating the atmosphere of the Globe Theatre in London. From a makeshift tower that tottered precariously, Bryarly Lee crooned to Stephen Joyce, "Romeo, O Romeo, wherefore art thou Romeo?" Someone with a Spanish accent yelled, "Give it to her, Pepito! Give it to her good!" There was laughing and a couple people yelled, "Hey, shut up." Shakespeare, born again.

After playing in four of the boroughs the show arrived in Central Park. Critics said we had reinvented Shakespeare. Walter Kerr wrote this nice review in the *New York Herald-Tribune*.

New York Herald-Tribune
" 'Romeo and Juliet' Opens City Tour in Central Park"
June 28, 1957
by Walter Kerr

. . . There is a further small miracle to report. That lout Peter is funny. Peter is the go-between who is unable to read the messages he is supposed to deliver and who is not a bit quick to defend the Nurse's honor. You probably remember him. I doubt, however, that you have ever really laughed at him. In Jerry Stiller's playing, the long-buried comedy of the role rises easily and lightly to a surface bubble, then happily explodes. Nor is this a matter of added "trick" business; we have finally—and simply—met the character.

I got around those days in a used '54 Dodge that acted as a shrunken limo for my fellow actors.

"I got room for eight," I would holler after the show. "Five in the back, three in front. We play kings and queens on stage. This car was built for royalty." Two of the royals, George C. Scott and Colleen Dewhurst, were getting warmly acquainted in the back seat.

"Can we pay for gas?" Suddenly all these actors were throwing dollar bills at me, little greenbacks floating over the front seat.

"I don't need all that. I was going home anyway."

The automobile ride made me feel big time. Whoever rode in that '54 Dodge had some luck: Roscoe Lee Brown, George and Colleen, J. D. (Jack) Cannon, Leo Bloom, Stephen Joyce, Ed Sherin, David Amram (who wrote the music for Joe's shows and later the score for Kazan's *Splendor in the Grass*). Driving actors home made me feel important. I didn't do it to suck up, I just loved the camaraderie. When I was in shows at the Phoenix, with people like Zero Mostel, Blanche Yurka, and E. G. Marshall, I'd similarly considered it a privilege. I always drove Miss Yurka and her sister home. Blanche was sweet to me, kissed me goodnight, treated me like a son. I would drive Zero, Bea Arthur, and Carroll O'Connor home whenever I picked up Anne at the Rooftop Theater on Houston Street, where they were all starring in *Ulysses in Nighttown*.

With the Papp company, Colleen Dewhurst was special. She was playing Lady Macbeth. I was the Porter. On opening night for the press, under menacing skies in Central Park, there was a crash of thunder on the line, "So fair and foul a night I have not seen," and the rains poured down, drowning the show. During the run Colleen, as Lady Macbeth, stood and shook her fist at a TWA flight passing overhead every night during her soliloquy. She got Joe to hold the opening curtain five minutes in the hope that the jet would have passed. Of course, the flight was often delayed.

One day Colleen said, "Why don't we all go out to Riis Park on our day off?"

"We can use my car," I was quick to suggest. Everyone agreed. Roy Poole, Jack and Alice, Roscoe, Leo, Colleen, Anne, and I put some beer, cold cuts, potato salad, and ice into a cooler and headed out to the Rockaways. On the way out we sang songs and told stories. It was a rare occurrence for actors to hang out together on their day off. As we reached the toll gate to Riis Park, the engine conked out. I tried the choke. Nothing. The engine wouldn't turn over.

The toll-keeper said, "What'd you do, run out of gas?"

I looked at the gauge. It was low but not empty.

"Must be some mistake," I said.

"You'll have to get this heap out of here," he said.

"How?" I said.

Colleen Dewhurst jumped out of the car and started to push. The others followed suit. I remained behind the wheel.

"Choke it!" Colleen hollered as the car picked up a little speed. It started to putt-putt. "Now the gas," she said, and the engine turned over. "Keep driving it," she yelled.

I drove around the parking lot while she kept spurring the car on. The gas line had been clogged. Colleen got back in. When we got out we gave Lady Macbeth a standing ovation.

When *Romeo and Juliet* was at the end of its run, Joe Papp had asked if I would like to do Launce, the servant and clown in *Two Gentlemen of Verona*. I told him I'd like to, but I couldn't afford to on the $35 salary.

"Why can't we hire Anne?" he suggested. "She can play Julia and the third witch in *Macbeth*."

I immediately agreed. It would solve the Stiller/Meara rent problem as well as the situation that occurs when one member of an acting family is working and the other is not.

"By the way," Joe said, "would she mind taking her clothes off? The director wants to do one of the Julia scenes in a bathtub."

This was before frontal nudity was commonplace. There was never any of this in Shakespeare, I thought.

"I don't know, Joe. She was brought up Catholic."

"We can get her a dispensation," Joe said by way of a jest. "The audience will never really see the nudity. It's going to be done behind a screen on a raised platform, too high for anyone to see. It's just another way to play the scene."

"Okay," I said, without asking Anne.

"Oh, by the way, you're going to have to work with a dog. Have you ever worked with an animal before?"

"I worked with a dog in *The World We Make* at the Equity Library Theater. The dog got a lot of calls as a result of my performance."

"Okay, then, we're set," Joe said.

I began rehearsing for my part as Launce on a blistering hot summer day in a little park in the shadow of the Brooklyn Bridge. Also in the play, attached to Launce, was—as Joe Papp had indicated—Crab the dog, a character in the play. A few days into rehearsal, Joe asked if I had found a dog yet.

"No. I'm rehearsing alone, Joe. When he arrives, I'll work him in."

"You'd better get on it," Joe warned. "If you leave it to the last minute, you'll be stuck with whatever you've got."

I asked the stage manager, John Robertson, to go to the ASPCA. John returned with a beautiful young brown collie, full of life and sparkle. He started licking me and seemed eager to be adopted.

"He's wrong," I said.

John said, "Okay, I'll take him."

Suddenly I was Louis B. Mayer looking for the perfect Scarlett O'Hara.

At that moment Ed Sherin, a fellow actor, said, "What would you think of me playing the dog?"

"You're wrong for it, Ed."

"I'll get a dog outfit."

"It wouldn't work, Ed," I said, trying to let him down easily.

"Okay," he said with a shrug. Ed gave up acting, married Jane Alexander, and today produces the television show *Law and Order*.

In show business, miracles sometimes do occur. Just at that moment a dirty, grayish-looking animal approached, walking very gingerly on the hot sidewalk. He seemed oblivious to everything around him. He was bowlegged, and his head was turned aimlessly to one side. The hot sun was beating down on the Brooklyn pavement, causing him to wince as his paws touched the ground.

"That's him, that's the dog!" I said. It was like Lana Turner being discovered in Schwab's Drugstore. "He's what Shakespeare would have wanted. He's a mutt, he's great, they're going to laugh at him. Get him!" I yelled.

John and I caught the poor animal, who cowered in fear. He obviously had been beaten by someone, somewhere.

I looked around for the owner, but there was no one nearby. The dog had no collar, no license. Who'd own a dog like that anyway, I thought.

"Look at his ribs," I said to John, admiringly. "He's so pathetic, he's perfect," I said, as if I had just crowned a beauty queen. I looked into the dog's eyes, which were tearing. He had hairs growing out of something in his eyes. It made him look like he was always crying.

"What kind of dog is he?"

"Who can tell; he's a mixture," John said.

Just then an old man walked by. The dog whimpered as he passed. He must've been beaten by some old man, I figured. He was so sad-looking, I knew people were going to pity him when they saw him on stage.

"Come on," I said. "Come on, Crab." I was calling him by his professional name. I extended my palm. The dog slowly walked over and sniffed my hand. "Here, Crab. Here, baby, I'm not going to hurt you."

He listened to me. I knew he was going to be great . . . as long as I could get him to come onstage with me.

The director came over and suggested I try rehearsing with the dog.

"You think so?" I said, a little tentatively.

"Try it."

"Come on, Crab," I said. "Come on, Crabbie."

He wouldn't budge. I picked him up, and his body stiffened. I cradled him in my arms, carried him onto the truck/stage, and started my opening lines, "My mother wailing, my sister crying, my nurse bawling, yet did not this cur shed a single tear at my departure . . ."

Crab didn't say a word, and I knew that being onstage with him would be memorable.

I arrived home with Crab. Anne said incredulously, "You're *not* going to have the dog *live* with us?"

"Just until the end of the show."

"Why?" she asked. "Why can't he live somewhere else, and just rehearse with you?"

"Don't you understand? We've got to get used to each other."

"What about me?" she said. "This is not a puppy. He'll probably hate me. He's big and gawky. Where's he going to sleep?"

"I'm going to put him in front of our bed. I've got an inner tube that I'll put a blanket over, and he curls up in it. He was beaten, you know." I was trying for sympathy. "I'm going to have to get him to trust me. If I lift my hand quickly, he cowers and cries. If that happens onstage, I'm dead. They'll think I'm the one who beat him. He's got to learn we love him."

"What do you mean 'we'?" Anne asked.

"Think of him as a pet."

"*You* think of him as a pet. You talk about him like I gave birth to him."

Crab moved into our now smaller three-room West Side apartment. Prior to the opening of the show I cooked chicken wings and necks for him. He loved them. Crab took to Anne and me. At night he'd hop out of his inner tube and into our bed, and as he wedged in between Anne and me, he'd sigh. Things had changed for him; he'd come a long way in just a few days. Love really works.

Crab and I rehearsed well together. I had won his trust. When the show opened the audiences adored him, and so did some of the reviewers. And so did I. Anne threatened to divorce me. She said she would name Crab as the co-respondent.

When the run had ended the score might've read: Crab 99, Stiller 0. He got all the acclaim. He appeared on the CBS-TV show *Eye on New York*. An article was written about him in *Theater Arts* magazine. I was often greeted by people on the street with the words, "By thy dog thou shalt be known." At a party that the Shakespeare Festival threw, a man approached me, saying he loved Shakespeare. Then he confided that he'd contributed $25,000 to the Festival because of Crab's performance. And here I was making thirty-five bucks a week.

As Crab's popularity grew, I found myself riding on his coattails, or on his tail anyway. I thought I might share some of his glory. Hardly so. To make matters worse, Crab was now so completely at home onstage, he'd yawn on my lines. He'd stare at the audience at the end of a joke. Maybe he'd been Jack Benny in another life. When he was really loose, Crab would turn facing upstage and wag his tail on my punch lines. Then he'd turn back to the audience as though he'd done nothing wrong. Luckily my next line was, "Oh, 'tis a thing sad when a mangy dog plays the cur with him."

Many people brought their dogs to the show. Crab would invariably sniff them out while onstage, again stealing my thunder. I complained to Joe about this, so he agreed to ban dogs at all performances. People got around that edict by bringing their dogs in lunch baskets. Crab had become a full-blown celebrity.

Since no one could determine Crab's breed, I called him my Shakespearean Retriever. Whatever laughs I missed, he retrieved just by his presence.

When the play ended its run, Anne and I decided to keep Crab. It was his reward for making me look good onstage. Now Crab was just a dog again, an ordinary dog, but I soon learned that without the footlights he would always have the heart of a stray.

Crab never could be curbed—which, translated, simply means he wouldn't pee unless off his leash. As the saying goes, you can't teach an old dog. . . . Over the years Crab incurred hundreds of dollars in fines for being off the leash. At one of the court hearings I claimed Crab was neurotic. The lady judge hit me with a $100 fine.

"It's usually five dollars," I pleaded.

"Say one more word and I'll hold you in contempt," she shouted.

"But—"

"Shut your mouth."

I mentioned working for Joe Papp in the park.

"I'm warning you."

"But . . ."

"One hundred dollars!"

I fished out my last hundred bucks and left the courthouse. The irony was that the man who preceded me, a Madison Avenue executive who had urinated on a subway platform while intoxicated, was given a suspended sentence on the promise he'd never do it again.

Syracuse, New York
October 23, 1957

Mr. Jerry Stiller
153 West 80th St.
New York, New York

Dear Jerry:

Seeing your picture in the current issue of Theater Arts *magazine (or I should say, you plus your dog) stresses the fact that I should have written to you long ago. In one breath, then, let me say what should take many pages. My thanks for your letters and phone calls during the summer. I had not realized until I had been hospitalized what these things really meant, and how much a token of friendship they were. Believe me, every letter and call helped me somehow to get better. At present I am at home, trying to gain back some of the thirty pounds I lost. I was a little despondent for a time about my progress, but in the last week or ten days I have improved much beyond my expectations.*

It will, however, be some time before I am able to come to New York, so I will have to count on your keeping me up-to-date about your activities. I imagine you are still affiliated with the Shakespeare group since you and it got such favorable notices. Is Anne also still with the company?

Mrs. Falk joins me in sending affectionate regards to both of you.

Sincerely,
Sawyer Falk

153 West 80th Street
New York, New York
October 25, 1957

Dear Professor Falk:

It was wonderful hearing from you. Life on this planet (NY, that is) is still a paradox. Despite the good notices, somehow I'm not in the right place at the right time and all that to land a B'way play. Not that I crave being a Broadway actor anymore. Who am I kidding? No one. I'd love to be on Broadway but nobody's asked me.

I'm very happy to be working with Stuart Vaughn, where through a certain rapport, understanding, and common sense we get the meaning out of the comedy (and comedy it is despite the constant reference to Shakespeare's tedious clowns). They're not tedious, they're simple, and the acting should be simple.

Since I've been called by some the hottest Shakespearean clown in Central Park, I'll tell you my secret:

In the early stages of rehearsal, my stuff is completely improvisational. I keep changing from rehearsal to rehearsal (always studying the script between rehearsals, of course), but never forcing myself to stay set. When I finish a rehearsal I go over the script and try to find the impulses—call them the needs of the character that forced me to say the line or do something in a certain way. When I can pinpoint these needs, impulses, then the acting becomes set (not set dull, but set in a reasonable architectural layout).

This process takes two to three weeks and Stuart knows this. He goes along with it although I'm the only actor in the company who works this way.

With John Houseman I would be forced to set the improvisation after two or three rehearsals. And so for three or four weeks I would be doing what was essentially my first day's work. Houseman would say, "What was good yesterday was good; don't change it." This would lock up the creative valves and force you to act out what you did yesterday. I gather you gather that I do not like this approach to comedy. . . .

If I have been too flip about my experiences, I guess it's because I'm letting off steam. Needless to say, I would never have got this far without your great faith in me.

One of the most vivid incidents of the time I spent with you was the morning following the opening of The Bourgeois Gentleman. *You called us all together and told us we had a great show despite what was said.*

This was so important to all of us, but especially to me. You don't know how responsible I felt, and was, for that matter, but you lifted the burden off me. When you were finished, regardless of how young, inexperienced, and inept we were, we felt like Duses, Bernhardts, and all the rest. Around here, in a similar situation, they're looking for someone to mutilate when something goes wrong.

I thank God for you, Mr. Falk, and pray you will soon feel well enough to do whatever and go wherever you desire. A small reward for giving so much of yourself to so many like me.

> *Regards to the family,*
> Jerry Stiller

Syracuse, New York
November 5, 1957

Mr. Jerry Stiller
153 West 80th St.
New York, New York

Dear Jerry:
    Thank you for your long and interesting letter of October 25 . . . [particularly for its] descriptions of your creative processes as an actor.

*And I am most grateful, of course, for the very kind things that you said
about me and whatever help I may have given you. The greatest
satisfaction that a teacher may have is the knowledge that he has
perhaps opened a door.*

*I enjoyed very much seeing the pictures of the productions you have
been in and of reading the press clippings about you. You have done very
well indeed, and it is to your credit that you have kept working most of
the time. As one of the newspaper accounts says, you have really become
a fixture at the Phoenix Theater . . .*

*Since writing to you I have improved greatly, although I still have a
good part of the thirty pounds I lost to gain back. As I told you before, it
is fortunate that I have a sabbatical leave for this semester which allows
me leisure for recovery. . . . It seems that I will be well enough to come
to New York sometime in the early part of December. I am counting on
seeing you then.*

Mrs. Falk joins me in sending affectionate regards.

Sawyer Falk

My connection to Joe Papp came crashing down when I was cast in
Richard III as the second murderer. The show starred George C. Scott as
Richard. The role of second murderer turned into an off-stage feud between myself and the actor playing the first murderer. We hated each
other.

I asked Stuart Vaughn to step in. I was shocked when he sided with
the first murderer, who was a professional puppeteer. Stuart then went
on to criticize my rehearsal process, which he called debilitating. He said
this had gone back to *Two Gentlemen*. I was devastated. I called Joe and
told him that I couldn't work with Vaughn anymore.

"Okay," Joe said, "quit." I did.

Six months later, Joe called again. He asked Anne and me if we'd be
willing to play William and Audrey in *As You Like It*. J. D. (Jack) Cannon
played Touchstone and George C. Scott did a magnificent Jacques. Since
I didn't hold a grudge, I agreed. My favorite memory of Scott was him
playing bridge in the basement with the other cast members. When he
heard his cue, George would drop his cards, walk upstairs to the stage,

deliver the "Seven Ages of Man" speech—there was always applause—and then return to the table and finish his hand. In 1972 Joe called yet once more for the role of Launce in the musical version of *Two Gentlemen of Verona,* the same role I played in 1957. The '72 cast included Raul Julia, Clifton Davis, José Perez, Norman Matlock, Jonelle Allen, and Frank O'Brien, and was directed by Mel Shapiro; John Guare wrote the book and Galt MacDermott the score. In the earlier version I had played Launce as a contemporary Brooklyn guy, more like a gofer than the traditional Shakespearean servant. I left out the "Hey nonney-nonneys" and the stylized Elizabethan shtick that most Americans tried to emulate from their English counterparts. To my delight, that interpretation worked. It came off great.

I was excited when Joe Papp asked me to recreate my original role. By then, Crab had gone on to a heavenly rest and the new Crab was to be played by a dog who had understudied Sandy in the Broadway musical *Annie.*

I quickly discovered that the musical version of *Two Gents* was completely different. The role I felt so perfect for in 1957 did not work in a Black/Hispanic '70s setting. I felt ethnically displaced. Next to Clifton Davis's Harlem street talk and Raul Julia's Puerto Rican lilt, I felt at sea.

As opening night approached, I said to Mel Shapiro, our director, "Mel, what I do in the part doesn't seem to mean anything. You don't need a white guy in this cast. You need Godfrey Cambridge. I want out."

"Stick with it," Mel said.

My frustration grew. Even the new Crab was wrong. He was a well-groomed wirehaired terrier with a Broadway credit, and did everything on cue. I hated him.

After a particularly frustrating rehearsal, I said to Mel, "I've got it!"

"What?"

"I'll play him like an Italian. The show takes place in Verona. Everybody in it is supposed to be Italian, but they ain't, so I'll do Launce as Chico Marx."

"Try it," Mel said.

That night at dress rehearsal with an invited audience, I came out doing Chico. I remembered the scene of Chico selling ice cream in *A Day at the Races.* "Get your tutti-frutti ice cream here."

I made my entrance and with great confidence said, "My momma cryin', my sista wailin', and my entiah household in tears—disa dog did notta shedda one teah."

Not a laugh from the audience. Total shock. It was Hiroshima in Central Park. I couldn't wait for the end of the show. I wanted to sneak out of my body and disappear from the face of the earth.

Shapiro, who never seemed to show any upset, said, "Listen, we'll just have to cut one of your monologues and you can go back to doing it straight." I was totally destroyed, but I knew that he had no recourse. He was right.

The day of the first preview, I was still searching for some hook into the character. I refused to accept what promised to be an empty performance. At about 4:30 P.M. I felt a little tired. I returned to our apartment a few blocks from Central Park. I lay down on Amy's bed for a nap. I closed my eyes, and as I felt myself dozing off I heard myself doing my opening lines, "My sister weeping, my mother wailing, my nurse . . . yet did not this dog utter one word." I also heard myself reciting the *Fier Kashes,* the Passover ritual known as the Four Questions that are asked at the Seder each year by the youngest member of the family to commemorate the Exodus from Egypt. "Why is this night different from every other night?" the child asks in Hebrew. The questions and answers, done part song and part verse, strike a familiar chord in every Jewish family.

As my eyes closed, I could feel myself slipping into the stages of sleep, first the drowsiness and then slumber. I was aware of sounds entering my consciousness. I heard Shakespeare's lines in the meter of the *Fier Kashes.* I was doing Shakespeare like a Jewish chant. The sound made me laugh, even in my half sleep. I could hear myself listening to my own performance. I wanted to stay asleep, to enjoy my dream, but I knew that next I would fall completely asleep and forget whatever was spinning around. I woke myself up and went over what had just occurred in the dream stage.

I looked at my watch. I had been asleep a total of seven minutes. Now I knew what I had to play that night. Launce was the Jewish servant to Proteus, his Puerto Rican master, the switch I needed to bring my once-buried character to life. That night, the monologue worked for the first time. Being part of *Two Gentlemen of Verona* from that moment on was one of the greatest theatrical experiences of my life.

"To sleep, perchance to dream. . . ." Ahh, that Shakespeare really knew what he was talking about.

Through the years Anne and I stayed in touch with the Public Theater and Joe Papp. In the late '80s we received a call from Yivo—the Yivo Institute for Jewish Research—which was throwing a tribute to Joe Papp at the Shubert Theater on Broadway. Would Anne and I be part of the evening? It was a kind of reunion. We'd be part of an elite regiment of artists who had all worked for Joe at some time. Mandy Patinkin, Peter Bogdanovich, Meryl Streep, Kathleen Turner, David Amram, and many others would be there.

"We need someone to lighten the evening," Fred Zollo said. "Could you two do a scene?"

"Of course. Let's talk."

We met at the Public, the beautiful old HIAS (Hebrew Immigrant Aid Society) building on Lafayette Street that Joe had turned into a huge, buzzing creative beehive of American theater.

"You can do something out of *Romeo and Juliet*," Fred said.

"Yeah," Anne said, "we could do the balcony scene with Jerry trying to climb the balcony and hurting himself."

"Anne could climb the balcony," I interjected, but then the idea suddenly fell flat in my own head. "No, the joke's over after the first couple of lines."

"You don't have to do anything like that," Fred said. "You can do something else."

"We'll think about it and call you."

As the list of stars grew, all of them performing something, Fred called back and asked if we would mind just coming out, introducing people, and saying a few words. "Joe really feels you are a part of all this."

"Of course," we said. Anne and I sighed a breath of relief. "We're good at that," Anne said, running an eye over the names whose credits included Pulitzers, Tonys, and Academy Awards.

To "say a few words" meant to say lines that would relate to Joe, Shakespeare, and Yivo, an organization dedicated to the preservation of Yiddish heritage. Joe had once himself taken to the spotlight in some heartwarming cabaret renditions of the Yiddish songs of his youth.

Me at four months. My mother was in labor for forty-two hours, I was told. (Author's collection)

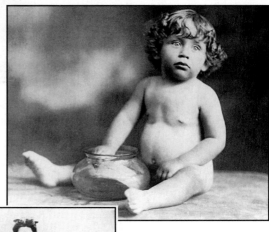

My parents, William and Bella Stiller, near the Vladeck projects on the Lower East Side, circa 1940. (Author's collection)

My brother, Arnie, age twelve, and me, age fourteen. Arnie always got the girls. (Author's collection)

My father, Willie, and my sister Doreen, in front of a stoop in Brooklyn, 1938. (Author's collection)

Eddie Cantor. I wanted to be funny like him. (Courtesy of Brian Gari)

My army buddy Private Joe DiSpigno and me goofing around at the Armored School in Fort Knox, Kentucky. As the only two New Yorkers in the company we had a lot in common. (Author's collection)

Sawyer Falk, my mentor at Syracuse University. Sawyer created the National Theatre Conference. His belief in me was unending. (Courtesy of Francy Falk Phelps)

Anne, ten years old, and her mother, May Meara. May died tragically soon after. (Author's collection)

No formal wedding photo, just this one taken by our friend Walt Witcover, 1953. (Courtesy of Walt Witcover)

Anne and her dad, Ed Meara, San Francisco, 1963. He baby-sat Amy while we performed at the Hungry i and other nightclubs. (Author's collection)

Me feeding four-week-old Amy while Anne was typing a sketch in the other room. (Courtesy of Walt Witcover)

Mommy, daddy, and eighteen-month-old daughter, Amy, while living in Washington Heights. (Courtesy of Walt Witcover)

Gene Saks, me, and Jack Klugman in *Coriolanus* at the Phoenix Theatre. We never auditioned. John Houseman cast us sight unseen. (Photo by Fred Fehl)

Me as Launce with my dog, Crab, in *Two Gentlemen of Verona,* Shakespeare in Central Park for Joe Papp, 1957. Crab became a permanent member of our family when the show closed. (Photo © by George E. Joseph)

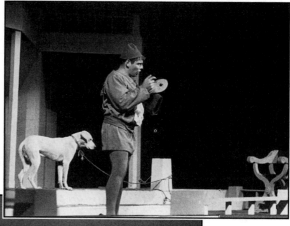

Anne as Julia in *Two Gents.* I got her the job. We were with Joe Papp from the beginning. (Photo © by George E. Joseph)

Ed calling us over after a sketch on the *Sullivan* show. "What's a *megillah*?" he asked. This was in the early 1960s. (CBS Worldwide, Inc.)

At the Royal Box, Hotel Americana, late 1960s. Anne's pearls were stolen while we were performing onstage. I had just gotten the news. (Author's collection)

F. Murray Abraham and myself in *The Ritz*, 1976, directed by Richard Lester and filmed in London. (*The Ritz* © 1976 Warner Bros. Inc. All rights reserved)

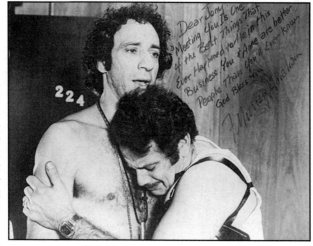

The cast of *Hurlyburly,* 1984, Barrymore Theatre. Left to right: Christopher Walken, Harvey Keitel, William Hurt, Sigourney Weaver, me as "Artie," Judith Ivey, and Cynthia Nixon. Directed by Mike Nichols. What a great cast. (Photo by Martha Swope, © by Time, Inc.)

Robin Williams as Tommy Wilhelm and me as Tamkin, the charlatan, in *Seize the Day.* (Courtesy of Bob Geller and Learning in Focus)

Me and Divine: Mr. And Mrs. Wilbur Turnblad in John Waters's *Hairspray,* 1987. (Author's collection)

Henny Youngman: a great friend and an intellect in the disguise of a clown. (Photo by Oscar White, courtesy of Marilyn Kelly)

The Costanzas: Estelle Harris, Jason Alexander, and myself. A quiet moment on *Seinfeld*. (Courtesy of Castle Rock Entertainment)

Michael Richards as Kramer, demonstrating the "mansierre" (or was it the "bro"?) to Frank Costanza. (Courtesy of Castle Rock Entertainment)

Seeking serenity as Frank Costanza. (Courtesy of Castle Rock Entertainment)

The two Jerrys on the *Seinfeld* set during the filming of the Korean War episode, in which I almost fatally poisoned my company with tainted food. (Author's collection)

My Dad, age 100, and me in 1996, three years before he passed away. (Author's collection)

The Stiller family: me, Amy, Ben, and Anne at a New York restaurant in the late 1980s. (Author's collection)

Leah Remini, Kevin James, and me in *King of Queens,* the hit CBS comedy. (© CBS Worldwide, Inc. Photo by Monty Brinton)

Anne and me on the set of HBO's *Take 5.* This is one of our favorite photos. (Martha Holmes, *Life* Magazine © Time Inc.)

For two days I worked on making humorous analogies between Shakespeare and Yiddish. I finally bounced some stuff off Anne.

"What do you think of this? Joe is an Anglophile. He loves the English language, especially Shakespearean words like 'forsooth,' 'methinks,' 'perchance,' 'henceforth' . . . but he also loves his mother tongue, phrases like *paskudnyak, nudnick.*"

"What does that mean, *paskudnyak?*" Anne asked.

"Just listen," I said, quieting her. "Joe went to the Jewish Theological Seminary, where he studied the ancient texts."

"Joe was a Yeshiva Bucha?" Anne asked.

"That's funny, use that," I said. "He was a scholar. He discovered certain phrases in Shakespeare that were interchangeable with Yiddish. Take the word 'perchance.' It could be *efsher.*"

"*Efsher?*" Anne asked.

"Yeah, like in *Hamlet,* Act I, Scene 1, when Horatio sees the ghost of Hamlet's father and says: '*Efsher* it's the King.'"

Anne repeated this. It was funny, her saying the Yiddish.

"And the word 'methinks' is *ver veist.*"

"*Ver veist?*" Anne said.

"It means, 'Who knows?'" I said. "Or *veir viest* if you're a Galitzianer."

"Joe is a Galitzianer?" Anne asked.

"I don't know," I said. "We're making this up."

"Wasn't your mother a Galitzianer?" Anne said.

"No, my mother was a Litvak. My father was a Galitzianer. There were a lot of problems there."

"Because of the ethnic difference?"

"No, because my grandmother never invited my mother to Friday-night dinners," I said.

"That's a *shonder,*" Anne replied.

"Yeah, there was a lot of alienation there."

"Alienation?" Anne said.

"Yeah, of the way my mother made gefilte fish. She made it sweet, and Galitzianers make it with salt."

"And that's why your grandmother never invited your mother to dinner?" Anne asked. "Jerry, we shouldn't be talking about our own *mishegaas.* This is Joe's night."

"Hey, I think the thrust of the evening is that Joe Papp is convinced that William Shakespeare was Jewish. His real name was Velvel."

"Velvel Shakespeare?" Anne asked. "Shakespeare's name was Velvel?"

"Yeah, it's my father's name. His first name. It's Willie, short form. Good—that's a good line, isn't it?"

Anne shrugged. *"Ver veist,"* she said.

7

Stiller and Meara

*H*ow did Anne and I ever survive? Actors must be the craziest breed of the human species. If we did on the streets what we do on the stage, we'd be locked up. We were each other's keepers.

In the mid-1950s Anne was busy at Equity Library Theater, doing *Maedchen in Uniform* with Barbara Barrie (who would be so brilliant in Anne's *After-Play* four decades later). Their director was a man named Walt Witcover.

For me, Walt was the teacher who taught actors how to deal with fear: Make the audience part of the play and they are no longer the faceless mass sitting in the darkness judging you. Create an intimacy between them and yourself, personalize them and they are no longer strangers.

In 1956, when Walt asked Anne, me, and Charles Nelson Reilly to do three one-acts, we jumped at the chance. It was the beginning of a long and warm relationship with Charles, one of the funniest men in the business.

Box and Cox; How He Lied to Her Husband; and *John John, Sir John, and Tyb* were plays that represented three centuries of theatrical styles.

Anne and I had now been married three years. This was the first time we would get the chance to play opposite each other. Would it separate us, or was this what marriage was about? So here we were in Little Italy on Mulberry Street, rehearsing in Walt's cold-water flat with a bathtub in the kitchen. Was this the beginning of a theatrical partnership?

Walt was not a blind visionary. Theater was his life. The weeks leading up to our opening in a small theater atop the Chanin Building at 42nd

Street and Lexington Avenue did not go smoothly. Anne and I were completely at odds. When I asked Anne recently why we hadn't got along back then, she said, "I guess it's because I hated the way you acted."

"But," I said, "was that any reason to throw a chair at me in rehearsal?"

"Yes, it was," she said. Thank God she missed.

At the time I wondered whether the marriage was working out.

When we finally got to the opening, the big shock was that there was hardly anyone in the audience. The Chanin, we learned, had some kind of jinx. Nobody wanted to take the elevator to the top of a skyscraper to see a show.

What I had learned about playing to a small house—in this case, five people—was invaluable. I used all of Walt's techniques, personalizing each member of the audience. I could practically smell them. I never got more laughs from five people in all my life. They became my best friends. What I'd learned then, I've since used at every nightclub performance. It meant being in the moment and bonding with whoever was out there.

At around this time I had started working as a team with a comic actress named Nancy Ponder. Stiller and Ponder (or Ponder and Stiller) never quite got off the ground. All we did was make each other laugh. But Nancy then introduced me to David Shepherd, the founder of the Compass Players. In 1959 we became replacements for Mike Nichols, Elaine May, and Shelley Berman, who had split from the Compass Players and were now stars working on their own.

Compass, later to become Second City, performed both rehearsed pieces and suggestions taken from the audience that built a scene on the spot.

Nancy, Alan Arkin, and I worked on our improvisational techniques in David's apartment on West 86th Street. Irvin Arthur, then an agent, booked us into the Alpine Village in Cleveland.

The Alpine Village was run by Herman Pirchner, an amiable, smiling impresario, who, we were told, had a circus background. We were the headliners. The opening act was Beverly, a blonde beauty who twirled flaming batons to Khachaturian's "Ritual Fire Dance." Alpine, a popular club in Cleveland, had a rising hydraulic stage similar to the one at the Paramount Theater in New York. Frankie Yankovic, the Polka King, usually sold the place out. Our big number was a sketch called "Fundador," in which Alan Arkin played a young bullfighter and I an old one. Nancy

played the seductive lady in the grandstand flirting with the young tore-
ador. The rest of the evening was to be made up of taking suggestions
from the audience on which we were to build instant improvisations.

Before we went on, Herman, who was also the MC, asked how he
should introduce us.

"The Compass Players," we told him.

"And where have you played before this?"

"No place," I said.

"Okay, I'll introduce you as 'Those international favorites.' "

That night we watched Beverly. The stage was pitch black except for
her batons ablaze and flying through the air. The music was ear shatter-
ing. When she finished and the cheers subsided, Mr. Pirchner, wearing an
elegant tuxedo, came out and said, "Ladies and gentlemen, the Alpine
Village is proud to present as its star attraction, for the first time in Cleveland, those international favorites, the Compass Players."

Alan, Nancy, and I strolled out together. We started to speak together
to explain what we were there to do. It was as if we had turned the club
into a classroom. The audience did not know what to make of us. When
we asked for suggestions there was dead silence. We then took suggestions from each other. After we'd spent about twenty minutes talking
among ourselves, the orchestra played us off. Pirchner ran backstage, a
huge smile on his face, saying, "That was wonderful. The first show is always like that."

Once in our dressing rooms we panicked.

"They don't understand that what we're doing is comedy," I said.
"Next show, why don't we put Nancy in a chair and drag her out on stage
like she was some kind of Egyptian queen. Then they'll know we're a
comedy act."

The second show, equally disastrous, had the audience dropping dinner rolls on the hydraulic stage as it lowered. The ride was dangerous, but
at least we had something to eat.

The next day I said, "I know what's wrong. We need clothes that make
us look like we're an act." Everyone agreed so we went downtown and
bought matching ponchos. Nonetheless, we bombed every night, every
show. At the end of the week Pirchner, still jolly, walked in and said, "I'm
holding you over." We were doing the Gettysburg Address of comedy:
They finally understood us when they got home. We still died each show.
Two weeks later, we were back in New York. Why had he held us over?

Somebody finally turned the light on: "Don't you realize you guys were a tax write-off?"

David Shepherd did not give up. Back in New York, Irvin Arthur was trying desperately to get us a booking on the *Jack Paar Show*. He got a one-night audition at the Den in the Duane, a small club on Madison Avenue whose audience loved avant-garde acts. Milt Kamen, Dick Cavett, and Lenny Bruce all worked there. It seemed perfect for us.

That night we entered the club as Mike Nichols was leaving. He said he and Elaine had just finished doing a set. He looked pained and a little sweaty.

"Mike," I said, "How are you?"

"They're tough," he said. "Do you want a Valium? I'm having a Valium," he joked, and he disappeared around the block. Minutes later Alan, Nancy, and I were introduced and went on. We did some set pieces that went over well enough. The lights went up and Nancy said, "We'd like to take some suggestions from the audience." Sitting in the first row were two guys who had to be goodfellas. Next to them were two flaming red-headed ladies with beehive hairdos. I had an immediate connection to them. I still had a childhood need to make it with the tough guys. Suggestions were flying from the audience. Someone said, "A baseball player."

"Okay, we got a ballplayer, what else?" Nancy said.

"How about a stripper," another one hollered. The audience wanted to play. We just let them suggest until we got characters we were comfortable with.

"How about you guys?" I said pointing to the foursome. "What character would you like to see?"

"A politician," one of them answered kind of sullenly. I was going to cheer him up.

"Okay," I said, "I'll be a politician." The name Carmine DeSapio flashed into my mind. I knew DeSapio was the Democratic district leader in Greenwich Village who had recently been jailed. I could run with this, I thought. "How about a place?" I asked.

One of them said, "Jail."

"We've got enough," Nancy informed the audience. "We've got a politician and we've got a jail."

I took the stage first. I paced back and forth and ran an imaginary tin cup against some imaginary prison bars. Alan Arkin quickly became a prison guard. I already knew my punch line.

I thought I was being hilariously hip. I was doing the headline in tomorrow's newspaper.

I ordered Alan as the jailer to send out for a bottle of wine and a hooker.

"Who do you think you are?" Alan asked.

"I'm Carmine DeSapio," I said.

"You got it, boss."

Blackout. Huge laughs except for the table with the guys who'd made the suggestion. The two of them looked up at me. I could see that they were furious. I couldn't understand why. They looked like they wanted to get up on the stage. "You son of a bitch," one of them muttered, loud enough for me to hear. The women, aware of this, were trying to cool the guys down. The audience was applauding. We thanked them and headed back to the dressing room, congratulating ourselves on a great set.

Suddenly the door opened and there were the two guys standing there with the women behind them.

One of them grabbed me by the arm and pulled me out of the room into the hallway. He lifted me off the floor by the lapels and held me up against the wall fully a foot above his head, my feet dangling. He was very strong.

"Why did you say that?" he asked.

The guy behind him said, "We ought to kill you."

One of the girls with the beehives implored, "Leave him alone, Joey, he's only a comedian."

"What did I say?" I asked.

"You said Carmine DeSapio, you bastard."

"What's wrong with that?" I asked.

"You don't get it, you schmuck!"

"It was a joke," I said, "I thought you'd laugh."

I was still up against the wall and unable to believe what was happening. Now he started banging me against the wall. The girls kept pleading, "Leave him alone, he didn't mean it."

"I could kill him," the guy said.

Suddenly he was relenting and I was being lowered to the floor. The guy had some mercy. As they left I kept thinking how I'd always considered the stage a place where I could say anything. It had never occurred to me that it was also a place where I could get killed.

As they left I wish I'd taken Mike Nichols up on his Valium offer that night.

David Shepherd finally got Compass a three-month gig at the Crystal Palace in St. Louis, where we could put our improv techniques into practice. At my insistence David hired Anne at $75 a week to become the fourth member of the Compass Players. Although she had no improvisational experience, Anne agreed to come along.

We loaded Crab (still part of our family) and our two kittens (now cats) into David's Volkswagen and drove to St. Louis.

Once we began performing, it was apparent that neither Alan nor Nancy nor I was comfortable taking suggestions and schmoozing with the audience. Anne quietly took over the job. With Anne taking the suggestions, Compass went from didactic to hip and entertaining. Anne sparked an instant intimacy and gave Compass a stand-up feeling. Anne's chat became funnier and funnier. Some nights, the audience couldn't care less about suggestions.

At one performance she said, "I need a setting."

Someone shouted, "My pad."

"Something you write on?" Anne asked.

"No, it's where I live."

St. Louis was where we learned that "pad" meant where you lived. St. Louis was a very hip town.

One night a woman wanted us to do a scene with a merkin. "What's a merkin?" Anne asked. The audience was convulsed.

"You don't know?" someone shouted. "It's a toupee for the unseen hairy place on a woman's anatomy." Everyone in St. Louis seemed to know this.

Once, while Anne was asking for suggestions from the audience, Professor Irwin Corey, sitting in the back, shouted, "Why don't you do an improv group taking suggestions from an audience?" I wanted to tell Irwin to go fuck off. In the Witcover sense, I felt that was as personalized as I could go.

Anne and I had learned that simply by taking suggestions, playing characters, and improvising a story, we were becoming writers. This was the beginning of what was to become Stiller and Meara.

When we had finished ten weeks at the Crystal Palace, David Shepherd said there were no plans to continue Compass. Alan was going through a marital break-up and was caring for his son Adam. Nancy was in love with Jerry Zucker, an ABC Television executive. Anne and I were out of work.

We needed a vacation, so I bought a car. A Nash Ambassador with a hundred and twenty-five thousand miles on the odometer was a steal at seventy-five dollars. It had been American Motors' breakthrough model. It featured a backseat that could open into a bed. The big Henny Young-man joke that year was about a guy who got a ticket for dirty sheets. The car had a new feature in family cars: It was equipped with a new four-wheel-drive transmission.

We decided to return to New York from St. Louis by way of Weston, West Virginia, where we'd visit Anne's friend Ursula's parents.

On the day we left St. Louis we had been travelling almost fourteen hours and were only a few hours from our destination, passing through St. Mary's on the West Virginia–Ohio border. The road got steeper. We began to descend. As the Nash picked up speed, I applied the brakes. The pedal went to the floor—there was no pressure on the brakes. We picked up more speed. I looked at Anne, sitting beside me, and said, "I don't think we have brakes." We went faster and faster. I pumped the brake pedal, hoping this would produce some resistance. It didn't. The pedal still went to the floor. My Adam's apple was in my mouth. Anne didn't seem at all upset. It was as if the two of us were meant to be together in whatever this was all about.

I rolled down my window. I could hear the sound of the wind whistling in my ears. I wanted to shout to passing cars, "No brakes!" be-seeching them to inform someone ahead. In the backseat the cats in their kitty boxes were meowing, and Crab sat petrified, farting. I wondered how this tale would play in the newspapers. Anne started singing "Rock of Ages." I figured we were going too fast for her to jump out. I started to pray in Hebrew. Does God understand Hebrew in West Virginia? As we kept picking up speed I could hear the whistling wind getting louder. *One minute,* I thought, *we've been free-falling at least one minute.* And there were still a couple miles to go on this huge hill.

I quietly locked in two thoughts: (1) we'll all die; (2) we'll live. It all depended on what was at the bottom of the hill. I realized there was noth-ing I could do. So I turned off the ignition, hoping that by some miracle this would stop the car, then just sat back. We kept shooting along. It was eerie. No sound. I could see the bottom of the hill now. The road inter-sected with a main highway. There was a traffic light. I figured if we had the green, we'd live. If the light turned red as we hit the intersection and a car was coming across our path, we'd probably be killed. I had enough time to ponder this.

I looked at Anne and started to curse quietly. "Fucking seventy-five-dollar car. I thought it was a bargain."

I was counting down the seconds to when we would reach the traffic light. A quarter of a mile to go. I could now see moving cars.

"It was all the money we had," Anne said as she touched my hand.

I turned to look over my shoulder at our cats and our dog. *They'll all live,* I thought. *Animals don't die in car crashes.*

The speedometer read sixty-five miles an hour as we sailed through the red light. Miraculously, no cars were coming from either direction. As our $75 baby hit the flat straightaway, we started to slow. Now the brakes were working again. I was shaking, my shirt was soaked with perspira-tion, and I wanted to cry. I looked at Anne. Had this really happened? I knew somebody was watching over us.

When we drove the car into a nearby gas station and described what had happened, the attendant pointed to the four-wheel-drive transmis-sion with its special box, which I never paid any attention to. It was a fea-ture that was meaningless to me. The attendant explained that when engaged manually this four-wheel-drive shift could act as a kind of brake and would slow the car when going downhill. I was unaware until that moment what those gears were for. I'm an actor; what do I know from gears? I thanked him, and we continued on our way.

Safely home from St. Louis, Anne and I started working on our own us-ing stuff we learned. Bob Weiner, a young producer, called. He said we could open in a new cabaret in Chicago doing a revue. "I can guarantee you six months' work at five hundred bucks a week." It was a fortune. So on Bob's recommendation, Oscar Marienthal hired us to open in *Medium Rare* at the Happy Medium on Rush Street right off Delaware. We stopped working on our act.

Medium Rare was a compilation of the best songs and sketches lifted from the sophisticated Julius Monk and Ben Bagley revues of that era. Os-car, who owned Mr. Kelly's and The London House, was a gentle, bear-like man, a benign father figure in the tough Chicago nightclub world.

After two weeks of rehearsal, we opened. *Medium Rare* got mixed notices. We thought surely we would close. Following the opening-night performance, Oscar, director Bill Penn, producer Bob Weiner, and the actors gathered in the darkened cabaret. Oscar started reading the reviews. The cast was waiting for the ax to fall.

"I thought it was a good show," Oscar said, looking around for some agreement.

"Yes," we all softly agreed.

"They call it my white elephant." After a long silence, he said, "I'm going to keep the show open. I believe in it and in all of you."

We were stunned. "What about the million you invested in this place?" Bob Weiner asked.

"It's only money, kids," Oscar said with a smile.

The company adjourned to Mammy's, an all-night restaurant on the corner of Rush and Elm. At 2 A.M. Mammy's would still be alive with the likes of Kaye Ballard, Dave Lambert, Jon Hendricks, Annie Ross, Phil Tucker, Norman Wallace, Jack E. Leonard, Sam Levene, Molly Berg, and other players from touring Broadway shows, talking away the night. Entertainers, mob guys, and hookers were all downing 2 A.M. breakfast, waiting for the sun to rise before finally giving up and going to bed. It was pure Chicago.

Oscar's belief paid off. *Medium Rare* became a hit. It ran for years. Anne and I looked to save $25,000 in six months.

"Now we have enough money to have a baby," Anne said to me one night after we'd taken our final bow.

I silently panicked.

"I'm not waiting for the security of a TV series," she said. "Playing mother to Squeaky, Sniffles, and Crab is like playing New Haven. I want real kids."

We had never spoken of children before. We were show folk. I suddenly realized that the only people I'd ever cared about other than myself and Anne was the audience. It was a shock to hear Anne's pronouncement. Suddenly, I was being told that I was to be a father, with all its consuming responsibilities.

"If you really love me, you'll go along with this," Anne said. "Doesn't it mean anything that I care enough about you to want to have kids?"

I could see that my dream of our becoming the Great American comedy team would have to take a backseat to the realization that my life did not depend solely on getting laughs. Being on stage should not take away from being a dad, I told myself. So I started working to become one.

When Anne became pregnant, *Medium Rare* had been running for three months. There was no doubt in our mind about the night when Amy was conceived.

Five months later, Anne's large appearance on stage turned each sketch into a pregnancy joke. In one scene she played Medea's nurse, rocking in a chair, knitting, as she chided Medea about Jason. In another bit, "Poet's Corner," she played a ninety-year-old woman who wrote erotic verse. When she got up to recite her poem, the audience, seeing her huge belly, was wiped out before she spoke her first line.

Although we were signed for a year, Oscar reluctantly admitted that he would have to replace us because of the pregnancy. He promised us a gig at his other club, Mr. Kelly's, as soon as we had an act. Although Stiller and Meara was still a pipe dream at that time, Oscar kept his promise: We were to play Kelly's for him twice before he passed away.

During the run of *Medium Rare* Anne and I *did* save $25,000, an astronomical figure. Twenty-five grand was more money than my father had earned in his whole life. That was the only measure of wealth I could go by.

Before returning to New York, Anne and I decided to take a vacation and visit our dear friends Charlie and Joanie Robinson, two transplanted New Yorkers now living high up in the Hollywood Hills.

After spending some relaxing time with our friends, we wanted to return home. Anne was now in her seventh month. We left the Robinsons, Anne in full bloom with Amy, and set out in the old Nash, the same car that had almost killed us in West Virginia.

"You're lucky you don't drive," I said to Anne.

"I wish I could drive," Anne replied. "I feel so helpless just sitting here."

"Do you want to stop in Vegas?" I asked. "Maybe we can get lucky."

"What can we lose, a couple of hundred bucks?" I said. "Besides," I assured her as we headed east into the desert, "I've got a system."

"What is it?" Anne asked.

"It's simple. We just double our bets after we lose. You have to come out ahead."

"I don't believe it," Anne said.

When we got to Vegas, we checked into a hotel and I proceeded to demonstrate my theory to Anne.

"See, I'll show you with these matches." I had bought a box of wooden matches. I gave Anne half a box and I took half a box.

"Who taught you this?" Anne asked.

"Lew Rose, my buddy in the ASTRP. He was a mathematical genius. He said this is foolproof as long as you have money to double up every time you lose. Look," I said, pulling out a deck of cards.

"You mean we're going to go downstairs and double our bets every time we lose?" Anne said. "What if we run out of money?" she asked, laughing because I was serious.

"How can we?" I said. "I'll show you with the match sticks."

"Those are match sticks, not money," she said.

"I'll show you," I said, clearing a dresser of everything. "You be the House and I'll be me. We're playing Black Jack, 21."

I dealt one hand after another. As I lost, I kept doubling my bets. Anne kept beating me. I kept doubling up until the dresser was full of matches. There was no room and we had to lay matches on the bed, then on the floor. By the time I won I couldn't figure out how much I'd lost. Anne was in tears laughing.

"You think they're going to allow you to do that?" she said. "They got guys watching for that. They'll take us out of here in a box."

We spent two hours working on my system before we called it quits and decided to go downstairs and just gamble. We lost a thousand bucks at craps and slots but still felt very rich as we left Vegas.

A couple of hours outside of Las Vegas, I noticed steam pouring out of the hood of the car. We were in the desert and the radiator had over-heated. Never having been cross-country before, I had no idea that we'd need to carry extra water to cool off the engine. The temperature gauge on the dashboard did not work, a minor failing until now. The car came to a halt. The sun blazing, I lifted the hood, and swirls of steam filled the air. I carefully removed the radiator cap, allowing the radiator to cool. Occasionally a car rolled by asking if we needed help. I refused the offer.

"Just the radiator cooling off," I said.

Anne, sitting in the car, looked like a lump. "What can we do?" she said.

"I'll just try to start it up and get some water in the next town," I said, acting totally in charge. This car was my tank, I thought. Nothing could hurt it. One half hour later the car started and we moved.

"I'm going to take it slow," I said. We saw a sign that read IMLAY,

NEVADA. When we got to Imlay it was dark and the car, steaming again, stopped at the railroad station which, coincidentally, was also a hotel— an overnight stopover on the Santa Fe Railway for workers who had to catch forty winks before getting the next day's assignment.

The car would not start and I knew there were serious problems that would have to wait until the following day. Anne was exhausted.

"Where are we going to stay?" she asked.

"Right here, I guess, until I get the car fixed."

"You really love this car," she said.

"What can I tell you, the gauge wasn't registering."

We checked into the hotel. The man at the desk said, "This is a railroad hotel. There's only one room available. It's not too comfortable," he said, looking at Anne's stomach, "but it's all we got."

"We'll take it," I said.

"Twenty-five bucks," he said.

I gave him the money. We hauled our bodies and the bags upstairs to the room, which had a double bed, a table, and a small lamp.

"Where's the door?" Anne said. I looked. There was no door. I went down the hall. None of the rooms had doors.

This was a stopover for railroad men. They all knew each other. Kind of a communal barracks. Too tired to think, we both lay our heads down and slept. During the night, the Santa Fe trains would stop and conductors, engineers, firemen, and other personnel would go noisily into the rooms along the hall as Anne and I slept fitfully until morning. We had the car towed to Winnemucca, a few miles down the road, where a bona fide gas station repairman looked at the damage. The owner looked at me quizzically, then said, "You guys better get settled in a motel. You need a new gasket and we're going to have to send for it. You blew right through your housing."

"How long to get the parts?" I asked.

"Could be three days," he said.

"You're kidding," Anne said.

"That's how long it'll take, unless you want to leave the car," he said.

Leave the Nash? Never. I loved that car. "We'll wait," I said.

Anne and I got a room at a motel in what appeared to be a small desert metropolis a few miles away, and unpacked our bags. The next day I went to the station to check. The gasket had not arrived. I sat and talked with the owner and his two men. They asked what we did. I told them we were actors.

"Have we ever seen you in anything?" they asked.

"Probably not," I said. "We've been in Chicago, in Central Park in New York." They were fascinated by my little droplets of showbiz information. After a while I said, "Would you call me if the gasket arrives?"

"Sure," they said.

The next day I arrived again, hitchhiking the three miles from the motel. "Has it come yet?"

"Nope," they said.

"Where is it coming from?" I asked.

"Elko," they said.

"Where's that?" I asked.

"A couple of miles," they said.

"Why is it taking so long?" I asked.

"It's coming by mail," they said.

"By mail?" I said. "Why didn't somebody pick it up?"

"We didn't think you wanted it that way," the man said. "Anyway, we liked talking to you."

I couldn't believe my ears. "I'll go pick it up," I said.

"You want to?"

"Sure," I said. "How do I get there?"

"There's a bus you can take on the highway."

I picked up the gasket, brought it back, and gave it to the gas station guys. It took about an hour to replace. It was a cutout piece of thickened cardboard that fit between the metallic housings. When the job was finished the radiator was filled again and we headed east. The Nash sputtered again, not quite as bad, and we just made it to Laramie, Wyoming. There we picked up a used Dodge and kissed the Nash good-bye.

The Dodge, although it could never compare to my beloved Nash, did its job and got us home safely. We arrived at our 80th Street apartment, opened the door, and were welcomed home by finding the place ransacked. Everything had been dumped into the yard. Birth certificates, insurance policies, memorabilia, all lying in a pile of wet, sopping rubble. Our unemployment books were the only things that were undamaged. Welcome home.

As fatherhood stared me in the face, I could feel responsibility creeping into my life. I understood the meaning of the term "breadwinner." Now I knew what my father must've gone through. For the first time I *had* to get a job. I had given someone life. I was now responsible for that someone. I was watching the twenty-five grand disappearing and knew I needed an acting job.

Bill Penn, who'd directed *Medium Rare,* called and asked if I would play Ozzie in *On the Town* for Lee Guber on the Guber, Gross, Ford circuit. I would be working with Jimmy Kirkwood (who was yet to write *Chorus Line*) and Jane Romano. I said yes even though it would mean being out of town. The words "getting paid" freed me from any hesitation about being away from Anne during her final weeks of pregnancy. Besides, the show was to close a few days before Anne's due date.

At the same time, Ursula and her husband Pat Campbell told us of an available apartment on Riverside Drive in Washington Heights.

The apartment was a dream: five rooms on the fifth floor facing beautiful trees and the sunset every night. Morning and afternoon sunlight, something we had not seen in the three apartments we'd had in seven years, flooded all five rooms. One hundred twenty-five dollars a month.

I raced up to 160th Street and met the super and his wife. She was Hell's Kitchen Irish, he was older and Jewish. The ethnic mix so similar to ours (and the one-month's rent under the table) undoubtedly influenced them into renting us the apartment.

On the day of the move I was to start rehearsing *On the Town.* We hired the Crabtree Movers, a group of out-of-work actors who were part-time moving men. They were cheap, friendly, and totally honest.

As the furniture was being moved into our new apartment, I felt a sudden shortness of breath. Rehearsals were due to start later that day. I had never had a sick day, and suddenly I felt my life coming to an abrupt end. I could not breathe. I looked at Anne surrounded by Crab, the two cats, and tons of boxes and gasped, "I can't breathe. I've got to call a doctor."

"I'll call Bob Weiner," Anne said. Bob was a friend of ours and also something of a hypochondriac. He knew all the best doctors. Bob gave Anne the name and address of his doctor on 55th Street. She jotted it down for me on a piece of paper.

I jumped in a cab and got out in front of a house on East 55th Street that looked like a slum. The hallway was marked with graffiti. My breath was now coming in shorter bursts, and I was beginning to panic. I looked at the address on the paper. I had misread it. It was *West* 55th, not *East.*

I flagged down another cab, jumped in, and told the driver I was having a heart attack. He sped off and got me to the building on West 55th Street in record time. He probably didn't want me dying in his cab.

I ran to the receptionist and said, "I'm a friend of Bob Weiner's and I'm having a heart attack. I can't breathe. I've got to see the doctor."

"There are people ahead of you," the receptionist said, pointing to the many elderly and infirm people sitting and watching with indignation as I tried to buck the line. I couldn't care less if any of these people were ahead of me. I started to speak louder. "You don't understand. Shortness of breath. I'm dying."

That got her. She ran inside. I looked around the waiting room. Angry faces seemed to say, "You're young, you should be ashamed." I ignored the deadly looks. I could see myself on the *Titanic,* the Captain shouting, "Women and children first!" Jerry Stiller exclaiming, "*Me* first!" as he jumped into a lifeboat.

The doctor came out, escorted me inside, and asked what was going on.

"I've got shortness of breath, I can't breathe," I said.

"Take off your shirt."

I did, and he listened with his stethoscope.

"Anything?" I said, waiting to hear the bad news.

"Nothing," he said. "Give him an EKG," he said to the nurse. They hooked me up to wires and read the results. The results were normal.

"Well, it's not a heart attack," the doctor said. "What's going on in your life?"

"I'm about to have a baby, this is my first day of rehearsal, and we just moved."

"Stress," the doctor said. "There's nothing physically wrong."

"Thanks," I said, running out of the office past the angry waiting room. I was no longer out of breath.

"Give Bob a hug for me," I shouted to the receptionist as, a moment later, I hopped a cab to the rehearsal of *On the Town.*

Not long after this, in August, 1961, I was performing in Owings Mills, Maryland, outside Baltimore when Kay Falk called to tell me Professor Falk had died. He'd been with students in a theater in Paris and collapsed. He died on August 31 at age 61. Kay asked if I could get up to Syracuse to be a pallbearer at his funeral.

When I arrived at Hendricks Chapel, I was told that the professor had left instructions that I be his first pallbearer. I was overcome. Was I that important to him?

The chapel was full of students, teachers, and alumni. As the choir sang I could see his eyes looking straight into mine telling me I would someday make it as an actor. I could see the man who gave me strength when things got tough. As I and the others lifted the casket, the choir sang "Swing Low, Sweet Chariot" and we carried Professor Falk out. He was buried at a cemetery not far from the house at 128 Circle Road, where Kay could see him every day from her window. On Yom Kippur, when I say Kaddish for my mother, my father, my uncles, and my father-in-law, Eddie Meara, I also send up a prayer for Sawyer Falk.

For the eight years Anne and I had been married I had submerged my feelings about my Jewishness. But guilt about marrying outside my background was simmering on the back burner. I had never severed myself from my Jewish roots, nor did I want to.

Seven years after my mother died, Anne converted to Judaism. She said she was taking instruction so that we could raise our children Jewish. On July 24, 1961, Anne became Jewish. Why did she do this? I wondered how Anne's father, a devout Roman Catholic, would take it. Did Anne consider this? She surely must have.

In hindsight, I could have waited to marry Anne. Anne too could have waited to convert, but didn't. Anne's conversion brought us closer together and we've never discussed it since, as odd as that may seem.

I was still in Baltimore in *On the Town,* when Amy arrived three days early. How could I not have anticipated this? How could work be more important than being with my wife when my first child was born?

When I reached the hospital the next day, I saw Anne and our beautiful baby girl, who smiled at me. I felt an immediate change within me, a loving feeling I had never experienced before. Something had been awakened. I wondered why we had waited so long.

Amy arrived only a short time after Sawyer Falk's death, so we named her Amy Belle Sawyer Stiller. Amy means "beloved." Belle is for my mother and Sawyer for Professor Falk.

Amy brought us luck. She brought Anne and me even closer together and motivated us. Anne and I had talked about doing an act together. Now we began writing and rehearsing.

Our first outing was at a Women's Strike for Peace benefit at BAM, the Brooklyn Academy of Music. The performance consisted of two pieces. The first we called "Psychodrama." It was an interview in which Anne plays a Geraldine Page–like character who talks about how psychodrama can help neurotics. She gives an inane description of how psychodrama works while all the time exhibiting off-the-wall behavior. Anne was hysterically funny.

In the second skit Anne played a stripper with a social conscience and I was a bogus doctor. We pretended to be pacifists seeking the end of nuclear testing, and our slogan was "Bump the Bomb."

In the sketch I exhorted the audience to get up and bump.

"Peaches, our expert in bumping, will demonstrate how to bump."

Anne, in a cheap tutu and clearly enjoying her work, does just that. "We must all ban the bomb," she pleads in a sweet baby voice. "Let's all get up and show the world how we feel about nuclear testing. Let's all get up and bump for peace."

The audience—the Women's Strike for Peace audience, which really was trying to ban the bomb, had just heard Nancy Walker read letters from mothers in Hiroshima—was in shock.

"Get up!" Anne insisted. The audience cautiously obeyed.

"Now, I want everyone to put their hands behind their heads and bump."

They did.

"Now didn't that feel good? That's wonderful. Now turn to the person next to you, and bump him or her. Think of this as an innocent orgy for peace."

The peace-loving audience responded and was caught up in the ridiculousness.

I said, "Ladies and gentlemen, let's show the warmongers and politicians how we feel about nuclear testing. Let's all sing 'God Bless America,' and *bump*."

The audience joined me in singing "God Bless America."

"Now let's all march out onto the streets and get everyone to bump. Bump the cop on the beat, bump the fireman, the postman, bump the person sitting next to you. Come on, do it."

The audience started marching up the aisle. They were ready to hit the sidewalks until we told them to stop, that we would need a permit. They applauded and laughed enthusiastically, and we left the stage feeling great.

Jerry Adler, a classmate from Syracuse, called not long afterward to ask if Anne and I would audition for Orson Bean's upcoming Summerhill School benefit, to be held at the Alvin Theater. Jerry, who was stage managing, thought the psychodrama sketch would work. The Juilliard String Quartet, Orson and Jack Gilford, and Margot Moser and Larry Keith (who had taken over from Julie Andrews and Rex Harrison in *My Fair Lady*) were also performing.

The benefit audience loved us. We were told we were *original.* Our dressing room after the benefit was like something out of a 20th Century-Fox movie. Agents were swarming out of the woodwork. Art D'Lugoff, who ran the Village Gate on Bleecker Street, approached us.

"How would you like to play at the Gate?" he asked. "You can go on next week with Herbie Mann."

An agent piped up, "I can book you into the Bon Soir starting this Sunday night." The Bon Soir was a small, chic club on West 8th Street, a few blocks above Bleecker, which had headliners like Kaye Ballard, Phyllis Diller, Dick Cavett, and Felicia Sanders, one of the great cabaret singers of the 1960s. That gig sounded perfect for us, so we asked Art for a raincheck.

"Anytime," Art said. "And I'll pay you four hundred dollars a week."

My mouth watered at the thought of that kind of money.

As instructed, Anne and I arrived at the Bon Soir on Sunday night. Its bar was the hippest—wall-to-wall laughers. If they laughed, we were in.

Our newfound agent met us. "I'll be back here, waiting," he said. "You go on after Louis Nye. It's his last night here. This is an audition night, and if they like you they'll probably hire you."

Anne and I looked at one another. We had thought we were booked.

We were prepared to do "Psychodrama" and a piece called "The Farnsworths." These particular Farnsworths, winners of a *Ted Mack Amateur Hour,* were siblings from Indiana whose parents had been killed in an auto accident. Anne sings "Bye-Bye Blues" while I tap-dance into the mike with my tongue and teeth. The untalented sibs are doing their first professional engagement after winning the talent hour. The pressure causes them to disintegrate in front of the audience.

We readied ourselves to go on. Louis Nye, the "man on the street" who would always come onto Steve Allen's TV program with "Hi, ho! Steverino!" was tremendous in his closing performance. The audience was packed with Nye's friends and well-wishers. As the customers were paying their checks and departing, the maitre d' walked briskly up to the microphone and barked, "Stiller and Meara!" We started "Psychodrama" as the crowd headed for the doors. No one was listening. I looked at Anne. There was disbelief on her face. Welcome to the world of night-clubs. I thought of the benefit we'd just done at the Alvin Theater. Where were all those people tonight? I realized we were unknowns; nobody cared about us. We finished the first sketch to faint applause. My shirt was wringing wet. Anne said, "Let's get out of here," but I wouldn't leave the stage defeated.

"Let's do 'The Farnsworths,'" I said to Anne, desperation in my voice. I was sure it would take only a few more minutes to grab the audience. We did the sketch—still totally ignored. I was angry. How could the agent not tell us it was an audition and not a booking?

When it was over, we waited for him to come backstage. My black suit was still soaking wet. I felt as if we'd given it our all, and now I wanted some feedback. We did good, I kept telling myself. Where was our agent? The maitre d' told us he had left.

We went home to Washington Heights. Amy was asleep. Eddie Meara, our baby-sitter for the night, asked how the gig went. "Terrible," I told him.

I tried reaching our erstwhile agent for weeks. He never returned our calls. We later learned he was busy booking a new "wunderkind" named Barbra.

We decided to take Art D'Lugoff up on his offer.

"Do you think he heard about how we bombed?" I asked Anne.

"What's the difference," she said. "Let's see if he meant it."

"You mean about the four hundred dollars a week?"

We called him. Art was as good as his word. "You'll open for Herbie Mann for four weeks. What do you say?"

"Terrific!"

There was still life on the planet.

We arrived at the Gate in the afternoon of our opening night. Amy was in a stroller given us by Fritz Weaver and Sylvia Short. We rehearsed "Peaches and the Doctor" as Amy watched. The Village Gate was big on jazz, with comedy the usual opener. Our names boomed out over the loudspeaker. "Here, for their first engagement at the Village Gate, Jerry Stiller and Anne Meara."

I came out as the bogus doctor and talked to the audience about the bomb, and how it was endangering all of us. About the need to stop nuclear testing. They seemed in total agreement. This was not a satirically minded audience, I thought. I then introduced Peaches, who, I said, was working with me to awaken the country to the danger of a nuclear war by bumping the bomb. "We want to bump the bomb," I said. "We need your help."

The onlookers sipped their drinks, chatting quietly among themselves, politely ignoring us. We didn't seem to be interrupting their evening.

"We'd like you all to get up and bump," I said.

No one moved.

"Peaches, tell them to get up and bump."

"Please"—there was a sob in Anne's voice—"please get up and bump for peace."

Nothing.

"Let's get up and sing 'God Bless America,'" I said. "Let's show the Atomic Energy Commission we mean business."

The conversations in the audience continued. No one got up. No one stopped chatting. We started to sing "God Bless America." Anne started to bump. No one responded.

Don't they have any feelings about nuclear testing? I thought. *About the fate of humanity?* I was taking myself seriously. What kind of world are we living in? No one cares about life? This is the Village, the home of Edna St. Vincent Millay, Eugene O'Neill, W. H. Auden, the freethinkers. Don't these people have any social conscience?

"Let's get up and bump each other," Anne's sweet baby voice pleaded with them.

We went from the bomb to "The Farnsworths." Nothing. They're so stupid, I thought. The Village audience, stupid. We finished as Herbie Mann's flute, Willie Bobo's congas, and Dave Pike's vibes softly came on to get us off. Applause, for leaving. In the dressing room, Anne and I pondered what went wrong. They weren't mean, I thought.

"Do we have to do that again tonight?" Anne asked.

"Yeah. Maybe it'll go better the second show."

Art didn't come back to talk to us. Did he see it? *If it was terrible, he'll tell us,* I thought.

For two weeks, twice a night, Anne and I would go out. We'd try new approaches. One night I did ten minutes of talking about anything that came into my mind. D'Lugoff never gave up on us.

Maybe we're not that bad, I kept telling myself. The audiences were always polite. They just talked while we were on. I started thinking perhaps they could not accept the premise that we were actually a doctor and a stripper. It was not believable to them. On Sunday night between shows I said, "This ain't working." Dejected, I said to Anne, "Let's take a walk." Across from the Waverly Theatre on Sixth Avenue was a little park; we sat on a bench. I said, "We have our last show coming up, and I know what's wrong."

"What?"

"The audience doesn't know who we are. We assume too much." The hip Village was not so hip. "We've got to do something they can associate us with."

"Like what?"

"How about a man and a woman?" I said. "Let's put them in a situation that anyone can relate to." On the marquee of the Waverly Theatre facing us I could see the name Ingmar Bergman.

"How about two people who go to an 'Ingmar Bergman' movie? Let's do it."

"Do what?"

"An improvisation, like we did in St. Louis. I'll be Hershey," I said.

"And I'll be Harriet," Anne said.

Right on the park bench, as people were passing by, we worked up an improv. I put my arm around Anne's shoulder.

"Hershey, please," she said. "I'm watching the movie."

"Harriet . . ." I said, pleadingly.

"You're missing the picture. It's Ingomar Bergman. *Please!*"

"I gotta have you."

"Hershey, don't be pushy. Look at the symbolism."

Anne went on and on about the Bergman movie. The more she rejected me, the more passionate I became, begging, imploring her to go to bed with me. Finally I asked for a single kiss.

"Don't get dirty," she said.

"But Harriet, we've been married eight years."

We even had a punch line.

"Come on, let's try it. Our last show of the week," I said.

We went back to the Gate. We were introduced. Anne said, "Ladies and gentlemen, we'd like to show you two people who are at an Ingomar Bergman movie." We did the sketch. Laughs. Laughs! After two weeks, it was like rain after a drought. They loved it. It was so simple. Why didn't we think of this before? You say, "Ladies and gentlemen, we'd like to show you . . ." and suddenly people listen. Hey, we could do this all the time. Red Skelton had said it, Sid Caesar—we learn from the masters.

As we prepared to leave for home, Edith Gordon, who managed the place for Art, said, "Art told me to tell you we have to let you go."

"But we just found it."

"I know. But he wasn't here."

We packed our stuff and left the Gate. Art had been kind enough to keep us for two weeks. "At least he paid us while we bombed," Anne said.

"I know. But we found it tonight. We'll find it again."

After bombing at the Bon Soir and being fired at the Village Gate, trying to support a wife and child led me to the idea of quitting show business and going back once more to selling. I loved cooking, and had a special recipe for Chicken Gai Yung.

I decided I could sell the delicious chicken legs door to door. I told Anne my idea. I'd marinate the legs overnight, broil them in the morning, and then hit every apartment building on the West Side. A dollar a leg. I figured it was an idea whose time had come, and it took me away from the pain of rejection. We'd become rich and possibly franchise the idea. You're sitting at home, watching TV. A knock on the door. "I'm selling Chicken Gai Yung. It's only a buck." Who could resist?

Anne looked at me and started to laugh.

"We're going down to the Phase II tonight and audition. They're looking for an act to take over down there," she announced.

I was out of business before I began.

At this time Vaughn Meader, completing his stint at the Phase II, a little club next door to the Lafayette Bakery, just off Seventh Avenue on Bleecker Street, was about to open at the Blue Angel and attain national acclaim for his Kennedyesque press conferences—but not before putting us on stage at the Village coffee house one rainy Monday night as his replacement.

We inherited his comedic pulpit, and our nightly appearances before a Bleecker Street crowd, mostly wandering in off the sidewalk, gave us a chance to try anything. It was the slow end of Bleecker Street, and people weren't expecting much, so we had lots of opportunity to half-fail. If something did get a laugh, passers-by would peek through the doors out of curiosity to see what was going on. We'd reel them in like fish, with some ad libs and several overlong sketches. One was about a boss and a secretary, based on Paddy Chayevsky's *Middle of the Night;* another had Amy Vanderbilt teaching a bus drivers' courtesy course; and another had TV news correspondent Pauline Frederick interviewing a man named Mr. Jonah who is miraculously swallowed by a whale while visiting his daughter in Miami Beach. We had started to draw audiences and attract attention.

Larry Holofcener, a talent coordinator, came in to check us out for a possible appearance on the Merv Griffin daytime TV show. Larry was also the composer of *Mr. Wonderful* on Broadway, starring Sammy Davis, Jr. He had written the song "Too Close for Comfort," a big hit. After watching our act, Larry came back and suggested some cuts. The next night we tried the revised act and it exploded. Larry then booked us on Merv's show, our first national TV appearance.

The Village was now abuzz about the tall girl and short guy whose names Stiller and Meara sounded like a trucking company. The aficionados of comedy would come back more than once to check us out. I decided that comedians are created like geraniums in a minefield.

Six months later, we were voted *Cue* magazine's 1961 "Comedy Finds of the Year."

Now agents and managers were coming by to catch us. One night after the show, a man came back and introduced himself as Milton Blackstone. He was distinguished looking and wore a business suit, hardly anything like the Village types who dressed down. An uptown guy, I thought.

"I like your work very much," he said. "Can we talk someplace?"

The only space available was our cellar dressing room. It was very damp, and we could sometimes hear the rumble of the Seventh Avenue subway beneath us. A piece of burlap served as a ceiling. To complicate things, a rat, huge and aged, also made his home somewhere in the sagging burlap. We invited Mr. Blackstone downstairs, where with no objection he took a seat on a mildewed couch. The damp, murky cellar didn't seem to bother him.

"I manage Eddie Fisher," he said quietly. "And I like you two and your act very much."

"Thank you," Anne said in a subdued voice. Was this for real?

I could feel the excitement fill me. I couldn't believe we were sitting in our dungeon of iniquity while the manager of one of the biggest names of that day was sitting two feet away, telling us this.

"I'd like to manage you," Milton Blackstone said.

I turned to Anne. She looked at me with a kind of "he's got to be kidding" smile.

"I'm serious," Mr. Blackstone said. Seeing our faces, he went on. "Let me tell you what I have in mind. Eddie's going into the Winter Garden, and I'd love you to be on the bill with him."

Just then, above our visitor, the burlap moved. The rat was walking across. It was slow motion, like a drunken circus acrobat-clown staggering his way across on a high wire above a net. I prayed that Mr. Blackstone would not see it, for fear that it would blow everything, that he'd run out to the street and forget he'd ever seen us.

The rat seemed to sense this. He stopped, turned around, and discreetly headed back. I looked straight ahead during the whole process.

"Well, what do you think?" Blackstone asked.

Anne and I sat silent.

"You want to think about it?" he asked.

"Yes, we'd like that," Anne said.

"Give me a call," he said, handing us his card and leaving. There was no pressure from him. It was all just matter-of-fact. Are the big boys like this? I wondered. He didn't act like he was anybody. He was a gentleman. He'd acted like we were stars, even in that place. He'd treated us as if we were stars.

Anne and I went upstairs and sat at an empty table.

"Did you see the rat?" I asked.

"No, where was he?" Anne said.

"In the burlap. I thought he'd fall through and land on Blackstone's head. That would have been the end of everything. Well, what do you think?" I asked.

"About what?" Anne said.

"About going into the Winter Garden. With Eddie Fisher."

"I'm not sure," Anne said.

"What do you mean?"

"We're not ready yet. It scares me."

I sat speechless. I knew she was right, but how do you turn down a thing like that?

"We've got to wait," Anne said. "He knows we're good, but he also knows we're not ready. He just wants us. It's good that he wants us; it means other people will want us too."

After Milton Blackstone there were lots of others. We asked ourselves who we wanted; who would take us to the next level? Was there someone out there who saw something special in us, someone who could help boost us to the top?

Jack Rollins was our manager of choice. He had thrust Woody Allen and Mike and Elaine into prominence. He had an amazing eye for what was new, and he could market talent.

I called Jack and asked if he'd come down to the Phase II to see us. He and his partner Chuck Joffe obliged. That night, after the performance, the four of us sat together in the empty coffeehouse. "What did you think?" we asked. Anne and I were praying that this was our man.

Immediately, I knew we were not his cup of tea. "I think you're both talented, but I can't handle you." If he rejected us, we must be less than perfect, to say the least. Out of desperation I said, "Jack, is there anything you saw tonight that you liked?" Maybe I was begging for a hit on the head, but if this man is the top of the line, perhaps he could pass on some piece of wisdom we could use.

He then mentioned the sketch in which Anne, as Amy Vanderbilt, lectured me, a New York City bus driver, on the rules of etiquette.

"That's it?" I said.

"That's it, Jerry."

My heart sank. "Well, do you have any advice for us?"

"Yeah," Jack said. "Wear a suit with a shirt and tie, and Anne, you put on a nice dress. Get rid of the ponchos." Ponchos were the "in" thing in the '60s. Folksingers, like the Kingston Trio, were wearing them at the time, and we did too.

With that, he and Joffe said goodnight.

Anne and I sat a little bewildered. The whole world wanted us, but we couldn't get the one manager we wanted. When we got home, I looked at Anne and said, "This guy knows something. Tomorrow night I'm wearing a suit and tie."

The next night we came out dressed as Rollins had advised. I looked like Madison Avenue. Anne looked like a young schoolteacher, and bingo!—laughs like we'd never had before. Something about my being in a suit and Anne in a proper dress, in Greenwich Village, made us funnier. Who would think it? I thank Jack Rollins for that advice to this day.

Marty Farrell, a young comedy writer, came in a couple of weeks later. He had written for Jackie Mason and Topo Gigio, the Italian mouse character on the *The Ed Sullivan Show*. Farrell came back one night and said, "I usually never tell comedians how much I like them. They usually get suspicious. But I had to tell you how much I love you guys. Would you mind if I brought a friend of mine down to see you?"

"No," we said.

His friend was a young lawyer named Bob Chartoff, who at the time was managing a stable of comics including Jackie Mason, Charlie Callas, and Jackie Vernon.

Chartoff came to see us at Phase II. He too visited our damp dressing room. "I think you two are wonderful, and I'd love to manage you," he said. He was very matter of fact.

"Really? Why?"

"I'll make you lots of money," he said. "You'll travel all over the world and meet presidents." I sensed this guy was serious.

"How do you know you can do all this?" I asked.

He said, "I'll give you a thousand dollars."

I laughed. It sounded like a bribe. "What would I need with a thousand bucks?" I asked.

"Buy some clothes for you and Anne," Bob said. "You'll pay me back."

I looked at Bob. Anne looked at Bob. His thick glasses magnified the pupils of his eyes. There was a silence. I could see Bob was a gambler, a guy who would bet money on anything.

"You're a gambler," I said.

"Yeah, I love it." There was no macho in his voice. He just meant it. I looked at Anne.

"We'll let you know," I said.

"Okay," he said. When he left, Anne and I quickly agreed that this was the guy for us. We signed on.

A few weeks later Bob induced Max Gordon, the legendary co-owner of the Blue Angel and the Village Vanguard, the jazz spot on Seventh Avenue, to come down to see us. When Max left, Bob said, "He likes you. You're going on at the Blue Angel." The Angel had made big names of Mike and Elaine, Shelley Berman, Mort Sahl, Carol Burnett, and Vaughn Meader.

Six weeks after Bob first spoke with us we were heading for a Sunday-night special guest audition at the Blue Angel. I wondered if this was going to be another Bon Soir disaster. As we pulled up in our '56 Chrysler, Sonny, the doorman, who'd been at the Angel since forever, said, "You're gonna make it tonight, kids. Let me park it." As he slid in behind the wheel, I prayed it wouldn't stall.

We walked through the fabled doors on East 55th Street. Bobby Short's trio was uptempoing "I've Got Your Number." The room was packed. Max Gordon, a small, balding man from Eugene, Oregon, met us and escorted us backstage.

"How do you guys feel?"

"Nervous," Anne said.

"It's natural," Max said softly. "Carol Burnett felt the same way. She went on for me on a Sunday and CBS saw her." She became a star, and it could happen to us, he seemed to be saying.

"Listen, you can do fifteen minutes and we'll see. I love that thing you do, 'Jonah and the Whale.' Who wrote that?"

"We did it based on my uncle," I told him.

Meader was onstage, winding up his presidential press conference, taking questions from the audience.

"You'll follow him. You can do it, I'm sure," Max said.

The audience and Meader were in synch. His Kennedy was more an essence than an impression. It was brilliant because he captured Kennedy's psyche. The audience wouldn't let him off. They kept asking one more question.

"He's a tough act to follow," Max said. "You have to go on right away. Otherwise they want to pay their checks, and they're walking out while you're on. You gotta grab 'em. I'll see ya."

He disappeared as Meader finished. I saw Henry Morgan, the acerbic and hilarious radio wit, who'd been at the bar, slip into the back of the room.

"Ladies and gentlemen, for the first time at the Blue Angel, Jerry Stiller and Anne Meara." We walked on. Anne's opening line, "Ladies and gentlemen," spoken with hesitancy as if she was not really sure they were ladies and gentlemen, was immediately picked up on. "We're just two people—"

"—Actors," I interjected. It brought a laugh.

"—Who do these things up here." She sounded like someone studying to be a nun. "Yeah, you see, what we do up here in front of you allows you to get in touch with your own feelings."

"This is called catharsis," I said.

"And you feel better afterwards," Anne said.

Tremendous laugh. Bigger than we ever got at Phase II. I instantly realized that in an uptown nightclub, when people pay big money, they laugh louder. These people could have seen us last night for a buck at the Phase II. We went over big and stayed on for thirty minutes.

When it was over, whistles, cheers. They clapped with their hands above their heads like they wanted us to know it. They're all hip. We've made it. The Upper East Side chic. It's the way I dreamed it. "You're clever, witty . . . we love you." Somebody shouted, "A little like Mike and Elaine, but hey, these guys are married!"

We walked off. The room was still applauding.

"Go ahead, take a bow," Max Gordon said.

Max hired us and we ended up working at the Angel off and on for fourteen weeks with Phyllis Diller, Barbra Streisand, Rolf Harris, The Tarriers, and Carol Sloan. Sometimes we'd open, sometimes go on second, and sometimes last. We earned $300 a week. Bob Chartoff had taken us out of the coffeehouse and up to the glamorous East Side. Each night, Sonny the doorman parked our '56 Chrysler, and at 1 A.M. we returned to our Washington Heights apartment at Riverside Drive and 160th Street, where Ed Meara, now retired from the American Radiator Company, baby-sat Amy.

We needed new material. We had to come up with something for people who stayed for the second show. When we were on first, they would sometimes stick around to see if we'd really ad-libbed it the first time. Bob Chartoff asked if we wanted to hear some stuff that two guys named Kander and Ebb had written.

"We can do our own stuff. We don't need anybody," I said. "Besides, I never heard of them." They had not yet written "New York, New York" or *Cabaret*.

In one year, from 1961 to 1962, we'd gone from the Phase II on Bleecker Street to the Blue Angel on East 55th and then got our biggest break, *The Ed Sullivan Show*.

When Bob Chartoff told us we were booked on Sullivan it shocked us. We were right out of a coffeehouse. Is this the direction we wanted to go?

I asked myself. The truth was, we had no idea where we were going with our lives, let alone our careers.

I wondered how many Sawyer Falk students got to do comedy on the "Really Big Show"? I'd been a kid watching vaudeville stars, and now Anne and I would be on the same bill with the greats. But, I asked myself, Do I really belong up here with, say, Jimmy Durante?

I asked Bob, "How did this happen?"

Ed Sullivan saw the kinescope of "Jonah and the Whale" on Merv Griffin's show and loved it.

I also had to believe Ed connected with Anne and me. His wife Sylvia was Jewish. But we knew this was the big break—and we had to deliver.

One afternoon, around that time, I took a walk through Central Park, going over new material in my head. I left the park and walked out on the Upper East Side. I passed a brownstone that had a sign that read Metropolitan Psychoanalytic Institute. I rang the bell and asked to see someone. I didn't have an appointment, just a look on my face that said, *Take this guy in immediately.*

I was ushered in to meet a gentleman in his sixties who wore thick-lensed glasses and a business suit, and spoke with a soft German accent. It was like meeting Freud himself. I knew on the spot that I would like this fatherly, sensitive man who, just on sight, knew I needed help. Somebody who could figure out why I was sad, weepy, and fearful just when we were signed to do three Ed Sullivan shows.

"Why are you here?" he asked.

"I'm sad."

"How sad?"

"Very."

"Do you want to kill yourself?"

The thought had never entered my mind until that moment. I realized instantly that this was the reason I was being seen so quickly. I was somewhat amazed that anyone would care. It dawned on me how lucky I was that I didn't want to kill myself. It lifted me just to realize that.

"What do you do?" he asked.

"I'm a comedian."

"Oh," he said. It seemed to intrigue him. "Are you funny?"

"Yes, believe it or not, when I'm on stage—so I think."

"Are you working?"

"Yes."

"Where are you playing now?"

"The Blue Angel," I said.

"What's the problem?" he asked.

"I freeze before starting a sketch. It started a while ago. It's very upsetting. I must come to see you."

"I think we can help you," he said.

His manner was comforting, like that of a grandfather. I immediately felt a great affection toward this man. His accent itself made me feel safe. A Freudian accent is very reassuring, I told myself. This man through his knowledge would take care of me.

"Can you afford fifteen dollars a week?" he asked.

"I think so," I said.

"And come for therapy twice a week?"

Twice? That bad, I thought. "Yes," I said, thrilled that I could see this man twice a week. I felt better already.

"You're going to treat me," I said gratefully.

"No, not me," he said. "You need a better detective than me. I teach, and the man you will have is also a teacher. I'm sure it will work out."

Who could be better than Dr. Freud himself?

My seeing a shrink was admitting that I was now overwhelmed by forces I could not see or understand. I was desperate enough to put my life in the hands of a stranger. I needed someone who could help me untangle knots that I had tied myself into and I couldn't unravel.

I had read Erich Fromm. I had read *Our Inner Conflict* by Karen Horney and identified with every psychological dysfunction described in the book. I finally had to stop reading.

My hangup was the hesitancy that came over me before I would start a sketch. It would stop me from saying my first line. Why was this happening when we were doing so well? What if I froze on the Sullivan show?

I wanted the doctor to zap it. I needed a kernel of understanding of what was causing this and an insight that would free me from the terror I was now experiencing. Help me, doctor. Give me a mantra that I can use. One word that will free me to soar creatively like I know I can.

All this wonderful material we had written—and me frozen. Free me of this existential hell I've put myself into.

When I entered into analysis I wondered whether another human being could help me, just by talking. If so, did his brain really understand mine? Did he ever experience this himself? I somehow assumed that he had traveled the same route and therefore could help me.

My newly assigned psychiatrist looked like a leading man. We talked about my Jewish background, and he told me what it was like growing up Catholic in the Midwest. Wow, not Jewish, not from New York: a new look in shrinks. The all-American type. All my self-hate at being Jewish—repressed, of course—could come out just by looking at this guy. If only I could be like him. Become the all-American Jew.

He sat in front of me in a chair. I too was sitting in a chair. (Where was the couch? What do I want for fifteen bucks?) He taught other psychiatrists, he told me.

The phone would ring during our sessions. "Pardon me," the doctor would say, and he would take the call. Why would he do this, I asked myself. Is this part of the treatment? Was he testing me? Why not ask him, I wondered to myself. Of course he'll say, "Yes, it's part of the treatment, I'm glad you asked that." So I didn't mention it. I realize now that if I could have mentioned it then, I wouldn't have had to be in therapy in the first place.

I also wondered whether I'd be treated differently if I were paying twenty-five bucks a session. Would he have shut off the phone?

I droned on about my childhood—growing up poor, the Depression. How for the first time I was making some money.

"What's wrong with money?" he asked.

I found it difficult to answer that question.

"What's bothering you? What's wrong with money?" he asked again.

He's going to raise the fee, I said to myself. I've been here twice and he's sucked me in. He's going to want twenty bucks next time.

"Tell me about money," he persisted.

I exhaled deeply. "I got this thing about money," I said. "I feel like . . ."

"So you hate money," he said. "You know where that comes from, don't you?"

"Where?"

"Money is the root of all evil. 'The poor shall inherit the Kingdom of Heaven.' That's what it says in the Bible."

"But I love money," I said. "Someday I'm going to have a lot of it. I'd like to give you a lot of money. Buy you a town house," I blurted out, feeling like a jerk.

On our many sessions we talked about everything but the act. I was afraid to bring it up. I wondered if he had been down to see us perform at the Blue Angel. It seemed to me that that would be uppermost in his mind. He could see firsthand what I was referring to when I mentioned the freeze.

I asked him if he'd seen Anne and me perform.

"No," he said.

I told myself he's lying; he had seen us but didn't want to tell me.

"How could you be treating a comedian without watching his work?" I asked.

"I'd rather not see your work," he said.

"Why?" I asked weakly.

"I'm treating the whole person, not the performer," the doctor said.

Was he telling me if I were emotionally more stable I wouldn't be on the stage? That my need to perform was a symptom of some emotional sickness? Was I the character in the old circus joke: A man is sweeping up elephant manure; somebody tells him to quit. "What," he says, "and give up showbiz?"

I thought if becoming a great performer means I'm nuts, then I want to be nuts. I want to be *more* nuts. The more nuts the more success. I want to be the nuttiest comedian in the world. My real trouble is I'm not sick enough. But I never said that to the shrink. Instead, I thought he was informing me that he was just dying to see me do my stuff but was repressing his feelings.

I looked up. His eyes were shut. He was dozing. "You're asleep," I said, surprising myself with my frankness as his eyes blinked open. How long had he been out, I wondered. Now, I wondered whether the time I'd spent spewing out my deepest secrets had any meaning at all. When I asked why he'd been asleep, his answer was that I hadn't been saying anything interesting. Being the sickee, I could possibly agree with that.

Was I a boring patient, which also made me a bore?

The treatments continued. During one session I asked, heart in mouth, "By the way, did you see us on *Sullivan* last Sunday?" We had been on for over a year. I was hesitant, afraid to hear his opinion. Maybe he hated us, or hadn't watched the show. Then I would have really hated him, and myself for asking.

"Is that important to what's going on here?" he asked.

In my mind it was the most important thing in the world, but I couldn't bring myself to say it. If he had seen me on *Ed Sullivan* and said he hated me, I would have been destroyed. That bothered me.

I readily accepted his non-answer without pushing it further.

When he'd asked about hobbies, I confided that I had none. He listened intently as I proudly listed the many pastimes I'd scrupulously avoided. I don't play bridge or poker. I don't play golf or tennis, and I don't go dancing. "I don't even go to the movies," I said.

"Why not?"

"I'm not in any of them."

"What do you do?"

"I jog at the Y. I love watching basketball, but I'm lousy at it."

"Let's shoot some baskets some day," the analyst said.

"You mean that?"

"Sure. Someday."

At one of the sessions he suggested we go to a comedy club. I took him at his word and brought him to the Improv. Dick Cavett was on. When Dick finished his set, I introduced them, not mentioning to Cavett that the other man was my shrink.

"Why are you so hostile, Dick?" the doctor asked. Cavett gave me a look and we said good-night. A few minutes later Milt Kamen, friend and brilliant satirist, got up to perform.

When Kamen finished, the shrink said, "Why don't you introduce me to him?" I couldn't believe the same thing would happen twice so I naively agreed. "Why are you so hostile, Milt?" he asked. "Hostile" was the *in* word in psychiatry. Milt said to me, "Is he a shrink?" And I laughed. We said good-night.

When I asked the doc why he had done what he did, he replied, "Because I was being direct, which is what you should try to be." I wondered if he wasn't right. I was never direct.

The following week he asked if I'd like to shoot baskets at the Y. I didn't hesitate. I came to the conclusion he was an avant-garde shrink. Go with it. Maybe I'd learn something. We met at the Y, changed into our gym stuff, got on the court, and started shooting baskets.

He was taller than me and better. He made his shots. "You gotta get different shots," he advised. Is this some kind of metaphor for my life? Were we playing hoops, or analyzing? Go with it, I told myself again.

We played one-on-one. I played hard. He beat me. I figured he was still analyzing. When we finished, he said, "Let's take a shower." I knew he wasn't gay. In the shower we looked at each other. His eyes dropped, and I knew why we were here. He looked at my penis. I didn't look at his. I was afraid to. Was his bigger than mine? Would it make a difference?

"You have to learn a few more shots," he said kind of cryptically as we toweled off and got dressed.

He didn't charge me for the session in the gym.

At the next session in his office we talked about penis size and its re-lationship to the sexual act. He spoke in medical terms. He didn't embar-rass me. When I left that afternoon, I was gratified that some part of me was bigger than I had allowed myself to imagine.

In the ensuing sessions we spoke about my freezing on stage during the act. Nightclubs were getting Anne and me off the ground. I told him I'd made more money in the past year than in my entire theatrical career, but after expenses I had barely enough to pay for the analysis.

He looked at me and said, "What are you complaining about? You're already making more than me."

I couldn't believe my ears. Was he serious? Was this a psychological ploy? Another avant-garde shtick? Perhaps he was tricking me into re-vealing some hidden repression. If so, a feather in his cap for getting me a step up on my id.

He suggested Anne join the sessions, which she agreed to. The three of us had very little rapport together. At one of the single sessions, I men-tioned the possibility of leaving Anne. There was a long pause.

"You gotta be strong about this," he said. I knew then that I had to leave *him*. I had been with him about five years by that point. Why? Schmuck bait.

On the night of our first *Sullivan* show we learned we would be on with Ella Fitzgerald and Jimmy Durante.

We were last on the bill. Thank God we didn't have to follow Durante. I was grateful and less scared. We had the dressing room on the top floor. We took the elevator down from there as our turn came close.

We heard Jimmy Durante doing his stuff on stage. The sound of his voice brought me back to seeing him at Loew's State. I was maybe eleven. The movie was Max Fleischer's *Gulliver's Travels,* one of the first feature-length cartoons but my father and mother had really taken us three kids to see Durante. On the bill were Jesse Block and Eve Sully, a husband-and-wife comedy team. They did about fifteen minutes and were funny. And then Clayton, Jackson, and Durante came on:

The house lights go up. The music blares "Who Will Be with You When I'm Far Away, When I'm Far Away from You?," and Jimmy Durante struts out, hat in hand and face in profile, showing off that wonderful schnozz. The audience applauds, a full house at the morning show. It's like the greatest event in history. He grabs the microphone like he's going to choke it. The music, the trumpets, the trombones, quiet momentarily. "Good morning, ladies and gentlemen. This is Jimmy, and I'm glad you all could be here at these prices."

"Who Will Be with You When I'm Far Away? . . ." The audience applauds. Eddie Jackson shouts, "Sing it, Jimmy boy." Eddie Jackson, with a top hat and cane, provides a high falsetto harmony as he starts to cakewalk behind Jimmy, bumping him along. Durante, annoyed, tries to maintain his cool dignity. Jackson keeps bumping him. Jimmy shows frustration as Jackson, singing a cappella, seems to be off on his own, distracting Jimmy. Totally frustrated, Jimmy flaps his arms down against his thighs, making a slapping sound. The audience is stifling its laughter. "Stop the music, stop the music," Jimmy demands. Silence, total silence in the theater. There's a slight noise. Durante turns and says, "Surrounded by assassins." The music starts again. "I'm Jimmy, that well-dressed man." Once more the great schnozzola is struttin'.

Jimmy sits at the piano, starts to play some arpeggios. A pianist on the opposite side of the stage does likewise. Jimmy does one arpeggio. The other piano does exactly the same arpeggio but adds a note. Jimmy suppresses his indignation. He is now engaged in a duel of arpeggios. The piano player matches Jimmy each time and adds a note. Jimmy finally rips off part of the upright and hurls it across the stage, chasing the other guy off.

My mother and father are laughing. When I see my mother and father laugh, I'm happy. Jimmy now explains to the audience that he had a lot of trouble getting this engagement. "They said I wasn't high-class enough to play Loew's State, that I didn't have a tuxedo. I want you to know I'm wearing tails."

Jimmy removes his tails. He calls Jesse Block on stage. "Jesse, come on out here." Block comes out. "I want you to show every person in this audience my tails." Jimmy hands Block the tails. "Put on your house lights," Jimmy tells the electrician. All the lights in the theater go up. Loew's State has become a courtroom. *Jimmy vs. The State*—Loew's State. We are the jury. Block is walking into the audience, showing us Jimmy's full dress outfit. We are all laughing. I want to get up there and be like him. I want to make people laugh.

"Show the audience my tails, Jesse. Show them to 'em. And they said I couldn't play Loew's State." ·

The tails are passed down a row. "Feel it. Let the people feel the material, Jesse. Show 'em how strong it is." Now the people in their seats are feeling Jimmy's tails. "And they said I couldn't play Loew's State." A huge laugh. "Show 'em how strong those tails are, Jesse. Pull 'em apart."

"What?" Jesse asks, "Are you sure, Jimmy?"

"Do it!" Jimmy says.

Jesse yanks the tails. Rrrip! The tails split. There is an ominous silence followed by snickers. Jimmy's face is now a mask of indignation like he's been betrayed. "Get off the floor, get off the floor!" Durante barks. Block half-walks, half-runs into the wings.

I look at my mother and father, who are are in tears from laughing. Arnie and Doreen are also laughing. We are a family. I don't want to ever go home again. I want to be in this place forever.

The show ends and we leave. We are back out on Broadway. It's one o'clock in the afternoon. We get on the subway and go back to Brooklyn. Something has happened to me. I'll never be the same again.

I snapped back to the present, to Anne and me standing in the wings waiting to go on. "Ladies and gentlemen, for the first time on our show, Stiller and Mara!" Ed Sullivan had mispronounced Anne's last name. We did "Jonah and the Whale." When we got back to the dressing room, Bob Chartoff said, "You were wonderful. He wants to sign you for three more shows. By the way, Anne, didn't he call you 'Mara'?"

"Yeah," Anne replied. "That's the way it's pronounced in Gaelic."

And that's the way Ed Sullivan pronounced it thirty-six times over the next seven years.

The sketch that was the breakthrough for us was the meeting of Hershey Horowitz and Mary Elizabeth Doyle through a computer dating service. The William Morris Agency, where we had gone to discuss our future, told us Ed Sullivan would never allow this sketch on the air. When we asked why, the agency said because most of the country was Protestant.

Sullivan let us run with it.

Here's how the first Hershey and Elizabeth sketch opened.

ANNE: Ladies and gentlemen, we'd like to show you two single people who, having been matched up by a computer, are meeting for the first time.

JERRY: How do you do?

ANNE: How do you do?

JERRY: I'm Hershey Horowitz.

ANNE: I'm Mary Elizabeth Doyle.

JERRY: Doyle?

ANNE: Yeah. . . . Horowitz?

JERRY: Horowitz. . . . H-o-r-o-w-i-t-z. Hershey. . . . My friends call me Hesh.

ANNE: Doyle. . . . D-o-y-l-e. My friends call me Mary Elizabeth.

JERRY: Is Doyle your real name?

ANNE: Well, sure. Why wouldn't it be my real name?

JERRY: I don't know. . . . I was just hoping.

ANNE: No, no . . . we're Doyles. You see, we're Dempseys on my mother's side.

JERRY: Dempsey, huh?

ANNE: Horowitz?

JERRY: Yeah. Shmulowitz on my mother's side. This computer is supposed to be a very good thing . . . I was reading about it in the *New York*—

ANNE: It's scientifically worked out so you can't make any—

JERRY: —mistakes. . . . Mary Elizabeth, you come from a large family?

ANNE: Me? Sure!

JERRY: I mean, you have a lot of sisters . . . ?

ANNE: In my family I got plenty of sisters. . . . Sister Mary Monica, Sister Bernadette Marie, Sister Mary Virginia. . . . Do you have any brothers and sisters?

JERRY: Three brothers . . .

ANNE: Oh . . .

JERRY: Buch, Bujie, and Sol.

ANNE: Buck?

JERRY: No, no, Buch. B . . . uch.

ANNE: Buck?

JERRY: No, it's Bu-uch.

ANNE: Bu-uck.

JERRY: No. . . . Bu-uch.

ANNE: Bu-uch . . . oooh! I think I hurt myself.

JERRY: Where do you live?

ANNE: Me? I'm from Flatbush.

JERRY: So am I. East 42nd Street.

ANNE: That's my block. . . . *I* live on East 42nd Street!

JERRY: How do you like that.

ANNE: Hey, do you know Richie Flanagan?

JERRY: No. . . . Do you know Moishe Bader?

ANNE: No, I don't know any Moishes. I'd know—

JERRY: Do you know Stanley Auster?

ANNE: No, I don't know him either.

JERRY: Adolph Hausman?

ANNE: Do you know Tommy Toohey?

JERRY: Tommy Toohey? No, I don't know Tommy Toohey.

ANNE: Timothy Sheehy?

JERRY: No, I don't know Timothy Sheehy.

ANNE: Vinnie Dougherty?

JERRY: Vinnie Dougherty? I don't know him either, no. Do you know Raymond Kisch?

ANNE: Kisch? No, I don't know any Kisches.

JERRY: Leon Wahaftig? Seymore Ehrenpreis?

ANNE: Eleanor Dempsey?

JERRY: I don't know her, no. . . .

ANNE: Patsy Jo Shannon?

JERRY: Patsy Jo Shannon? I don't know her. . . . Well, that's a pretty big block, that 42nd Street.

ANNE: Very long . . .

JERRY: Listen, you like to dance?

ANNE: Oh, I'm crazy about dancing.

JERRY: Well, maybe we can go dancing some night.

ANNE: Oh, I'd love that. Do you wanna go dancing tonight?

JERRY: I'd love to go dancing tonight.

ANNE: They're having a dance tonight at my Sodality.

JERRY: At your what?

ANNE: My Sodality.

JERRY: What's that?

ANNE: Well, it's a girls' organization in my parish.

JERRY: You mean like the Hadassah?

ANNE: What's that?

JERRY: It's a girls' organization in my parish.

ANNE: This computer . . . it really . . .

JERRY: Oh yeah. . . . It really did a job on us there, didn't it? . . .

That night Hershey and Mary Elizabeth got a tremendous audience response. Ed's eyes watered as we performed. He called us over and said to us on the air, "Someday they're going to change all that in Rome."

When I thanked him later, he said smilingly, "I loved the sketch but these mixed marriages, they never work out."

The next day at the YMHA when I was in the sauna, Georgie Lieberman, one of the directors there, said to me, "I saw you on *Sullivan* last night."

"Did you like the sketch?" I asked.

"Forget the sketch," he said. "It's what Sullivan said about changing things in Rome. Is he going to talk to the Pope?"

Some weeks later Ed confided to me, "We got lots of nice mail on the last sketch you did between the Jewish boy and the Irish girl."

"From the Catholics or the Jews?" I asked.

"The Lutherans," he replied. "They all want kinescopes."

Ed Sullivan had a great sense of humor. He especially loved comedians. One day I mentioned that the *Dean Martin Show* was taped. They cut out the bad parts and sweetened it by adding laugh tracks.

"Wouldn't it take a lot of pressure off if you taped your show?"

"But it isn't honest, Jerry."

"But what about when the comedians aren't funny and bomb?"

"Yeah," he said, "but it's honest."

Of course, I was thinking of how it could lighten our load. Ed knew the audience brings out the best in you. He was right.

I think our sketches grew on Ed, and he'd often call us over for a quick on-camera chat. "Come over here," he'd say waving at us after we finished. He'd ask some questions—like "What's a *megillah*?"—and we'd have two seconds to answer. The call-over meant he liked you and the audience liked you, and you'd be back.

Ed loved everything we did until we performed our astronaut sketch. We had just finished the Sunday-afternoon dress rehearsal. In the sketch, Walter Flonkite (me) interviews a weeping woman (Anne) whom he mistakes for the mother of an astronaut who's just completed the first manned space flight.

"How does it feel to be the mother of an astronaut?" Flonkite asks.

The lady replies, "I'm not the mother, I'm the cleaning woman."

Flonkite, nonplussed, forges ahead.

"Why are you crying?" he asks.

"I have to clean it, Walter, clean the capsule. You don't know what it's like in there."

The rehearsal audience laughed hard. The sketch was topical, Alan Shepard's historic flight still being fresh in everyone's mind.

Off-camera, Ed Sullivan's face turned beet red. He had always trusted our taste. As the make-believe interview continues, the cleaning woman gets more and more graphic about what a mess the capsule is. Who doesn't laugh at bathroom references? Before she can say the "s" word Flonkite cuts her off with, "Be sure to be with us next time for the launching of Gemini, the twin capsule."

"Two of them!" Anne screams. "I can't handle it!" Lots of laughs.

When the dress rehearsal ended, Sullivan's producer, Bob Precht, sent word that Ed would like to see us.

"We'll see what he has to say," Bob Chartoff said, leading the way to Ed's second-floor office. He knocked on Ed's door. Precht opened it.

"Come on in," he said. "Ed wants to talk to you."

I walked in. The door behind me slammed shut. I realized immediately I was alone with Ed Sullivan. I'd somehow lost Chartoff and Anne.

Sullivan, standing in the middle of the room and very upset, asked, "How could you bring in a piece like that?" He was clearly holding back his anger.

"Because it's funny," was all I could think of saying. There was a pause.

With disbelief in his voice, he said, "Do you know what this sketch is about?"

"It's about a cleaning woman who's cleaning a space capsule," I said, playing bewilderment.

"It's about s--t!" he said.

The reason I was alone arguing the merits of our sketch with Ed Sullivan was that Ed was so furious he didn't want a woman in the room. Bob Chartoff just never made it through the door.

"I've got it here," Ed said, pressing down the "play" switch on a reel-to-reel tape recorder. "Do you want to hear it, Jerry? It's not funny." I listened. There were laughs. I felt abandoned—the lone sailor on a raft, lost at sea with no compass. Suddenly I felt responsible for foisting bad taste on Ed Sullivan and his worldwide audience. Why me? Was I the sacrificial lamb?

"Do you know what this sketch is about?" Sullivan repeated. I looked him squarely in the eye and said, "Mr. Sullivan, this is a sketch about a woman who cleans a space capsule."

With a look of mild surprise and without missing a beat, Ed said, "Well, you're not going to do it on my show, Jerry. You and Anne have done too many good things to blow it now. I won't allow you to do this kind of material." His eyes turned soft. He suddenly became very fatherly. "You can do an old piece tonight, and come back in a couple of weeks with something new."

In seconds, his anger had dissipated. I had made the biggest name in show business mad. Was I that important? For an instant, I no longer resented Anne or Bob. I actually wanted to thank them for giving me the chance to prove I had balls enough to stand up to Sullivan, although no one was there to witness it. Downstairs I said to Anne, "He wants us to do an old piece of material."

We did as he asked, but I figured Sullivan had had it with us. This was the kiss-off. I was wrong. Ed was true to his word. Six weeks later we were back on his show.

What was it like being on the most popular television show of its day all those years? Anne would say, "It was what Jerry wanted." I think she was really a reluctant traveler, unlike me—the Brooklyn kid who aspired to be a vaudevillian. Never did Anne mention that her dream in life was to someday appear on *The Ed Sullivan Show.* Nor did she ever aspire to be another Gracie Allen, with me as the straight man. Her love was theater, the stage.

"I love Kim Stanley. If I could only be as good as her."

But could Kim Stanley get laughs, I asked. Somehow I'd schlepped this beautiful young acting wunderkind into my dream world, and she'd married me into the bargain. She was living *my* dream.

I wanted to be a comedian so badly that when Anne came into my life I figured the two of us would do it together. Doing an act together would satisfy my dream, and we'd *tummel* through life as husband and wife. What *chutzpah*. Did I want a wife or a comedy partner? Good, sweet-natured Irish people, they'll go along with anything—up to a point.

Anne went along just as some vast sea change was taking place in 1960s comedy fashions. Comedians were going cerebral, developing a new style from classroom exercises. Improvisation, which goes back to *commedia dell'arte,* was all the rage. All this school stuff was birthing a new intellectual connection with the audiences. The old titans of laughter were being replaced by New Age comics.

Mike and Elaine had suddenly come onto the scene. Shelley Berman. Dick Shawn, Flip Wilson, Bill Cosby, Pat Morita, who talked about his Japanese-American heritage. Jack Burns and Avery Schreiber, who also were funny doing ethnic comedy. George Carlin. Mort Sahl. David Frye. Richard Pryor. Vaughn Meader and the Kennedy press conference. The doors of comedy were now open to a new breed. Lenny Bruce would kick those doors open even wider.

As a result of the *Sullivan* show, we were in demand and began to tour. Bob Chartoff called us. "The Establishment in London wants you and Anne to fly over." It was 1963 and the Establishment's four stars—Dudley Moore, Peter Cook, Jonathan Miller, and Alan Bennett—were at that moment performing their show, *Beyond the Fringe,* on Broadway. Lenny Bruce, who was to take over at the Establishment in the interim, had been banned the night before by the Lord Chancellor—the official censor—after a reported onstage altercation between Bruce and Siobhan McKenna in which, it was said, fists flew and blood flowed.

"They've heard great reports about you two, and want you to replace Lenny. You open tomorrow night."

Words like this brought me back to life and thawed the onstage freeze. With additional *Sullivan* bookings coming up, we were certainly on a roll.

Within hours we decided to go to London. But what about Amy? Our friends Ursula and Pat Campbell agreed to care for her for the length of the three-week London engagement. We flew the Atlantic.

Cook, Moore, Miller, and Bennett had spawned an audience who treated acts the way the British Parliament treats its members. They hiss you if they hate you and stamp their feet if they approve.

The folksingers who opened for us got boos. "Rubbish! Rubbish!" one highly vocal patron bellowed. We were terrified. The manager of the club did his best to put us at ease. We had barely an hour to rehearse our New York–oriented material, in the wild hope that it would be understood by these Anglos. There was no time to wonder. The urgency of the situation must have blasted my freeze away. We did our act, about fifty minutes, and the English audience ate us up. At the end they stamped and then rose for an ovation. We suddenly felt international.

As we passed through the audience, the boisterous patron whom I had heard earlier stopped us and offered his congratulations in a thick Irish accent. "I'm Dominick Behan, Brendan's brother. You were terrific. Both of you."

"Thanks," I said. "But you hated the other act?"

"Rubbish!" he roared. "They were terrible. If you were terrible, I'd say, 'Rubbish,' but you weren't."

The three weeks in London were a great success for us. Bernard Levin, the toughest London reviewer, gave us a rave in *The Daily Mail*.

During the run, we resided at Olivelli's, a theatrical hotel in Bloomsbury. The hallways were filled with photos and letters from acts such as the Marx Brothers, thanking the hotel for its hospitality. One such letter was charred as if burned in a fire. It was from Ben Dova, a juggler I'd seen at the Roxy Theater as a boy. Typewritten at the bottom were the words, "Mail Salvaged from the Hindenburg." Here we were performing in London, married nine years, and wondering how life had changed us.

We flew back to New York and our apartment in Washington Heights. We had not seen Amy for three weeks, and in that time she had started to put words together. I figured she must have wondered, "Where the hell have those two been?"

The success of our London engagement started us on a cross-country tour, beginning in Detroit. We opened a week after the terrible race riots. Opening for us was a young singer whose admiration for our work was boundless. Before the first show in the dressing room, he recited every line of our routines. We were flattered. After doing his first song onstage, he then did our act word for word. We were mortified.

Next stop was Milwaukee. When we arrived at the Holiday House, we saw our names on the marquee, just above a permanent sign that read, "Where Every Night Is New Year's Eve."

We had no idea of the significance of the motto until on opening night at precisely midnight, in the middle of our second show, we heard the strains of "Auld Lang Syne" being played by a small band. At that moment, a door leading to the lounge swung open and we could see customers wearing party hats, tooting horns, and making noise with paper whistles that untwirled, as confetti rained down from above. It was the middle of July and people were celebrating New Year's Eve. This went on every night for the entire two weeks we played there.

Before going on that first night I had the urge to pee. I opened the door to what I thought was the bathroom. It was a small closet with an empty jeroboam bottle. I realized immediately that we had no bathroom. On the wall of the closet was some graffiti that said, "Never Again—Ella Fitzgerald." Other stars autographed the walls with similar sentiments. I knew I wasn't the first to use the empty jeroboam bottle.

The overriding factor in getting us through clubs like these was the knowledge that we had another *Ed Sullivan Show* coming up. We knew we were going to be seen nationally, and the next *Sullivan* show could possibly get us out of nightclubs. But to where? In the middle of the act we would sometimes bravely attempt to break in a new *Sullivan* piece. It was unfair to inflict it on a paying audience, but we tried.

One such sketch dealt with a man buying a doll for his daughter that could eat, drink, talk, and pee. He had to prove to the saleswoman that he was a respected member of the community, had a job, and could provide a decent home for his new offspring. The audience barely understood what we were talking about. Weeks later on the *Sullivan* show, the same sketch got a great response.

The final leg of the cross-country tour brought us to Gene Brown's Crescendo in Hollywood. We were on the bill with Pat Suzuki and Arthur Lyman. We would be seen by the bigwigs in movies, radio, television, and recordings. We had reached the entertainment capital of the world. This was the engagement that would give us the visibility to make us stars.

We couldn't afford to stay at the Chateau Marmont so Anne, Amy, and I moved in with Charlie and Joanie Robinson on Whitley Terrace, high in the Hollywood Hills. Charlie had recently filmed *Sand Pebbles* and Joanie had done *Middle of the Night* on Broadway in a company headed by Edward G. Robinson and Gena Rowlands. The Robinsons would care for two-year-old Amy while Mom and Dad were hoping to take Hollywood by storm.

Anne and I had known Charlie since he and Joan decided to tie the knot. At that time Anne and I were just toying with the idea of doing an act. At Charlie and Joanie's wedding reception on Bank Street, we did a takeoff of the play Joan had been in. The improvised skit convulsed everyone and prompted Charlie to say, "Why don't you two do an act?"

I said at the time, as a joke, "If we ever do this in public, we can say it started here."

Charlie's enthusiasm was overpowering. It was so strong that it was unreal, sheer belief. I could never feel the same sureness that Charlie felt, not about myself. But now we were doing an act, just as he'd said, and we were playing Hollywood.

During the countdown of the days until we opened, Charlie advised me to get a haircut.

"You must go to Jerry Rothschild's," Charlie said. "In Beverly Hills. If you're going to open at the Crescendo, go there. It's good for everyone to know you're getting a cut at Jerry's."

"How much?" I asked.

"Twenty-five dollars. Everyone in Hollywood is seen there."

Charlie made the appointment, and I arrived on time. I parked the car and entered the shop. A woman asked me for the parking stub, which, she said, she would have validated. I was asked if I would like a shoe shine while I waited. I said yes. A gray-haired Black man in a sweater, shirt, and tie, who carried himself like one of my uncles in the Bronx, started shining my shoes. He attended to them with a dignity I'd never realized any pair of shoes could deserve. When he was finished, a woman took me to a stainless-steel sink to shampoo my hair. She wore a smock and was made up like a courtesan in the palace of an eighteenth-century European king. It was difficult not to surrender to her strong, expert hands as she massaged my scalp with fingers that were sending messages my Orphan Annie secret decoder would blush at. I was toweled vigorously and placed under a dryer to await the call from my particular barber.

"Are you Jerry Rothschild?" I asked him when he appeared.

"No, I'm Harry Gelbart. I'm Larry Gelbart's father," he said.

"The writer?"

"Yes, he's my son."

"He's a funny writer," I said.

"Yes. He just finished *A Funny Thing Happened on the Way to the Forum*. And I know your wife, Anne," Harry Gelbart said. "You're very funny also, the two of you. Do you write your own material?"

"Yes. We're too egotistical to think that anyone could write it as well," I said, trying to act Hollywood.

"Maybe you can meet Larry sometime."

"Does he know you work here?" I asked.

"Yes. I was a barber before he was a writer. I enjoy this. I meet a lot of interesting people."

As Harry Gelbart expertly cut and coiffed my hair, I thought this must be more like a hobby to him than a job. In New York he would be going to work every day like everybody else. In Hollywood he was having some fun. Then I wondered, what do you tip a man whose son the comedy writer has just written *A Funny Thing Happened on the Way to the Forum*?

"By the way," Mr. Gelbart said. "Have you met Brad Dexter?" He pointed to the man in the next chair, reading a paper.

Should I know Brad Dexter? I thought. People had names out there that sounded as if you should know who they were. They often seemed to have first names that were famous by themselves, and then when the second name was mentioned it'd just confuse me.

"Brad, this is Jerry Stiller. He and his wife are opening at the Crescendo next week."

How did Harry Gelbart know that? I asked myself.

Brad looked like an actor I was sure I'd seen on TV or in the movies.

"Jerry, how are you?" He shook my hand. It was a very macho grip. A Hollywood grip. "I've really enjoyed you and Anne on *Sullivan*."

"Well, thanks," I said. *He's probably a producer,* I thought.

"Good luck at the Crescendo next week. I'll be down to catch you."

He got up and said good-bye to Mr. Gelbart.

"Do you know who he is?" Mr. Gelbart asked a moment later.

"No," I said.

"He saved Frank Sinatra's life last week. Frank was swimming off Malibu. He got a cramp and Brad went in after him. Didn't you hear about it?"

"No, I didn't," I said, acting amazed, trying desperately to be part of the event now past.

When Mr. Gelbart was finished fixing my hair, I took no chances and put down $10 as the tip. I knew I was overtipping, but I didn't care. I wanted to be well thought of, like Willie Loman.

When I got home I showed everyone my haircut.

"It's great," Charlie Robinson said. "As good as Sebring, and half the price. Who did you have? Larry Gelbart's father?"

"Yes," I said.

"Yeah, I told him all about you," Charlie said. "I gave him your credits. This gets around, you know. He'll tell everyone you're opening next week. It'll get a lot of important people in."

"He knew all about us."

"This is California," Charlie said.

The next day Charlie asked if I wanted to go out to 20th Century-Fox to see him shoot. "I'm doing a couple of days on *77 Sunset Strip.* It'll be good for you to come watch. They give me a limo, and you can meet some of the people on the show."

"Okay," I said, "but I don't want to embarrass you. I'm going to wear my best suit, the one I wear in the act. It'll go with the limo," I told him.

The next day the temperature was close to 105. I wore my black shantung, got in the chauffeur-driven, air-conditioned limo, and Charlie and I headed for the lot.

"How did you manage the limo?" I asked.

"It's in the contract," Charlie said. "My agent, Paul Kohner, put it in. You've got to fight for it. They respect that. It's like being seen in the right restaurants."

What he was saying ran totally against my grain. I could never fight for stuff like that. When we reached the studio gates the car window moved down electrically. "Jerry Stiller and Charles Robinson," Charlie informed the guard.

"Go right in, Mr. Robinson," the guard dutifully replied.

"They seem to know us," I said to Charlie.

"They treat everybody like he might be the head of the studio. It's called fear."

On the set, Charlie introduced me to the makeup man, who greeted me with startling warmth and enthusiasm. As Charlie changed, the costume lady, a woman with a Cockney accent, mentioned that her parents were British music-hall performers. She talked as if she knew me. I was fascinated. She said she'd been raped backstage in Birmingham, England, by an acrobat, when, as a six-year-old, she'd been watching her parents perform. This was more information than I wanted to know. By the time Charlie came out to shoot his scene, I knew everything about her. I thought of Hollywood in a new way. It's a place where everyone has a story and is willing to share it with strangers.

"You look fine, Charles," the costume lady said.

"Come on," Charlie said to me. "You'll meet Edd Byrnes."

"Nice meeting you," the costume lady said as we went off.

"Same here," I said.

I was introduced to Edd "Kookie" Byrnes, the kid with the duck's-ass hairdo. He seemed in a rush but was very nice. Charlie then short-circuited Efrem Zimbalist, Jr., who was changing costumes. Zimbalist stopped everything, came over, and made me feel at home. I couldn't get over his warmth and hospitality. I was sweating profusely. The heat was unrelenting and my shirt was wringing wet. I did not dare unloosen my tie. I wanted to look good for Charlie.

"I've got to get ready for my next scene," Zimbalist said apologetically. "Nice meeting you, sir."

"Same," I said.

When Charlie finished shooting we headed back to the limo.

I said, "Charlie, I can't get over how everyone treated me. You must've said something. They told me stories about their lives. They called me 'sir.' They were all over me."

"That's because you were wearing that suit and tie in 105 degrees. They all thought you were Jack Warner's son."

"You're kidding?"

"I'm not. The costume lady told everyone you were Jack Warner's son. It got around the studio."

Our opening at the Crescendo in December of 1964 was a Hollywood dream. Every TV name in the business came to see us. Our "Jonah and the Whale" routine, which we changed to a man visiting his daughter at Laguna Beach instead of Miami Beach, stopped the show. The trade papers gave us raves. Before the run ended we were signed for a return engagement. By the end of the week, we were signed for *The Danny Kaye Variety Show* and three more *Sullivan* shows. Oscar Marienthal booked us into Mr. Kelly's in Chicago with Helen O'Connell; Shelley Berman had us on his "The Sex Life of the Primate" album; and we had an engagement with the Supremes at the Flamingo.

We opened for the Supremes in Vegas.

On one *Sullivan* show we had written a sketch in which I played a forty-year-old son telling his mother he was in love and wanted to marry a girl. But he had some qualms because the girl was of a different ethnic background.

"That's all right, she'll convert," Anne said in a typically motherly way.

"But, Mom, you don't understand, she's . . . "

"Bring her around, we'll talk," Anne says. "What does she do?"

"She's part of a group, a singing group."

"What do they call themselves? I know them all."

"The Supremes," I would say. Blackout. Huge laugh.

After doing the sketch on the *Sullivan* show we received a postcard with an illegible address and the following message: "We used to like youse people but since you had that sketch where the white guy wants to marry the colored girl we're writing CBS and Sullivan to take youse off the air." The postcard made me wonder whether Sullivan too had received bad mail about the sketch. When I mentioned the card and its content to Ed, he looked at me and said, "You let me take care of that." At that moment, he was our mountain.

Seeing the sketch on *Sullivan* must have given some imaginative booker the bright idea to put Stiller and Meara and the Supremes together at the Flamingo. We did the Supremes sketch in the show. None of the Supremes ever mentioned seeing it.

8

Family Man

The tour was over. We were back in Washington Heights. Our careers were in high gear. With all the good things happening we decided it was time to have another child. And we had saved enough money to think about moving to a better address.

"We're doing *The Ed Sullivan Show*," Anne said, "and we're living like we're broke. If we paid more rent we'd make more money," she argued. "What you put out, you get back, and more."

She scared the hell out of me. What had I married? She wasn't like this when we first went out and she stole the silverware from Longley's Cafeteria.

"We've been here five years. Find another place before I go into the hospital."

"Otto Harbach, George Gershwin—they all lived here in Washington Heights," I said

"And they all moved," Anne said. "Gershwin didn't write 'Rhapsody in Blue' on 160th Street."

I could see she wasn't kidding. "You don't know what we're giving up," I said.

"Me. If you don't find another apartment, you're giving up *me*."

I took the subtle hint. I started by bribing janitors on Riverside Drive. I'd do this every time I saw a janitor who looked like he might come through for me. The farther downtown I got, the more I'd *shtup*. I was hoping some superintendent would recognize me from *Sullivan*, and like the act enough to give me an apartment on the spot.

I'd ring a super's bell and introduce myself. "I'm looking for an apartment," I'd say. "We have an infant daughter and my wife is pregnant."

I'd stand there for a second, waiting for some response. Invariably there was a language barrier followed by, "My wife talk to you."

I would explain to the wife that I desperately needed an apartment and I would be willing to give them one month's rent as a gift.

"Dinero por una apartment," I'd say in broken Spanish.

"You give me your telephone number."

I'd write down our phone number, then take out $25 to show I was serious and that there was more where that came from.

"Gracias," they'd say.

"My name is Stiller. Jerry Stiller," I'd say in a loud voice.

They'd repeat, "'Jerry Stiller.' Thank you."

I put seed money in about ten apartment buildings. I figured if even one of them called it'd be worth it. I got no calls. Meantime Anne and I were working on our next *Sullivan* date, scheduled for two weeks after the baby was due. We couldn't afford to cancel the date. On our last *Sullivan* show, Anne had been in her fifth month. This time it was conceivable the baby could be born on the show. It would be a first for *Sullivan*. "But could you do it in six minutes?" Sullivan might ask.

A week before Ben arrived, Arthur Brendel, a real-estate agent, called and said that Dick Shawn had said we were looking, and there was an apartment on Riverside Drive in the 80s that Dick had turned down. It had just become available. "Get right over."

I raced over. Five rooms, three facing the river. "How much?" I asked the agent.

"Two hundred and fifty dollars plus a month's rent in advance and a month's security. You paint it yourself, but you must meet the building agent."

I called Anne to tell her the great news. "We have just enough to cover the first month's rent plus the security," she said.

"We'll have enough once we do the *Sullivan* show."

Ed Sullivan had just bought us for five shows. He had no idea we were hanging by a thread financially.

"I'm supposed to go see the building agent," I told Anne. "Right now."

Mr. Brendel was Viennese and his office was on Fifth Avenue. A secretary asked me to sit. A few minutes later he walked in and introduced himself. He seemed proper, authoritative, and sensitive. He wore a brown business suit that matched his eyes.

"What do you do, Mr. Stiller?" he asked.

"I'm an actor," I said.

"Have I ever seen you in anything?"

I could see that somehow I had to prove I was not unemployed.

"I don't know," I said. "Do you watch Ed Sullivan?"

"Sometimes," he said, "but I don't recognize you."

"My wife and I have been on a few times," I said.

"What do you do?"

"I'm a comedian," I said. This was like Claude Rains, the chief of police in *Casablanca,* interrogating Paul Henreid as Victor Laszlo. I was being interrogated, but I desperately needed the apartment.

"What kind of comedian?"

"My wife and I are a comedy act, Stiller and Meara."

"Who's the funny one?" he said.

"She is," I said quietly.

"Where is she now?"

"She's home."

"Why isn't she with you?"

"She's pregnant," I said. I suddenly felt a wave of guilt sweeping over me, as if I had impregnated some innocent woman.

His eyes examined me like a man who knew he was in charge of another person's fate. "I know a little about show business," he said. "I worked at a nightclub in London. I like show people."

I looked at him soulfully.

"You know who had this apartment years ago? Lou Walters."

"The owner of the Latin Quarter," I said.

"That's right. I'd come to the apartment and put Barbara on my lap and play with her when I collected the rent. She was a nice girl. And now she's on the *Today* show."

I listened, captured by his sudden eagerness to talk show business.

"This apartment, you know, was most recently leased by a man for his girlfriend. He decided to give her up and she couldn't meet the rent, so I need someone right away to take it over. Are you willing to paint it yourself?"

"Of course," I said.

Landlords were supposed to paint when an apartment was turned over, but I was not going to quibble.

"One month's security and one month's rent in advance. But I must meet your wife."

"Why?" I asked.

"I want to meet her. I have a right, don't I?"

"Yes," I quickly agreed. I was beginning to like him.

I picked up the phone and told Anne we had the apartment if she could get down to say hello to the renting agent.

"I'm writing something for Sullivan," she said.

"You gotta come down," I said.

"Okay." She sensed the urgency in my voice.

"Go out and get yourself a cup of coffee," the agent said to me. "I'll see you and your wife in an hour."

An hour later Anne, all 185 pounds of her, walked into the office.

"Sit down," the man from Vienna said. "Your husband told me you're comedians."

Anne looked at me, wondering if this was really happening.

"Yes," she said, her maternity dress ballooning over her slightly parted legs.

"How long have you two been married?"

"Twelve years," I said.

"Twelve years, hah! May I feel your stomach?" he asked Anne.

"What?" Anne said.

"I want to feel your stomach."

Anne looked at me. She seemed to be saying, I'm your wife, don't let him do this to me. Is he some kind of kinky guy?

"Go ahead," I said, turning my head slightly away as if I couldn't bear to watch.

How badly do I want this apartment? I was thinking. And why does he want to feel my wife's tummy? Why would I subject Anne to this?

Anne shrugged and threw her head back as if to say, "Be my guest."

His hand came gently down upon Anne's stomach. He held it there a few seconds.

"You really are pregnant, aren't you," he said.

"You mean you didn't believe me?" I said.

"Oh, Mr. Stiller, you don't know what people will do in this town to get an apartment. They'll say or do anything. Okay, you got the apartment," he said to us. "When can I see you on television?"

We gave him the date of our next *Sullivan*. We signed the lease and he wished us luck.

A few weeks after we moved into our beautiful new apartment, Ben was born at Mount Sinai. I had just left the hospital to pick up Amy at pre-school when Anne delivered. She had an emergency C-section. Eddie Meara was notified and was with Anne at the time. Eleven days later, Anne and I did the *Sullivan* show. Ed permitted us to do one of our "Mrs. Santa Claus" sketches, updated. It went over fine.

Some months later, on Johnny Carson's *Tonight Show*, while we were sitting down chatting with Johnny, he asked what it was like living in New York City. Anne said, "We have cockroaches. They're so friendly and big, we call them by their first names."

The next day we got a call from Mr. Brendel. "How come you said my apartment has cockroaches?" he asked indignantly.

"Because it does," I humbly replied.

"You hurt my feelings, Mr. Stiller."

"We never mentioned you or the building," I said. "I'm really sorry if you were upset."

"I love your act," he said, and hung up.

The next day a very well-dressed man in a dark business suit, white shirt, and tie rang our doorbell. He was carrying a black valise.

"Who are you?" I asked.

"I'm the exterminator. The renting agent sent me over to take care of anything in the apartment."

"You're dressed like a Madison Avenue executive," I said.

"The renting agent's orders. He wanted you to know he loves your work and told me I should dress appropriately. Incidentally, I saw that show, the one where you mentioned cockroaches. You're right, everybody in New York has them. I just came from"—and he whispered the name of a prominent show business personality who lived on Fifth Avenue.

"He's got them too?"

"Yes, him."

The name he'd whispered was . . . Johnny . . .

• • •

It was close to Thanksgiving 1966. Ben was one year old, Amy five. Ed Meara was in Boston attending the American Radiator Company's convention. Anne and I were busy writing material for the Perry Como Christmas show when Anne got a call from Dr. Julian Aroesty of Beth Israel Hospital in Boston.

Anne's face was frozen. I knew something terrible had happened.

"What is it?" I asked.

"My father's had a heart attack."

We packed a few things, flew the shuttle to Boston, and took a cab to the hospital. Ed was wide awake as we entered his room. He was being given oxygen.

"How are you, Totsie," he said to his daughter with a joyful smile.

It's the Irish shit, I'm thinking. It's a re-enactment of every Pat O'Brien, Jimmy Cagney, Warner Bros. movie ever made. They laugh at death. This isn't funny to me. Why can't they admit pain or suffering? It helps a doctor know what to do.

"How are you doing, Jerry boy?"

Ed started to sit up.

"Sit back," I said. "Don't move."

"Here, let me fix your pillow," Anne said.

I told myself to act happy. I envisioned myself as Myron Cohen doing three garment-industry stories the Irish would love. But I contained myself.

"What happened?" Anne asked.

"We were at the Statler. There must have been ten of us at the table, and I just got this pain. They took me to my room, and Dr. Aroesty was in the hotel. He got me into the hospital right away. They gave me oxygen. Right now I just feel a little weak."

"Are you eating?" Anne asked.

"I'm not too hungry. I've been trying to lose weight, you know. Now's a good time to do it. How's Amy, my little darling?"

"She's fine," I said.

"And Ben?"

"They're okay," Anne said.

"Who's with them?"

"We've got someone taking care of them."

"You gotta take it easy and get some rest," I said.

"I miss the kids," Ed said. "I feel a little tired."

A nurse came in and motioned to us. We followed her out. "Dr. Aroesty would like to talk to you."

Dr. Aroesty, a fortyish man with sensitive eyes, told us the prognosis was not good. "We'll treat him with medication and see what happens."

For five days we watched Ed's condition steadily improve. Anne and I remained at his bedside past visiting hours, kibitzing with the staff and other patients. The floor took on a festive atmosphere. Ed's spirits perked.

"These two are doing the Perry Como Christmas show," Ed announced to everyone within earshot.

"We're not doing the show, Dad," Anne said. "We've canceled. It's more important we're here with you."

Anne read Ed a letter from Perry Como saying how he was sorry we'd had to bow out, and hoping Anne's father would be better soon.

"Why the hell *don't* you do the show?" Ed said. "I told everybody in Rockville Centre you were going to be on."

During the following day, Ed's condition worsened. He was having trouble breathing and would periodically lose consciousness.

Anne and I stayed close.

"How'm I doing?" Ed would whisper when he could get the words out.

A few days later Dr. Aroesty said, "I need your permission to perform a tracheotomy. It will help his breathing."

Anne agreed.

The sight of Eddie Meara with a breathing device got to me. Anne handled it. She talked a little louder to make him aware that we were nearby.

"Jerry's going to shave you in the morning," she told Ed. She fully believed my shaving him would make him feel better.

Francis Mannion, a Paulist priest, quietly introduced himself in the corridor near the nurses' station. He said he'd been informed of Ed's condition. "How Catholic is he?" Father Mannion asked.

"Real Catholic," Anne said.

"I know who you are," Father Mannion said. "You give us lots of laughs at the rectory. I know this is tough, but how would your dad feel if I said a few prayers?"

Anne got angry. "You're not going to say any last rites. I won't have him listening to that."

I took Father Mannion aside and told him this was not the right moment.

He said, "Jerry, when I ask people if they want the last rites, I'm doing it for the family. The person dying doesn't even know what I'm saying, but it's important that everyone knows he died in a state of grace. You know what I do when I'm outside the room where someone's dying? I make jokes."

He told me the one about the drunken Irishman falling down a flight of stairs with a bottle of whiskey in his back pocket, discovering his pants dripping red, and thanking God it was only blood. To me, it wasn't funny, but I understood his point.

"You sure you don't want me to go in?" he asked Anne once again.

"Just wait," Anne said.

Anne asked her dad if he wanted Father Mannion, and Ed said, "Not at this time."

Around 11 o'clock the next morning, Ed went into a coma, and Anne had Father Mannion give him last rites.

We had been in Boston ten days and never thought he would die.

"You've got to get him a good obituary," Anne said to me. "Go downstairs and call Dave Rush and tell him, if he wants to keep doing PR for us, he's got to get my father a decent obit. I don't want one of those death notices in small type, you understand? I want all his friends on the Island to know."

"I'll take care of it," I said. I ran to the lobby to make the phone call to Dave Rush.

"Dave, I'm in Boston."

"What are you doing in Boston?"

"My father died. I mean Anne's father."

"I'm sorry," Dave said.

"David, we want an obit."

"That's not PR," he said.

"I know, but I want it anyway. I want you to call whoever you know to get Ed Meara a decent obit."

"What can I say about him?" Dave asked.

"He baby-sat Amy on the road when we were playing clubs."

"I can't put down baby-sitter in an obit," Dave said.

"He helped us out with the rent when we couldn't pay. He took us to dinner every Friday at Vorst's Restaurant." I knew I was running on empty.

"That's not enough," Dave said.

"Make him our road manager. He was with us in Cleveland, Chicago, Milwaukee. Give him a title."

"What else?"

"He did our lighting," I said.

"How old was he?"

"Seventy-three."

"And he was doing lights? They're not going to believe that."

"Okay, how about this: He wrote all our material."

"Are you kidding?" Dave's voice lit up as if he had just stumbled onto a major scoop. I knew I'd finally hit home.

"Every single piece you've ever seen on *Sullivan* was written by him." I was on a roll. I sensed that Dave really believed me, or wanted to believe me.

"He wrote all that? Okay, I'll call the papers. Tell Annie how sorry I am."

"Okay, Dave. Thanks." I hung up.

I rushed back and told Anne, "I got the obit."

"What'd you say?"

"I told him Ed wrote all our material."

"You didn't," she said.

"It was the only way we could get it in the papers."

Next day an obituary notice appeared in both *The New York Times* and the *Daily News,* with a picture. The one in the *Times* began, "E. J. Meara, creator of comedy material for the team of Stiller and Meara . . ."

The wake was held at Macken's in Rockville Centre, Long Island. Mr. Macken had been Ed's poker buddy, and we thought he'd be Ed's undertaker of choice. The wake, attended by the Knights of Columbus and scores of friends and relatives and employees of the American Radiator Company, was a happy one.

At one point Gene Brown, another poker buddy, drew Anne and myself aside and said, "Jerry, Anne, I read the obituary and I wanted to cry. He was a great guy, your dad was. He used to tell me he took you out to dinner and once in a while paid the rent, but he never let on that he wrote all your material. God bless him."

For the next year, Anne and I would receive requests from colleges and from the New York Public Library, asking if we would donate the comedy material written by E. J. Meara to their archives.

Ed left us with wonderful memories and his blessings. He was catholic with a small c, meaning worldly. As an example of his beliefs, when Amy was going to nursery school at the Stephen Wise Free Synagogue, Ed would sometimes pick her up in the afternoon. He'd wait in the lobby until she came out. He always wore a hat, which is mandatory only in an Orthodox or Conservative Synagogue. Rabbi Klein once passed by and greeted Ed.

"Why are you wearing a hat, Mr. Meara?" Ed explained he was in a synagogue and did not want to seem disrespectful. "But this is Reform, Mr. Meara. It's optional." Ed kept his hat on.

Ed left Anne and me with the feeling that we could make it. From that point on, our Riverside Drive apartment turned into a writing factory. Inspiration came from all places and at all hours.

One day I was in the playground near our apartment with the kids. Anne was shopping. We'd just been booked into Lou Walters' Latin Quarter, long a fixture of the Broadway nightclub scene. In my mind, this was the dream come true. The marquee on 48th Street would herald our names as headliners. This was where Sophie Tucker, Harry Richman, Joe E. Lewis, and Jack Durant had played. We had made it.

I was sitting on the park bench, adapting our material for the Latin Quarter. Ben and Amy were climbing the monkey bars with another little boy. The boy's father, sitting nearby with a stroller, asked if I was Jerry Stiller of Stiller and Meara.

I said yes. He had a newspaper in his hand. "You're opening at the Latin Quarter?"

The opening was a week away, and the day before I had gone into Cye Martin's on Broadway and bought a $200 tux, a dress shirt with ruffles, cuff links with real stones, and a set of studs. I wanted to look elegant.

"Who does your hair?" the father asked.

"My barber," I said.

"I'm the world's second-best barber," he said, hauling out some newspaper clippings.

"I was just in a contest worldwide," he said. "I was chosen second best in the entire world. I'd like to do your hair."

Sure enough, there was his picture in a Paris newspaper that hailed him as *le deuxième barbier du monde*.

I said, "That's too bad." I wanted to say, "That's terrible." What if somebody told me I was the second-best comedian in the world? It's not a compliment.

"Yes," he said. "You'd be surprised how people respond to that. I can't put that up in the shop. People get upset. They feel funny when they see it. But never mind all that. I'd love to do your hair. It'll look great. You'll have it for your opening."

Whatever it was—pity, identification—I made an appointment to go to his shop on Third Avenue two days before our opening. We had been rehearsing all morning. I was exhausted.

"Just sit down, I'm going to make you look great," he said. I closed my eyes and fell asleep in the chair. When I awoke and looked in the mirror, my hair was jet black. He had also straightened it and had given me a razor cut. I didn't recognize myself.

I could feel sweat breaking out over my entire body. What had I done? I'd trusted this guy.

"What did you do?"

"Why, don't you like it?"

I knew it was too late. Second best, I said to myself. Fucking second best. Now I knew why.

"How long will it stay this way?"

"About nine months," he said.

My heart sank. That's as long as it takes to make a baby. How could anybody do something like this? I got up out of the chair, paid him some inordinate amount, and walked down Third Avenue, feeling sheared.

Jack O'Brian, a columnist on the *Journal-American,* was walking toward me. He stopped, stared, and said, "What happened to your hair?"

I smiled weakly. "It's a new image," I muttered.

"Good luck at the Latin Quarter," Jack said.

When I got home, Anne made no mention of my hair, so I knew there was something wrong.

We opened at the Latin Quarter, played one week, and were canceled. Was it the hair, the act, or a new tax ruling on business deductions? It didn't matter.

I didn't see the world's second-best barber again until years later when I was flying down to my cousin Florence's funeral in Fort Lauderdale. Somewhere over South Carolina, a man on the plane approached me and said, "Remember me?"

I knew immediately it was him. He had a smile on his face as if he had just given me the greatest haircut.

"I've got a shop in Florida now," he said. "It's a great place. Visit me if you get a chance."

He gave me his card. I put it in my wallet with a lot of other cards. You never know when you're going to need a second-best haircut.

It was around this same time, while Amy was still a tot, that she was cast in *Lovers and Other Strangers*. Anne was playing Wilma opposite Harry Guardino. David Susskind, the producer, thought it would be rather nice to have both Amy and myself playing family members in the wedding scene. In the ceremony, I would put Amy up on a piano and she would sing "I Love You Truly."

On the day of the shoot at the Tarrytown Inn in Westchester, I was late in leaving the city. Although I had only about three words to say, I was very nervous. I don't know whether it had to do with the fact that I was not cast as Anne's husband and I was playing a walk-on or what. The upshot was that I was late getting to the set. I rented a car and sped up the Henry Hudson Parkway. Amy was about to do her first acting job. She had no interest in show business. We'd never pushed her into it.

We're late, I kept thinking as I exceeded sixty-five miles per hour. Amy could not help but feel my strange vibes.

"What am I supposed to do, Daddy?"

"You sing a song," I told her. "I put you up on a piano and you sing, 'I Love You Truly.'"

"Where's Mommy?"

"She's on the set. Now sing, 'I love you truly, truly dear.'" I started to sing.

"Daddy, you're going too fast."

"I can't help it, we're late," I said.

"Daddy, please. I'm scared."

We hit a bump. A little rise in the highway that when taken at sixty-five or seventy sent the little car flying in the air as if it were a toy. Amy screamed. My God, what the hell was I doing? Filling my kid with anxiety just before she was about to do a scene in a movie. I slowed down, wishing I could erase the tape and shoot the last few minutes of my life over again. When we arrived at the Inn, they were still in the midst of shooting Anne Jackson, Gig Young, Diane Keaton, Bob Dishy, Marian

Hailey, and Richie Castellano. We were early, as it turned out. The usual movie routine—hurry up and wait. Diane Keaton played games with Amy while we killed time.

Anne was doing a scene with Harry. They were both in the buff under the sheets in the bedroom, attempting to make love. Anne tells Harry, an ex-Marine who's having trouble getting into the moment, "You owe me one."

Anne and Harry were students at the Dramatic Workshop. Some years earlier, Anne had mentioned that Harry had written her once. He had had a crush on her. In the scene, they worked wonderfully together. I told myself I wasn't jealous; I only wished that I had been cast in the role.

My scene with Amy was next. They shot it quickly. Amy was adorable, not the stereotypical precocious brat that I figured they'd want her to be. *Lovers and Other Strangers* was a big success for Renee Taylor and Joe Bologna.

Anne had just been cast as Bunny Flingus opposite Harold Gould and Katherine Helmond in John Guare's *The House of Blue Leaves*, playing at the Truck and Warehouse Theater, when we registered Ben at the Calhoun School, then located about six blocks from our home. After being taken to and from school by Anne or me for the first week, Ben suggested that he walk home by himself.

My first fears were that he might be kidnapped. This was quickly followed by the fear that a child molester would be lurking in every doorway on West End Avenue, ready to pounce on him. Anne sensed my apprehension and said, "You've got to give him a chance to grow up. He wants to walk home. Let him walk home."

Reluctantly, I gave in. With great fanfare I announced to Ben one morning that he could walk home by himself that afternoon.

"Can I, Dad?" He asked. "You really mean it?"

"Yeah," I said, a slight lump in my throat. "Just make sure you don't stop for anybody."

I could hear myself filling Ben with my foreboding, which he sensibly ignored. I didn't quite say, "Don't take candy from strangers," but it was implicit in my tone.

I drove him to school that morning, kissed him good-bye, and went back home. At about 2:45 P.M., fifteen minutes before school was dismissed, I got into my car and drove up to the school. I double-parked outside the school and waited until I spotted Ben leaving, his book bag on his shoulder.

He strode along the street, turning his head to see if he really was alone. I slunk behind the wheel. As he walked toward West End, I started the car and trailed after him. I stayed a good half-block behind. He kept a steady pace, occasionally looking behind him. He seemed to be reassuring himself that no parent was following him. As I trailed along, other cars either passed me or formed a small procession in my rear. I was going five miles an hour and I'd get the horn, the finger, or a questioning look as other drivers passed me.

About halfway home I noticed a police car practically on my rear bumper. It too was crawling along, obviously checking me out. I continued to follow Ben, ignoring the squad car until it pulled alongside and a cop motioned to me to stop. One of the cops got out. Fortunately the cop recognized me and was friendly. He said, "We noticed you driving along the street, Mr. Stiller. Is there any reason you're going so slow?"

"Yeah, I'm following a kid home from school," I said, making a joke.
"Really?"

"It's my own kid," I said laughingly. "He's going home by himself for the first time, and I'm very nervous."

The cop laughed. "Give Anne our regards," he said, as he and his partner drove off.

That day Ben made it home safe and sound, and gained a little confidence along the way. So did I.

Ironically, fifteen years later Ben made his Lincoln Center and Broadway debut playing Ronnie in *The House of Blue Leaves*. This was a prelude to *Permanent Midnight* and *Something About Mary*.

As we were becoming more popular, our five-room apartment was slowly becoming our unofficial office. Each morning we tumbled out of bed and went straight to the typewriter. The apartment was our own little kibbutz on Riverside Drive. We even built bunk beds in the living room, which now became our work room. Who said you need to separate family from work? We were not shutting the kids out of our life just because we were in show business.

One day Anne and I were rehearsing our "Hate" sketch, which is about a husband and wife who can no longer restrain themselves.

Anne: "I hate you."

Jerry: "You hate me? I hate you."

Anne: "You don't know what hate is, the kind of hate I have for you. . . ."

At this point Amy, about two years old, tears in her eyes, came into the room and said, "Daddy, Mommy fight?"

I took Amy into my arms and said, "No, no, Amy. Mommy, Daddy rehearse."

A couple of days later Anne and I got into an argument about whether a joke was funny. The argument got heated. Amy must have heard it in the other room. She ran in and smilingly said, "Mommy, Daddy rehearse?" I had to be honest. I said, "No, honey, Mommy, Daddy fight."

This setup lasted about a year. There was no way two married people with children in New York City could live in bunk beds with no locks on the doors. But at least we had tried.

Show business was in our kids' blood before they were born. Amy was on stage with us twice a night for five months when we were doing *Medium Rare* in Chicago. She was privy to our every punch line in every sketch twice a night. All the kicking she did in Anne's stomach was either her laughing or telling us something could be funnier. Ben was on *Sullivan* no fewer than three times before he was born.

Both have chosen the same profession as Anne and myself. God help them.

One day Mike Douglas, whose show we were guest-hosting, asked us if we would like Amy and Ben to come on. They had just started taking violin lessons. Anne tried desperately to stop me from opening my mouth.

"Yeah, they play the violin," I said proudly.

Ernie DiMassa, Mike's talent coordinator, said, "That's great. Why not have them play a piece together?"

"We're pushing them," Anne said. "People will think we're just pushy parents."

"It'll be great." I thought, *the kids will love it.*

"People love you and Jerry. It'll be great," Ernie reassured me.

Despite Anne's protests, I made the decision for Amy and Ben to appear on the show. Anne fumed. That night I informed Ben and Amy that they were going on *The Mike Douglas Show.* I expected them to be elated.

Instead, they informed me that all their friends would be watching, and they could only play one song, badly.

Whatever sensitivities my children had about being on television escaped me. I saw it as their rite of passage into the world of show business, perhaps the beginning of a theatrical dynasty. We'd be like the Barrymores, the Cohans, the Foys. I said to myself, who has a better right to show off their kids than someone in the business? It's taken years, I thought, for me to get my foot in the door. The echoes of rejection are still with me.

Anne, on the other hand, said, "Let them learn on their own. Don't force it. It's the only way they'll get a sense of themselves."

The next day Amy and Ben arrived in Philadelphia with their tiny Yamahas. They played "Chopsticks" for a national audience. They started on time and ended on time. The studio audience applauded enthusiastically. When it was all over and I went to congratulate them, they said, "Dad, our friends are going to hate us for this."

We did get a letter from some women who said, "How could you have done that to two such nice kids?"

What words of wisdom can I give my children? See past the hype and the glitz and ask yourself why you want to perform. It may take years to arrive at the answers, but understanding the reasons will help you to keep the dream alive and reach your goals.

9

Radio, Stage, and Screen

*A*nne and I had never done a commercial together before Blue Nun came into our lives. Anne's hand had been shown testing a harsh dishwashing detergent that purportedly reddened her skin. I had once played a short silhouette telling a tall silhouette at a dance that he—the tall silhouette—had bad breath, and Colgate toothpaste could change everything for him. I earned about $300.

One night Jerry Della Femina, then a copywriter for the Ted Bates Agency, walked into the Phase II, saw us perform, and said he would someday own his own agency and use us. Years later, true to his word, he telephoned and asked us to drop down to see him. "I want you to improvise something," he said.

We met in a room with Jerry—baldish, wide-eyed, hardly a Madison Avenue type—and two of his young copywriters, Mark Justein and Sara Bragin.

"I guess you remember me telling you that someday I'd come to you," Jerry said. "Well, now I'm on my own and I have an account for a wine. I've wanted to use comedians, and I think you two would be perfect."

I asked the name of the product.

"It's called Blue Nun Wine," Jerry said.

"Why is it called Blue Nun?" Anne asked.

"Blue Nun is a name we created."

It was a German table wine, Jerry said, a Liebfraumilch that would sell for around $3 a bottle.

Anne then and there improvised a story into a tape recorder about nuns who worked in the vineyards of Bavaria picking grapes. These nuns would jump up and down, stomping the grapes until the grapes were crushed and put into vats and fermented.

The barefoot nuns were not permitted ever to taste the fruits of their labor. As a result, the nuns became very depressed. The mother superior, seeing all the sad nuns, their heads hanging low, declared a holiday to cheer up the convent.

"Ring the bells! Let's cheer up our blue nuns!"

The bells rang, and some monk ran in with a cask of wine that had fermented. He filled a lot of flasks and made a toast: "Here's to our blue nuns!"

They drank the wine . . . and got sick.

At this point, Jerry Della Femina was on the floor, laughing. He asked if I knew how to order wine.

"No," I said.

"That's it. Men are afraid to order wine when they go out. Do you order red or white?"

"If it's meat you order red, if it's fish you order white."

"Not necessarily," Della Femina said. "White wine goes with anything, so does red, but we're talking Blue Nun—the delicious white wine that goes as well with meat as it does with fish."

Anne said, "Is this supposed to get a girl to go to bed with a guy? Because he orders Blue Nun wine? Boy, if the nuns ever hear about this."

"We'll give it a try," Della Femina said. "You two meet in a restaurant. It's your first date. Jerry, you're trying to impress Anne. Just be yourselves and see what happens. Anne, you're Lola; Jerry, you're Phil, and this is a real fancy restaurant."

"I hardly expected such elegance on a blind date," Anne said. "I *like* French cooking. They've got some great *mussels meunière*," she said, as if scanning a menu, "and their specialty is *coq au vin*."

"Well, I do lean towards fish," I said.

"Then the *poisson de maison* is what you want."

"Good, here comes the waiter," I said. "She'd like the *poisson de maison* and I'll try the veal cordon bleu and some wine. . . ."

"May I suggest a little Blue Nun?" said Jerry Della Femina as the waiter.

"Excuse me? I never heard of Blue Nun," I said.

Anne said, "Wasn't she on *The Ed Sullivan Show*?"

Della Femina broke up. He said, "That's it. You guys have got it. Those are the people."

I said, "But wait, when people laugh at a commercial, they usually don't remember the product."

"This time they will," Jerry Della Femina said.

He was right.

"Have you got any Blue Nun?" people would shout over to our table when we ate at the Russian Tea Room.

"We bathe in it," Anne would crack back.

"Do you really drink that stuff?"

"I drink it," Anne would reply. "Jerry doesn't. One in the family is enough."

The tag line, said by the announcer, was always, "Blue Nun, the delicious white wine that goes as well with meat as it does with fish." The *Wall Street Journal* in a front-page article said Blue Nun sales jumped 150 percent as a result of our commercials.

At Zabar's, the legendary specialty food store on upper Broadway, a male shopper loaded with bags of eats remarked to me one day, "Jerry, what's the delicious white wine that goes as well with meat as it does with whitefish?"

Anne and I were now spokespersons for Blue Nun. We read in *Ad Age* that we had broken the oldest rule in advertising: That funny could never sell a product. Jerry Della Femina said you could sell through humor. We proved him right. The sales of Blue Nun jumped from 140,000 cases a year to over 1,400,000.

The irony of those commercials is that we had actually done thirty takes. I remember noticing somewhere around take twenty-four that Anne always did it the same way. I could never do it the same way twice. It's her parochial school background, I told myself. Those nuns making you do things, forcing you, made her one wonderful actress. At my school, they allowed me to do whatever the hell I wanted and look how it screwed me up. Next to her, I'm inept.

When we finished recording that day we took the elevator downstairs.

"Let's have a drink," I said to Anne.

"Okay," Anne said.

"You did great," I told her.

"You did great," she said.

"I'm sorry I couldn't do it better and faster," I said, "but that's the way I work."

"I know," she said. "We're different."

Years later I called Jerry Della Femina and asked him, "Do you remember doing thirty takes on that Blue Nun commercial?"

"Sure. You had it on the first take, but you were doing so great I figured we could make it even better."

At that time, in the late 1960s, I had agreed to read the names of the Vietnam war dead at the Cathedral of St. John the Divine as part of a protest organized by psychiatrists from St. Luke's Hospital. I was one of many who agreed to read the names. My feelings about Vietnam were confused. As an actor, my life was concerned with day-to-day career decisions. As writers, Anne and I never really got into political issues. We dealt with man/woman stuff. It was a safe place.

But some part of me was upset by the terrible stories about the war and the casualties we saw each week on TV. When I heard of the protest, I didn't want to forgo the opportunity to say something. I remembered what had happened during the entertainment blacklist of the 1950s. Blacklisting could be silent, too, I told myself.

On the day of the reading, I simply arrived at the cathedral and read some names. I was interviewed briefly by *The New York Times*. My name, along with that of Leonard Bernstein and others in the entertainment world, was mentioned in the story. We did not lose the Blue Nun account. During the following years, we wrote and performed in many, many commercials. We always insisted on a soft sell. That meant the spots had to be funny and have a punch line. Clients like the Amalgamated Bank, United Van Lines, Jack in the Box, Lanier, Harrah's, and Food Emporium went along with us, resisted the hard sell, and came out winners.

Had we sold out? Siobhan McKenna and Maureen Stapleton were once asked in an interview what they felt about actors doing commercials. McKenna said it was obscene. Maureen said, "For an actor, poverty is the only thing that's obscene."

Thanks to Blue Nun and our appearances on the *Sullivan* show, people now knew our names. We were no longer the tall girl and the short guy. But they never got our names quite right. "Schiller and Myra." "Jerry Stiller and Moira Shearer." Trini Lopez once introduced us as "Stella and Maria." Tony Martin, in a tent in Holyoke, Massachusetts, just gave up and said, "Ladies and gentlemen, those people with the two *fechachta* names." Bernard Levin, when he gave us a rave in the London *Daily Mail,* called us Steara and Miller. The next day he wrote a follow-up review saying, "The team I admired, was not Steara and Miller but Stiller and Meara—py amologies."

Our Blue Nun popularity grew to the point that we were booked on a summer tour of Neil Simon's *The Prisoner of Second Avenue.* One afternoon in Dayton, Ohio, Mary Ellyn Devery, our lifelong friend, who produced and managed the tour, came backstage with two nuns who politely asked if we'd autograph some bottles of Blue Nun wine, which they had in their handbags. They were in street clothes, of course. While doing *Prisoner* for John Kenley in Dayton we were assigned a police officer, Fred Sandoval, to "guard" us and make sure we were not harassed by autograph seekers.

"It's not like we're Robert Redford and Jane Fonda," I told him. "You don't have to guard us." This did not deter him in his duties. Amy and Ben were out of school and traveling with us. Fred would entertain them backstage. One of his bits was taking a photo of Ben with a "Most Wanted" headline beneath his face. Here we were, in Sherwood Anderson country, with a cop making us feel like we were the Barrymores.

Perhaps it was because we'd done good business and the audiences had loved us that I innocently remarked to Fred on closing night, "Come see us if you ever get to New York."

Some years later I received a letter from him. He described his arthritis and the terrible pain he was suffering. He mentioned something about coming to New York. Remembering my promise in Dayton, I wrote back, "Call us if you get in," not expecting he would take me literally. One evening when Anne was in bed with the flu, I received a phone call at about 9 P.M. "Jerry, it's me, Fred."

"Where are you?"

"In New York."

I was in shock. He named a fleabag motel on Ninth Avenue. Not the Waldorf, I thought.

"The room is terrible," he said.

"I'll be right over," I told him. What could I do? I had made a promise.

When I reached the motel, there was Fred. Once so active and full of life, he now seemed crushed by his affliction.

I had no idea what to do, but I could see the pain he was in.

I looked at the dilapidated surroundings.

It suddenly hit me that the purpose of his traveling to New York was that he really believed me when I'd said to look us up. In Fred's mind, Anne and I were Ozzie and Harriet from TV, the most ingratiating two people in the world. What would Ozzie do? I looked at the cheap paintings on the motel room walls, the windows overlooking a hostile city.

"Come on," I said. "It's late and Anne's not feeling well, but you can't stay here. You can stay with us."

I checked him out of the motel and drove up to our apartment on Riverside Drive. Anne was asleep. I didn't wake her. Fred and I talked about Ohio and then had a snack. I told him he'd see Anne in the morning when she felt better. He went to bed and I finished working on a script in my office/bedroom.

When I awoke in the morning, Fred was looking out over Riverside Drive and the Hudson River from one of our windows.

"How about lox and eggs?" I said. He looked at me bewildered. Eggs he knew. Lox was terra incognita, but I fixed it anyway. I brewed some coffee. Anne was still asleep. How could I tell her we had a guest? Let her find out for herself, I thought.

Suddenly the bedroom door opened. There was Anne, in a beat-up bathrobe, still groggy from the antibiotics.

Fred said, "Anne! How are you?"

I said, "You remember Fred from Dayton?"

"Dayton?"

"Yeah, when we did *Prisoner* for John Kenley."

Anne's face scrunched up as she searched for some connection. She said, "I look terrible. Don't kiss me. I'm sick."

Instantly, this man's fantasy disintegrated. I was now just Joe Schmo introducing him to my sick wife. I suddenly felt like a fraud inviting him to the Big Apple to meet stars, as though I was trying to be someone I wasn't. But I could only guess that, just like me, Fred had dreams. As far-out as they may have seemed, he tried to act on them.

We sat down at the table and talked some more about Dayton, John Kenley, and the good times we'd all had together. When breakfast was finished, Fred said, "I really have to get back."

"Must you go so soon?" I said. I could sense he couldn't wait to leave town for home.

"It was nice seeing both of you," Fred said. "Give my regards to the kids." I wanted to say, "Come on, Fred, we're going out tonight, we'll see *Pippin.* We'll paint the town red." But if the truth were to be known, Anne and I never painted any town red. We were just actors putting on a show, and some people believed it a little too hard.

Thanks to the Blue Nun radio commercials, Stiller and Meara were still alive. However, we kept turning down lucrative nightclub offers around the country in order to stay in New York, where Amy and Ben were going to school. The only way we could stay together as a family was to stop performing together. We vowed that one of us always had to be with Amy and Ben. This led me back to the theater, where I no longer had to hear a metronome in my head, ticking, telling me that the audience had to laugh every fifteen seconds.

I wanted to get back to doing a play. But could I still act?

Walt Witcover cast me, Bob Snively, and Nancy Ponder in *Bou-bouroche* by Georges Courteline, a nineteenth-century French play-wright. The show was performed in a former New York City jail and courthouse in the East Village. It was wonderfully received. But gone were the big checks.

It must've gotten around to the industry that we were bona fide stage performers. Together Anne and I did *Next* by Terrence McNally and *Last of the Red Hot Lovers,* selling out on the summer circuit. On my own I did *Red Hot Lovers* in Atlanta in early 1974 with Jane Curtin, who had not yet appeared on *Saturday Night Live.* Anne was to receive the first of four Emmy nominations for her work on *Medical Center,* so the split was pay-ing dividends financially.

In 1974 Alixe Gordon, the casting agent of the old *Studio One* days, called and said she'd heard one of the Blue Nun commercials.

"I have a role for you in *The Taking of Pelham One Two Three.* It's a subway thriller, and you play a transit cop, Lieutenant Garber. You're Walter Matthau's sidekick."

In the film, a New York subway train has just been hijacked, and the passengers are being held for one million dollars ransom. My first day on the set I was in my camper putting on my transit cop's outfit when the as-sistant director knocked on my door saying they were ready to rehearse. I finished lacing my shoes and trundled over to the production trailer, where I met Matthau and screenwriter Peter Stone for the first time. I knew the director, Joe Sargent, from my days apprenticing at the Cherry Lane Theater in the Village.

Joe introduced us.

"Walter, this is Jerry."

"Hi, Jerry. You're playing . . . ?"

"Lieutenant Garber," I said.

"And who am I playing?" Matthau asked.

"Revill," Joe replied.

"Revill? What kind of name is that?"

"It's the name of the guy you're playing," Peter Stone said. "Here, here's the book," Joe said, handing Matthau a paperback of John Godey's *The Taking of Pelham One Two Three.* "You're a Transit Police lieutenant."

Matthau started leafing through the pages. "Revill doesn't sound right."

"He's black," Stone said. "The guy in the novel is black."

"I'm not Revill," Matthau said. "I don't feel the name is right."

"Well, what name would you like?" Stone asked.

"I don't know. Jerry"—turning to me—"what did you say your name was?"

"Garber."

"That's Jewish, right?" Matthau asked.

"Yeah," I said. "The way I figure it."

"Well, that's what I should be," said Matthau. "I'm Jewish. I should be Garber. Jerry, would you mind switching names with me?"

I couldn't believe what I was listening to. Is this the way movies are made? Major decisions about character are made on the spot? This being my first movie, I'd immersed myself in the role. I'd worked on my character to the last, finest detail—to the extent that I knew Garber's wife's maiden name, his birth sign, and even the date his father and mother became citizens.

In as nonconfrontational way as possible, I said, "But I'm not Revill either."

"Well, can't we find you another name?" Walter said. "Let's look at the book."

The three of them and Gabe Katzka, the producer, started leafing through, looking for a name.

"Here, here's one. Patrone. Rico Patrone," someone said.

"How about that?" said Matthau. "You can be Patrone."

All eyes were now on me. Would I accommodate everyone? A simple adjustment. A good actor can make an adjustment. But it's not so simple: If Walter Matthau couldn't be Revill, why should it be so easy for me to be Patrone?

"I have to think about it," I said.

The assistant director walked in. "We're ready to rehearse."

Suddenly I started to laugh. "I'm an actor. I can adjust. Sure, I'm Rico Patrone, the product of a mixed marriage; my father's Italian, my mother's Jewish. I was abandoned on a doorstep and sent to the Hebrew Orphan Asylum. But I kept the name Rico Patrone."

Matthau was laughing out loud. "One more thing, Jerry," he said. "Garber needs a first name. What would you call me?"

Looking at Matthau, I said, "Walter, to me you're a tall, skinny Zero Mostel. I'll call you Z."

"Zachary," he said. "My name is Zachary. Zachary Garber." Looking at everyone he said, "Remember, Jerry Stiller here gave me my name."

"Let's go rehearse," said Joe Sargent.

As we were about to shoot, Matthau said, "What do you say in this scene, Jerry?"

"I got no lines."

"I'll give you mine."

And he did.

During the filming, Matthau stayed at the Carlyle Hotel, a Madison Avenue elegance. At 6 o'clock each morning he'd pick me up in his white Rolls-Royce, and we'd run our lines on the way to the locations.

One day Walter took me to lunch at Oscar's Catch of the Sea. I sat with him and his agent, Lee Stevens, in a booth, talking basketball. While we were waiting to order, a lady approached and said to me, "I really enjoy those Blue Nun commercials you and your wife do."

"Thanks," I said.

As she left, Walter joked, "I did *The Odd Couple* on Broadway and you she knows from Blue Nun wine."

And he picked up the check.

My dream of performing in a speaking role on Broadway came true when I got a call to audition for the role of Carmine Vespucci in the New York production of *The Ritz,* a play by Terrence McNally to be directed by Bobby Drivas. Drivas cast me despite a terrible audition. After my reading he told me to go down into the cellar to go over the script, which I did. When I came back up he asked me to drop the script and do an improvisation. I did and I ate the scenery. I pulled out all the stops. I went bananas. I played Carmine Vespucci as a deranged "crazo." Drivas cast me on the spot. The play gave me the chance to costar with Rita Moreno, Jack Weston, and F. Murray Abraham. This was to be a very merry adventure.

The cast included Paul Price, Steve Collins, George Dzundza, Tony DiSantis, Ruth Jareslow, and Vera Lockwood. While the publicity photos were being taken, Rita told a joke about an actor playing the gravedigger in *Hamlet* with Sir Laurence Olivier. The actor riffled through the script saying, "Bullshit, bullshit, bullshit . . . ah, my part, my part."

We rehearsed at the New Amsterdam Rooftop Theater on 42nd Street, once a jewel of a playhouse where the likes of Eddie Cantor, Al Jolson, and Fanny Brice had starred.

There was no steam heat in the theater now; the seats were broken, the ceilings were peeling. The stage looked like pipe-rack city, a mock-up of the Ritz Baths. This show has all the earmarks of a hit, I told myself. Every time I work in a miserable rehearsal space, I feel a hit. I love substandard conditions. It makes me work better. But these were the worst.

One night after a late rehearsal, Philip, the night maintenance man, took us down in the elevator. As we were walking on 42nd Street toward Eighth Avenue, I realized I had forgotten my script. I told Bobby I was going back to get it.

Bobby said, "You won't have much luck."

"Why?"

"You'll find out. We're going to have a drink at Downey's. Come meet us."

I went back to the New Amsterdam and rang for the elevator. I asked the maintenance man to take me upstairs.

"I can't, Mr. Stiller," he said.

"Why not?" I asked.

"There's somebody up there."

"Who? Who's up there?" I asked.

"This woman," he said, looking at me in a strange way. "She's only there at night," he said.

"What woman?" I asked.

"She cries at night," he said. "I'm not going up there. If you want to go, you'll have to walk."

"It's twelve floors," I said.

"I wouldn't go if I were you."

"Are you saying there's a ghost up there?"

"I'm not saying nothing. I'm just letting you know what I hear."

"How long has this been going on?" I asked.

"As long as I've been here," the maintenance man said.

"Who is she?" I asked.

"Some famous actress who was shot by her husband when he caught her doing it with some big producer."

"Well, I think I'll leave the script till tomorrow," I said.

"Good idea, Mr. Stiller."

"Good night, Philip."

"Good night, Mr. Stiller."

We spent the final days before the opening in Washington, D.C., rehearsing at a scenery warehouse in a burned-out area near Yankee Stadium. We'd work from late night till morning.

"It's going to be a hit," I said. "Nothing can be lower than this dump."

During this period, Bobby Drivas seemed oblivious to everything. "It's good to get used to this," he'd say. "We can catch the desperation of the characters in the show."

The Ritz opened in Washington to terrible notices. The theater was close to empty at each performance. Adela, the producer, would not close the play. Drivas and McNally went to work, rewriting each night, switching the order of scenes. Jimmy Coco, Will Holt, and Dolly Jonah also pitched in, reshaping the play. Two weeks later we had something that seemed to work, but still no audiences.

Thanks to Adela Holzer's unflagging belief in Terrence McNally, *The Ritz* opened at the Longacre in New York on January 20, 1975. The reviews somehow gave the impression that the play was especially tailored to a gay audience. In truth, for the first month on Broadway, most of the people in the audience *were* gay. Many came more than once, wearing different outfits. Miraculously, word of mouth on the show started attracting a straight audience who viewed it as an out-and-out farce. Rex Reed's great follow-up review in the (N.Y.) *Daily News* undoubtedly turned the show into a hit. When busloads of women started arriving from Wilkes-Barre and Scranton on Sundays, we knew we were in. The women were our best audiences.

One Sunday matinee, Totie Fields came back after the show. "I loved it," she said, "and did you hear those women laughing? Can you imagine how much harder they would've laughed if they knew what they were laughing about?"

Larry Ford, the stage manager, was put in charge of the asylum. At times the offstage madness was as bizarre as what took place on stage.

One night, during one of my scenes, someone broke through the iron bars of my dressing-room window and stole the .38 revolver and mink coat I needed for my next entrance. Here I was, playing a Mafioso tough guy, and a real crook rips me off. I was humiliated and panic-stricken. I dashed down to the stage and told Larry what had happened.

"What do I do? I can't go on without my gun."

Larry said, "Follow the book," handing me his stage manager's script as he bolted out the stage door. I was now the stage manager running the show. Five minutes later he returned, carrying a mink coat and a gun.

"Where did you get them?" I asked.

"I borrowed the coat from a lady in the audience, the gun I got from a cop on 48th Street. Now go ahead, do your scene." And he went back on the book.

Around the fifth month into the run, Jack Weston, who played Gaetano Proclo and always cracked me up offstage, decided to try to break me up onstage. At one turn of the plot, Jack dons a mink coat and a blonde wig, slaps on lipstick, and joins an amateur show already in progress, impersonating one of the Andrews Sisters. This was all done while lip-synching to an actual Andrews Sisters' recording of "Roll Out the Barrel." In my zeal to prove to my sister that Jack is gay, I interrupt the act at gunpoint and order him to take off the wig, the mink coat, and the lipstick. At this particular performance Jack added a Groucho nose. Looking me square in the eye, he dared me not to crack up.

I did the lines. "Okay, Gaetano, take off the wig."

Jack removed the wig.

"Now take off the mink."

Jack obeyed.

"Now the lipstick."

He wiped off the lipstick.

I could see him anticipating my breaking up. I said, "Okay, Gaetano, take off the Groucho nose." Jack took off the nose, slowly. I took one look at his face, I paused and said, "Put it back on."

Jack fell to his knees, convulsed in laughter, which set the audience off, stopping the show.

When we got offstage we expected Larry Ford to give us hell. All he said was, "If it happens again, Jack, you could rupture yourself laughing so hard. I don't want to see that happen to you."

One matinee day my dressing room door burst open, and before I could see who it was, a man grabbed me in a huge embrace. His head was over my shoulder, and I heard weeping. I still didn't know who he was as I pulled his body off mine and stared at him, trying to figure out if I knew him.

He was still sobbing. "It's me, Zinger," he gasped.

"Zinger?"

"Zinger, one of the Harmonica Rascals."

"Borah Minnevitch and the Harmonica Rascals?" I asked.

"Yes," he said. "Remember? We played *Sullivan* together."

"Of course I remember," I said. "The Harmonica Rascals. You're the one who . . ." Suddenly I recalled the seven original harmonica players and a poor little midget they kicked around. "You're the one who kicked . . . Johnny. . . ."

"Yeah! Johnny Puleo. The audience loved it."

"What happened to Johnny?" I asked.

"He disappeared."

At this point Zinger or whatever his name was broke down, sobbing inconsolably.

"You were wonderful," he said, the words choking in his throat.

"How are you?" I asked.

"Not so good, Jerry. She's not going to make it."

"Who's not going to make it?"

"Fran."

Fran?

"She's bad, Jerry."

"What's wrong?" I asked.

"Oh, Jerry, Jerry. You were so wonderful, Jerry. You were the best."

"I'm sorry about Fran." Who was Fran? I asked myself.

"We're broke, Jerry. Not a dime. We have nothing. Can you believe that?" More tears poured out.

"Take it easy," I said. "How much do you need?"

"How much have you got?"

I checked my wallet, asking myself what was going on.

"About thirty-five dollars," I said.

"I'll take it." More tears and a hug.

Other visitors were knocking on the door, coming to tell me how much they'd enjoyed the performance.

"Here," I said. "I don't carry money at the theater."

"This is fine," he said. "God bless you, Jerry. I'll tell Fran."

He left, and I never saw or heard from Zinger again. If he wasn't telling the truth, it was the greatest $35 performance I'd ever seen in my life.

The Ritz ran at the Longacre a year. Bernie Kukoff and Jeff Harris caught a performance and subsequently cast me as Gus Duzik opposite Richard Castellano in *Joe and Sons,* an upcoming CBS TV sitcom. A month later I left *The Ritz* and was on my way to Hollywood.

Richie Castellano's acting mantra was, "If you don't want to do a bad take, don't do a bad take." Opposite *Joe and Sons* was a new show, *Welcome Back, Kotter,* which swept the hour. After ten weeks, William Paley of CBS made the final decision to cancel us.

At the same time Fred Silverman, the reigning head of CBS, cast Anne as Kate McShane, described as a Kennedyesque lawyer, in a one-hour TV drama of the same name. We rented the home of the daughter of Victor Fleming, the director of *Gone with the Wind* and *The Wizard of Oz.* She was a most generous woman and spoke about her father in glowing terms.

Unfortunately *Kate McShane* was up against *Starsky and Hutch* and disappeared after thirteen episodes. So 1975 was our proverbial fifteen minutes in television, but Anne would resurface on TV many other times over the years. She starred with Carroll O'Connor in *Archie Bunker's Place,* played the mother-in-law on *Alf,* and with her friend Lila Garrett would coauther the Writer's Guild–award-winning *The Other Woman,* which starred Anne and Hal Linden.

In December 1975, the movie version of *The Ritz* was to be shot in London. Richard Lester, who had directed the Beatles' films *A Hard Day's Night* and *Help!,* cast me in my old role.

I arrived at my hotel in London. My room, figuratively speaking, was the size of a closet, equipped with a tiny refrigerator, a coin-operated liquor-and-snacks bar, a single bed, and a TV.

I was to play the third lead in the movie, and my contract stipulated that I was to have accommodations at a first-class hotel. Jack Weston was staying at the Connaught, Rita Moreno at the Mayfair. I'd expected to awaken to Big Ben and the sight of Buckingham Palace. My hotel was miles away from the theater district. Five weeks in a room no bigger than a cell. I was furious.

I bolted into the lobby, where I ran into F. Murray Abraham.

"What's wrong?" Murray asked.

"My room! It's too small," I sputtered. I couldn't finish. "How's yours?" I asked.

"Small," he said.

"Are they all that small?"

"I think so."

We approached the desk clerk. Suddenly Murray shouted loud enough for the entire lobby to hear, "This is Mr. Stiller! This man is a major Broadway star, and you have given him a terrible room. I demand that you change his room at once."

The desk clerk looked at us in amazement.

"Well, that's the room we were told to give Mr. Stiller," he whispered.

"You don't understand," Murray exclaimed. "This is a great actor, an artist, and you're treating him like dirt. This man is a major, major star in the United States." He drew a breath. "Do you hear me?"

"You'll have to stop shouting or I'll have to call security."

"I'm not shouting," Murray screamed.

"Murray," I said, "it's okay. I love what you're doing. I'll just call California and straighten this out."

"It's 7 A.M. in California," Murray said. "They're all asleep. The only way to get these people here to change your room is to scream at them. It scares them."

While Murray was still screaming, security men arrived.

Murray turned on them. "We're American actors shooting a movie in your country, and you're treating us like dirt."

"All the rooms are the same size," the desk clerk said. "The airlines use this hotel."

"There's got to be a better room for this man. This is an American star."

I was beginning to feel a lot more wounded now, believing the things

Murray was saying about me. The clerk went into the back office and returned.

"All right, sir," he said to Murray, "we can make two adjoining rooms into one for Mr. Stiller and yourself."

A few years later when Murray was nominated for his Academy Award for *Amadeus,* a Texas newspaperwoman called and wanted to know what I knew about this comparatively unknown long shot for an Oscar. I told her that I'd once seen him give an even better performance in a London hotel lobby.

I went to Twickenham Studios to meet Richard Lester for the first time. He was between scene setups. I introduced myself.

"You're playing Vespucci," he said.

"Yes."

"We'll have to darken your hair," he said, on the run.

The hair stylist, a forceful English lady, said, "Come with me. We'll do it at my hotel." She called a driver.

Minutes later we were sitting in her room, my hair now being dyed black. She worked very quickly, inundating the hair with a thick gooey substance. When she finished she said, "Good, now get in the shower," directing me toward it. "Go ahead, get in."

I was taken aback.

"Get in," she said.

Without questioning, I removed my clothes and got in the shower. I told myself, *You're in England, and I guess this is the way they dye their hair here—naked.* I could feel the water going down past my navel. *It's probably dyeing all of me,* I thought.

After a few minutes the forceful English lady said, "All right, come on out."

I needed a towel, I said.

"Just come on out."

I felt like a hostage being released. There was nothing in her voice, no emotion.

"I'm going to put the conditioner in," she said.

"Okay," I said, locating a towel.

She applied the liquid and said, "Get back in the shower. Rinse."

"Okay," I said. I rinsed.

"Tip top," she said. "You're ready to shoot."

Two weeks later my hair needed a touch-up. Again we went to her hotel, and again she applied the dye. Then she said, as before, "Get in the shower." I did. It was like a dance step, like the "Lambeth Walk." Only naked.

The next day we were about to film the death scene between myself and my father, played by George Coulouris. Mr. Coulouris had appeared in many Hollywood pictures of the '40s and early '50s—notably *Citizen Kane*—and had then moved to England during the McCarthy period, which put a number of actors, writers, and directors into exile. As Coulouris lay on his movie deathbed, waiting for action, I introduced myself.

"Tell me," he said. "I know I'm supposed to die in this scene, but is this movie a comedy or a tragedy?"

"You mean they didn't send you a script?"

"No. It's only one scene. I just need to know whether it's supposed to be funny."

"Well, it's funny—I think. You're my father, and on your dying bed you tell me to kill my brother-in-law, Gaetano Proclo, whom you hate because he's fat and you think he's a sissy."

"Okay, I've got it," he said. "There's a difference, you know, when you die funny or serious. A lot more going on when it's funny."

On the word "Action," Coulouris became a volcano. He bellowed like a bull and died like a buffalo.

There was a scene in *The Ritz* in which the gay bathhouse customers tie me up, dress me in a green sequined gown and red wig, gag me, and throw me in a steam room. When I finally break loose, I scream vengeance from a New Orleans–like balcony.

During the run of the Broadway show the sight of me in the green gown and red wig provoked some interesting reactions. My kids said, "Dad, green is your color." Leo Bloom, a Syracuse buddy, loved the outfit so much he sent me a huge hand-painted button that said "Think Green." I kept the button in my shoulder bag, a kind of knapsack, and had forgotten about it. Now the bag was in London with me. Coincidentally, this was a period when the IRA had recently set off some bombs in the London Underground, and security was tight. Kaye Ballard, who played my sister in the movie, invited me one afternoon to go with her to see Albert Finney in *Hamlet*. She asked me to pick up our tickets at a booth in the lobby of a West End hotel. As I walked up to the ticket booth,

I was suddenly pushed against the wall by two large men, one of whom immediately grabbed my shoulder bag while his mate searched me.

"Keep your 'ands up against the wall," the first guy said. He was in civilian clothes. "We're Scotland Yard," the other informed me, flashing his identification, "and we'd like to see what you've got in that bag."

"I'm an American," I said. "I'm in a movie."

This didn't deter them.

The second gentleman, going through the contents of my bag, pulled out the button that said "Think Green."

"What's this all about?" he wanted to know.

I suddenly realized I was dressed kind of scruffily and they had somehow suspected me of being a member of the IRA. The button confirmed it.

"Look," I said. "You may not believe this, but I'm here in London shooting a movie. I'm an actor, and I play this Mafioso character who gets thrown into a steam bath by these gay guys in a bathhouse."

The two policemen stared at me. "Go on," they said, in fascination.

"Anyway, these guys in this bathhouse put this green sequined gown and a red wig on me, and they tie and gag me. When I finally break loose and the audience sees the gown, it's hilarious. A friend complimented me on the gown when we did it in a theater in New York. He said green was my color. It goes with my eyes. And he gave me that button."

The two cops didn't say a word. Finally one of them started to laugh. "When does the fill-um come out?" he asked.

"In about a year," I said.

"You're sure you're an American?" the other fellow asked.

I took out my wallet and showed them some credit cards—not that they proved I wasn't an IRA bomber.

"Look," I said, fishing in my pocket, "these things prove I'm an American." I had two Kennedy half-dollars on me, brand shining new. The policeman suddenly relaxed. "Would you take these as a gift?" I said.

They were enthralled by the coins, and each accepted one, telling me how sorry they were for the inconvenience they'd caused and hoped I'd understand.

"By the way, Yank, what's the name of the picture?"

"*The Ritz*," I told them.

"We'll be sure to watch for it."

• • •

Fifteen years after the Broadway production of *The Ritz* I heard that Bobby Drivas had died. He was only fifty. Terrence McNally organized a memorial service at Frank Campbell's. July is a bad month to die if you're in the theater. Everyone is either in the Hamptons or doing summer stock, but at 11:30 A.M. the chapel was filled. I saw Colleen Dewhurst, Ken Marsolais, Renee Taylor, Joe Bologna, Ken Friedman, Jack Betts, Jane Bergere, Adela Holzer, Rex Reed, and a lot of people I didn't know. I saw F. Murray Abraham, whom I hadn't seen since the filming of *The Ritz*.

We were all seated. Cy Coleman walked over to a piano and started playing something. It was almost like an overture to a show. I had been in this same room for Ed Sullivan's wake. I remembered telling Bob Precht, Ed's son-in-law, that Anne and I would not be at the funeral mass for Ed at St. Patrick's the following day because we'd be working.

"That's the one thing Ed would've understood," Bob said.

As Coleman played, I wondered how the piano had gotten in here. You don't find that at Jewish funerals. I remember Bob Fosse at Paddy Chayevsky's funeral, when asked to say something, doing a time step. He did it a cappella.

McNally got up and said Bobby was a tough taskmaster.

"He'd say to me, 'You've got a pretty fair first act, a decent second act, but you've got no third act.' Bobby had three actors whom he loved. I want them to say something."

Jimmy Coco, Paul Benedict, and F. Murray Abraham got up and spoke; then Colleen recited one of Shakespeare's sonnets. There was a moment of quiet. Five men appeared and quickly wheeled the casket out.

Terrence McNally said, "Let's give Bobby a hand." The standing ovation lasted two minutes. No one would stop.

In 1976 Anne and I took one of our few non-working vacations. We packed up and headed for Nantucket, an island off the Massachusetts coast. The four of us stayed in a small room in a bed-and-breakfast. Although we were somewhat near the water, the room was tiny and faced an alley. There wasn't much light. At least on Riverside Drive we could see trees.

Anne was ecstatic. She loved the island, the quaint shops, even the overpriced restaurants. One day she took me to a ramshackle house and said she would love to live there. I didn't understand. Yes, it was near the water, but the house was falling apart, we would be the only Jews for miles around, and there were no kosher delis. What was so great about this place?

We returned to New York and I forgot about Nantucket. The next year Anne returned to the island, this time by herself. I thought nothing about this until she returned home and announced, "I bought the house."

"What?"

"The house on Children's Beach. I bought it. Our first house, Jerry."

I was stunned, to say the least. But I trusted Anne and she proved to be right. Nantucket has become a very special place for both of us. And now they even sell kosher franks.

Coming from the sidewalks of NYC, owning a second home was a dream. To look at the trees, the ocean, the stars at night. But I forgot about fog. Nantucket was one hundred miles away from New York by air if you weren't fogged in. I was told that during World War Two American pilots learned how to land in fog by training on the island. Nevertheless, over these many years I've learned to love Nantucket, fog and all.

As the island's reputation grew, though, so did the airfares. Nantucket became the island of the rich, and after a while the $140 round-trip cost $400, possibly more.

The idea that there were people desperate to bolt from the Big Apple speedily and inexpensively must have struck a young aviator living on the island as a good business opportunity.

Sam flagged me down one day while I was riding my bike past his house. He asked if his business manager might call on us to discuss the matter of the rising cost of airfares. I said sure. Two days later the four of us—he, his business manager, Anne, and I—sat on our porch sipping vodka tonics, watching the sky change from fiery red to orange, then disappear as the harvest moon emerged above the horizon.

"We have an idea which you two might be interested in," the business manager said. "We all love this place. The problem is, how to afford to get up here? Sam has a twelve-seat passenger plane. He thinks he can start a service to get people like yourselves up here whenever you like. We've already got ten people interested enough to put up money. Sam has been flying up every week for five years."

Sounds good, I thought. "What would it cost?"

"We're thinking of everybody putting up $25,000 each. We can start an airline. You guys fly free. You also become stockholders, so you're investing and collecting dividends."

The idea excited me immediately. To own a share in an airline that could get me to Nantucket in an hour was the answer to a dream.

"We'll get back to you on it," I said. Anne was in agreement. I called our business manager and told him of the idea.

"I don't like it," he said. "You don't know the people. Are they legitimate? I don't recommend you put $25,000 of your hard-earned money into it."

I was devastated by his pessimistic attitude, but aware that his conservative approach came from hard experience.

I notified our two entrepreneurs of our decision not to invest. "Can we meet again?" they asked. I said yes. The dream was still alive for me despite the forewarning.

Back in New York, the two pioneers sat and laid out an alternative plan for Anne and me. In lieu of payment, would we write commercials for the new airline? We would not have to invest and would still get free passage to Nantucket whenever we wanted. I asked how I could get an idea of what the service would be like.

Sam said, "When you're back in Nantucket again, call me and we'll fly to New York."

So one weekend I met him at the waiting room in Nantucket Airport. "Just follow me," Sam said. I carried my bags to a remote part of the runway and stared at the strange craft whose fuselage seemed to sit practically on the ground. It had tiny wheels, a double tail, and a single engine. It looked like the Edsel of the aircraft industry. I told myself not to make any quick judgments.

Sam loaded my bags into the baggage compartment. "Do you want to sit in the copilot's seat?"

"Of course," I said. Another adventure.

I sat to his right as he coolly hit the ignition and turned on the engine. It's only a hundred miles, I said to myself. A milk run. We got clearance, and minutes later were in the air, circling Nantucket, then heading to New York. There was no conversation between us, not even, How're you doing? The guy had enough to do, looking at the altimeter, checking the gas, and being in contact with the control tower. There was really no time for small talk. He had earphones on anyway, listening to the weather. I likened it to being on stage. You're there to act, not to converse with the stagehands.

Out of curiosity I looked behind me and examined what was in the back of this flagship of our fledgling airline. The seats were not all in the upright position. Some seemed to have torn upholstery. And there was a strange smell.

I glanced at Sam. Still no voice contact between us. Martha's Vineyard was off to the right. My eyes dipped toward his feet, which were on some pedals, controlling the ailerons or the rudder or something. I noticed the soles of his shoes were flapping. They were not sewn to the shoes themselves. I immediately experienced a severe loss of faith in the airline.

For the first time I spoke to Sam, who seemed to be in an entirely different world than the one I remembered on our porch. "This is a very unusual plane," I said. There was a long silence. I hoped my question was not interpreted as impugning the credibility of the airline. "The fuselage has a lot of space," I said.

"That's on account of the fish," he said.

"Fish?"

"Yeah, that's how I make a living, I transport fish from Nantucket."

"Oh, I see," I said. That explained the smell. My business manager's warning words were suddenly ringing in my ears.

My remark seemed to evoke a quiet anger in the pilot. He had a mood change. It was scary. I immediately realized that I had gotten to the heart of the matter. The dark side of this guy was emerging, and here I was five thousand feet in the air. I'd better shut up. We didn't say a word to each other for what seemed like an eternity. I gazed at Long Island, now below us.

Without warning Sam started his descent. "Is this La Guardia?" I asked.

"No, we're going to Islip," he said.

"Why? That's hours from New York."

"There's a landing fee at the other airports."

Minutes later we were on the ground and I stood in a small terminal with my bags.

"Where can I drop you?" Sam asked.

In semi-shock I said, "Gee, I didn't expect door-to-door service."

He said, "I'm going into Midtown. How about 34th Street and Eighth

Avenue? I'd take you home, but I've got to be someplace at eight." We drove from the airport in silence. I asked myself how I'd gotten into this. I was just riding my bike past a guy's house, and I end up delivering fish and almost buying into an airline.

When we reached 34th and Eighth, Sam helped me onto the street with the suitcases. He said again, "Sorry I can't take you all the way." I hailed a cab and arrived home a half-hour later.

Some years later I ran across a story in *The New York Times*. It was about Sam, who had been sentenced to prison for transporting arms parts to Iran. It described how he flew from an airfield at the tip of Long Island across the Atlantic. He must have been a pretty good pilot, after all.

One day in the early '80s I was jogging and discovered I couldn't do five miles. I could barely do three. I felt winded. The experience frightened the hell out of me. It seemed so precipitous. I felt I had been betrayed by my body.

Up until the *Sullivan* years, and even during the *Sullivan* years, I'd eat anything, drink limitless cups of coffee, and enjoy a couple of scotches two or three times a week. My body seemed resilient. It could withstand anything. Now I was at the YMCA on West 63rd Street, circling the oval with the regular crowd, when I realized that guys I'd once lapped were passing me. I attributed everything to pollution.

During the next few weeks I continued to hit the Y and struggled to do my three miles. The frustration now made jogging painful. I visited my internist, who did an EKG.

"You've got low T's," he said, meaning a dip in the cardiogram.

"What does that mean?"

"It could be nothing. It's indeterminate. You should have a stress test."

I didn't take the test. The thought scared the hell out of me. Instead, I decided to fast.

I envisioned cleansing myself in Biblical fashion. I'd purge myself of all the impurities I had ingested in those jogging years. I could see huge chunks of my body dropping off. All the coffee, pastrami, and booze would be washed away by going to a fasting farm.

I arrived at the fabled Health Manor in Pawling, New York, with two suitcases. One contained necessities—underwear, toothpaste, etc. The other, all the Super 8mm film I had ever shot of Anne, myself, and the kids, and a splicer. My intention was to keep occupied during the difficult days ahead, during which I'd be fasting.

I'd heard about the Health Manor from actor friends. There was also a nutrition program, where non-fasters could enjoy food that appealed to the mind as well as the body. Sy Travers, an actor who'd toured with Anne and me in *The Prisoner of Second Avenue,* spoke of his having "gone up to Dr. Gross" as a child with his family. I envisioned an entire overweight family stuffed into a Buick, plodding up the Taconic Parkway for a fast. It almost sounded as if they'd been going on a picnic.

"What's the longest you ever fasted?" I asked Sy, wondering if I could handle one day.

"A month," he replied, his eyes suddenly ablaze.

"What did you do after it ended?"

"I ate a cheesecake," he said, as if that was the stupidest question anyone could ask.

"A whole cheesecake?"

"Made with ricotta cheese, Italian. It's less fattening."

Of course, I thought, you always binge after denial. It's like when Prohibition was repealed. People went out and got drunk.

I saw myself attacking a cheesecake after losing a pound a day. After thirty pounds, I'd have a right.

I was told that some of Dr. Gross's famous clients included Shelley Winters (whom he'd ordered off the farm for sneaking in a pizza), Grace Bumbry, and Charles Mingus. Of incidental interest was the fact that Cus D'Amato, the manager of Floyd Patterson and José Torres (and later Mike Tyson) trained his prospects in a gym next to the main house. The boxers were also on Dr. Gross's regimen.

Intellectually I was prepared to stop eating, but emotionally I knew I'd have to psych myself. I called Anna Berger, an actress friend who'd also been up to Dr. Gross. "How much did you lose, Anna?"

"Lots," Anna said, "but it's not easy. Bring up lots of books."

Instead, I brought all the old family movies.

When I arrived at the Rhinebeck railroad station I was met by Dr. Gross himself. He looked like an "in the pink" bantamweight boxer, with curly hair, eyes that twinkled, and skin that glistened.

"Jerry," he said, shaking my hand with enthusiasm, "I'm Dr. Gross. Come on, let's get in the car." Each of us grabbed a bag. "Glad you're up here."

"Me too," I said, marveling at his health.

"I'm a great admirer of you both. How's Anne?"

"Fine," I said.

"What's in those bags?" he asked.

"Oh, books, and some Super 8mm film. I'm going to make a feature film out of all the home movies I ever took," I said, joking.

"Nothing else?" he asked, discreet admonishment in his eyes. "No food?"

"No, no food."

"Good. I'm going to put you in one of the deluxe cabins. It's a single. You're not far from the main house. You know who's up here?" Dr. Gross asked. "Sugar Hart. Jimmy Jacobs thinks he can be a champ. We're trying to bring him down a class to welterweight."

"Fasting?"

"Yes."

"You're in great shape," I remarked. "How do you do it?"

"I'm the same weight I was when I boxed in the '20s," Dr. Gross said.

"You boxed?" I suddenly thought of Sam Jaffe in *Lost Horizon,* who lived to be two hundred.

"Yeah, under the name Baby Gross. I won a lot of fights."

The car pulled up to a huge mansion on a hill.

"This is the main house. You can register and meet the staff. They'd love you to say hello."

I entered the spacious old house with its high ceilings. We walked past the living room filled with people, mostly ladies in bathrobes, conversing, watching television, all losing weight.

"Come with me to my office."

We passed the kitchen. I could smell food. I saw carrots being shredded, tomatoes sliced, potatoes being made ready for baking.

"See?" said Dr. Gross. "All vegetarian. I haven't had meat in twenty-five years. Not everyone up here fasts. Some come just to change their eating habits. But you're going to fast."

I was getting hungry.

We reached his office.

"Sit down and fill this out. I'm going to examine you."

He took out a stethoscope and placed the ends in his ears. "Open your shirt." He was listening. "Okay." He made a notation. He checked my blood pressure.

"Okay," he said. "I'll show you where you're staying."

We walked down a hill to my cabin.

"Let me explain. You're not supposed to eat. If you get hungry, drink some water. There's a pitcher with ice cubes and water on the night table. If you feel like eating, put an ice cube in your mouth. The first two days are the toughest. If you get dizzy, there's the buzzer," he said, indicating it. "Just ring it and I'll bring you an orange. We can put in a TV if you want."

"Yeah, I'd like one," I said, suddenly feeling isolated.

"I'll have one sent over," he said.

A young man appeared with my suitcases. "Where can I put these?" he asked.

"Under my bed?"

"Not enough room," he said. He slid them in the closet.

Minutes later the TV was hooked up.

The cabin had a double bed, shower, and a bureau. Outside was a porch. Halfway through unpacking, I decided to say hello to my neighbors. I strolled past their cabins. They were all women.

"Hello," I said, trying to be as unobtrusive as possible. Privacy seemed to be the order of the day. The women all nodded politely and went back to losing weight.

I returned to my own cabin, turned on the TV, and finished unpacking. I took out the Super 8 film and set the splicer on the bureau. I had also brought along some bouillon cubes, a heating filament, and a ceramic mug. I figured that if by some chance my willpower failed me, I could make a little bouillon. It seemed harmless. How much damage could water and a bouillon cube do? The filament was a piece of metal shaped like a deformed triangle. It plugged into an electrical outlet. When inserted into a mug of water it made the water boil.

I went into the bathroom, dropped a bouillon cube into the mug, and filled the mug with water from the faucet. I plugged the filament into the outlet near the medicine chest. I watched as the bouillon bubbled, my mouth beginning to water. Suddenly the television went off and I could hear women shouting, "What happened to the lights?" The mug had cracked, and muddy soup was oozing into the sink. The cabin door flew open. Standing in the doorway was a livid Dr. Gross. Had he been waiting outside?

"You got a filament, right?" he demanded, like a teacher who'd caught a kid throwing a spitball.

"Yeah," I said.

He surveyed the evidence in the sink.

"I'm sorry," I said.

"You blew a fuse, Jerry. It happens all the time. They come in, they say they want to fast, and they cheat."

I looked and saw a man who hadn't eaten meat in twenty-five years, and I felt terrible. I started to tremble.

"I'm sorry," I said again.

"Give it to me," he said.

I handed him the filament.

"Made in Japan," he noted. "Remember, if you get hungry, suck on the ice cubes."

"Okay," I said.

He left.

That day I occupied myself by visiting the Roosevelt Mansion in Hyde Park, just up the road. I tried to substitute historical artifacts for pastrami. It filled me for three hours.

When I got back I pulled out reels of Super 8 film and examined them through the viewer. I started to splice. My eyes got blurry, so I stopped and switched on the television. The ever-present pitcher of water and ice cubes sat staring at me. I survived the night.

The next day Dr. Gross visited me. "How're you doing?" he asked.

"Fine," I lied.

"Come on, I'll take you up to the gym. You'll meet Sugar Hart. He's from Philadelphia. He's won all his fights, all knockouts. Jimmy Jacobs and Cus D'Amato are training him."

"That sounds great," I said, following Dr. Gross up a hill.

We watched Sugar Hart work out. Dr. Gross promised me tickets to Hart's next fight in Madison Square Garden.

I decided to return to my cabin to work on splicing the film, and after working for a few minutes heard a knock. My cabin neighbor stood at the door. She introduced herself. She said she taught school in Queens. "How much are you trying to lose?" she asked.

"I don't know," I said. "I've got no big goals. I just want to feel better."

"I've lost fifteen pounds. I'm happy to lose twenty-five," she said. "Have you met the rest of the girls?"

"No, I haven't."

"You're the only man in the cabins."

"I noticed," I said. "It's like I've got a harem."

She laughed. "Yeah, fasting gets you horny."

"Why is that?" I asked.

"I don't know," she said, smiling, "but it's true. Come on, I'll introduce you to my roommate."

We walked next door, and I met another chubby lady who said she was in advertising.

"I love your ads," she said. "Does Anne fast?"

"She doesn't have to."

"Listen," the teacher's roommate said, "it's nice to have a man around."

"Okay, I'm here if you need me," I said by way of a joke.

Around 5:30 that afternoon the northern sky took on a strange yellowish glow and the birds stopped singing. It was as if nature had suddenly gone on strike. I don't know what made me turn on the television, but I did. The regular programming was interrupted by a local announcer, who said there was a tornado watch in Dutchess and Putnam counties. I remembered the scene in *The Wizard of Oz* just before the tornado, when everything stopped. I watched the sky getting darker. I could hear silence. Tornadoes in New York State? But this was for real.

I suddenly wanted to eat. If I was going to die, I wanted at least to have a last meal. It seemed bizarre to die while fasting. Maybe this was a dream. I'll check with the ladies. I walked into a cabin full of anxious women watching the tube.

"Is it true?" I asked.

"Yeah, it's a tornado."

It dawned upon me that when Mother Nature strikes, both sexes have the same thought: Save your ass.

"What do we do?" one of the women asked. "Do we go to the main house?"

"Are you kidding?" another one said. "That's the last thing to do. It's wood. It'll get blown away."

"Where's Dr. Gross?"

"What can he do?" said someone else. "He's just like us."

"But he must know a place to go."

"What place? Listen to the TV. This never happened around here before."

Nobody turned to me for manly advice. I just stood and looked. I could hear a whistling, like a far-off wind. Suddenly it started to pour.

"Maybe we should all get under our beds," one woman said.

"That's ridiculous," the advertising lady said. "We'd never fit."

"Let's get in my station wagon," the teacher said. "There's a state troopers' station on the highway."

Everyone agreed, including myself. We piled unceremoniously into the groaning station wagon and headed north. The rain and wind buffeted the car, and its windshield wipers were almost snapped off by the gusts. We peered out the windows, searching for the state-trooper station. Someone spotted it. We stopped and, dripping wet, bolted into the station. A trooper in a neatly ironed shirt sat writing at a desk.

My teacher neighbor, now the spokesperson, said, "Excuse us, we're from—"

"I know," the trooper said. "You're from Dr. Gross's."

"Yeah," she said, "and we heard about the tornado watch, and we—"

"It's a warning," he said, "not a watch."

"Well, it's coming down heavy. What do we do?"

"Go back to the Manor," he said. "There's nothing to worry about."

The teacher got angry. "Don't tell us to go back there. It's a tornado."

"What do you want me to do?" the trooper asked.

"We can't go back. Wooden houses aren't safe. What's this place made of?"

"Cinder blocks. But you can't stay here."

"Then where can we go?" one of the ladies shouted hysterically.

"We could go to the movies," the ad lady calmly suggested.

"Yes," the trooper agreed. "The movie house is made of cinder blocks."

"But what's playing?" the hysterical one shouted.

"*Blazing Saddles,*" the trooper said.

"That old thing. I saw it," she screamed.

"So did I," another yelled. The movie house was vetoed.

"Try the Rhinebeck Inn," the trooper said. "It's been there two hundred years. It's safe."

Good idea, everyone agreed.

We fought our way back through wind and rain to the station wagon, and drove the five miles to the Inn. The manager, watching the news reports, broke away from the TV long enough to usher us into the dining room and to say, "I know you're from Dr. Gross. I can only serve you club soda. That's Dr. Gross's standing orders."

"Fine," we said.

The table was suddenly filled with bottles of bubbles.

For two hours we told stories and burped. We rejected each other's excuses to break the fast. When the storm subsided, we drove back to the Manor.

I remained at Dr. Gross's for three days, fasting fastidiously. On the fourth day Anne called from New York. I had to read for a show. I bade Dr. Gross and his staff good-bye.

A couple of weeks later, true to his word, Dr. Gross phoned to ask if I wanted to see Sugar Hart fight at the Garden.

"I'd love to," I said.

"We can meet, and Jimmy Jacobs, Hart's trainer, will take us back to see him before the fight."

When I arrived at the Garden I was greeted by Gross and Jacobs, and was introduced to the luminaries at ringside. I was thrilled. The crowd anxiously awaited Hart's appearance.

"Come on, Jerry," said Jacobs, whom I'd first met at the Y long ago, when he was a national handball champion. "We'll say hello to Sugar."

"Does he like to meet people before a fight?" I asked.

"He's asleep," Jacobs said.

"What?"

"That's how relaxed he is. And remember, he came down from a middleweight. Come on, I'll show you."

Jacobs led us through the catacombs to Hart's dressing room. He opened the door a crack. There, lying on the table, sound asleep, was Hart.

"How does he do it?" I asked.

"He's just completely relaxed," Jacobs said.

"I guess it's the fasting," I said. "It really relaxes you."

At 10 P.M. Hart entered the ring, followed by his opponent, Wilfredo Benitez. Sugar looked like a champion. The announcer introduced the fighters and the loudspeakers gave us the national anthem. The referee called the two men together for their final instructions. The bell rang and the bout started. The action was furious. The crowd was on its feet. Just before the end of Round 1, Hart was hit and went down. He was out cold. The referee counted to 8. The bell rang. The Garden was in an uproar.

Hart, odds on to win, was dragged to his corner and revived by his han-
dlers in time for Round 2. Seconds later he went down again, this time
for good. The crowd was stunned. Jacobs was stunned. Dr. Gross was
bewildered.

I didn't dare say, That fasting, it really relaxes you.

In 1980 I was playing an Italian American man married to an Ozark
woman in Albert Innaurato's *Passione,* the next to last play produced at
the Morosco before that historic theater was demolished by the wrecking
ball. After a preview, I took a nap. When I awoke, I was unable to move
my back. Somehow I managed to go onstage and perform, but the problem persisted, and it eventually led me to the offices of Dr. Milton Reder.
I'd first heard of his wizardry when, at the YMCA, a handball player of my
own vintage volunteered at the end of a game that he knew I had a bad
back.

When the game ended, my partner said, "Go see Dr. Reder. Five visits and you're cured."

My back *was* hurting me, so I took the advice and visited Dr. Reder's
Park Avenue office. A matronly receptionist spoke into a phone, and in
seconds Dr. Reder himself, a jovial Santa Claus–like man, greeted me.

"Jerry Stiller," he said warmly as his eyes brightened. "Come with
me." He was like a friendly uncle welcoming a long-lost nephew.

He led me past the waiting room, filled with patients chatting or reading, many of whom I recognized as celebrities. What they all had in common were two prongs protruding from their noses, making them look like
a school of walruses.

"Did you notice who some of those people were?" Dr. Reder said as
we entered his inner sanctum.

"Yes," I said. "Yul Brynner, Virginia Graham. But it was hard to recognize them with those things sticking out of their noses. What are
they?"

"Would you like something to eat?" the doctor said. "I'm sending
out."

"No thanks," I said.

"I'm going to the Friars tonight with Goodman Ace. Are you free?" he
said as his fingers twirled a steel prong wrapped with a thin layer of ab-
sorbent cotton in a bottle of some solution.

"You write those commercials?" he said. "You and your wife? Who writes them?"

"Anne, mostly," I said.

"She's terrific. I like her." He quoted one of our United Van Lines punch lines.

I was flattered.

"Now, this doesn't hurt," the doctor said, preparing to insert what looked like a bandillero into my proboscis.

"Wait a minute," I interjected. "Before you start, can you tell me what we're doing?"

"If I told you, you wouldn't understand." His hands were now moving toward my nose.

"Please," I said. "I'd like to know."

"Did you see those people out there?"

"Yeah," I said.

"Well, they've all got bad backs. Look," Dr. Reder said, pointing to a crest on the wall. "That's from the Prince of Morocco. He wanted to fly me over in his plane. I wouldn't go."

"Why not?" I asked.

"My people, the people I take care of here, they need me. Trust me," he said, moving once more to insert the prong.

"First tell me what these things do," I begged.

He pointed toward two prongs crisscrossed like a coat of arms on the wall. "I invented this procedure. You really want to know?"

"Yes," I said.

"Okay, I'll make it simple. This is the ganglia," he said, pointing to a spot on his forehead. "We block the ganglia with one of these," he said, indicating the prong in his hand, "and that cuts off the nerves to the back. You do this for forty-five minutes and your back doesn't ache."

It seemed so simple and immediately made sense. That was all the cajoling I needed.

"Okay, be my guest," I said.

Seconds later I was rhinocerized. It was painless. The two cotton-swathed prongs in my nasal passages imparted a soothing feeling.

"Now just sit. You got a book?" the doctor said, leading me back to the waiting room. "You know Virginia Graham, don't you," he said, smiling down on her.

"Virginia," I said, "it's you."

"Yes," the good-natured *Girl Talk* TV hostess said. She pointed to the prongs. "I'm writing a book," she said. "I'm calling it *Up Your Nose.*"

"Does this stuff work?" I asked her.

"Who knows? Ever since Harry died"—her husband, Harry—"I've had this back. When I leave here it feels great. They say five treatments. Listen, I've seen everybody sitting in here, and it's twenty-five bucks. You can't beat it. The place is never empty."

"Twenty-five bucks whoever you are? For anybody?" I said.

"Anybody," Virginia said.

At this moment a bent and hobbling man and his equally bent wife entered. Dr. Reder again emerged and escorted them back into his office. Seconds later, he returned. "You know who that is?" he said. "One of the richest men in the world and his wife. He owns hotels . . . supertankers . . . When he was a kid he bought an abandoned boat on the Mississippi River and floated it."

Minutes later, the husband and wife were seated next to us, pronged.

"We're going to the Friars tonight; want to join us?" Reder again asked me.

"No, thanks. I'm sorry. I've got to write a commercial."

"He's got a great wife, Virginia," Reder said to Virginia Graham, with a nod toward me.

"I know," Virginia Graham said. "Anne's been on my show."

The forty-five minutes—*my* forty-five minutes—sped by. Dr. Reder's introductions, asides, and jokes seemed to be part of the cure. A camaraderie developed between us, a bonding. People hated to leave. Miraculously, after forty-five minutes, everyone seemed able to stand up almost pain-free. This was true healing, I said to myself—the physician who healed through laughter and the heart.

"Come back the day after tomorrow," Reder said jovially as I reluctantly hit the street, ready once again to take on New York. The wealthy couple's chauffeured limo awaited them. I turned around to see them entering their car. They were no longer bent. My spirits soared.

I returned a few more times, then told myself I really didn't need the treatment anymore. My back was cured.

Some time later I read scorching headlines in the newspapers saying that Dr. Milton Reder was accused of using a diluted cocaine solution to treat patients. All I know is that for twenty-five bucks it was forty-five of the most delightfully pain-free minutes I've ever spent in the company of some terrific people.

Following our Blue Nun success, Anne and I got into commercials in a big way. It began when we were hired by the J. Walter Thompson ad agency to do a very brief daily radio program as a vehicle for advertising. John Davis, an agency executive, suggested we call it "Take 5 with Stiller and Meara."

"You'll have an office, a budget, writers, and you'll shoot ten two-minute sketches per week without an audience," he said.

We jumped at the idea. We would be producing. Wow.

We turned out 360 sketches, which are now in storage. At the time, they were shown after the Sermonette at 2 A.M. or in Korea for the Armed Forces and wherever else.

For two years we had an office on West 57th Street just across from Carnegie Hall and Chock Full o'Nuts, courtesy of J. Walter Thompson. The office gave us the discipline necessary to come up with material. It allowed us to work in the city where our kids were attending school. When "Take 5" ended we decided to keep the office. Now we were paying rent. When you pay rent you produce. It's magic.

During that time we wrote commercials for clients such as the Amalgamated Bank, Lanier, Nikon, United Van Lines, and Food Emporium. The office was our workplace for over fifteen years.

The front office, a combination kitchen and reception area, seemed cluttered. The walls, full of Clio Awards, plaques, theatrical posters, and framed album covers, resembled a French general's chest, bedecked with every medal ever created. Our show-business background was splattered there for all to see.

The phone would ring. Our secretary, Arnie Duncan, would pick it up. Sometimes it would be my sister Maxine calling before arriving at our office.

"I'm coming over. Is that okay, Jerry?"

"Where are you?"

"I'm in Coney Island."

"Okay," I'd say, "come on over."

My younger sister Maxine would be coming to our office to pick up some spending money. The time it took for her to get there gave me an hour to decide whether I could deal with her that particular day. It's her state of mind that would concern me. She's been living at an adult home but would come to our office periodically.

I never understood how Maxine arrived in the world. On one level it seemed that with all the fighting between Willie and Bella, there was still some love left after all. At forty-four my mother had given birth again.

I was seventeen when Maxine was born. Years later, when my mother was in the hospital, dying, she instructed me not to bring Maxine into the hospital room. (At the time, Maxine was living with Anne and me on Cornelia Street in the Village.)

My mother said, "I don't want her to see me this way."

So Maxine and Anne would stand on the street, and Anne would point up to my mother's hospital room and my mother would wave to Maxine from the window. Maxine was nine when my mother died. From that moment on, she became part of Anne's and my life.

Maxine's early years were filled with the aroma of showbiz, things that must've lodged in her mind as part reality and part fantasy. I would take her with me to rehearsal of *Diary of a Scoundrel.* She got to meet Roddy McDowall and Margaret Hamilton, whom she recognized as the Wicked Witch in *The Wizard of Oz.* On another occasion, Uta Hagen and Herbert Berghof, whose extended family included their students, invited us all to their home during the Christmas holidays. Under the tree were gifts for all, including Maxine.

After my mother died, the last semblance of our family disappeared. My father, who managed to pay every doctor bill and hang on until the end, was free at last. We were all on our own. The question of who was to care for Maxine was left unanswered. When my father remarried, there was a problem with caring for her. I requested the guardianship of my sister, and my father agreed. When our theater schedule made it no longer possible for Anne and me to take care of Maxine, she spent the following years living with different members of the family, each doing their best to maintain their life as well as hers.

Sandra Zemel, my first cousin, extended herself to take care of Maxine, as did my sister Doreen and her husband, Joe, and Arnie and his wife, Linda. When she was old enough, Maxine started working as a waitress at a restaurant in Greenwich Village. She had already lost several jobs because of anti-social behavior. Soon there were problems at the new restaurant. She got into fights with customers. "She had become difficult," they said, and they let her go. At the age of nineteen, after several such incidents, Maxine was diagnosed as paranoid schizophrenic. I learned that she had taken LSD. From then on she performed in her own world, on her own stage, in her own mind.

Each week she'd arrive from the adult home in Coney Island. I would give her spending money each week and order lunch. She'd smoke a cigarette and tell me that Roddy McDowall and Sammy Davis, Jr. were staying with her and Tanta Faiga and Tanta Chaila where she lived. Jumbled reality. Sometimes she'd take the money and immediately take someone she met on the street to lunch. She'd then need more money for cigarettes before the week was over. We'd give it to her.

The doorbell to the office rang twice in quick succession. *It's her ring,* I thought.

"Come on in, Maxine," Arnie Duncan said. She gave him a big hug. "Are you my brother, Arnie?"

"Of course, Maxine."

Then she hugged me. "I love you, Jerry," she said.

Her lips were cracked because of the medicine. At forty-three years old, she looked twenty-six. Mental illness seems to slow the aging process. Actors have to fight to stay this way, I told myself. She wore jeans, a polyester shirt, and boots. She was always clean. She must have showered every day. Some part of her cared.

"Can I have some coffee?"

"Sure," I said.

"I take it black. Jerry, are you my father?"

She knows I'm not, but it zings me.

She pointed to her boots. "Sammy Davis gave me his boots," she said.

"They're nice," I said. I didn't pause or question.

"It's a mixed marriage," she said, quoting lines from some of our routines and laughing, knowing she's making me laugh when she says them.

I would tell myself she's not really sick; she is just fantasizing a little too much. I kept thinking this would all change. She would someday behave normally. If she did, it would change my entire life. I'd be taller. I could smile more. I could go out onstage with less on my shoulders before each performance.

"I love you, Jerry," Maxine would say as she headed out the door and back to Coney Island.

"Your sister's a hoot," Arnie would say. "You gotta give her a part in a show."

For a decade our secretary, Arnie Duncan, was an important part of our lives. His presence in the office and his gentle manner, contained in his lanky 6-foot-3-inch frame, were everyday reminders that Anne and I were some kind of corporate entity. His "Good morning, Stiller and Meara," backed up by the testimonials on the walls, were daily reassurance that we did indeed belong in the world of stars, superstars, and mini-stars.

More important to us was his sensitivity to our immediate needs—our instantaneous flip-flops in making decisions, our family responsibilities, all the rest of it. He accepted these as if they were the facts of life. His sense of humor and flexibility helped us to survive and stay human.

Every routine we had ever written was stored somewhere in the office. I had little idea where—I was too busy to keep track. If I needed an old *Sullivan* routine, I'd yell, "Where is it, Arnie?"

"I'll get it for you," he'd respond.

"I'll get it, just tell me where."

"I'll get it," he'd repeat.

"Why won't you tell me where things are?"

Without missing a beat, he'd answer, "If you knew where everything was, then you'd know where everything was and then you wouldn't really need me, would you? There would be nothing for me to do."

I wanted to kill him for it, but it made perfect sense. As the saying goes, if it ain't broke, don't fix it. I never knew where things were, but I gave it up to God. Things were working out.

Arnie Duncan and I had first met as undergraduates at Syracuse University when I was directing that student revue called *Long Live Love*. He walked in and auditioned. He sounded like Billy Eckstine, minus the vibrato. He was good and he was cast.

Some twenty years after graduation I ran into him on the street, and he told me he was no longer the office manager for the Edward Marks music-publishing company. He needed a job. Anne and I, being a nightclub act, worked out of our apartment. I said, "Well, if you ever do need me, I'm there for you."

Once we had our office we hired him. I had always loved him back at school. I pictured Arnie turning our office into a computerized comedy corporation, with sketches and punch lines at our, or his, fingertips.

On a typical day the phone would ring.

"Stiller and Meara," Arnie would coo, just like a bird. "Yes, I'm their secretary. My name is Arnie. Yes, I'm black." They hired a black guy, he's telling whoever it is on the other end of the line; it's implicit in his tone. He's too social, I'd tell myself. Get to what they want.

But people liked talking to him. Strangers talked with him as if they'd known him all their lives—and he'd never seen any of them, nor they him. What did they talk about? He was very elegant. *It's very European,* I'd tell myself. This place was turning into Grand Hotel.

One day the phone rang and Arnie picked up.

"Stiller and Meara, can I help you? I'll see if Mr. Stiller's in. . . . Are you in, Jerry," he said to me.

"Who is it?"

"Bob Kelly, from United Van Lines in St. Louis."

"Tell him I'm not in."

"He said he's not in, Bob."

Then Arnie turned to me and, without covering the mouthpiece of the phone, said, "Bob said, can you call him when you get in?"

"Tell him yes."

"He said yes, Bob."

You would expect people to be highly offended by a conversation like that, but they weren't when Arnie was on the line. This happened a lot. But if the phone rang and I answered it, the caller would say, "Where's Arnie?"

"Oh, he'll be back in a minute," I'd mumble.

"I love that guy," the caller would remark.

"How come?" I'd ask.

"He's great on the phone. He's so nice. Where'd you find him?"

I'd never realized the telephone could be so important to relationships. "If you ever decide to let him go, I want him," people would say. Suddenly I was some genius who had found a jewel in life's sandbox. I enjoyed the unearned praise—but now I could no longer fault Arnie for not putting "Mr." or "Ms." in front of proper names on envelopes addressed to celebrity friends.

"It's *Mr.* Frank Langella, Arnie. Please type it again."

"Why?"

"Because it's proper to address him as 'Mister.'"

"He's important enough to know who he is already," Arnie would answer. Retyping the envelope, he'd say, "Do you want me to save the stamp?"

"Of course," I'd say, and he'd laugh.

His logic was such that I understood it completely, and denied it wholly.

"Here, Arnie, retype this—a commercial for the Amalgamated Bank." I'd hand it to him and walk away, knowing he'd read it as he retyped it. Would he like it?

I heard him laugh.

"What are you laughing at?"

"This line breaks me up," he'd say, repeating it. "It's great. Only I'd have it at the end instead of the middle."

"It's that funny, huh? Anne, Arnie loves my Amalgamated commercial!"

"I'm writing one myself," she'd answer.

"Tell her my commercial's funny, Arnie."

"Jerry's is really funny, Anne," he would say to oblige me.

"Want to read it?" I'd ask her.

"I'll read it later. Leave me alone, I'm busy," she'd say.

"Okay. Arnie, I'll do it over with that punch line at the end. . . . Oh, by the way, you misspelled 'commercial.' It's not 'commerical.'"

"Sorry. You're the speller around here. My spelling's terrible," he'd say.

"But don't you proofread?"

"Yes, I do, but even when I proofread it, it still comes out wrong."

"You've got a dictionary right there."

"That's unabridged, and it's so *big*."

I wanted to die. His spelling was getting better, I had to admit, but the word "commercial" always came out "commerical."

I stopped kvetching. Funny punch lines are more important than typos, I told myself. And if I needed something, I could call him at home at midnight and he'd do it for me. But most important, Arnie loved working for us—he had become a part of our family.

While we were in California in 1985 to discuss a possible CBS series with producer Mort Lachman, we found out Arnie was not well.

"I can't sit at home," he said. "I'll come to the office and lie down. I can take phone calls and relay any messages."

"Fine with us. Rest. Don't feel obligated to do anything."

He'd been diagnosed with lung cancer. We arrived back in New York after a week of talks with CBS.

"What's the series about?" Arnie asked.

"Two people, Anne and myself, married, living in a New York apartment on the West Side. They have two grown kids and a thirteen-year-old. I'm a deputy mayor. I see myself roaming the city streets, checking broken parking meters, closing open fire hydrants, saving New York City's water supply, and a myriad of other tasks. A job which could lead to some wonderful story lines."

"Let me type up your outline. But I have to take an hour first to get through the radiation treatment."

"How often do you go?"

"Every day," Arnie said. "Except weekends."

"What do they do?" I asked.

"They lay you down on a table and hit you with X-rays. Next week they tell me if it's doing any good."

"How do you feel? Are you eating?"

"I ate some Chinese food today."

"Good," I said.

"I'm going down to Florida next week to see my sister," Arnie said. "It's my vacation. Or do you need me?"

"It would be good for you to go," we said. "How do you feel right now? Do you want to go home?"

"I'd rather be here . . . if it doesn't get you down."

It was always a squeeze before Christmas. I'd go pick out items that had to be individually engraved. Whom did we forget?

"We have to send cards," I said.

"No," Anne would say. "No Christmas cards. Let's make it a rule."

"But I love to get cards. Why shouldn't I send them?"

"You're Jewish. Why do you have to send cards? You must've been sick as a kid."

"I never received any presents. So I love to give them and receive them, because I'm still a kid."

"Let him do it," Arnie said.

Arnie would patiently address our Christmas cards to friends and keep it a secret from Anne.

By now Arnie had even stopped going to Knicks games.

"Why?" I asked.

"I hate to see them lose."

It was the year Patrick Ewing arrived, and Cartwright, Cummings, and

Bernard King were all out with injuries. Arnie was super-critical when it came to basketball. At the Garden or watching the tube, he would let out his feelings when a play was not executed well enough. He had his pet players and the guys he disliked. He owned a season ticket to the Knicks home games and so did I. We'd talk between halves, about the plays, the players. At the end of the game, we'd leave the Garden happy.

A week after he flew to Florida, he came back to New York in a wheel-chair. We took him to Doctors' Hospital. He started to sink.

"Jerry, don't let them give me bad blood," he said. He died December 13, 1985, at the age of sixty-one. It was six weeks from the day he told us he was ill.

That night I saw him in a dream. I was in a jazz club in Greenwich Village, maybe the Vanguard. I looked out of the basement window and saw Arnie's feet. As I looked closer, I could see him staring in silently through that window at the woman jazz singer. He suddenly entered the club, said nothing to me, which was uncharacteristic, and went directly to the singer. He whispered something in her ear and then left.

The dream frightened me, and I woke myself up.

In my dream, he was mad at me. I had never seen Arnie angry before. Why was he mad? I could not bear the thought. How could he die? How could he leave us? Our office wasn't even our office. It was his, and he was still running it.

I told myself that Arnie had only decided to take some time off and would be back. I could not mourn anyone who had not left my consciousness. I would still feel upset with him when I couldn't find something in the office. He was still there for me, always and forever, and he knew it.

The funeral was to be held at a funeral home in Harlem. As I prepared for the service, I remembered the name of the song he'd sung in *Long Live Love,* the school show. Arnie had put a bunch of tapes of the show on a shelf somewhere in the office. I reached for a box at random, looked at the label—and there it was, "The Things I Miss Most," written by Ross Miller. I played it. Arnie's voice, much higher than I remembered: "The things I miss most are just the little things / the flowers in springtime / the birds on the wing . . ." *God, they'll cry at this tomorrow,* I thought, *unless I make it funny.*

I went to the Audio Department—the studio where Anne and I

recorded our commercials—and got the engineer, Gene Coleman, to clean up the tape that Leo Bloom had recorded in 1948.

The chapel was full. The service was scheduled for 11:15 A.M. Friends—white, black, women, men—relatives, people I had never seen or known, filled every row. There were actors, house managers, musicians, artists, writers, DJs, a policeman, and members of the African-American Society, of which Arnie had been president. A black woman walked to the organ and played a gospel-blues rendition of "You'll Never Walk Alone." She played and sang it with meaning.

A young minister asked if anyone wanted to speak. A couple of people got up and praised Arnie as a wonderful, giving person.

Then I got up. I knew I had to say something meaningful. Arnie had told so many people that Anne and I were his life.

I raised a Sony ghetto blaster to my shoulder. It was surely a shock, I knew, for everyone in that chapel. I said, "Forgive me, but these things do have a value other than for the street. I don't know any other way of playing for you a tape I've found that Arnie made thirty-seven years ago. If the song 'The Things I Miss Most' brings a single tear to your eyes, I know Arnie would kill you if he could."

They laughed.

I held the blaster at arm's length and prepared to press the switch.

"Before I play this," I said, "I have to tell you that Arnie did a lot of things wrong." Huge laugh. "Let me tell you a few things."

How wonderful to list a man's faults and still know he was a giant. I told them the Bob Kelly story—Arnie on the phone, to the United Van Lines guy in St. Louis, "He says he's not in, Bob," and then, turning to me, "Bob said can you call him when you get in?"

They never stopped laughing.

I said, "Arnie always thought of himself as Dick Powell." I played the tape.

When it ended I said, "Did you know his favorite movie was *All About Eve*? And he loved Anne Baxter. He knew every word in the movie. Well, Anne Baxter died on the same date Arnie did. Maybe they planned it that way."

The funeral ended, and everyone got into their cars or cabs and headed back where they came from.

• • •

I read somewhere a motto attributed to Paul Muni, whom as a kid I was likened to by my uncles, aunts, and cousins. When I mentioned to any of them I wanted someday to go on the stage, they'd call me "Paul Muni." For me it was like someone saying I could be president of the United States if I wanted to. Paul Muni was a hero of mine because he made it from the Yiddish theater to Hollywood stardom. Muni was quoted as saying in an interview, "An actor must act," meaning that the true test of an actor was his constant need to perform. It didn't matter whether he was a good actor or bad actor, he just had to do his thing someplace.

In May 1985, I got a call from Donald Schoenbaum, the director of the Guthrie Theater in Minneapolis, asking if I'd be interested in playing Nathan Detroit in *Guys and Dolls.* I was informed it was to be the first musical ever done at this illustrious playhouse. We'd rehearse seven weeks. I was assured that this was to be a first-class production, with Roy Thinnes as Sky Masterson, Mike Mazurki as Big Julie, and Barbara Shaema as Adelaide.

After days of procrastination I said, Why not? I'd have the opportunity to rehearse long enough to do my best work. There would be no big-city distractions. I imagined performing in a peaceful city and not fighting traffic. It was a chance to play the best role ever written in an American musical.

On the first day of rehearsal I realized that the Guthrie, a three-sided theater, created a special problem for actors, namely to share the performance with each third of the audience. A part of me kept saying that this was wrong, I didn't feel right, moving on this line or that. Another part of me said, You're an actor, you can make anything work. Within a few days I started to feel lonely without Anne. This grew into a sense of isolation. I wondered as to whether I'd bitten off too much.

As rehearsals continued I pictured the ghost of Sam Levene, the original Nathan Detroit, hovering over me. At the first preview performance I was terribly nervous. I never listened to a word being uttered by the character of Adelaide. I was too busy acting. When the show opened I received the worst reviews of my life and felt totally miserable. A couple of weeks after we opened we were rereviewed. The critics still hated me.

But the show played three months and did 97 percent capacity. The theater was out of the red. Among the many people who came backstage during the run were Garrison Keillor and his son, who told me how much they'd enjoyed the show. Lots of young actors also came back, many of whom had played Nathan Detroit in a school play or a community theater production. The young Nathans would invariably advise me on how to get more laughs.

One night after a performance, around 2 A.M., I was half asleep watching Charlie Rose on *Nightwatch* on a black-and-white TV set. He was reporting the passing of Ira Gershwin. It was a particularly hot summer evening and the windows in my apartment were open because the air conditioning was on the fritz.

Suddenly I heard a noise, turned, and saw a pair of wings through the open window. The wings zoomed straight for my head. I screamed, "Bats, fucking bats! What the hell am I doing in Minneapolis," and tore the sheets off my bed, throwing them over my head as the bat zoomed straight at me.

I kept watching that bat circle the room blindly. I was standing on the bed pulling the sheet hard over my head like a sheik. I could hear myself screaming, "fucking bats!" as though this was the last of the plagues that were visited on me for wanting to do *Guys and Dolls*. It was right out of Dracula.

I reached for a record album. I would wait for the bat's next swoop and swat. I didn't think of the consequences. What would I do if I did hit it? Would it turn killer and go for my jugular? Once more the bat sailed toward me. I stood on the bed and swung as it flitted past. I could hear the hit, a soft thud against the wings, and the bat fell to the floor, wounded. I ran for the light switch and flicked it on. There on the floor was a small bat. It was crawling rapidly toward the radiator, and before I could grab it, it escaped underneath. I tried using the album cover as a shovel to pull it out. I felt nothing.

I awakened the superintendent of the building. He arrived with some tools. "Yeah, we have bats in the summertime, Mr. Stiller," he said as he removed the radiator cover, "but we've never had anything like this." As the radiator cover came off I expected the worst, a dead bat. Nothing. Where the hell was it? Had it been a hallucination? I noticed a metal ring encircling the radiator pipe where it goes through to the floor below. There was barely an inch between the radiator pipe and the metal ring. I asked the super, "Could a bat escape through that size pipe?" The superintendent said yes, "They shrivel."

I said goodnight to the super, put the sheets back on the bed, turned on the television, and tried to get to sleep. Suddenly I heard the sound of

wings. Once more a bat flew into the apartment and once more the sheets
went over my head. Could it be the same bat? I picked up the album cover
and hit it. Down it went. One shot. I had gotten good at this. I turned on
the light and there was a bat crawling toward the crack under the door. It
disappeared into the hall before I could make a move. I stopped and wondered what to do. Follow it out? Never. It could fly back in. After a full
minute I opened the door. Nothing. Gone. But where? I looked down the
stairs.

That summer I got bad notices, but I knew that if I ever got to play
Dracula I would win an Oscar.

A few weeks later the run of *Guys and Dolls* ended and I flew back to
New York City. My old pal Joe DiSpigno was being honored that night by
parents, friends, and the faculty of King's Park Public School. He was re-
tiring as their principal. Joe and I had been in touch on and off for
twenty-five years.

"Could you come out and be part of the evening? It would thrill
everyone to know we're friends," he said.

This was one event I didn't want to miss.

When I first met Anne I had called Joe. "I met an actress and I'm
thinking of marrying her. She's Irish Catholic," I said.

"An Irish girl, huh?" Joe was picturing us together and laughing.

"I want you to meet her," I said.

"I will."

Anne, Joe, and I met someplace. We talked in generalities. He seemed
to be my protector, as if he were screening Anne for defects. He was
never sharp with her, just there to intimate, "If you ever hurt this man, I'll
get you if I have to travel to the end of the earth."

Through the years Anne and I would have get-togethers with Joe, his
wife, Italia, his son Dominic, and his daughter Thalia. Now tonight it was
Joe's big event.

I flew in from the Guthrie, rented a car at La Guardia, double-parked in
front of our apartment building, and ran upstairs to change into my tux.
The schedule was tight. Anne was already dressed and ready to go. When
we came back down my rental car had been towed away. The doorman,
who was new, had gone to dinner and had not told his relief man to call
me if the police came by. I went totally pale and screamed at the poor
handyman, who didn't understand a word of English. Anne and I ran up
and down the streets looking desperately for the tow truck. No luck.

Dressed in my tux, and Anne in a gown, we hailed a cab that took us to the impound lot at 12th Avenue and 54th Street. Every New Yorker who owns a car—and many out-of-town visitors—know this place. At that time, seventy-five dollars in cash, plus your driver's license, would get you your car back. The victims lined up in front of a booth on a dock on the Hudson River. It was a scene out of a Chekhov play—bureaucracy in action. Explanations fell unheeded on the ears of the clerical help, who'd locate your car and issue a receipt to allow you to drive away.

Anne and I were on line. The man in back of me handed me a card. "I'm Alan King's tailor," he whispered. "I make his tuxes. I can make one for you."

"I'm wearing one," I said.

"You can use another."

I took his card so as not to offend him. I saw a policeman who seemed to be in charge. I ran up to him. "Please, I need my car." I was hoping he'd recognize me.

"Aren't you . . ." A smile of recognition.

"Jerry Stiller," I tell him.

"Stiller and Meara," he said, like he'd discovered treasure. He was smiling. That miserable, depressing atmosphere didn't affect him. He worked there. This was home for him. He loved his work, and I was the icing on the cake he'd been baking all day.

"Come with me. Your car was towed away, huh?"

"I've got to get to King's Park, Long Island. We're doing a show for my best friend."

"Come with me."

He took us to the back of a makeshift office that looked like something out of a shanty town in the Depression. The walls were filled with locations of vehicles.

"Here it is," he said, pointing to a pushpin. "That's seventy-five dollars, Jerry."

How wonderful, I told myself. The magic of being recognized. I could get my car back without waiting on line. I paid him the seventy-five bucks. "You don't know how much this means to me," I told him.

He said, "Hey, can you do me a favor? Could you send us a picture?"

"Sure," I said.

"You know who else we got?" He pointed to the wall. Opera stars, football players, other actors, people I respect were all up on the wall. I suddenly felt good all over—I was in with the best. A cop arrived with our car. "Here it is, Mr. Stiller." It was like valet parking. I'm on a pier on the Hudson River, my car has been hijacked from in front of my house, and I'm grateful. I took out a five-dollar bill and handed it to him.

"You don't have to do that," he said.

"I know that, I want to do it."

"Thanks," he said. "Don't forget the picture."

Two hours later Anne and I arrived at the Smithtown Inn. We were an hour and a half late. Once we were onstage, our first fifteen minutes were about being towed away. Half of Long Island was there to honor my pal Joe, a principal who gave kids vision, insight, and inspiration. It was an overwhelming expression of love. *He's like the pillar of the community,* I thought. *What happened to the rebel I once knew?* I told the audience of our adventures in the army, throwing chairs overboard, his meeting Italia and falling in love. When it was over I realized that as a school principal Joe had changed people's lives. It was fifty years since he'd stopped me from jumping overboard on the *General Howze,* and I was still able to call him my friend.

Some time afterward Anne answered the phone.

"Jerry, it's Mike Nichols, pick up."

Mike Nichols? What could he want?

I picked it up. "Mike . . . ?"

"You're the Jew," he said laughing.

What was he talking about? It was about thirty-five years since I had worked with Mike in Isaac Rosenfeld's *The Liars,* my first experience performing without a script, improvising. I had replaced Shelley Berman and was working with the original members of the Compass Players, Tom Aldredge, Walter Beakel, and Mike.

We were trying to raise money at a backer's audition for the New York company of Compass. I asked Mike, whom I'd never met, what I had to do.

"The outline is up on the board," he said. "Just follow it."

"I make up my own lines?"

"Yes. You just have to listen and follow the scenario. You'll see."

Working in that sketch was a turning point in my life. I had no memory of time passing on stage. I could hear the audience laughing but I didn't want to stop the flow of the scenario. We were four people breezing through acting space like it was pure oxygen. No resistance. No stops.

No pauses to think. Just one continuous flow of acting energy. What did I say? It didn't matter. I was on to something else. When it was over, a wonderful response. How long were we on? Someone said forty-five minutes.

After that, Mike and his partner, Elaine May, were also performing a sketch, in the middle of which an argument broke out between them. I had no idea they were performing a sketch called "Pirandello."

I called Anne immediately after the performance to say, "Anne, I had the most wonderful experience I've ever known in the theater. It's called improvisation. We've got to try it."

Postscript: The following night, Mike and Elaine opened for Mort Sahl at the Village Vanguard, were discovered, and soon became stars.

"You're the Jew," Mike said again.

What was he talking about?

"I'm doing David Rabe's new play, *Hurlyburly,*" Nichols said, "and I'd like you to play Artie."

"You're casting me on the phone?"

"You're Artie. I'll send you the script."

The idea of being cast by the hottest director on Broadway without having to read blinded me.

Greg Mosher had called a week earlier and asked if I would be willing to read for him and David Mamet for *Glengarry Glen Ross.* I hated having to audition. I hadn't seen either script, but Mike was now an icon. So I called and bowed out of *Glengarry,* disappointing Greg.

Two weeks passed, and I still had not received a script of *Hurlyburly,* or a confirming phone call to my agent. I was getting very uneasy and I finally worked up enough nerve to call Mike and ask if this was for real and when would I get the script.

"You'll be getting it. We've lined up Chris Walken, William Hurt, Sigourney Weaver, Judith Ivey, Harvey Keitel, and Cynthia Nixon. You're set."

I was dazzled to be part of this assemblage of the hottest talent on the block. Show business. Lots of crazy twists. One minute down, the next up. Mike Nichols wants me. "You're the Jew" was ringing in my ears.

David Rabe's long script arrived. It was two months prior to the start of rehearsals. I fought my way through it and found myself falling asleep. The characters made no sense. It suddenly occurred to me that everyone in the play was on drugs.

My part was that of Artie, a third-rate hack writer who makes his entrance delivering as a present to Walken and Hurt a "CARE package"—a sixteen-year-old nymphet who'd been living in a hotel elevator. This creep I'd be playing so repulsed me that I had to ask myself what Nichols saw in me as an actor that allowed him to cast me for the role without even a reading. I was equally upset at myself for not asking to see the script first before agreeing to play the role.

The other characters, I soon noted, were no better in their lifestyles than Artie. I found myself wondering how I would be perceived in this lowlife role. Rabe's writing probed into places I was not comfortable with. I had to examine what kind of human being could deliver a teenager as a sexual present and still live with himself. I then had to ask myself why I'd want to play this Artie. Rabe had written a modern-day morality play.

We started rehearsing at the Manhattan Theatre Club, on East 74th Street. At the first reading, Judith Ivey knew all her lines. She never referred to the script. I had attempted to learn mine, but I never imagined I'd know them by rote at a first reading. I felt left in the dust.

Welcome to the brave new world of theater, I told myself. The fact that no one else except Judith knew his or her lines didn't make me feel any more comfortable. The last time I'd encountered this unease was when I'd played the Second Murderer in *Richard III* for Joe Papp, and a newcomer from Missouri named George C. Scott knew every word at the first reading. It was a shock. I'd asked myself if Scott was for real and if he'd be able to pull it off in performance. He did.

The rehearsals of *Hurlyburly*—in which we just sat and read—went on for two weeks. Mike explained we were trying to understand the play. At times we were comatose, just reading it over and over.

"Let's all have some pizza," Mike would say. We were not under any pressure. There was no opening date, he said.

In my memory, as we read and reread the play, we became bored, then angry, at the slowness of the gestation process. The anger started to overflow into the relationships between the characters in the play.

One day Harvey Keitel offered me a ride home in his car. Harvey played Phil, a sociopath who was on a collision course with Eddie, the William Hurt character. As we kept driving toward the West Side, Harvey started discussing the play and his character. It soon dawned on me that Phil was enlisting Artie as his ally against Eddie. We were no longer Jerry and Harvey driving home, we were Artie and Phil in a sociopathic triangle with Eddie. So much for not taking a cab. I was also learning a lot about Jerry Stiller. All the personal bilge that existed in my own cellar was beginning to manifest itself during the car ride. *Hurlyburly* was going deep.

Nichols was in constant search for what he called "The Joke." "What's The Joke in the scene?" he would ask. I learned that The Joke did not mean funny, like a piece of business, but making sense of the scene. This, to Mike, was The Joke.

Once we were on our feet, the relationship between me, Chris Walken, and Bill Hurt started to internalize. "You're the Jew" slowly became clear. I was suddenly in touch with the part of me that hated myself and my being Jewish, feelings that were unconscious but not inaccessible. And I knew that I'd been cast in a role which, if played truthfully, was that of a parasitic, untalented piece of *dreck*.

To survive, amoral Artie has to make it with the *goyim*. No more perfect pair ever existed to accommodate Artie's neurosis than Bill Hurt and Chris Walken as Eddie and Mickey. My bestowing a sexual gift was the equivalent of what the actor and teacher Michael Chekhov described as the psychological gesture.

All of this character-probing was overwhelming my capacity to perform freely. Had I fully grasped whom I was playing when I jumped into this play? I had no idea it would set off so many unresolved issues in my own life, feelings about my marriage, Judaism, sex, and on and on. Did I really need this? Was this a good career move? What career, I immediately asked myself? Stiller and Meara were no longer performing as a team. Was there a marriage without a career? Before I met Anne I was an actor. And before Anne and I joined hands she wanted to be an actress. The stage was the real bond between us.

Yes, I told myself, I'm still an actor. And as Paul Muni said, "An actor must act." I could play this guy, but I must find out what in myself would not allow me to play a character I disliked so intensely.

We were now in Chicago rehearsing for our New York run. As we got closer to opening night Mike and David Rabe had opposite views about whether Phil should be allowed to beat up Donna, the sixteen-year-old played by Cynthia Nixon, in full view of the audience. Rabe said it was the way he wrote it. Mike said it would make the audience walk out. Mike agreed to rehearse the scene, but not immediately put it in the performance. A violent argument took place in front of the cast. I thought Mike might actually get hurt. I felt loyalty toward Mike going back to the first time we met, but couldn't let Harvey, Bill, and Chris think I was sucking up to the director. Artie and Jerry were intersecting in this drama within the drama.

The next day Mike cut many of my lines. I was shocked. That'll teach me, I thought. The hammer falls on the loyal subject, I told myself. I'd signed on to this, had given up a shot at *Glengarry,* which by then was a big hit on Broadway and was up for a Pulitzer, and here I was in Chicago in the middle of a pit fight while my role was disappearing.

I wondered if I should quit the show. I asked myself whether I had compromised myself by getting sucked in by the name Mike Nichols. What did this say about me, my desperation? Mike Nichols knew that I was perfect for the role of Artie.

Artie's character became even more clear when, during a rehearsal of one of my scenes, Mike shouted, "Schmuck bait!" That was The Joke when it came to Artie. A schmuck was, among other things, someone who could be manipulated. Mickey and Eddie tore into this and were now given the handle on how to mind-fuck Artie. They already knew that making it with *goyim* was my subconscious need. Oddly enough, "schmuck bait" was a phrase Mike had used when he and I were in *The Liars* back in the '50s.

The night before we opened at the Goodman Theater, Cynthia Nixon, Sigourney Weaver, and Judith Ivey wrote their own feminist version of *Hurlyburly* and Mike threw a party for the cast in his penthouse at the Delaware Towers.

We played four weeks to quiet audiences. At the end of that run, the question of whether we would open in New York had still not been answered. Was this another joke? But after our final performance at the Goodman, while in the van returning to our Chicago hotel for the last time, Mike quietly asked, "Where do you think we should open—on or off Broadway?"

There was a moment of silence. Was he kidding? Were we voting in a bus? What a way to learn that we were actually opening in New York. We threw around names like the Barrymore, the Royale, the De Lys, etc. The final decision came weeks later, when we were back in New York. We were to open at the Promenade, a four-hundred seat Off-Broadway house.

As the New York opening got closer, I became more and more conflicted with the character I was playing. During the first preview I started blowing my lines. I was in a panic mode. Why was I afraid to play a man who offers the services of a sixteen-year-old girl? After all, it was just a show, and I'm an actor.

I realized that this role was unmasking me. My first performances were ragged. I blew more lines, two nights in a row. I thought Nichols would fire me. He didn't. I was back on track by the third performance. Had I actually gotten in touch with what was bothering me? My guilt about portraying a bad Jew in front of an audience had blocked me psychologically. At that moment I knew that in taking part in *Hurlyburly* I had learned more about myself by *being* an actor than I'd ever learned about acting. I suddenly started feeling comfortable with Cynthia Nixon, who would lie on the floor with me before our entrance, as if we were together in the elevator. In some way, Cynthia sensed all my angst and was going through it with me. What a nice girl she was. Being in touch with my conflict loosened me up.

We played a couple of sold-out months at the Promenade and then moved to the Barrymore on Broadway, where Ron Silver replaced Chris Walken.

When the show moved uptown, I learned that the audience loved Artie, at least on Saturdays. I was very attractive to the matinee ladies. It inspired Ron Silver to say that on Saturday afternoon the show should be called "Jerry's Girls." For some reason amoral Artie had turned into a sex symbol. Those matinee ladies loved me.

Opening night on Broadway brought all my fears to the surface—the fear that I would be unmasked and discovered not as a king but a pretender, that I'd be found unworthy of applause, that failure would bring humiliation to Anne, Amy, and Ben. For the first time in my life I was in touch with those feelings and aware that a play illuminates more than the audience. It also enlightens the actors.

I was aware that I was competing with everyone in the cast, down to sixteen-year-old Cynthia. Next to the rest of them, I felt invisible. So it was a great moment when Enid Nemy, who wrote the Broadway column in *The New York Times* called to say, "I want to do a profile on you for Friday, and Al Hirschfeld wants to do your caricature."

"How about the others in the show?" I asked.

"We want you," she repeated.

During the run of *Hurlyburly* I invited my father to come see the show.

"Come see me, Deddy." He was retired now, after driving the bus for more than twenty years. His enjoyment came from riding free on a bus pass that was good for a lifetime. He and his third wife, Marsha, also a bus-pass recipient, would hop a cross-town bus, ride a couple of stops, change for an uptown. "I can ride anywhere," he bragged playfully.

They were like world travelers. I'd never seen him so happy.

He made a matinee performance. I knew *Hurlyburly* was not my father's cup of tea as far as entertainment. He loved comedy. Olson and Johnson's *Hellzapoppin'* thrilled him. But this was a chance for my father to see me onstage with some great actors. At the conclusion of the matinee I met him in the lobby.

"I'm gonna take the subway," he said.

"I can call a cab."

"No, I'll take the subway."

We were walking toward the subway entrance. I waited for some word about the show, my performance. Then, out of the blue, in a non sequitur, he said, "Harvey Kite-le." He had mispronounced Harvey Keitel's name; it now had a vaguely Yiddish inflection, to rhyme with *title*.

"Harvey Kite-le," my father repeated. There was a smile in his voice. He liked saying it: "Harvey Kite-le."

"You liked him?" I said.

"Very good." My father had put his stamp of approval on an actor I was working with. He never mentioned me, for which maybe I should be grateful. Zero Mostel once told me, "Don't ever ask anyone for an opinion of your performance, they're liable to tell it to you."

We got to the subway entrance kiosk.

"I'm going up to the Bronx. I got my pass," he said. He started down the steps, turned to say good-bye, then disappeared onto the platform. I stood for a minute. Why was I hurt? I thought Harvey was fine. Was I jealous?

I remembered the night in the late '60s when I introduced my father to disk jockey William B. Williams when Anne and I opened for Charles Aznavour at the Royal Box in New York. The press said we stole the show.

"How do you like your son, Mr. Stiller?" Williams asked.

"He's okay, but she's great!"

He was telling the truth. What else did I expect from the man who took me as a kid to vaudeville and said of a no-talent comic on the bill, "He's a faker."

It took years, but I also learned that despite loving Anne onstage he never approved of our marriage. But he never said a word about it to me.

At age ninety-eight he and Marsha, his wife for over twenty years, separated. I had to arrange for him to enter an adult home, a retirement hotel outside the city. He would spend almost five years at the hotel. Between *Seinfeld* shoots in Hollywood, I would visit him. I wanted to close the distance between us.

After each *Seinfeld*, he'd ask, "Jerry, when will I see you again?"

"In a couple of weeks, Deddy. You know I work in California." I didn't mention *Seinfeld*. I had never mentioned any of the shows I'd been in since *Hurlyburly*, I had stopped looking for a thumb's up.

"How old am I, Jerry? Am I a hundred?" he asked.

I didn't want to tell him that he was over a hundred years old.

"I feel young," he said. "How old am I? Eighty? Am I eighty?"

"Don't you know?" I asked softly.

"I feel like a kid. I drink a lot of milk. I drink a lot of milk," my father repeated. "How old am I, Jerry?"

"Where were you born, Deddy?" I asked. We had no birth certificate for my father.

"Two-fifty-three Stanton Street," he replied, clear as a bell.

That was only blocks away from where I got the hell beat out of me by Ralphie Stolzman.

My father was the oldest of ten brothers and sisters. They lived with my grandparents in a six-room railroad flat on the Lower East Side. Where did ten kids sleep? How did they eat? How did his parents pay the rent? My father never mentioned his upbringing, not a word. I wanted to hear about it from him. I wanted to connect, to hear his stories.

"I played baseball in Hamilton Fish Park," he said.

"What position?"

"Third base."

"Were you good?"

"Yeah, I was good. My father used to smack me because I wore out the soles on my shoes. I loved baseball. I played all day. They had to come get me out of the park."

"Did you work?"

"Yeah, sure, I delivered tuxedos on Canal Street."

"That's a long walk from Stanton Street, Deddy. How did you get there?"

"I walked. On Saturdays I would sometimes take the Third Avenue El."

"Did you have a girlfriend?" I said, knowing I was stepping on dangerous ground. Was I wondering if he'd been a crazy, horny kid?

He laughed, but never answered. I didn't pursue the question. "Who were your favorite comedians?" I asked.

"The Avon Comedy Four—Smith and Dale," he replied.

I'd seen them myself at Loew's State many times. I could almost do their lines. "Are you the doctor?" Joe Smith would say. Henry Dale would answer, "I'm the doctor," and Joe Smith would say, "I'm dubious." I started to do their lines. My father laughed.

"You remember?" he said.

"You took me," I said.

"Did I?"

"Yeah. You took me a lot of places. You took me to a circus in Brooklyn. It was in a tent on Flatlands Avenue." I remembered the day he sneaked us under a tent flap. I knew I hadn't made this up. "Do you remember?" I asked.

"No."

It was like a door slamming shut in my face.

"Do you remember taking me to Yankee Stadium?" It was the day Lou Gehrig made that speech thanking everybody.

"I can't remember," my father said.

"Do you remember Dexter Park? You took me to see the Bushwicks playing the House of David at night. The House of David players all had beards. When we got there it started to rain and we all went home." I knew I hadn't made this up.

"I can't remember," he said.

Was it me fantasizing? I knew my father had taken me to these places when I was a kid. He must have loved me. He's a hundred years old, but he had to remember something. The reason for his silence suddenly hit me. I remembered Ursula saying that on the day of the wedding, she and my mother got out of the cab, but my father refused. I know now forty years later he was angry that day because I had married Anne. And he was still angry.

There was a Hebrew National Delicatessen near the retirement hotel. I would drive him there, and my father would order matzoh-ball soup. The owners knew us by now, and always treated us royally. After the soup I ordered a corned-beef sandwich that I split with Deddy. After we finished eating I'd drive him back to the hotel and help him back to his room. He had photographs of Anne, myself, Ben and Amy, an old 8 x 10 glossy of Anne and me, Ben on a seesaw, Amy on a swing. It was a connection to us. Marsha had given up on him. Would I give up on Anne or she on me? I wondered. Who knows. What if one of us is disabled, crippled? It happens. Willie and Bella never got divorced. They were married over thirty years, stuck it out. Anne and I have been married almost forty-seven years; I hear the ticking.

I put my father to bed. He lay on his side. I didn't want to leave, so I lay down beside him. I put my hand on his back, rubbed it, and nestled next to him. When he was asleep, I figured I'd leave. His eyes were now closed. Quietly I got out of bed. I got to the door.

"Jerry," he whispered.

"What?"

"When are you coming back?"

"I'm going to L.A." There was a silence.

"You're in a show. Well, you gotta work."

"Yeah. It's called *Seinfeld*."

"You'll call me?" he whispered.

"Yeah."

"Jerry?"

"Yeah."

"Come here." I walked over to the bed. His eyes opened. He looked up at me. "You did good."

What?

"You did good, Jerry." His eyes closed and he was fast asleep.

I kissed him and left.

I was in Los Angeles shooting a new show, *King of Queens,* when I received a call from Anne one night.

"Your father is in the hospital. They took him from the home. You'd better get here."

I hung up, called the producer, and told him I had to go back to New York to be with my father.

"We'll shoot your scenes in the morning and you can leave at noon," he said.

I learned my scenes that night and shot them the next day without an audience. As I was ready to leave for the airport Anne called again.

"Your father died at nine this morning." Just as I had finished shooting.

When asked what his headstone should read, I said, "Never a Faker."

10

Anne: Act Three

One afternoon in 1985, during the run of *Hurlyburly,* Anne and I and Ben were sitting in Mike Nichols's office at his town house in the East 80s. We were there for a reading of Anne's play *Victims,* and we were the first to arrive other than Sid Armus. Sid was dressed in white Calvin Klein overalls, a strange getup for a sixty-year-old man. He had a circular Band-Aid over his left upper lip.

"What happened to your lip, Sidney?"

"Acting," he says.

He's an Actor's Studio member. It was his preparation, of course. I'm not psychic, but I knew this. He was to read the role of the father, who's recovering from a stroke, he told me.

Olympia Dukakis, Joanna Gleason, Ken Welsh, and Ruth Uhle, actors invited by Mike, arrived on the scene. John Mahoney, just nominated for a Tony, would read Joel. We were awaiting Sam Cohn, who represents Anne, myself, and Mike, as well as Meryl Streep, Dianne Wiest, and lots of other people. Sam has been called the world's top agent. He'd read *Victims* and called Anne to say how much he loved it. *Victims* had been on Mike's dance card for almost a year. I'd been at home one night when he called.

"I read Anne's play. Don't you think it's great?"

"I don't know," I said, "what do you think?"

"It's the funniest thing I ever read."

"Why don't you call Anne in Nantucket and tell her," I said.

"Give me the number."

Anne was in bed when his call came at 9:30 P.M.

"I want to have a reading of it," Mike said.

"Who do you think should play Joel?" Anne asked.

"I'd like to do it with Elaine May."

Anne called to tell me. I was elated, surprised, and relieved. My reservations about the play—Anne's first—suddenly disappeared. I turned on a dime. My reticence in expressing all-out enthusiasm for *Victims* had hurt Anne. When Nichols not only expressed interest but said he also wanted to play my role, I felt like a fool. I remembered the schmuck joke that had been going around.

The wife, after thirty-five years of marriage, wakes up one night calling her husband a schmuck. He looks at her in dismay.

"Why?" he asks.

"Because you *are* a schmuck," she tells him. "You are a world-class schmuck. You're the quintessential schmuck. Schmuck City! Schmuck to the *nth* power! If they had a contest today for the world's biggest schmuck, you'd come in second!"

"Why second?" he asks, somewhat bewildered.

"Because you're a schmuck," she tells him.

"It's you, the part is you," Anne said. "Can't you see it?"

She was right. The part was me.

But, I didn't tell her I was fearful of taking the responsibility for pulling it off or that I felt the tenor of the play was too abrasive. I could never confront Anne with my feelings. Rather than confront, I played it safe and was noncommittal.

Mike arrived. On the table in the living room office were sandwiches along with cookies and coffee. He was dressed in a blue suit with a yellow silk tie and looked informally elegant, like a visitor in his own home. He was giving the event some credence. Mike does not overpower you with his theatrical intelligence yet you know it's there. His commitment to the reading was apparent.

During the successful run of *Hurlyburly,* I once asked Mike what he feared most about the business. "That it might never happen again," he answered without hesitation.

Sam Cohn arrived. I sat on Cohn's left. The reading began. Sid Armus, playing the old man, was now wearing a white jacket over his overalls. It was on backwards. Whatever he was up to as the character was discreetly ignored by everyone. He was funny.

The reaction to the play was stunning. Nichols was in tears laughing. Sam Cohn was laughing. John Mahoney's reading captured Joel. His gravelly voice is musical. His delivery never stretches for a laugh. He's an Irish Joel. So what's wrong with that? The reading was over. Sam Cohn said, "It's a great play." Ben, who had been sitting in the background all this time, said, "I loved it, Mom."

"I want to talk," Mike said. "Let me say good-bye to everyone."

Sam Cohn told Anne, "We'll be talking," and left.

Mike said, "Let's sit down."

We arranged ourselves on the couch. He said, "I want you to know I'll never be able to look at *Long Day's Journey into Night* the same way. There are silences in it. We have to know that and not feel some need to think of it as anything else. It's not O'Neill or Neil Simon." It's *O'Neil Simon* but no one says it. The meeting ended. Mike tried to make *Victims* a theatrical reality, but it never got further than the great read we had in his office.

On June 16, 1987, I was at the Symphony Space Theater on the Upper West Side. The theater was filling up with West Siders hungry for a literary banquet. The neighborhood was jumpin' with Joyce. In the lobby the literati mixed with the not-too-literati. On stage, scores of Broadway and Off-Broadway actors were reading aloud from James Joyce's *Ulysses* as if it were the Torah. From midnight to 3 A.M. Anne was to climax the whole event by reading the Molly Bloom soliloquy that ends this great novel.

I pressed my way backstage to the Green Room, which was filled with people from Charles Kuralt's *Sunday Morning* CBS show, lugging cameras, lighting equipment, and electrical hookups.

A woman grabbed my arm and asked, "Are you reading tonight?"

"I'm not Irish," I told her.

"Half of them up there aren't. You've got my permission," she said, and disappeared into the crowd. I ran into Malachy McCourt, whose liberal viewpoints made him a controversial radio talk-show host in the '70s. His brother Frank (this was a dozen years before *Angela's Ashes*), along with Carroll O'Connor, a young Brian Dennehy, the Clancys, Tommy Makem, Dermott McNamara, Pauline Flanagan, and Helena Carroll, are the Irish cultural connection in America. Anne might have been part of that crowd, but she took another route.

"I didn't get here in time to hear you tonight, Malachy. I was saving myself for Anne."

"I understand, Jerrrry," the brogue bursting through. Malachy had the good grace to forgive me.

I passed a table heaped with exotic cheeses, cold cuts, Irish soda bread, and jugs of wine. Someone offered me an Irish whiskey. I figured I'd need it to fortify me for the three-hour soliloquy.

It was Anne's turn tonight to pay homage to her background.

The Molly Bloom reverie has no punctuation. When read with no meaning, the Irish lilt can easily lull the senses. Joyce is a somnambulist's dream. Anne and director Isaiah Sheffer had created a makeshift variorum: a road map with stops and pauses along the way—something Joyce, for whatever reason, chose not to do. Anne and Isaiah had opted for clarity. That day, she and I had been up since 6 A.M. It was the same day we received the Orson Welles Imagery Award from the Radio Advertising Bureau. What a segue.

I'd just poured myself a shot of Bushmill's and a glass of Guinness Stout—a boilermaker—when Anne spotted me.

"There you are. You got here."

"Of course I got here. You wanted me here, didn't you?"

It turns me on when I see her onstage, all alone. Tonight she would be up there alone. I'm her audience. If she's great, is it because of me? I want to think so.

"I'm glad you made it." She kissed me. "This may not go three hours," she said. "It could go faster."

"Take your time," I told her.

She knows you can't milk an audience's generosity. You're only there with their permission.

The lights went up. Isaiah Sheffer, who resembles a learned Talmudist, walked to the apron and introduced Anne. Larry Josephson, the National Public Radio producer, humorously warned the audience that what they would be hearing might be construed as erotic. Keep the children away from the radio.

Anne entered in a blue, flowered cotton dress that cloaked her youthful figure. It was an artful disguise. How lucky I am to have a beautiful wife. I imagined my Tanta Faiga, my mother's oldest sister, who kept *kashruth* and would never drink anything more than a glass of water when she visited our family during my childhood, saying to me, a now-grown Jerry, "You have a beautiful wife. Why don't you smile?" I couldn't believe my Orthodox aunt was saying that. She was telling me it was okay to be passionate about a woman of another faith.

Anne's performance that night was remarkable. Joyce's words were no longer book stuff. Anne's reading filled the theater with sensuality. *God,* I thought, *is that Anne talking or is it Molly Bloom?* Molly's fantasies affirm every Jewish mother's admonition about boys who marry Gentile women. Suddenly I was Leopold Bloom, asleep next to Molly.

I was watching Anne turn on the world, and it was okay.

When the reading ended at 3 A.M.—"Yes I said Yes I will Yes"—the viewers and listeners, some of whom had followed the text on their laps, disappeared into the night.

"You were wonderful," I told my wife.

"Was I? I lost my place a couple of times."

"I never noticed it."

"I did it in less than three hours."

"I don't care. You got me excited," I said.

A week later I was in Baltimore shooting the film *Hairspray.* I ordered room service and turned on the TV.

Charles Kuralt's *Sunday Morning* billboard cited "Bloomsday" along with George Abbott's one-hundredth-birthday celebration. The wide-angle shot showed Malachy McCourt, David Margulies, John Rubinstein, Stephen Lang. No Anne. I began to get nervous. I remembered watching the TV crew during Anne's reading. There had seemed to be technical difficulties. The sound people were suddenly talking to one another. My worst fears were that they had somehow run out of juice after seven hours, and Anne's stuff would not be on the air.

As Charles Kuralt was about to wind up the segment, he said, "Last came Anne Meara reading, for three hours, Molly Bloom."

A long shot of Anne. The camera dollied in, and Anne's face was now clearly in view during the final speech. "Yes," she said about her willingness to love the man lying next to her. "Yes" again. The word "Yes" was like a drumroll. In my mind she was telling her people, my people, everyone, that I was her man. Her voice was saying all of that through Joyce. She's my Molly, I'm her Leopold.

I suddenly thought, *This marriage is beginning to work out.*

At that moment I felt close to Anne personally, but careerwise it was clear that what I wanted to achieve as an actor was no longer connected to her. Our paths had taken us in different directions. In mid-1985 I had recently come off what I felt was my best work, playing Tamkin in the screen adaptation of Saul Bellow's *Seize the Day.* The chance to play this role had come two weeks after I had agreed to play a bit part in the same film. The cast included Robin Williams as Tommy Wilhelm. When the producer, Robert Geller, a winner of several Peabody awards and producer of the award-winning PBS *American Short Story*, called to ask if I'd be willing to read for Tamkin, I could feel excitement fill me. The audition for director Fielder Cook and Chiz Schultz turned into a performance. That night I was told the role was mine, with rehearsals beginning the next day. The rehearsal ritual was at best a familiarization process, with me stumbling, script in hand. Robin and I were chosen so that Bellow's remorseful characters would somehow have a comic edge to lift them from the somberness of the novella. Williams's poignancy was heightened by a sense of his being a decent *nebbish.* Tamkin is a self-licensed psychoanalyst and amateur inventor who preys on troubled and naive minds. He entices Tommy into a commodities scheme while treating him as a patient. The role is wonderful. Cook's direction was to keep Bellow's work dramatically alive by showing Tommy caught in a web of uncertainty in his desperate search for security.

The message of the film was "Seize the Day," live in the now, this moment. *Seize the role,* I whispered to myself. Do it, grab the golden ring. I was aware that this opportunity was not accidental. I had made steps in my work. Someone other than myself thought I could play this role. I asked myself if I could cut it. I was alone with Robin in scenes that ran whole pages.

In one of the scenes, set in a restaurant, Tamkin's greed and gluttony become apparent to Tommy.

The table was filled with food.

"I want you to eat during this scene," Fielder said. I rebelled against the eating. I could have played the scene convincingly without eating the food but I listened to Cook.

"I want you to eat with your hands, do everything, gorge yourself. Go to the moon with this. I want you to go all out, the bigger the better."

Bellow's script has Tamkin, a hog of a man, shoveling pot roast and red cabbage into his mouth and biting huge chunks of watermelon as he psychoanalyzes Tommy with unerring accuracy. Between the lines I dunked chunks of French bread into my soup and stuffed them into my mouth. My fingers were drenched and the soggy bread dripped down my chin. "Perfect," Fielder said.

For me, the shoot was three weeks of bliss. The best of the best were all at the screening, including Glenn Close, Bill Hickey, Chris Walken, and Jack Rollins, who was now Robin Williams's manager. When the film ended, I could feel my entire life, my hopes and my dreams, at that moment made worthwhile. It validated me in the eyes of everyone who had ever hired me—on some intuition that someday I'd be someone. I remembered Morris Carnovsky's words to me: "Someday I'll pay money to see you." I remembered Jerome Moross, who composed "The Golden Apple," saying "Someday . . ." and my Uncle Charlie, at my Bar Mitzvah saying, "Someday, you'll play the Roxy." I wanted to cry. I was asked to stand up. I stood up and took a bow as my peers applauded. Anne embraced me. *Was that me?* I asked myself. I'd never need to act again; I told myself I'd done it, I'd proved it. It was a lock on my life. It didn't matter what would happen to this picture. They could play it in a schoolroom. I didn't want any more than this. I suddenly felt all my jealousies of fellow performers dissolving. I pictured critics who had been unscathing in their criticism of me suddenly having anxiety attacks in the middle of the night and printing retroactive apologies for being overly critical of my work.

Director Fielder Cook, whom I love to this day, then made an impassioned plea to the audience that the movie should not become lost forever in public television. It should have a theatrical run. Roger Ebert wrote in the *Chicago Sun-Times* about the screening of *Seize the Day* at the 1986 Telluride Film Fest:

TELLURIDE, Colo. Saul Bellow is one of the great novelists of his era, but that certainly hasn't brought Hollywood knocking at his door.

The premiere here this weekend of *Seize the Day,* an intense tragicomedy starring Robin Williams, Joseph Wiseman, and Jerry Stiller, marks the first time a Bellow novel has been filmed. Although many Bellow novels have been on the bestseller lists, not even a star with Jack Nicholson's clout has been able, after ten years of trying, to find financing for a movie version of *Henderson the Rain King.*

Even now that *Seize the Day* has been filmed, it seems headed for television instead of the big screen. In the case of *Seize the Day,* there's

the added possibility that a theatrical run could win Oscar considera-
tion for Jerry Stiller's supporting performance, his best film work in a
long time, as the con-man who steers the hero into the stock market.

My own feelings were that no matter what happened to the film, I had
met Robert Geller, a great filmmaker who believed in me, and somehow I
had been fortunate enough to work with a comedic genius in the person
of Robin Williams. Robin had given of himself to me in every conceivable
way. His purity, his creative fairness, allowed me to be the character fully
and truly. What a mensch. "Don't be afraid," he'd whisper before each
big scene. I wanted to kiss him. This man, whose talent was so big it extended to the moon, could also share the aesthetic pie.

Alas, my thought that I never need act again after *Seize the Day* was
short-lived. I was asked to play a role in *Hairspray,* which was filming in
Baltimore, director John Waters's hometown. Sonny Bono and Deborah
Harry were also in the film.

I agreed to do Wilbur Turnblad, the husband of Divine. Pia Zadora
played a '60s beatnik and Ricki Lake played my daughter. The word
"crossover film" was heard in the industry. The script had all the makings
of a sleeper.

John Waters introduced himself. He was then forty-one years old. He
joked about his pencil-thin mustache. "I think I saw it on some actor in a
B-movie and decided to try it," he told me. He was funny; I liked him. I'd
chosen to be here, in a John Waters movie. It was like nothing I'd ever
done. Was this a career move? Nothing made sense. You do your best
work, and who knows. *Live this moment,* I told myself. Seize the day. I'm
in Baltimore in a movie. I'm alive. I'm acting.

"You'll have fun," John said. "See you on the set."

I was getting into costume and makeup when I met Glenn Milstead,
known as Divine, for the first time. He too was getting ready to shoot our
first scene. He was wearing a housedress and adjusting his wig.

"How's Anne?" he said in a very soft, womanly voice. I knew immediately we'd be perfect together as husband and wife.

"We're ready to shoot," someone said.

The Hardy Har Joke Shop actually exists. It's in a blue-collar area and
sells things like dribble glasses and cans of doggy-doo. That day, it had
been commandeered for a shoot. I sensed this was Waters's favorite

scene. He worked with childlike enthusiasm. He confided that the Hardy Har owner had been told to put a stop to the selling of snot. He hadn't been given a reason. But the owner said he could get a fresh shipment if someone needed it right away. John put his hand up to his nostril as if to demonstrate.

"Do you want to meet the guy?" Waters asked.

"I'd rather not," I said apologetically. "I always feel a little funny about meeting people I play."

"I understand," Waters said.

Divine, Ricki Lake, and I squeezed tightly in a doorway as the last-minute lighting changes were made. The scene deals with Divine and myself—mama and papa—describing the wonders of the whoopie cushion to our recalcitrant daughter, whose ambitions lie in other areas.

"Lock it up," said Dave Iselin, the cinematographer.

"Speed. Sound rolling. Action," Waters said.

The six-week shoot was fun. Lots of location shots around the city. The Baltimoreans lined the streets awaiting Divine's entrance. When we emerged from a trailer, the mostly blue-collar fans applauded. It was like a Hollywood movie, only on the other side of the tracks.

When we wrapped, the cast and crew had a final lunch together. A nice party. Divine and I sat next to each other.

"I can't wait to meet Anne in New York," he said. "I'd love to meet her. We'll have to get together.

"I'm so nervous," he said. "I'm going to Salt Lake City tomorrow to do my act for the Mormons. I know they're going to stone me."

"Not at all," I reassured him. "They'll want to laugh. If you have any problems just say you're a friend of Donny and Marie."

"What do you mean 'friend'? I'm one of them: Donny, Marie, and Divine Osmond."

About a year later the film was released. John asked me to do some publicity, so I shuttled to and from radio shows, touting *Hairspray*. The film was selling out, and I was staggered by the reaction. At a press screening, I was upset at the silences during most of the film. My scene demonstrating a whoopie cushion to Ricki Lake had been cut. When the screening ended, I'd escaped to the street and walked up Broadway to our office. Why had they cut the scene? was all I could think about.

I was also preoccupied with the results of a recent sigmoidoscopy. Doctor Belsky had found polyps and now recommended a colonoscopy, which was to take place in a few days. For two weeks I had avoided calling for an appointment because of fear that the polyps might be malignant. I had not told Anne of having to go in to have polyps removed. I'd deliberately set the appointment for the week she would be in Los Angeles doing *Hollywood Squares, Alf,* and *Win, Lose, or Draw,* plus writing a script on spec for Bette Midler.

Deep within, I knew I was clean, and that message in itself became powerful for me. I had safely kept Anne away from the polyp situation until just before she left. She'd opened the mail on our bureau and come across instructions for the colonoscopy.

I berated myself for not hiding the instructions, and attributed it, rightly or wrongly, to wanting her to discover what was going on. She looked at me in a soft, pained way.

"Why didn't you tell me?" she said. "Why do we have to play games? This macho shit doesn't work. It's an insult."

I knew she was right and that I was very lousy at pulling it off.

"When do you do this?"

"Next Monday. It's done in an office, not a hospital, so it can't be too bad. You'll be on the Coast. I'm okay, I know it."

Sunday morning, Anne left for L.A. and I prepared for my procedure the next day. No food for twenty-four hours.

I also squeezed in the press lunch for Divine at *Spy* magazine. I arrived at *Spy* headquarters. The room was filled with people. Most were gay. At two separate tables sat Divine and John Waters. The tables were crammed with food. I could see breads, salads, and wine. I was getting hungry. Waters saw me and stood up and gave me a big hug. Divine, at his own table, sat there smiling. A ridge of blond hair circling his scalp gave him the appearance of a Trappist monk. My own hair had turned pink. It had not been dyed in a month and had oxidized.

"What happened to your hair?" Waters asked.

"It's pink. It's changing color as you watch it," I said. The line seemed appropriate for *Hairspray,* I thought.

"Stick around," John said. "Have some lunch."

"I can't," I said.

A part of me wanted to say, "I'm having my polyps removed in a couple of hours. I hope they're benign." Just to see his reaction. I held back the temptation. The party was on a high.

John said, "*Time* magazine gave us a great review. So did *New York* magazine."

"Great. I gotta go."

"Where?" they asked.

"A reading," I said, and headed for the street.

I walked toward the medical building on First Avenue, trying to focus on something that would block out my fear. I still had forty minutes to kill. I entered a bookstore and walked quickly to the magazine rack, where I picked up *Time* and turned to the review. They liked it, just as John had said. I looked for my name. No mention. I checked *New York* magazine. Also good. I was not mentioned. A wave of melancholy enveloped me.

At 2:15 P.M. I started walking from the bookstore toward the doctor's office. The last mile. Two busted Vietnam vets sitting on some steps looked up at me and asked: "You're who we think you are, aren't you?"

"Yeah," I said.

"We love you and your wife." They were bearded and toothless. "We're both drunks," one of them said. "Could you help us out?"

"Sure," I said, reaching into my pants and pulling out two bucks.

Funny how fear of dying creates generosity.

When I got to the office, a nurse had me lie on my side, and Dr. Friedlander, a man in his forties with a sweet Jewish face, injected some Valium into my arm. A nurse from Jamaica prepared a long snaky tube that would be inserted into my behind.

"Mr. Stiller?" Dr. Friedlander pointed to the wall, where there was a map of the human anatomy. He explained what he would be doing and where he would be going.

"I'm going to go slow," he said, "and if I get to something, I'm going to cauterize it and save the tissue. If I break through the intestine, that would cause a hemorrhage. I don't anticipate that."

I lay quietly on my side as the long tube was inserted, praying that my intestines stayed intact. The doctor stopped once, twice, three times, explaining that he had discovered something. The anesthesia created a mellowing effect. Time seemed to evaporate. There was no sense of existence, and no pain. For almost two hours the doctor slowly, cautiously, did his work. I looked at the anatomy map and tried to visualize his stops as stations on the BMT subway line from when I was a kid in Brooklyn— Church Avenue, Newkirk, Brighton Beach. Last stop, Coney Island.

The doctor said, "We got them."

"How many?"

"Three," he said.

"Can I see?"

"I'll show you one," he said.

"Looks like part of an oyster," I said of the red-tinted tissue he showed me.

"The other two were bigger. Size of garbanzo beans," he said.

"Those are the culprits?"

"Yes. You can sleep peacefully."

This I didn't fully believe.

"They go to the lab and come back in a week, but they're okay," he said, breaking into a smile.

The nurse said, "You have to stay here till the anesthesia wears off. I love your work, Mr. Stiller."

"I love yours too," I said.

I called Anne in Los Angeles and told her I was okay.

I walked over to Third Avenue, then up Third toward the crosstown bus. Suddenly I was terribly hungry. I tried very hard to make myself remember this moment: the relief of knowing I was in good health, asking myself what greater gift could I have received than my life. I went into an Asian salad bar and bought a health cookie, the kind that tastes like soy and molasses. I slowly ate it as I walked up the avenue, relishing life.

The following Saturday night, when going for the Sunday papers, I saw huge lines outside Loew's 84th Street movie house. The ushers were telling everybody that *Hairspray* was sold out. *I've got to see it with real people,* I told myself. To see it from their eyes. The manager recognized me and escorted me inside.

"The picture's great," he said, "and you're wonderful. Just go right in."

The kids who ran the hot-dog stand hollered, "Ain't you in the movie?"

"Yeah," I said.

"Come here. Can we have an autograph?"

"Sure," I said, wondering how they could possibly have singled me out.

"You know, Divine and John Waters were here last night. They were signing autographs."

"Lots of people?"

"Sold out."

I found a seat in the rear of the theater. I could feel the audience's enthusiasm. For the first time I laughed out loud at Divine and myself, playing wife and husband.

That same week I appeared on Ted Brown's radio show and "Luncheon at Sardi's" with radio hosts Arlene Francis and Joan Hamburg.

"What's Divine really like?" they all wanted to know.

"He's someone who I love to watch iron my clothes," I said.

"Why did you do the picture?" Jerry Tallmer asked during an interview for the *Post*.

"I've done Shakespeare, Saul Bellow. Why not Waters."

A couple of weeks later I was at my health club when a phone call came from producer Stanley Buchtal. "I've got some sad news, Jerry. Divine is dead."

"What?!"

"It's true," Stanley said.

I wanted to cry. "How?" I asked.

"Choked on his food, in his sleep. Suffocated."

"He was so heavy" were the only words I could find at that moment. I meant to say, "How could he have done this to himself?"

Shocks of disbelief rippled through me. I saw Divine as a class person. The guy had finally found stardom, and had been rewarded unfairly. He'd been in Los Angeles shooting an episode of *Married With Children*. In my mind I saw him celebrating his triumph in a most innocent way. Enjoying food. What a vice.

The day of the funeral in Baltimore was two days before I was scheduled to perform with Joe Grifasi in a Cole Porter tribute for Isaiah Sheffer's "Selected Shorts" at Symphony Space in New York. I called Waters to explain that I could not make the funeral.

"We'll miss you," John said in a shaken voice. "The wake's tomorrow night."

"Send my love. I'm sorry I can't be there."

The following day I called the funeral home in Towson, Maryland, to ask if my letter to Divine's parents had arrived.

"No, but if you'd like to speak to his mother, she's here."

Divine's mother got on the phone.

"Jerry, he really liked you," she said.

"I'm so sorry for you and Mr. Milstead," I said.

"He said you were always there for him," she answered.

"I'm not going to be able to make the funeral. I'm working tomorrow."

"I'm sorry," Mrs. Milstead said. "We'd love for you to be here. Your flowers arrived. They're beautiful."

There was a pause. There was no pressuring.

"I'll be there tonight."

I took the Amtrak. We passed through Philly. It was nightfall. I went over the words and music to "Brush Up Your Shakespeare" for the show at Symphony Space. The train pulled into Baltimore. Baltimore Film Festival producer George Udel and his artist wife Joan Erbe picked me up at the station, and twenty-five minutes later we were in the Ruck Funeral Home in Towson. The place was filled with people, decks of flowers. Divine once said jokingly, "When I go, I want lots of flowers. Give them in lieu of a donation to a worthy charity." His request was granted.

To left and right of the open casket were lines of floral arrangements. I walked to the casket and stood there a moment. Waters and his assistant, Pat Moran, came to me. We hugged and then looked at one another and said nothing.

"I saw the picture the other night in New York," I told Waters. "They told me you and Divine were there the night before."

"It's a big hit," Waters said.

"Yeah. What a way to celebrate."

"I'm glad you came," Waters said.

"I had to. I really had to. Where's his mother?"

"Right there," Waters said, pointing to a gray-haired lady standing next to a man in a wheelchair.

"That's Glenn's father," Waters said.

I went over to them. "I'm so sorry," I said. His father looked up and I shook his hand. I suddenly felt how important it was to be here.

There were flowers and balloons from Whoopi Goldberg, along with a note: "So you get a good review and this is what you do." From *Married With Children* came a message: "If you didn't like the show, you should've just told us."

I spoke to crew members Gary Lambert and Dave Insley, to actress Mink Stole, and to the costumer, who designed a golfball shirt I wore that got lots of attention. At one point the editing people gathered around me and mentioned my hilarious scene that had been cut. I listened—and knew for the first time that it really didn't matter.

The Night Owl arrived back in New York at 2:30 A.M. Twelve hours later, Joe Grifasi and I were doing "Brush Up Your Shakespeare" at Symphony Space. The number went well. I did it for Divine.

In the early 1990s Isaiah Sheffer called again, asking me to travel to Miami to do a reading of John Sayles's "At the Anarchists' Convention" at the Dade County Book Fair. The following day I called my Uncle Abe. He had moved to Florida, and I hadn't seen him in years. His wife, my aunt Anne, had passed away, and he lived alone.

Now, in Miami, I telephoned him.

"Jerry! You're in Miami?! Where?"

I told him at the Book Fair.

"You want me to come and meet you there?" he said.

"No," I said. "I'm driving. I'll come to you."

"I'm at the Casablanca."

"Okay, I'll find it."

"You're sure?"

"I'm sure."

My uncle Abe was ninety years old and wanted to pick me up. I'd almost said yes. When would I no longer be the kid being cared for by his uncle?

Minutes later, I was on Ocean Drive, passing small hotels that face the Atlantic. I parked and walked toward the water. There wasn't a soul on the beach. It reminded me of an empty stage set. I got back in the car and drove onto Collins Avenue, passing the once fabulous Fontainbleu and Eden Roc hotels. There were a few old people meandering at their own pace. They wore bright outfits and funny hats—costumes to deflect pity, to make them feel good inside.

I arrived at a huge oceanfront edifice. The Casablanca parking lot had lots of tow-away warnings but no cars. At the desk I asked for Abe Citron. The clerk asked me to write the name on a piece of paper. He pointed to three men sitting in the lobby on a bench encircling a palm tree.

"Mr. Citron, you have a visitor," the clerk's voice on the loudspeaker announced.

An old man with a cane stared at me. "Jer-r-r-y? Is that you?"

His soft Yiddish lilt awakened memories. His appearance shocked me. It was as if I hadn't been informed that he'd aged, but I could not act surprised. I too had aged. I wondered, *Does he notice any difference in me?* He played it perfectly. I was still the nephew.

My uncle got to his feet with the help of a cane. His warming smile was still there. He introduced me to one of the men sitting next to him. "This is Mr. Lou Harris."

Mr. Lou Harris, who wore thick glasses, asked if I was from Avenue U in Brooklyn. No, I told him.

"You look like someone from the block."

"This is my nephew," Abe said. "Come," he said to me, "we'll go upstairs. I'll show you my apartment."

"Tell them not to tow my car," I said.

"They never tow. Come."

We started toward the elevator. The movement was in mini-steps. I remembered when he was a vibrant seventy-five. "I'm on the top floor," he said as he hit the elevator button. "I've got a great view."

A heavyset man in his seventies, carrying a plastic shopping bag filled with groceries, got on at the third floor. He complained to my uncle how the hotel and its clientele had changed. He waited for my uncle to agree. After a moment Uncle Abe said, "As long as they wear nice clothes, they're just like me." He was putting down a bigot.

I remember my uncle meeting Anne for the first time. There was no shock in his face when he saw the *shikse*.

The man with the shopping bag got off at the ninth floor. "That's the first time he spoke to me in three years," my uncle said.

On my uncle's floor we rounded a bend in the hall where a fancy iron gate guarded the door to an apartment. An antique lamp hung above the door, throwing an eerie yellow light.

"That's the dungeon," my uncle said. "It belongs to the man who once owned the building. He sold the building but kept the apartment as part of the deal. It makes everyone else feel poor. Come," he said.

We entered my uncle's apartment, a large single room with a picture window overlooking the Atlantic.

"You like the view?" my uncle said.

It was spectacular. I could see cloud formations and squadrons of birds flying to an unknown destination. As far as the eye could see were miles of desolate beach and trash cans. It was ghostly. I said nothing. I took it all in.

"Tell me, Jerry, what are you doing here?"

I told him about reading the John Sayles story at the Book Fair.

"And where's Anne?" Uncle Abe asked.

"She's flying to L.A. to do a TV show called *Alf*."

"They call this a studio," he said with a wave of the hand. "A kitchen, a Frigidaire, and a closet."

Alongside the window was a roll-away bed; in the center of the room, an armchair facing a TV.

I had a feeling of emptiness. The room was depressing. The beautiful Atlantic seemed like a backdrop for despair.

When Anne and I were first married, we had won a huge turkey on *The Price Is Right*. Allan Shalleck, my friend from Syracuse University, was working as an assistant director on the show, and had set Anne and me up as contestants. We had brought the uncooked turkey prize to Uncle Abe's restaurant, and he gave us a roasted turkey in its place. Now, in his lonely room in Florida, I remembered Leo Bloom, Rex Partington, and Rudy Marinetti, my college roommates, driving down with me from Syracuse for the Barter Theater auditions in New York and Abe feeding us in his restaurant. I remembered him pouring schnapps and cutting sponge cake on a bridge table at my mother's unveiling in Montefiore Cemetery. His presence made a sad occasion less sad. I thought of the many things he had given me in a lifetime that I was now trying to repay in one fell swoop.

"Sit down. We don't have to go out. I'll make lunch," he said. He reached into a cupboard and took out two cans of Bumble Bee salmon, which he ran under the faucet and then placed in the refrigerator to cool.

His eyes sparkled. "You know, being alone is not the worst thing in the world."

He stared at my nondescript garb. "In Europe, actors wore capes. Why blue jeans?" he asked. "You know, Ludwig Satz was a great Yiddish actor, but nobody knows it. Moishe Nadir, he was a wonderful writer; nobody knows his name."

I listened, like a good actor. Then he was off on opera, and how he admired Jusi Bjoerling. All this while setting the table, laying out silverware and plates.

"I wanted to be an opera singer," my uncle said. "I used to sing at the Social Club. That's where I met *my* Anne. She loved my voice. She married me because in those days the educated women loved artists. We'd go to the opera all the time. It's what we had in common. I thought someday I'd be an opera singer."

"Do you listen to music?" I asked.

"No. To tell you the truth, my hearing isn't as good as it used to be."

I mentioned the possibility of a Walkman.

"What is that?"

"You've seen them. Those people wearing earphones."

"I always thought those people had hearing problems," he said.

He removed the cans of salmon from the fridge, along with a head of lettuce wrapped in plastic. He peeled off and placed each leaf like a work of origami on a large plate. He sliced some tomatoes.

"How about some onion?"

"Yes," I said, "I'd like some onion."

"What do you do when somebody you act with smells from onions?" he asked as he sliced away.

I laughed. "If they're good actors, you don't mind. You become a family. If they're lousy actors, you tell them to cut it out."

When he finished making the salad, he smiled devilishly and said, "How about a shot? You drink whiskey?"

"Sure," I said.

"I got Dewar's Scotch."

"That's good stuff."

He reached into the cupboard and pulled out a bottle obviously hidden away for just such an occasion. He poured a thimbleful into a milk glass.

"Tell me when."

"When," I said, making two fingers.

"That's all?"

"No ice," I told him.

When we finished eating, he poured boiling water into a cup and dropped in a spoonful of instant coffee.

"When I owned the restaurant," he said, "a coffee salesman talked me into switching to a more expensive brand. Would you believe the customers complained? They loved the cheaper coffee."

I knew he was apologizing for this instant coffee.

"Come, we'll go outside," he said.

I followed him, with no idea where he was taking me. Twenty minutes later and a few hundred yards up Collins Avenue, we arrived at the Sherry Frontenac, where seniors were frolicking in the lobby. A redheaded soprano at the piano was playing and singing *Kiss Me Again*. A few feet away a game of casino was in full swing.

"This place is nicer," I said.

"You think so?"

He led me to the terrace. I could see from a stenciled SHERRY FRONTENAC on the pool platform that this was no longer a luxury hotel. I asked him if he would like to move here.

"Yes, but there's no ocean view," he said.

"What about price?"

"It's the same."

"I'll talk to the manager," I said. "Maybe if they see my face they'll move you in."

"But I wouldn't have a view," he said. "I just wanted you to see this place."

Like two tortoises, we started back to the Casablanca.

Twenty minutes later we were there. I was hoping he wouldn't ask me to go upstairs.

"You don't have to come up," he said. "We can say good-bye here."

I felt a rush of sadness. He'd taken me off the hook, and I was relieved.

As we embraced, a car pulled out of the driveway and stopped. The man behind the wheel asked me what I was doing here. It was clear that he recognized me.

"Visiting my uncle," I said, pointing to Abe.

"This is my mother," the driver's wife remarked, indicating an older woman in back. "She loves to dance." The daughter was obviously trying to set up a *shiddach,* a love match.

Abe smiled and said, "We know each other."

"Well, it's nice seeing you," the younger woman said as they drove off.

"How did they know you?" Uncle Abe asked.

"Television," I said.

He looked at me and smiled.

As I got into my car he said, "I don't like it when people come, because I know when they say good-bye, it's tough for them."

I kissed him a wet kiss and headed into traffic. He was right. It was tough. That was the last time I ever saw him.

Actors in pursuit of "the dream" sometimes get caught in the trap of not listening to themselves. When you listen to someone else and go against your own instincts, you're courting trouble.

Such was the case when I accepted a role in *Sam's Spa,* a film later called *Little Vegas.* I was to play the title role, Sam. Intriguing, to say the least, except that the script was not really about Sam, but about five other people, at least two of whom were more important than Sam. But, having turned down a chance to be in *Dirty Dancing* because I hated the script, I didn't trust my judgment and allowed myself to be persuaded to do *Sam's Spa.*

Many times when asked to do something on stage that is physically dangerous, actors become courageous. In real life I would shrink at things I've been asked to do onstage. You learn how to do a fall, for instance, and when it works, you feel proud. It rids you of former feelings of cowardice.

In this film I was supposed to hold a rattlesnake in my hand and converse with it. I knew there would be no doubles, and did not object. I figured, hell, it was some pussycat snake that was defanged and lovable. I also trusted my instinct that no animal, bird, or reptile would harm an actor. Also, the trainers were Hollywood experts. I had all these things going for me.

On the given day I was introduced to a six-foot rattler named Coffee. Coffee and I were to rehearse in one of the cottages. He was with the trainer, who took him out of a box and held him close in an easy, relaxed manner. I thought I could see the fangs.

"Does he—?" I didn't have time to finish the sentence.

"No, he's tame. It's okay."

"How old is he?"

"A couple of years," the trainer said.

"How do I get to know him?"

"Here," the trainer said, transferring the beautiful slithery creature into my hands. "They're nice," the trainer said.

I held the snake pressed into the palm of my hand, and he made himself at home on my arms. I began to wonder whether I could actually say my lines with the snake on my arm.

"Has he been defanged?" I asked as he slithered about, his tongue constantly moving.

"He's harmless."

"How do you know?"

"We test him. We feed him a rat, and when he doesn't go for it, we know he's safe." I started to feel confident. I did my lines, put my face close to his, and got to like the feel.

"Okay, let's shoot it," said the director. I went down to the set and got into position for the take.

"Give him the snake," the first assistant director shouted. I was handed a huge rattler at least two feet longer and lots heavier than Coffee.

"What happened to the other snake?" I asked.

"Oh, he was just the rehearsal snake," the trainer said.

I survived.

Back in New York, Anne was performing on Broadway in a play by Richard Greenberg called *Eastern Standard*. Producer Jessica Levy lost her fight to keep the play alive until Tony nomination time. Anne's performance as May Logan, the bag lady hovering on the edge of schizophrenia, might have earned her a nomination. More than one voter informed me that he would have voted for her.

When the show closed, Anne, like any actor, was saddened.

Anne asked if I would drive her to Great Neck. "Would you take me out to the house on Baker Hill Road?"

"Sure," I said. I figured it would take her mind away from the show.

We drove over the Triboro Bridge and eventually onto the Northern State Parkway.

I played a tape. "Scott Joplin, you love him."

We exited the Parkway and were in Great Neck.

"I was thinking of this place when I played May. It's hard to get it out of my mind. That's the church. It's where I went to school, St. Thomas. Make a right."

We climbed a small hill.

"That's Baker Hill Road. Slow down. Stop the car."

I stopped in front of the house.

"Do you want to go in?" I said.

"No. Drive around the corner."

I made the turn.

"That's the hill where my father took me sleigh riding. That's the tree my father planted. I was eight years old. It was a sapling. Look at it, huge."

"Yeah, like the one in our backyard in Nantucket."

I realized that our Nantucket house is very similar to the one on Baker Hill Road.

"Let's go."

"Where?" I asked.

"To the other house."

The other house was where Anne's mother died. For some reason I thought it was on East 42nd Street in Brooklyn, next to Holy Cross cemetery. "Wasn't it on East 42nd Street?"

"No, that's where we all lived with the Gartners and Steenie Kearny and Tom and Mary." We drove past the church again. "This is where I was sent to school. My mother made me sandwiches and gave me money for soda or dessert."

"Didn't you walk home for lunch? You were close enough."

"Yes, I went home sometimes," Anne said. "It's up this street. Turn here."

I turned up another tree-lined street. Two-family houses, all middle class.

Traveling back in time with Anne, I was touching base with this part of her life for the first time. It was to know Anne as I had never known her. There was a sadness to her she had never permitted me to see. It was also a chance for me to get closer to her.

"That's the place," Anne said, pointing to a shabby stucco house that hadn't been kept up like the others around it.

We stopped. I remembered Anne describing coming home from school that day. The police cars were parked next to an ambulance. An ambulance outside a child's house makes a child feel like the most important being in the world. Something life-threatening was taking place. The neighbors congregating outside made what happened seem almost festive. Anne was nine. Her father called her in, telling her, "Totsie, something's happened to your mother."

My mind flashed back to Cornelia Street. "I want you to know my mother committed suicide. That doesn't change anything between us, does it?" Anne had asked.

"No," I'd said, "why should it?"

"You still want to be with me."

"Of course," I'd said. I realized I had been entrusted with her most private secret.

I wondered what Anne had submerged all these years. What would a little girl think of her mother's suicide? As we sat in the car outside the house I saw her as a child again.

"I want to go back to the church in Great Neck," Anne said.

I couldn't remember her ever going to church during the time we'd been married. I suddenly felt apart from her.

"Drive around and I'll meet you in front in a few minutes."

I drove around and waited.

A few minutes later she emerged through the archway. Had she become Catholic again?

"C'mon," she said. "Let's get something to eat. Wait a minute, there was a restaurant my father took me to called the Abbey. It's this way."

We drove a few blocks and finally gave up.

"It's gone," she said.

"You're doing me today," I said. "I'm the one always going back to the old neighborhood. You always made fun of me for doing it. Two people in one family doing the same thing is very sad. C'mon, let's get something to eat."

"Here on the Island?"

"Yeah, why not?" I said.

We drove past a steak house near Jericho Turnpike.

Anne said, "We haven't eaten steak in a year."

A valet parking guy took the Volkswagen. We ordered champagne cocktails and people came by and made a fuss over us. And the painful distance between the past and the present almost disappeared.

One of our great friends was Henny Youngman. Henny was a magician: His trick was that he could make anyone laugh. His only prop was his wit. He was an intellect in the garb of a clown. He loved opera. His delivery was like a shortwave radio sending out a distress signal. Sentences seemed to break up as they came out of his mouth an SOS: "My ship is going down. If you don't laugh, I'll sink." He was doing the *Titanic* every time he told a joke. Each sentence was a trip to a precipice. He dared you not to laugh. More often than not you would, and he lived to tell another joke.

Henny befriended Anne and me before we were married. I was at Grand Central waiting to catch a train to Erie, Pennsylvania, and standing there was Henny Youngman.

"Henny Youngman," I said,

"Where are you going?" he asked.

"Erie, Pennsylvania," I said.

"I'm going to Toronto. I'll see you."

And we did. Four years later Anne was appearing in *Bus Stop* at the Woodstock (New York) Playhouse. During the intermission I spotted Henny in the lobby. I walked up and said, "Mr. Youngman, what are you doing here?"

"Same as you," he replied.

"We met at Grand Central some years ago. My wife plays Cherie."

"She's wonderful," he said. "Why don't you come to my house. I'll pick you up in front of the theater at 9 A.M. tomorrow."

I was in shock. When the show ended I told Anne.

"He's got to be kidding," she said.

Nonetheless the next morning we drove to the Playhouse.

At 9 A.M. sharp Henny pulled up and said, "Get in the car." We drove to his home. He introduced us to his wife, Sadie, and the kids. For the next eight hours we ate and laughed. Not a single one-liner, just ad libs.

"See that mountain? I own that mountain," he cracked. "Tomorrow night I play on the other side of that mountain."

When Anne and I were working at Mr. Kelly's in Chicago, there were Henny and Sadie in the audience, laughing. When do comedians ever laugh at other younger comedians, I wondered.

It was the beginning of a long friendship.

Some thirty years later, early one morning, the phone rang. It was Henny.

"What are you doing?" he asked. "Come on over. I'm taking a bath."

"You really want me to?"

"It would be nice," he said.

"I'll be there in an hour."

When I arrived Henny was watching golf on the tube, a phone on the table next to him.

"I got over three hundred cards," he said. "My daughter Marilyn is helping me answer them."

He mentions a business associate who hadn't come to the shiva. The wall was full of pictures of Henny and Sadie. He pointed to one of himself, taken thirty years earlier.

"I think I'm going to send out that one of me. I'm going to Milwaukee tomorrow to do a commercial. I stopped taking jobs when Sadie was so sick. . . . Do you like golf?" he asked, still watching the tube.

"No, I don't play it."

"I don't know how they do it," he said.

He picked up the phone. I hadn't heard it ring. A red light went on and the word "Yes" was out of his mouth before the end of the first ring. When he answered, it was as if he was no longer in mourning. He pretended cheerfulness.

"Friends," he whispered. He hung up. "How did you get into this business?"

The golf game was no longer of interest. He turned off the TV set. Without waiting for an answer he rolled on. "My brother-in-law gave me a piece of material. I did it on an amateur night. How about you?"

I mentioned being taken to vaudeville by my father.

"No, I mean when did you start?"

"I was in the army."

"Did you perform in the army?"

"No, at the Henry Street Playhouse, but when I got out of the army I studied acting on the GI Bill."

Henny seemed bewildered. He thought in headlines. I was giving him a biblical tome.

"How'd you get into this?" he repeated.

"My Italian soap opera," I said.

He looked at me, puzzled, so I sang "Sorrento" and did my "Buona Sera, Signore, Signorina." Suddenly I was auditioning for him. He smiled. I didn't expect him to laugh.

While he was getting dressed, he talked of Danny Kaye. "We started in the Borscht Circuit," he said. "They'd hire you and tell you you were on vacation. They'd feed you, give you a place to sleep so they wouldn't have to pay you. Then you did the shows. Something new every couple of nights. Danny became a star. Did one number in a Broadway show that established him." Henny was talking about *Lady in the Dark*.

"Did you hang out together?" I asked.

"No, he hung out with a different crowd, not with Berle and the other guys."

"Why not?"

"I don't know," Henny said. "He was different. He hung out with the Broadway crowd."

"You mean Kurt Weill, people like that?"

"Yeah," Henny said.

"Couldn't you hang out with both crowds?"

"You could if you wanted to. I'd go to Lindy's when I started out. Walter Winchell would have me sit at his table. Berle was there, Jack E. Leonard, Joe E. Lewis. I told them some jokes. I made them laugh. I sat with them till six in the morning. I wouldn't leave. I'd come home, Sadie would want to know where I'd been. I tried to explain. She said, 'Six o'clock!' I was the funniest. They wouldn't leave."

I couldn't match him with any Anne stories.

We started walking toward the Plaza on Central Park South. People recognized Henny. "Sorry about Sadie, Henny." He acknowledged them.

We passed some friends who hadn't shown up during the mourning period.

"We didn't know there was a shiva," they said, and walked on.

"Millionaires," Henny said to me. "Now they're just spending it till it all runs out. They just have to stay in good health."

As we were walking, I told Henny that I hated people who don't drink.

"I don't drink either," he said. "I always thought Scotch tasted like medicine."

Henny said, "Did you know that Waxy Gordon, the gangster, loved my act?" I remembered listening to my father speak of the Jewish Mafia in whispers to my mother. I dreamt about Little Augie, a thug crawling through our bathroom window, trying to kill my father because he'd mentioned Little Augie's name. It made me fearful. Henny Youngman could walk among these terrible giants free of fear. Why? Because he was funny. You don't kill people who make you laugh. Creating laughter is an intimate act—it creates instant affection. The ugly toad becomes a handsome prince if he can make you laugh. Henny was the comedian my father wished he could be.

When we reached the Plaza, Henny said, "Come on, let's go to the Oyster Bar."

We maneuvered down the halls of the Plaza like two tortoises. Henny pointed to what was once the Persian Room and was now a boutique.

"I'm one of the only comedians who played that room."

Anne and I did, too, but I didn't say that.

"Hey, would you please tie my shoe? The laces slip out."

Henny was huge and by now had trouble bending. I was having trouble myself, so I could identify.

He put his foot out and I tied the knot.

"Now the other one. Thanks," Henny said. We sat down and ordered.

"Are you having a party this year?" Henny was always a big draw at our New Year's Eve parties. When I mentioned Henny was coming everyone wanted to be there.

We learned how to throw a great party from the fabulous bashes thrown by Milton Goldman, the legendary agent. Although we weren't his clients, Milton always seemed to remember us, inviting us to a Sir Laurence Olivier party, a birthday celebration for Maureen Stapleton, or an opening for Rex Harrison. Milton, the perfect gentleman, was also the master of introductions even at *our* parties. Milton would grab my arm.

"Jerry, this is Ethel Merman. Ethel, this is Jerry Stiller."

She said, "I know, Milton. We did the Boy Scout Jamboree together."

Of course, everyone knew Ethel Merman but Milton took no chances.

"Jerry just finished doing *Passione* on Broadway. He was wonderful. How long did it run, Jerry?"

"Two weeks, Milton."

"You were wonderful, Jerry. Ethel, come with me. I want you to meet Ernie Borgnine."

"I was married to him, Milton . . . for six weeks."

When Henny Youngman arrived, the attention turned to the King of the One-Liners. He held court the entire evening.

Some months later, I was asleep at our house in Nantucket when Henny called.

"He doesn't use me in his jokes anymore. Is he jealous of me?" I listened to Henny painfully describe how he was still waiting for Berle to invite him to dinner. "We've known each other sixty years. William Morrow is coming out with my book in October," he said. "It's from the vault."

I was still half asleep. What was he talking about? What vault? I never interrupted him, fearing I'd sound stupid. Sometimes he'd start the straight line to a joke in the middle of a sentence. I'd never know he was telling a joke until he was racing toward the punch line.

"You're not asleep, are you?"

"No, no," I reassured him.

"It's from the vault."

"What?"

"The jokes," he said. Was this the secret cache he'd been stashing, hoarded material he'd never used? The key to teaching how to tell the perfect joke. Almost like establishing a master race of comedians. And now in this latest book, was he giving the secret away to everyone? I could hear the mortality in his voice.

"I'm eighty-five years old, what do I have to hide? I'm giving it away. They're doing a show about Berle on Broadway. If he can have one, so can I. Look, I got a story too. You're a writer. You can do it."

Suddenly I was elevated to Henny's biographer. For half a second I looked back at my life and wondered how at sixty-four I was connected to the lives of Milton Berle and Henny Youngman, a generation older than me.

He said, "Look, I need something for my book. Something that would get people interested. This is a book that kids could use who want to be comedians."

"You mean you want me to write a preface?"

"Yeah, could you do that?"

"I think I know what you mean," I said.

"I love you, good-bye." Click.

I descended the attic stairs wondering what I was doing in Nantucket—"Goyville," as Henny called it—listening to Henny doing King Lear, railing against Milton Berle. Suddenly I was associating—actually or by proxy—with some of the world's best comedians, people who as a kid I dreamt about knowing.

I sat down to write in Henny's voice about why Henny was opening the vault. An hour and a half later it was finished. It was in longhand. I read it to Anne. She approved. I called Henny and asked him where to send it.

"Read it to me," he said. There was urgency in his voice. When I finished there was silence. "That's beautiful," he said. "I wanna show it to someone. Send it to me right away."

"Where?" I said. I myself was excited.

"Fax it to the Friars, I can pick it up."

I didn't want to fax it for fear that someone at the Friars might read it. I wanted it to be thought of as Henny's.

"Look, I'll mail it to you."

What am I doing in another comedian's life? I wondered.

I looked out at Children's Beach. It was a beautiful sunny day. I asked myself, Was this the way you thought this day would be spent? I told Anne I was going out for a short bike ride. I took a copy of *The Strife of the Spirit* by Rabbi Steinsaltz with me. At the Jetties Beach I soaked up sun while I highlighted in yellow passages by this brilliant scholar who put me in touch with Jewish ideas that until now had eluded me. I remembered Henny's parody of the song "What Kind of Fool Am I": "What kind of Jew am I that never went to *shul.* . . ." I sat at a wooden table overlooking a windy, sunny beach. Kids were flying kites, I was reading Steinsaltz. I biked home and took a nap.

Over the next few days Henny called three times. "I love the piece. I've shown it to a few people. They think it's great. Can I use it in the book?"

"Of course," I said.

"How much do you want?"

"Nothing. I wrote it for you."

"That's very generous."

I reminded him how he had picked us up outside the Woodstock Playhouse and had us over to his house the entire day. His unending delivery of jokes was a command performance. He spent the entire day telling us his life. He was so open. Then he drove us back.

"The piece is yours, Henny."

"By the way, the Friars are honoring Berle. Can I do it?"

"Do what?"

"Your story about me. I can switch it, make it about Berle. Do you mind if I read it at the Friars' Roast?" He did.

Henny's comedy was never out of season. But, Henny never knew he was a star. He'd do his act over the phone to people who were in a sickbed. He brought the priceless gift of laughter to everyone. Is it possible that God himself needed a laugh, and Henny said, "Take my life, please"?

11

Seinfeld

*I*n the early 1990s my manager of over twenty-five years called to tell me I was cast in an ABC pilot called *Civil Wars*, which was about tales of divorce. (Bob Chartoff, our first manager, was now living in India we had heard.) A few weeks later our manager called to say that although my performance was "spectacular," the show was too heavy and had been cut and replaced by a story about an Elvis impersonator embroiled in a divorce.

Thanks to Amy's persistence and her connection to the New Group, Sam Schact cast me opposite Amy in Neil Simon's *I Oughta Be in Pictures*. Amy was pure in the role of Libby. Aside from her splendid notices, she won my heart. She came through.

The show was followed by a long dry spell with no work, after which I received offers for jobs that seemed stupid. I felt as though our manager was cutting the cord. "You're too old, grandpa."

I wondered if I'd made a mistake becoming an actor. Did all the *Sullivan* shows, the Broadway plays, the films, and the commercials add up to nothing? Was I in some "old" pool in a Hollywood casting computer? It took a while for it to hit me: What had happened to other people of advancing age was now happening to me. What should I do? I could wait for a call saying, "You're playing Willy Loman in Denver." I should be so lucky.

Most of all I worried about how this downturn would affect Anne and me. When you're young you bounce back—the world is still out there for you. But now it seemed as though our future was uncertain.

In desperation, Anne and I, now in our sixties, decided to work together once again. The reunion came as a result of an offer to play Trump Plaza in Atlantic City. Lee Salomon, the agent who had booked Sinatra and many others, had been urging us to do this for some time. Anne and I hadn't done our act in more than fifteen years, but as we watched our careers disappearing, we had little choice. Thanks to Lee's persistence, we agreed to headline with Leslie Uggams. Lee said, "Don't worry, they'll love you." Maybe he was just schmoozing us, but Lee was great at it.

The night before we opened in Atlantic City, Anne and I were frantically brushing up our act in any comedy club on Theater Row that would have us. People were paying their checks as we were announced as a surprise act. It was like being back in the Bon Soir. It was a nightmare.

The next night in Atlantic City was like a homecoming. The audience stood up when we came on, shook our hands, and did the same when we finished. We were elated; we were back in the limelight. Lee Salomon had saved our lives. Oddly enough our manager didn't make any of the performances. That hurt me. Who keeps your career alive if not your manager? We wanted him to see us in front of a live audience, to see that we weren't a couple of museum pieces. We knew we still had it. That night in Atlantic City we learned once again that acting was all about believing in yourself.

A few days later, we sadly decided to drop our manager. Though we had been close for so long, it was up to *us* to cut the cord.

I first met Michael Hartig, an agent, at a birthday party in 1989. June Havoc invited Anne and me to her home in Connecticut. Michael was a close friend of June's. While I was eating at the barbecue, Michael came by and praised my work in *Seize the Day*. He described scenes I had almost forgotten. I knew I was being wooed. I knew he handled Helen Gallagher, Mercedes McCambridge, and Tyne Daly, a Tony winner. These were all phenomenal performers.

Here it was three years later. I couldn't get arrested. I wondered, Will Michael Hartig want to handle Jerry Stiller? I made the call.

"Let's have lunch at the Russian Tea Room," he said. The Tea Room was run by Faith Stewart Gordon, and it was a place where good things used to happen for us. It was late afternoon. The place was mostly quiet. We sat in a booth and discussed my career. I tried to be upbeat. I figured if I acted depressed and showed bitterness I could have blown it. But I still had to be honest, I was out of work and had no representation.

Michael listened as I talked to him about my hangups, where my life was at. I thought that if he wanted to handle me, maybe *his* business was in trouble.

What impressed me was Michael's understanding of the actor's process. We talked about my fears, stuff I would normally never have wanted or allowed an agent to know. He took it all in. He said, "If you were onstage as many times as Joseph Buloff you would never have fear." It astounded me that Michael mentioned the name Buloff, a famous Yiddish actor who'd starred in the role of Ali Hakim in *Oklahoma* on Broadway, opposite Celeste Holm. Joseph's daughter, Barbara, is Anne's and my therapist. I wondered if I should mention this, but I held back. Enough already. Our meeting ended. Michael left me with these words: "I never lie in the Green Room," which I understood to mean that if I was lousy onstage, he'd tell me.

"I'll send your contract, one year; we'll see how it works out," he said.

Soon afterward Michael called. "Tony Randall's doing a revival of *Three Men on a Horse.* He wants to talk to you."

Tony had founded the National Actor's Theatre on Broadway. He had invested much of his own savings and begun a collaboration with Laura Pels producing revivals.

The possibility of going into the George Abbott and John Cecil comedy on Broadway excited me. When I met with Tony, I was wearing a black-and-white checkered woolen coat that made me look like a zebra.

"What are you up to?" he asked, staring at my coat. I knew by the look on his face that I would not have to read for the role I was being considered for. The *coat* won the day.

"Jack Klugman's going to play Patsy and I'm playing Irwin. I'd love you to play Charlie." Bingo, I was cast. "We got Joey Faye, John Beal, Ellen Greene, and Julie Hagerty. John Tillinger is directing."

"Sounds good," I said. And so, I was back to work on Broadway. I was reunited with Jack, whom I'd worked with at Stratford, the Phoenix, and Equity Library Theater (ELT). My spirits revived!

Just as I was about to begin rehearsals, I got another call from Michael. "They'd like you to replace the father on the *Seinfeld* show. Have you ever seen it?"

"No," I said.

"It's a big hit," he said. "You must do it. They need you right away. They'll fly you out tonight and shoot Tuesday."

"Michael, it's the second day of rehearsal for *Three Men on a Horse.* I'm working with Tony Randall and Jack Klugman. They'll hate me. I can't do it."

"You can fly back Wednesday."

"I'll miss three days of rehearsal. I gotta pass."

"I'll tell them," Michael said.

As he said this, I was already telling myself I could do both. Actors do this all the time. When I was doing *Airport '75* at Universal with Charlton Heston, Heston was also doing *Earthquake,* another disaster movie, at the same time.

"They called again," Michael said a day later. "They want you desperately."

"I can't," I said. "Tell them I can't. Give me their telephone number. I'll tell them."

Already I was opening the door to a mercy plea. I didn't want them to hate me. I called Larry David, the producer and co-creator of the show, and thanked him for wanting me. But I told him I couldn't do it.

I opened in *Three Men on a Horse.* Two months later I was given a Drama League Award for my performance as Charlie, the third banana in the show. At the luncheon in the Plaza sat the royalty of New York theater. I was on the dais with every star on Broadway. Anne was sitting next to me. When a mike was handed to me and I was asked to say a few words, I proudly announced it was the fiftieth anniversary of my first erection. Why I said it I have no idea. Probably just to liven up the proceedings. My remarks startled everyone, to say the least.

"It happened when I was in the sixth grade and our English teacher was reading from Chaucer. 'A Nun's Tale' or something like that. Suddenly I felt a bulge in my pants. I had no idea what it was but it was very annoying. At the end of the class I went up to my English teacher and said, 'I have this . . .'

"She looked down and said, 'My God, you have an erection.'

"I said, 'Yes and it's very annoying. How do I get rid of it?'

"She said, 'That's not my department. Go downstairs and see the Hygiene people.'

"I went downstairs to see Mr. Tuttle. Before I could open my mouth, he spotted my bulge and said, 'Kid, you've got an erection.'

"I said, 'How do I get rid of it?'"

"He said, 'I can't help you, Jerry. Go to the library and look it up.'"

"So, I cut the rest of my classes and went over to the library on East Broadway and got hold of this book *Anatomy of Sex,* by Havelock Ellis, and turned to the chapters on erections. Just then a gong sounded and the librarian said, 'Everyone out, we're having a fire drill.'"

"I did something I'd never done before. I stuck the book under my jacket and started to leave. The library had a little wooden turnstile that you had to go through as you checked out your books. As I went through, the turnstile hit my erection, and lo and behold, it went away. Now every once in a while I still get an erection, and if Anne is out of town I go down to the subway, buy a token, put it into the slot, and walk through. I usually hit the turnstile and when I do, well, my erection goes away."

At this point, amid the laughs, Anne got up and handed me a token. She said, "Here, go down to the subway and maybe you'll get lucky."

"You broke the ice," Tony Randall whispered. Was this a compliment or was my theatrical career *finito,* I wondered. But I got laughs and I got their attention. It was no longer a stodgy lunch.

One month after that, *Three Men* closed and I was once again out of work. Another call came from Michael. "They still want you for George's father."

"Who's George?" I asked. I had never seen the show.

A few hours later I was flying to Los Angeles to do the first of what would turn into approximately twenty-five episodes on *Seinfeld.*

From that point, my life changed. Much of it had to do with an actor named John Randolph.

In 1947, when I was nineteen, I went to see *Command Decision* on Broadway. This play by William Wister Haines about an air force squadron flying out of England in World War Two starred Paul Kelly, but the actor I identified with was John Randolph. He played Jake Goldberg, bombardier on a B-17. His performance was so warm and so heroic that I decided at that moment I wanted someday to perform on Broadway. I went backstage to tell him this.

I knocked on his dressing-room door. He stood in the doorway, dripping with perspiration.

"Come in," Randolph said, without asking anything more of this strange kid.

"I loved your performance," I said.

He showed me a chair. "What did you like?"

"You," I said. "It's like you lit up the stage."

"What do you do?" he asked.

"I want to be an actor. If only I could do what you do!"

"If you've got ambition and the will, you'll make it," he said.

"You really think so? Maybe someday I'll work with you." I got up and left.

Six years later I was playing one of the three Volscian servants in *Coriolanus* at the Phoenix. The company included Robert Ryan, John Emery, Mildred Natwick, Paula Lawrence, Lou Polan, Will Geer, Jack Klugman, Gene Saks—and John Randolph.

On the first day of rehearsal I approached Randolph and said, "Do you remember me? I came to your dressing room at *Command Decision*. You told me I'd make it someday." He broke into a smile. I doubt he remembered, but he acted as if he did.

In the following weeks I learned that John, Robert Ryan, Will Geer, and many others in the company were either blacklisted or otherwise tagged as Communist sympathizers, fellow travelers. Nearly everyone in the company, including director John Houseman, was left-of-center. Houseman's interpretation of Shakespeare likened Coriolanus's banishment by the Roman Senate to the Un-American Activities Committee's bludgeoning of left-wing artists. The blacklisted John Randolph was ironically playing a Roman counterpart of Senator Joseph McCarthy.

During the run of the show I listened to stories of the broken lives of blacklisted actors. Randolph's unwillingness to squeal to the Committee still sticks with me. Though his job opportunities were virtually nil, the smile was always there and his belief in American justice was steadfast.

The actor I replaced on *Seinfeld* was John Randolph.

My first day on the set, Stage 5, in Studio City, I learned my name was Costanza. What kind of name is Costanza? I had never watched a minute of *Seinfeld*. I'd seen a couple of minutes of Jerry's special and had no idea what people were laughing at. I was still freaking out watching the Marx Brothers. Nobody was funnier than Milton Berle, Eddie Cantor, Jack Benny, Jimmy Durante, Fred Allen, and Henny Youngman. Their greatness haunted my memory.

Now came *Seinfeld,* the newest generation of comedy. Nichols and May and Shelley Berman were the distant past, as was the comedy team of Stiller and Meara. Now we had the new kids: Robin Williams, Billy Crystal, Whoopi Goldberg. And then came Seinfeld, completely different. He makes observations; no punch lines.

As the table reading started for the writers and network, I was already trying to figure out how to make my lines funny. I heard my cue, and added a few words. The table went silent. What had I done wrong? Then I got it: These written words were sacrosanct.

The unspoken message: "Put a lid on it, shut up and listen." If I didn't, I was telling them that I wasn't on their wavelength. But what was I supposed to be? The character of Frank Costanza was supposed to be out of step with the world. If I didn't speak up I was just saying words with no bite, and I'd always improvised funny stuff.

What's the big deal? I thought. *What have I got to lose?* I was a replacement. I could easily end up walking the same plank as Randolph. But I might as well give it a fight, be what an actor is supposed to be, courageous. I'd been a quiet Jew too long. *Fuck it,* I thought. *If they fire me, they fire me.* Don't hold back.

But I did hold back.

We finished the reading. We knew there would be script revisions but we started blocking the scenes. Then the announcement: Go home and wait for the rewrites.

We rehearsed for five days. On the day of the shoot, Larry David, who also played the voice of George Steinbrenner, asked how I'd feel wearing a bald wig that would approximate the hairline of Jason Alexander, the actor playing my son George. I felt uneasy about wearing a hairpiece but agreed. The makeup department worked for three hours trying to make me look like Jason. As we got closer to the camera blocking, I felt more and more estranged from my character, which was still very nebulous. When we started the final blocking I asked Larry if the bald wig was necessary.

"Try it," he urged.

"But it's uncomfortable," I said. I remembered Fielder Cook's directorial hand in *Seize the Day.* Cook's sharp insights made my performance as Tamkin better than I could have imagined. Was Larry right? Should I go with the wig?

We started blocking the scene with Estelle Harris playing my wife. Now the wig was beginning to separate from my sideburns. Estelle's piercing screams could shatter glass. In fact, this was the normal voice of her character. Larry advised me to reply in a monotone. The contrast, he said, would get some laughs. As the scene progressed I could feel the wig peeling and my nonconfrontational character disintegrating. There was no conflict in the scene.

I found myself desperately searching for some way to connect with Estelle's character. I suddenly saw myself on a bus, heading back to New York City and once more out of work. I was history in this role. I asked for a break, and called Larry over. "I can't do this guy subdued, and the wig is driving me crazy. Do you mind if I do it my way?"

"Do it your way."

We started the scene again, and this time I screamed back at Estelle. "You made him this way, you spoiled him. You slept in the same bed with him!"

Estelle went catatonic. The cameramen were hysterical. I continued shouting at Estelle, stunning her with the strength of my outburst. Jason, Jerry, Michael Richards, and Julia Louis-Dreyfus were laughing their heads off.

"Keep it up, do it," Larry said.

"Can I take off the wig?"

"Yeah, take it off," Larry said. "You don't need a wig." It so happened that my hair, which was dyed brown, had oxidized to a bright orange, Tang-colored, almost the same color as Estelle's. It was a happy accident. We looked ridiculous together.

At that moment, Jason, who seemed to be enjoying all this, said, "Jerry, don't be afraid to hit me."

"What do you mean?" I asked

He slapped his own head, a kind of glancing shot.

"You want me to hit you?"

"Yes," he said.

"You're thirty-five years old and my son, I can't do that."

"Try it," he said.

"I don't want to hurt you."

"Don't be afraid." Jason then ad-libbed some funny line about wanting my car. I let him have it right on his pate with the palm of my hand, sort of a hit and a bounce. It was as if the world stopped. The cast and crew and Jason exploded in laughter. At that point, Estelle said, "Can I hit him too?"

"No, Estelle," Larry interjected. "Only one person can hit Jason at a time."

That night Estelle and I performed before a studio audience for the first time. She was in a wheelchair. She had broken her ankle and had been rehearsing in a cast. It never showed on camera.

In the scene I was asked to present a good-luck coin to George. I came up with a piece of business. I held the coin between my forefinger and thumb and made it disappear. It was a magic trick every five-year-old has seen. Jason's reaction blew everyone away. The trick was meant to show him the value of money and make him agree to take a post office job. I can only imagine that the coin trick nailed down my future appearances on *Seinfeld*. I can still remember Jerry, Michael, and Julia hovering around me as we shot the scene that night. I felt like I was in a safe place. I was back in the womb. And I was making it with these kids.

When the shoot before the live audience was completed that evening, Jerry Seinfeld introduced the cast for curtain calls. When I took my bow, there was an audible increase in the applause. I was genuinely surprised. At that moment Jerry turned and gave me a look that said, "nice going." An acknowledgment that something had indeed happened that night.

While this was going on, a lot was happening for Anne. She had written a second play—a funny, harrowing play—called *After-Play*. The show launched Anne in a new way. She had become a playwright.

Casting the role of one of the husbands in *After-Play*, however, became a problem. The role of Phil was written for me, Anne said. Deep down I was wrestling with why I did not want to read the role at backers' auditions. If I could be truthful, I'd have to say I didn't understand how wonderful the play was—this comedy dealing with love and death, husbands and wives, parents and children. I really didn't get it. It was staring me in the face, and I didn't understand my wife's writing. I kept justifying my doubts by remembering stories of Bert Lahr in *Waiting for Godot* not knowing whether a joke was funny and asking people's opinions. I was no Bert Lahr, I told myself, and the possibility of screwing up frightened me. Jack Weston agreed to do Phil in a reading along with Tresa Hughes, Tony Roberts, and Katherine Kerr, for Lynne Meadow of the

Manhattan Theatre Club. Lynne loved the play and immediately scheduled it for production.

When casting time came, those set for the show were Rue McClanahan, Barbara Barrie, Merwin Goldsmith, Rochelle Oliver, John Venema, and Lance Reddick. But the role of Phil was still up in the air. Jack Weston couldn't do it. Something about "dental work." Jack, my pal from *The Ritz,* was in fact undergoing treatment for cancer, and died not long afterward. Larry Keith opened in the role of Phil.

When *After-Play* opened at the Manhattan Theatre Club, the notices from *The New York Times,* the *Daily News, The Post,* and *Newsday* all spelled "hit." What made the story so remarkable in the eyes of the media was that Anne in her sixties had written a play that was selling out.

It was during this period that the Frank Costanza character was heating up. Although my TV stock was soaring, I was what was known in TV parlance as a recurring character, meaning it was never known when or if the character would reappear. Rather than fall victim to just waiting for the phone to ring, I kissed *Seinfeld* good-bye in my head. Inwardly, though, I was wishing I'd become a more frequent flyer to the coast.

That summer, while *Seinfeld* was on hiatus, Jim McKenzie (the producer of the Westport Playhouse) and Carlton Davis (the producer of the Cape Playhouse) asked if I would do *Beau Jest* at their theaters. I loved those grand old summer stock theaters. I'd performed there with Vivian Blaine some years past. *Beau Jest* was a perfect vehicle for Estelle Harris and myself, so I called her and she agreed to do the show. David Saint, who directed *After-Play,* would also direct. Then my daughter Amy joined the cast. It was a great way to spend the summer. We sold out every performance for four weeks.

Meanwhile, Donald Margulies, who would later win a Pulitzer Prize and whom Anne and I first met when he wrote sketches for *HBO Sneak Previews* (a series of short sketches we did for HBO), asked if I would play Sid, the grandfather, in a Broadway production of *What's Wrong with This Picture.* The show had originally been produced Off-Broadway and now would reopen in the fall at the Brooks Atkinson with Faith Prince, Alan Rosenberg, and Florence Stanley.

My *Seinfeld* appearances were getting me work. Television actors were now drawing a Broadway audience. It was looking good until one day, while out on my daily walk (I'd stopped jogging some time back) I heard a crunch in my right hip. No pain, but it felt like two pieces of shredded wheat rubbing against each other. I knew this spelled trouble up the road. Nevertheless, the thought of opening in Donald's play on Broadway wiped away any concern over a stupid thing like hip degeneration. Besides, I could use it in the role. Actors use everything. I was playing an aging ex–New York cab driver who had progressing Alzheimer's disease. I could add a little limp.

I was thrilled I'd be opening on Broadway. Then, shortly before rehearsals were to begin, I received a call from my agent.

"*Seinfeld* needs you right away."

The "Chinese Woman" was the beginning of five years of hopping back and forth to L.A. After shooting "Chinese Woman," I flew back to New York and opened in *What's Wrong with This Picture* on Broadway.

The notices were not raves, but I felt it was the best work I'd done since *Hurlyburly*. I loved the play and was saddened when I heard that the show was to close after five weeks of performances.

Although *After-Play* was selling out at the Manhattan Theatre Club, the show closed to make way for a play MTC had previously scheduled. Now what? Anne had a hit show without a theater.

The idea that Anne's play might disappear affected me. I already felt guilty about not being in it for the first run, so I got on the phone and began trying to raise the $400,000 needed for a further Off-Broadway production. Many people came aboard: Judith Resnick, Nancy Richards, Evangeline Morphos, and Carol Ostrow. Then when Anne and I put some of our own money into the till, *After-Play* was reborn Off-Broadway.

Its second coming happened at Theater Four, on Manhattan's West 55th Street, in January of 1995, six weeks after closing at MTC. Once again, it was beautifully received.

I now agreed to step into the role of Phil. My biggest fear was how a limp, which was growing more pronounced, would read onstage. I sat down and talked with Anne about it.

Then I explained my fears to David Saint.

David said, "You could do Phil on crutches. That's how perfect you are. You could do it in a wheelchair." That's all I had to hear. Now I wanted to do it.

I would be playing opposite Rita Moreno, a Tony, Emmy, and Oscar winner whom I had worked with in *The Ritz*. What a gift. Anne agreed to replace Rue McClanahan, who was now working in London.

My continuing appearances on *Seinfeld* had been my career lifeline.

They had given me the cachet to extend the run of *After-Play* as well as allayed my fears of never being called back to appear on *Seinfeld* again.

No sooner had the play opened when one afternoon, as Anne and I were having lunch in a neighborhood restaurant, Dawn Eaton, the young woman who keeps our lives and everything else on track, called to say, "*Seinfeld* called."

"When?"

"Tonight."

"You gotta be kidding."

"They've booked you on the 6 P.M. out of Newark."

"You going to do it?" Anne asked. "Three hours' notice?"

This is exciting, I said to myself. Inwardly I was *kvelling.* In their minds Frank Costanza was still alive.

Then I wondered, What kind of person was I to let a TV show rule me? I'm performing every night. What more do I want? I mean, can someone just press a button and I turn into Costanza? I'm going to refuse this offer, I thought. Be my own man. I'll show them. I'll ask for a guarantee. Sign me for ten shows.

"You going to do it?" Anne asked.

"Of course." An actor must act. I forgot about the ten shows.

"What about your hip? It's killing you. Six hours on a plane."

"That's what cortisone's for."

"Have them fax me my lines," I said to Dawn.

Three hours later I was in the air learning my part from a mini cassette tape recorder. I landed in L.A., drove to the hotel, went to bed, and the next morning arrived on the Stage 5 lot.

In the "Fusilli Jerry" episode, Kramer (Michael Richards) and I get into a physical confrontation over who owns the rights to the "man-sierre," an upper body support for men. Michael and I improvised the scene, which got very physical. I was supposed to end up on the floor, landing on a corkscrew pasta. The fusilli Jerry trophy was to imbed itself in my *tush* and cause a visit to a proctologist.

I painstakingly avoided telling the cast about my hip out of fear that doing so would inhibit them. I did a lot of hopping. The question was, how to land after the fall without further aggravating my condition?

Since the action took place behind a couch, I figured that as Michael hit me I'd hook my arm onto the couch, lessening the impact, and the camera would then cut away. However, every time I fell, Julia, also in the scene, would break up laughing. We had to reshoot. My ego was delighted that I could make her laugh, and I almost willingly repeated the scene despite fear of injury.

"Are you all right?" everybody would ask.

"Fine, fine," I'd say. We finally got the shot.

During my breaks in *Seinfeld,* I got to play Vince Lombardi in a Nike commercial, film *A Fish in the Bathtub* for Joan and Ray Silver, and play Chebutykin in Chekhov's *Three Sisters* at the Roundabout Theatre on Broadway. I had done more as an actor in the *Seinfeld* period than I could ever have dreamed of doing. Someone had been good to me.

My appearances on *Seinfeld* had become popular enough that the New York State Council on the Arts and the National Endowment for the Arts, under Jane Alexander's chairmanship, called on me for an appearance at a fund-raiser. I was thrilled at my growing popularity and my power to persuade people to support a cause.

All this attention was filling me with the air I needed. My existence as an actor took on a new meaning. I could speak and people would listen. Suddenly I felt I had finally done something in my life—and alone, no longer feeding off Anne.

One day Ginny Louloudes of the Alliance of Resident Theaters (ART NY) called and asked if I would become a board member. ART NY was part of the New York State Council on the Arts (NYSCA), which supported hundreds of theater groups throughout New York State. It was my chance to pay back what the Henry Street Playhouse gave me.

One of the most thrilling days of my life came when I agreed to fly to Albany in a Cherokee Piper Cub along with Kitty Carlisle Hart (who chaired NYSCA), Tony Randall, Celeste Holm, and Ginny. We were to meet with Governor George Pataki and then lobby the members of the New York state legislature for money for the arts. A special Arts Day had been designated by the legislature.

The presence of Tony, Celeste, and Kitty speaking out for the arts really affected everyone. Sitting next to three stars fighting for the "have nots" was unforgettable. What was my contribution to all of this, I wondered as we were ushered into an auditorium filled with legislators and 3,600 people representing arts organizations who were lobbying for a piece of the financial pie.

The three stars spoke eloquently about their own beginnings, how important it was to nurture talented people who need a place to start. The arts have always been in the back of the line of funding priorities, behind education, Medicaid, the homeless, drug abuse. How do we get the message across that theater is the pulpit of the masses? After the big three made their pitch I was introduced by state Senator Roy Goodman, who was always a friend of the arts. He gave me a wonderful introduction as Frank Costanza on *Seinfeld*. *Be funny,* I told myself. *These people are expecting a few laughs.*

So I got up and started screaming in Frank's character, "Without arts we got nothing." Then I went into a parody of "The Name Game," a hit song from the '60s. The word I used was *shonder,* "shame" in Yiddish. "*Shonder, shonder,* bo bonder, banana, fanna, fo-fonder, mee-my-mo-monder—SHONDER!" chastising the legislature for not allocating money to the arts. Now I had them laughing and I had their attention. Tony, Celeste, Kitty, and Ginny were in shock but were nodding their heads in approval. Would Frank Costanza win bucks for the arts? I then explained how my life in the theater started with the Henry Street Playhouse, which had been partially funded by government grants. I explained that without Henry Street I would never have gotten the chance to become an actor. Thanks to House Minority Leader Sheldon Silver, A.R.T. / New York was given some needed funding.

After the event, I was amazed when I was surrounded by state senators and other powerful legislators asking for my autograph for themselves and their kids. The power of a hit television show.

All of this spadework for the arts made me feel beautiful inside—more joyful than I had ever expected. Suddenly I was a flaming activist storming the barricades. I was Robespierre invoking the spirit of Esther Lane and the Henry Street Playhouse.

It also occurred to me that my sudden outspokenness could make me controversial and might affect future appearances on *Seinfeld*. Why not, I thought. I'd be a martyr for the arts and I'd be remembered forever.

Toward the end of December 1995, while I was still performing in *After-Play,* an offer came in for the new *Seinfeld* season. I was guaranteed five episodes. "But can you fly this week?" they asked. "We heard about your hip. Are you okay?"

"Of course, yes, that's what painkillers are for. Just fax me the script."

Anne was reluctant to let me leave.

"I love your body. I want you in one piece," she said. "You need to get a new hip."

"I gotta go out there, Anne."

Seinfeld, here I come. The script arrived, and I planned to learn my lines in the air, as I always did. The first *Seinfeld* episode of that next-to-last season was to be shot without an audience. The cortisone shot was working as I boarded the aircraft.

What happened en route changed everything. After three hours aloft the pilot announced we would be landing in Cleveland. No explanation. A chill went through me. A few minutes later a stewardess informed us it was not a mechanical problem; a woman had confided to a flight attendant that she had packed firecrackers in her baggage. She was escorted off the plane in Cleveland.

The flight arrived in Los Angeles eight hours later, my hip killing me. I couldn't walk a step. I needed a wheelchair to get to baggage claim, and had to crawl into my rented car. When I arrived at the hotel I needed help. I could not walk. Once in my room, I made it to the bathroom on all fours. I wondered how I would get to the set the next morning. I called the actor Ron Guillory, who would be cueing me the next day. I asked him to pick me up in the morning and to bring some crutches.

Ron came through. I arrived on the set on crutches. "Bad hip," I said. Andy Ackerman, our gifted director, finessed every move. We were to shoot my scenes as I sat in a car. We rehearsed, blocked, and shot the scene.

The next day I visited a doctor in Beverly Hills, who gave me kind words and a cortisone shot. I worked the rest of the week—as they say, very gingerly. After shooting my final scene, I left L.A. on an early flight to New York and went on in *After-Play* that night.

The *Seinfeld* episode we had just filmed was "The Rye," in which I steal back the Schnitzers' marble rye, and it became the kickoff hit for the new season. It seemed incredible. Here I was performing Anne's play in New York twenty-four hours after shooting *Seinfeld* in L.A. Being in a hit TV series, a hit play, and hearing laughter take away pain.

Three weeks later. I checked into the hospital to receive a new hip. As I was being wheeled into the operating room on the gurney, a medical assistant handed me an audio cassette and said, "Mr. Stiller, I do voice-overs. Can you get this to your agent?" I stuck it in between my thighs and waited for the epidural.

• • •

On a winter morning in 1998, I had just gotten up and was in the kitchen preparing my coffee. From the breakfast table Anne said, "Look at the front page of *The New York Times*." Her words had a strange ring—something less than ominous, but still with a hint of foreboding.

This particular morning we were getting ready to go to the funeral of my ninety-seven-year-old Aunt Sarah. Three days earlier my cousin Eileen had died. Too much was happening.

"You've got to read the story in the *Times*," Anne said once more. How could a headline be that important when you lose two members of your family, I wondered, as I sipped my coffee.

"You've got to read about *Seinfeld*," Anne said. "It affects you." Her words still made no impact. "It's over," she said. I continued drinking my coffee, blocking out my feelings over the loss of my aunt and my cousin.

"Read it," she repeated. I finally did. There it was on the front page of *The New York Times:* SEINFELD QUITS. How often does the termination of a television show take precedence over world events? I read the story and realized that the show was really over. And so was a part of my life.

That part of my life—a television series—had given me instant recognition among people on the street everywhere. A woman stopped her car and shouted through the window, "Serenity now, you're a very sick man." Girls in the Hamburg airport ran up and asked me if I could get them a date with Jerry Seinfeld.

"Sorry, I can't."

"Then how about you?"

Israeli soldiers on the Golan Heights recognized me.

"*Shalom*, we love you," they cried out.

I finally got it through my head that *Seinfeld* was over, but what I couldn't fully understand was how big the ending of a TV series was in the eyes of the public. I soon knew. The press coverage said it all. It finally occurred to me that Estelle Harris and I were actually part of the *Seinfeld* phenomenon.

Seinfeld is over. Aside from the laughs, the show was saying something about America's changing attitudes about watching Jewish characters on television. Every character on *Seinfeld* was out of the closet except for maybe the Costanzas. How could a family that noshes on bagels and loves kasha have the name Costanza? They had to be a Jewish family in the witness protection program.

The show was successful because it never apologized for the behavior of its characters. Nor do most people in real life apologize when they step over the line. The show mirrored not just Jewish behavior, but everyone's.

Each *Seinfeld* episode had added to my feelings of self-esteem, and now it was over. What a way to feel good about myself, playing the role of a deranged father. Am I going to miss being Mr. Costanza, the fictional me? Will people once again know me as Jerry Stiller the actor or am I forever George's father? Who am I in *my* mind? It suddenly hit me that I'd-been on a great trip. I'd been given something few actors get. Jerry, Jason, Michael, and Julia were the greatest ensemble since the Marx Brothers, in my opinion. Estelle Harris could have been Margaret Dumont. In performance there was no air between us. And those kids did it for nine years—what an achievement.

I needed to get in touch with myself so I told Anne I had to get to Nantucket.

"I'll go with you," she said.

"I've got to be by myself."

It was a bumpy flight in the small plane. Whenever I'm in a small plane and there's turbulence, I wonder if the next air pocket we hit will be the last. Has the plane been inspected recently? Is the pilot qualified? What if we crash? Will Anne miss me? What did we have together? Sure we had the act, but what did we have *between us*?

I remembered when Anne and I were invited to be on a special in Vegas honoring Jackie Gleason. George Burns was also on the show. Burns was standing nearby when we taped. I had never met him so I figured why not introduce myself.

"Mr. Burns, I'm Jerry Stiller."

"I know you," he said. "You work with your wife."

I felt a little strange conversing with half of America's most popular husband-and-wife comedy team. Did he think Anne and I were some kind of interlopers comparing ourselves to George and Gracie?

"I like your work," he said. I was flattered.

I suddenly remembered something Artie Shaw had said when we'd first met, a few years earlier at the pool of the Sunset Marquis in Hollywood. He said, "Who do you think is the happiest married couple in Hollywood?" This coming from a man who'd been married ten times.

I thought for a moment. "Is it Burns and Allen?" I asked.

"How'd you know?" he replied.

"I don't know, I just guessed."

"You're right. Come on, let's get wet." We both jumped in the pool. So here I was talking to George Burns, now a widower.

"Artie Shaw said you and Gracie were the happiest married couple in Hollywood."

"That's right," George replied. "It's because we were never married."

"What?!"

"We were married to the business." He smiled. "Keep up the good work."

His words, although shocking, had an impact on me. I knew he was being truthful and I wanted to kiss him for sharing something that one revealed only to an intimate. I had seen and listened to Burns and Allen over the years. Besides enjoying them and laughing at their comedy, I always wondered how they came up with their material.

How did they rehearse? I knew they started in vaudeville, probably doing five shows a day between showings of movies. What did they do during the breaks? Were they in the dressing room writing? They had to be writing down things they said that were funny. Who did the writing? Did they argue about a line or a premise? Their timing was great. What went into it? Did they have a life? They had had children, so they were parents. What did they do together besides make people laugh? Suddenly George Burns's words made sense. "We were married to the business." I could only interpret this to mean the love of show business brought them closer. It created love for each other.

I asked myself if Anne and I were married to the business like George and Gracie. Me, I'd figured we could do it all—have kids and a career. Bring Amy and Ben on the road with us so we'd never be apart.

Anne never saw it that way.

"You want us to be another Burns and Allen," she had remarked.

"Sure, why not. They were great."

"Just remember, Jerry, Gracie's dead."

Her message was simple: "Don't make me do this for the rest of our lives—if you want me alive."

"But you're great in front of an audience," I said.

"Yeah, I learned that from being with you."

Anne and I had spent most of our married life working in front of people. On stage we had intimacy, a connection that made us feel whole, gave me a sense of being somebody. When a show ended I felt a void. I needed the audience to make me feel whole again. I can only guess that Anne loved making people laugh, but it wasn't her whole life. Maybe that's why she was so loose and funny.

Now we didn't have an act. The sketches were thirty years old. We no longer went out on the road, although there were offers. Without the act our lives were different. We needed to keep our lives together. We both wanted a closeness. We needed to keep something alive between us. No act, the kids grown and on their own—what did we have in common now? I asked myself. What a question after so many years.

I wanted us to hold hands and skip down life's garden path together. Travel, go to concerts, museums. But Anne liked to stay home.

"I like to read," she'd say, looking up from a book.

I'd rather watch the Knicks, see some jazz, go to shows, but I wanted more than anything to be closer to Anne. I tried to get on her wavelength, get her on mine. I didn't want us to lose each other.

Amy had picked up on our problems and suggested Barbara Buloff, a therapist she had heard about.

Amy knew that Barbara, who had been brought up by two actors, could understand the bond Anne and I had. With this background Barbara had an awareness that Anne and I truly loved each other and belonged together. During ten years of therapy, Barbara melted the walls that separated Anne and me. What a gift. In that time the freeze thawed between us and so had my freeze on stage. We grew incredibly close. It wasn't like the sudden mysterious healing that took place in the film *Spellbound,* where Gregory Peck is suddenly enlightened by the psychiatrist. It happened gradually. We started communicating with each other.

I think it started in our living room, overlooking the Hudson River. In the morning Anne would usually be doing *The New York Times* crossword puzzle. I hated this puzzle. It intimidated me, although I loved it when my name was mentioned.

On one occasion I put on some coffee and played a CD. It was Chopin. Anne put down the puzzle.

"That's nice," she said.

"I love music," I said. "All kinds. Chopin, Ellington.

"You like Scott Joplin?" I asked.

"Yeah, but I love Jim Croce, *Bad, Bad, Leroy Brown.*" She started to sing the words, moving her body the way she did in the '70s.

"I'll play it," I said.

"No, play what you like. You love Bill Evans, don't you? Put him on."

I put on Bill Evans's Paris Concert. We had been on the bill with him at the Village Vanguard. I loved listening to him between our sets.

"I don't understand jazz," Anne said. "Bill Evans used to lean over the keyboard like he was falling asleep."

"Yeah, he was making love to the piano. . . . What are you reading?" I asked.

"Seth Speaks."

Hooley wooley stuff, I thought.

This was the beginning of our many morning talks. It usually started with my playing music and asking what Anne was reading. It was the opening to get into each other's heads.

We were like people just getting to know one another.

"I've never understood jazz. Why don't I understand it?"

"Because you're orderly. Jazz can be chaotic. It's like some storm that suddenly erupts spontaneously in a musician's soul. It's somebody else's sunset—someone else's terror. Who wants to hear the musical version of someone else's problems? A lot of dissonance. Just when you're ready to say 'I've heard enough,' you hear the thread of a melody. It falls easily on the ears. The storm has subsided. You're suddenly caught up and now you're listening to Bill Evans's inner voice. He's taken us on a trip we've all been on ourselves at one time or another. Now he's out of his wilderness. The search for life's golden path is over." I was starting to sound like a poet.

"What about basketball?" Anne asked. "Why do you love it?"

"Because I can't play it. I love watching a sport where the outcome can change in seconds, where one player can take over and change the outcome of a game. What happens on a basketball court happens in life. On the court it happens in seconds. To me it's inspirational watching forty-eight minutes mirror life."

"I love Jorge Luis Borges," Anne said. "You've got to read him. He was blind, you know. He wrote about paths not taken. Short pieces, mystical, beautiful."

"Like if we hadn't married each other, what would we be doing now?"

"Yeah, something like that. Also like there are many Jerrys and many Annes out there taking those paths."

"That I don't understand," I said.

"Quantum probabilities."

"I still don't understand."

"Come on," Anne said. "Let's finish this conversation in the bedroom."

Every morning these talks became more enjoyable. Every day we'd talk about something else. We'd just sit and talk, listen to music, and drink coffee. It was a daily habit. It went on for months.

One morning I asked Anne, "What's your secret? How can you do a scene ten times in a row the same way while I do it differently each time? Were the nuns that strict? Did you get it across the knuckles if you didn't get it right? My Hebrew teacher chased me around the room with a ruler but even that didn't make me consistent."

"You really want to know?" she asked.

"Yeah."

"It's got to do with intention," Anne said. "Know your intention in the scene. When you hear your cue, make an entrance and the rest will follow."

I realized that when I waited in the wings, I hadn't fully decided and was still searching for my intention. I would hear my cue and be in no-man's land. How did this happen? It suddenly occurred to me that in all these years of performing I had never learned the meaning of structure. Anne was describing "technique." Technique is synonymous with structure. It's breaking down the scene, taking it apart, deconstructing it, then reconstructing it. It's what made *Seinfeld* so great. Each of the stars was a master of deconstructing. They understood the importance of structure.

I always thought that analyzing would rob me of spontaneity. But the next time I performed, I followed Anne's advice. I locked into my intention, worked on structure, and when I made my entrance, suddenly I was floating onstage. I was liberated. What a paradox: Structure had actually freed me. Working with *Seinfeld*'s young stars had taught me how to do this.

When I was a young actor, the absence of structure freed my imagination to run wild. My dreams could take shape and rule onstage. But a dream without structure, I soon discovered, evaporates. Acting is the flow of feeling without intellect, I believed. It's an uncapped geyser of emotion that spews without intelligence, I thought. My chief fear was that intellectualizing would interfere with the flow of feeling. The acting genie would not pop out of the proverbial bottle.

In those years, I depended too much on inspiration, and inspiration didn't show up at every performance. Why hadn't I gotten this message earlier? I was full of myself and scared. But it finally did hit me—very late.

I realize now that I've learned more about myself by being an actor than I have ever learned about acting. I no longer want to be Eddie Cantor. I want to discover myself onstage.

The small plane is approaching Nantucket. I can't wait to ride the bike without hands and maybe learn something new about myself. We land, we taxi, and I take a cab to our house, drop my bag, and open the bike shed. There it is. My steed.

Getting on a bike makes me feel like Columbus. But the landmarks I'm exploring are islands of thought hidden from myself. The bike is my release. When the wind shifts and propels me, my body becomes a sail. I stop pedaling. I soar silently like a gull. I own myself. I feel grand. An unfettering of the soul. The past becomes the present. I'm on a trip with no timetable, no limit on stopovers, and no destination.

Pedaling against the wind pumps blood into places in my brain that don't always get energized. My unexamined life flashes before me like soundless television. The ride clearly defines my life.

The ride makes me feel like an old engine that is still turning over. Toward the end of my ride, my legs seemed weighted. I entertain the thought of flagging a lift with some compassionate passing motorist. The bike wheels rotate slowly. A cab passes. I could stop him, but the thought of chickening out humiliates me.

A gust smashes me in the chest. I'm in a battle, but it's an imaginary war I've created between myself and everything in my life. Bullfighters take risks. Pilots. Deep-sea divers. I'm none of these. I'm an actor, and when I'm not onstage, riding a bike into the wind permits me to feel temporarily invincible. It releases me. I think of choices I can still make, if I'm willing to make them.

Suddenly I envision a Brooklyn street where a kid my own age was riding a red tricycle. I watch him circling the block. He must have guessed that I'd love to be doing what he was doing.

"Would you like a ride?" he asks.

Amazed at his generosity, I say yes.

"Take it around the block," he suggests.

In my vision, my feet would just reach the pedals, thanks to blocks of wood. When I finish the tricycle ride, I know I've traveled more than just around a city block. I've been given a passport to go to places I'll some-day visit. I too have discovered the wheel.

I get back to the house. Anne calls. "CBS left a message. They want you for a new show called *King of Queens*. You play the part of a de-ranged guy, somebody's father, living in a basement."

An actor must act.